AGGRESSION AND DANGEROUSNESS

Wiley Series on

CURRENT RESEARCH IN FORENSIC PSYCHIATRY AND PSYCHOLOGY

Series Editors

Professor John Gunn
Institute of Psychiatry
De Crespigny Park
Denmark Hill
London SE5 8AF

Dr David Farrington
Institute of Criminology
University of Cambridge
7 West Road
Cambridge CB3 9DT

ABNORMAL OFFENDERS, DELINQUENCY,
AND THE CRIMINAL JUSTICE SYSTEM

REACTIONS TO CRIME: THE PUBLIC, THE POLICE,
COURTS, AND PRISONS

AGGRESSION AND DANGEROUSNESS

AGGRESSION AND DANGEROUSNESS

Edited by

David P. Farrington
Institute of Criminology,
University of Cambridge

and

John Gunn
Institute of Psychiatry,
University of London

JOHN WILEY & SONS

Chichester · New York · Brisbane · Toronto · Singapore

Library of Congress Cataloging in Publication Data:
Main entry under title:

Aggression and dangerousness.

  (Current research in forensic psychiatry and psychology)
  Includes index.
  1. Criminal psychology—Addresses, essays, lectures.
2. Aggressiveness (Psychology)—Addresses, essays,
lectures. 3. Insane, Criminal and dangerous—Addresses,
essays, lectures. I. Farrington, David P. II. Gunn,
John. III. Series: Wiley series on current research in
forensic psychiatry and psychology.
HV6080.A35   1985   364.3   84-13112

ISBN 0 471 90556 9

British Library Cataloguing in Publication Data:
Aggression and dangerousness.—(Wiley series
  on current research in forensic psychiatry
  and psychology; v. 3)
  1. Criminal psychology 2. Aggressiveness
  (Psychology) 3. Psychiatric hospital
  patients 4. Violence in psychiatric
  hospitals
  I. Farrington, D. P. II. Gunn, John, 1937–
  364.3   HV6105

ISBN 0 471 90556 9

Photosetting by Activity Limited, Salisbury, Wilts
and printed by The Pitman Press, Bath, Avon

Contents

Preface ix

1. Introduction
   by DAVID P. FARRINGTON and JOHN GUNN 1

Part 1: Characteristics of Aggressive Offenders
2. The Neurochemistry and Neuroendocrinology of Sexual
   Aggression
   by ROBERT PRENTKY 7
3. Characteristics of Non-institutionalized Psychopaths
   by CATHY SPATZ WIDOM and JOSEPH P. NEWMAN 57
4. Psychological and Physiological Characteristics of Personality-
   disordered Patients
   by GISLI H. GUDJONSSON and JOANNA C. ROBERTS 81
5. Jealousy, Pathological Jealousy, and Aggression
   by PAUL E. MULLEN and LARA H. MAACK 103
6. The Psychodynamics of Borderline Personality
   by PATRICK L. G. GALLWEY 127

Part 2: The Management of Dangerous Patients
7. Dangerousness and the Mental Health Review Tribunal
   by DAVID HEPWORTH 155
8. Security in a Local Mental Hospital
   by MICHAEL CARNEY and JANE GARNER 185
9. The Impact of Deinstitutionalization
   by RONALD ROESCH and STEPHEN L. GOLDING 209
10. The Management of Dangerous Patients in Zimbabwe
    by TERRY BUCHAN and PETER SPARLING 241

Author Index 261
Subject Index 267

The Contributors

TERRY BUCHAN, *Professor of Psychiatry, Godfrey Huggins School of Medicine, Harare, Zimbabwe*

MICHAEL CARNEY, *Consultant Psychiatrist, Northwick Park and Shenley Hospitals, Harrow, Middlesex*

DAVID P. FARRINGTON, *Lecturer in Criminology, Cambridge University*

PATRICK L. G. GALLWEY, *Consultant Forensic Psychiatrist, St George's Hospital, London*

JANE GARNER, *Senior Registrar in Psychiatry, Middlesex and Shenley Hospitals, Harrow, Middlesex*

STEPHEN L. GOLDING, *Associate Professor of Psychology, University of Illinois, Urbana-Champaign*

GISLI H. GUDJONSSON, *Lecturer in Clinical Psychology, London University*

JOHN GUNN, *Professor of Forensic Psychiatry, London University*

DAVID HEPWORTH, *Principal Officer, Doncaster Social Services*

LARA H. MAACK, *Registrar in Psychiatry, Bethlem Royal and Maudsley Hospital, London*

PAUL E. MULLEN, *Professor of Psychological Medicine, University of Otago Medical School, Dunedin, New Zealand*

JOSEPH P. NEWMAN, *Assistant Professor of Psychology, University of Wisconsin, Madison*

ROBERT PRENTKY, *Director of Research, Massachusetts Treatment Center, Bridgewater*

JOANNA C. ROBERTS, *Research Psychologist, Henderson Hospital, Sutton, Surrey*

RONALD ROESCH, *Associate Professor of Psychology and Criminology, Simon Fraser University, Burnaby, British Columbia*

PETER SPARLING, *Charge Nurse, Mlondolozi Hospital, Bulawayo, Zimbabwe*

CATHY SPATZ WIDOM, *Associate Professor of Forensic Studies and Psychology, Indiana University, Bloomington*

Preface

This book is the third and last volume in the series *Current Research in Forensic Psychiatry and Psychology*, published by John Wiley and edited by ourselves. The first volume, entitled *Abnormal Offenders, Delinquency, and the Criminal Justice System*, was published in 1982, and the second volume, on *Reactions to Crime: The Public, The Police, Courts, and Prisons*, is being published at the same time as this one. Books in this series are concerned with the contribution of psychiatry and psychology to all aspects of crime, offenders, the law, legal processes, the treatment of offenders, and the criminal justice system. As the list of contributors to this volume indicates, our scope is international. Four of the five continents are represented. Our intention is not to compete with existing journals, but to complement them by publishing relatively long articles reporting the results of substantial programmes of empirical research rather than short papers. We also include substantial reviews of the literature and theoretical contributions, both of which are difficult to publish in journals. We hope that they show the contribution that psychiatrists and psychologists can make to our knowledge and understanding of aggressive, psychopathic, and dangerous offenders and of methods of dealing with them. We also hope that this book and the series as a whole will be useful not only to psychiatrists and psychologists but also to criminologists, social scientists, lawyers, social workers, probation officers, and others employed in the criminal justice and mental health systems.

D.P.F.

February 1984   J.G.

CHAPTER 1

Introduction

DAVID P. FARRINGTON AND JOHN GUNN

The chapters in this book include 'state of the art' reviews, theoretical contributions, and reports of empirical research projects. As the table of contents indicates, the book is in two parts, Part 1 is concerned primarily with characteristics of aggressive and psychopathic offenders and with methods of treating them, while Part 2 reviews methods of dealing with 'dangerous' offenders.

Part 1 begins with a detailed review of neurochemical and neuroendocrinological correlates of sexual aggression, by Robert Prentky. Recent years have witnessed a rebirth of interst in biology and crime, as seen for example in the detailed reviews by Shah and Roth (1974) and Mednick and Volavka (1980). Prentky's review of the biochemistry of aggression is the most extensive yet written on this topic. It demonstrates that there are clearly correlations between biochemical factors and sexual aggression, but also that more years of research are needed to specify fully the interactions between biological and social factors.

One problem in studying characteristics of aggressive offenders is that most of the research is based on institutionalized samples, making it difficult to disentangle correlations with offending from effects of institutionalization. The chapter by Cathy Spatz Widom and Joseph P. Newman describes an interesting attempt to assemble a non-institutionalized sample of psychopaths, by means of advertisements in newspapers, building on earlier innovative research of Widom (1977). They also compare different classificatory criteria for psychopathy, showing once again the difficulty of pinning down this widely used construct.

Gisli H. Gudjonsson and Joanna C. Roberts are also concerned with psychopathy. They investigate psychological and physiological characteristics of personality-disordered patients at the Henderson Hospital, an institution noted for its attempts to treat such patients within a therapeutic community. Gudjonsson and Roberts conclude that most of the patients were 'secondary' psychopaths, having a great deal of anxiety and emotional problems. The 'primary' psychopath, lacking anxiety, affect and guilt, described by Cleckley (1964) and Hare (1978), seems as elusive as ever.

1

Paul E. Mullen, Professor of Psychological Medicine in Otago, New Zealand, and Lara H. Maack present an interesting theoretical analysis of the concept of jealousy. They provide a useful review of the literature on morbid jealousy, and show the relationship between it and the more 'normal' variety. They point out that people can be morbidly jealous even if their delusions are in fact correct. Their empirical study of pathologically jealous patients reinforces earlier work in showing the degree and likelihood of violence associated with morbid jealousy.

Patrick L. G. Gallwey is a follower of Melanie Klein, who started an important British school of psychoanalysis. Gallwey's chapter gives an account of the way a Kleinian analyst approaches the difficult problem of a patient with severe personality disorder including intermittent or hidden psychotic elements. It is probably this clear theoretical approach which enables such an analyst to be a useful psychotherapist with this group of patients, who are rejected by most other types of psychotherapists. Not everyone will agree with Gallwey's theoretical premises, but the theory elaborated here is thought-provoking and will probably assist many therapists with the core issue of personality disorder in forensic psychiatry.

Part 2 is concerned with the management of dangerous patients. The subject of dangerousness has been widely discussed recently (e.g. Floud and Young, 1981; Hinton, 1983). David Hepworth provides a much-needed analysis of the process by which patients are discharged from Special (secure) Hospitals, showing the importance of the assessment of dangerousness. His conclusions are especially relevant since the Mental Health Act 1983 came into effect. This Act greatly increased the power of Mental Health Review Tribunals to order the release of offender-patients held in secure conditions, irrespective of the wishes of the Home Secretary.

Following the Butler report (Home Office, Department of Health and Social Security, 1975), most regions in the United Kingdom are slowly establishing regional secure hospital units—a system of secure care for mentally abnormal offenders who do not need to be held in conditions of maximum security. Michael Carney and Jane Garner report on the operation of a local secure unit set up in one particular hospital, and provide some interesting information about the later outcomes of their violent, disturbed patients. As a result of their experience, they raise doubts about the policy of establishing a regional system of secure care. However, it must be pointed out that there are probably a number of persons from their area (in the community, in prison or in Special Hospitals) who would not be referred to a local unit because of doubts about their suitability. In other words, their local unit probably only deals with a proportion of the mentally abnormal offenders in the area who need secure care.

Ronald Roesch and Stephen L. Golding review the movement to deinstitutionalize mental patients. This was grounded in the belief that many patients were unnecessarily detained, and was often based on marginally relevant arguments about the unpredictability of dangerousness. Roesch and Golding argue that deinstitutionalization has produced reinstitutionalization for many and no treatment for most. In conformity with their commendable concern for methodological rigour, they conclude with a plea for a longitudinal tracking system to follow persons through the mental health and criminal justice systems and between these systems and the community. We agree with their argument that large-scale changes in social policy such as the deinstitutionalization of mental patients need to be informed by methodologically adequate research.

The final chapter, by Terry Buchan and Peter Sparling, is an interesting commentary from a developing country (Zimbabwe) about the familiar problem of managing dangerous mentally abnormal offenders. The chapter shows how the imaginative psychiatrist can prevent the traditional bureaucratic response (of secure units) to the problem. It also suggests that there is an important role for the psychiatrist in preventive medicine. If a good standard of general psychiatry can be achieved in rural communities, potentially dangerous persons can be identified and dealt with at an early stage, before serious violence occurs. This might have a lesson for richer countries, to put their resources into community clinics rather than secure units. This chapter is also interesting in demonstrating that diagnoses of patients in Zimbabwe are similar to those in Great Britain, with the difference that the African sample had more neurological damage (a commonly found difference between richer and poorer countries).

REFERENCES

Cleckley, H. (1964) *The Mask of Sanity*. (4th edn.). St Louis, Missouri: C. V. Mosby.
Floud, J. and Young, W. (1981) *Dangerousness and Criminal Justice*. London: Heinemann.
Hare, R. D. (1978) Electrodermal and cardiovascular correlates of psychopathy. In Hare, R. D. and Schalling, D. (Eds) *Psychopathic Behaviour*. Chichester: Wiley.
Hinton, J. W. (Ed., 1983) *Dangerousness*. London: Allen and Unwin.
Home Office, Department of Health and Social Security (1975) *Report of the Committee on Mentally Abnormal Offenders*. London:HMSO.
Mednick, S. A. and Volavka, J. (1980) Biology and crime. In Morris, N, and Tonry, M (Eds) *Crime and Justice*, vol. 2. Chicago: University of Chicago Press.
Shah, S. A. and Roth, L. H. (1974) Biological and psychophysiological factors in criminality. In Glaser, D. (Ed.) *Handbook of Criminology*. Chicago: Rand McNally.
Widom, C. S. (1977) A methodology for studying non-institutionalized psychopaths. *Journal of Consulting and Clinical Psychology*, **45**, 674–683.

PART 1

CHARACTERISTICS OF AGGRESSIVE OFFENDERS

Aggression and Dangerousness
Edited by D. P. Farrington and J. Gunn
© 1985 John Wiley & Sons Ltd.

CHAPTER 2

The Neurochemistry and Neuroendocrinology of Sexual Aggression

ROBERT PRENTKY

The dearth of empirical data that address the problem of sexual aggression is certainly noteworthy, though perhaps not surprising. The relative absence of research in this area may be attributable to historical scientific timidity about sex in general. In 1922, Robert Dickinson wrote, 'In view of the pervicacious gonadal urge in human beings, it is not a little curious that science develops its sole timidity about the pivotal point of the physiology of sex'. Indeed, the first studies explored the sociological/psychological aspects of sexuality. It was not until 1948 that the entomologist Alfred Kinsey and his colleagues Pomeroy and Martin first published *Sexual Behavior in the Human Male*. The Kinsey reports, based upon extensive interviews and the files of Dr Dickinson, remain the largest collection of data on sexual experience in the world (Henderson, 1981).

Physiological studies of human sexuality lagged behind even these preliminary excursions. The laboratory research of William Masters and Virginia Johnson (1966), appearing less than 20 years ago, detailed for the first time the sexual physiology of females and males. Hence, while humans have been loving and begetting for thousands of years, only in the last 15 years have we had other than sparse and anecdotal information about reproductive physiology. This scientific neglect is even more surprising when we consider that in the study of human adaptation the interaction of physiology and behaviour is epitomized in sexuality.

It is certainly noteworthy that, despite the lack of sound empirical data on most aspects of sexuality, theoreticians have not been the least reticent to draw alliances between sexuality and aggression. From the classical *Freudian perspective*, both sex and aggression are biological instincts which interact in a hypothetically predictable fashion. Inhibited sexual urges may emerge in the form of aggressive behaviour, just as impulses to aggress may be sublimated into various sexual acts (Freud, 1966). From an *ethological perspective*, Lorenz associated affiliation with aggression, arguing that there is no love without aggression. In *On Aggression*, Lorenz (1966) marshalled evidence to support his thesis that over the course of human evolution social bonding and intraspecific aggression developed together.

Finally, from a strictly *biological perspective*, one again notes close ties between sexuality and aggression. The same hormones which activate the accessory sex glands are also involved in aggressive behaviour (Scott, 1971). MacLean and Ploog (1962) reported that electrical stimulation of areas which elicited immediate penile erection were situated within a millimetre of sites which produced a rage response. Although proximity alone need not necessarily imply anything, case studies have suggested possible interactive effects. Mark and Ervin (1970) reported a case history of a woman who evidenced hypermasturbatory behaviour (18–20 times per day) as well as dangerous physical assaults using razor blades and broken bottles. Thiessen (1976) noted that

> in mammals the development of sexuality is intimately tied to the development of aggression. The same steroids seem to be operative and the same critical periods seem to be involved. Unfortunately, too few studies have concentrated on aggression, but those that have suggest a close relationship between the mechanisms of sexual and aggressive differentiation (pp. 62–63).

At the most simplistic level, criminal activity often involves some form of aggression. Similarly, sexual offending (e.g. rape and child molestation), a variant of criminal activity, typically involve aggression. While there may in fact be no direct causal biological link between sexuality and aggression (sexual offending simply being a form of generic criminal behaviour), the weight of speculation, theorizing, and anecdotal evidence merits an examination of the potential for an association between these two cardinal features of human behaviour.

Needless to say, sexual aggression is clearly multifaceted, drawing on early developmental, familial, biological, historical, sociological, and economic roots for its impetus (Knight *et al.*, 1983). The victims may be males or females, children, adolescents, or adults. The crime may happen anywhere at any time. The act itself may be meticulously planned or impulsive; it may be carried out with only the intimation of violence, brutal assault, or murder. Any one of these outcomes may be premeditated or determined by the victim's response. In sum, sexual aggression is defined by a multiplicity of interrelated elements. On the positive side, however, it has been argued that focusing on one specific form of aggression, such as sexual assault, may make empirical testing more feasible than investigating generic aggression couched in global theories (Thiessen, 1976). Moyer (1971a, p. 30) stated that 'for the sake of completeness, it should at least be mentioned that sex-related aggression is probably also a class of aggression', though he does not include it in his typology because so little is known about it. While the existence of sex-related criminal behaviour is obvious, few attempts have been made to marshal evidence that would define and delineate this type of aggression. This review examines the possibility of identifying endocrinological and neurochemical correlates of sexual aggression.

GONADAL HORMONES

While research documenting the importance of androgens in aggression, primarily infrahuman aggression, is considerable (Conner *et al.*, 1969; Conner, 1972; Kling, 1975; Leshner, 1975; Dixson, 1980), evidence relating testosterone to criminal behaviour in general and sexual offences in particular remains sparse and controversial. The preponderance of research relating testosterone to aggression has examined animals, typically rodents and primates. Of this research, there are two main sources of evidence reported. One concerns pre- and post-natal androgen manipulation of normal developmental trends, such as the onset of puberty (when testosterone levels are increasing), and the coincident appearance of aggression. This research further suggests that exposure to steroid hormones early in ontogeny may influence aggression. Primate research reveals unambiguous sexual dimorphic behaviour patterns in which threat, overt aggression, and aggressive play are greater in males than females. Typically, pre-natal treatment of genetic females with testosterone (injected into the pregnant mother) resulted in behaviour more characteristic of genetic males (i.e. more aggressive and socially dominant acts).

A second major line of research has clearly documented the role of plasma testosterone (PT; see the Technical Appendix for the meaning of abbreviations) in influencing 'dominance' in social hierarchies (Ulrich, 1938; Mirsky, 1955; Rose *et al.*, 1971; Logan, 1971; Green *et al.*, 1972; Joslyn, 1973; Mazur, 1976; Dixson and Herbert, 1977; Cochran and Perachio, 1977; Smith *et al.*, 1977; Selmanoff *et al.*, 1977; Keverne *et al.*, 1978; Bernstein, 1970). Rose *et al.* (1975) found a progressive increase in PT with dominance in adult rhesus monkeys. Males who became subordinate to the dominant males showed an 80 per cent drop in PT from baseline levels. The dominant male of the breeding group evidenced a 23 per cent increase in PT 24 hours after he successfully defended his group and became the dominant member of a larger, newly formed group. Bernstein *et al.* (1979) found the same effects of dominance or subordination (defeat) on PT in male pigtail monkeys.

Testosterone and Human Aggression

In general, there is a dearth of information on the relationship, if one exists, between hormones and human aggression (Thiessen, 1976). While several reviews have dealt specifically with the relationship between PT and aggression in criminal and non-criminal populations (Rada, 1981; Rada *et al.*, 1976; Rose, 1975), the evidence is conflictual, with many studies reporting both positive and negative results (Doering *et al.*, 1975; Ehrenkranz *et al.*, 1974; Kreuz and Rose, 1972; Rada *et al.*, 1976). At least one study has reported positive results (Persky *et al.*, 1971), while others have reported marginally positive findings (Mattson *et al.*, 1980) or negative ones (Meyer-Bahlburg, *et al.*, 1974; Monti *et al.*, 1977; Rada *et al.*, 1983).

Several studies have looked at the relation between PT and mood states in non-criminal male populations. Persky *et al* (1971) related PT level and production rate to scores on the Buss–Durkee Hostility Inventory in a group of 18 healthy young men, averaging 22 years old; 15 healthy older men, averaging 45 years old; and 6 male psychiatric ('dysphoric') patients, averaging 39 years old. The investigators found a highly significant correlation between testosterone production rate and factor 11 (aggressive feelings) of the Buss–Durkee in the group of young men ($r = 0.69$). Interestingly, while production rate did not correlate with age for the young group ($r = 0.07$), it did correlate with age for both normal groups combined (age range 17–66 years, $r = -0.62$). Production rate in mg/day averaged 10.1 for the young men and 5.2 for the older men. PT level in ng/100 ml averaged 685.6 for the young men and 404.3 for the older men. None of the psychometric variables was related to testosterone rate or level for the older men. Another study looked at the relationship between three mood states (hostility, anxiety, and depression) over a 2–month period and PT in a sample of 20 paid male volunteers, averaging 23.4 years old (Doering *et al.*, 1975). Intra-subject correlations were significant in the positive *and* negative directions. A notable lack of homogeneity indicated that the relationship between affect and PT levels varied considerably among subjects. Inter-subject correlations between affect and PT levels were, by and large, all non-significant.

Olweus *et al.* (1980) looked at the relationship between PT and an extensive battery of personality inventory scores in 58 normal adolescent Swedish boys (average age 16). PT levels correlated significantly with self-reports of physical and verbal aggression on the Olweus Aggression Inventory ($r = 0.44$). This finding reflected responsiveness to provocation and threat. The only other inventory variable that related significantly to PT was lack of frustration tolerance ($r = 0.28$). The investigators concluded that 'dimensions reflecting intensity and/or frequency of aggressive responses to provocation and threat were most clearly related to testosterone' (p. 263). Importantly, however, there was only a weak, non-significant correlation ($r = 0.15$) between PT and self-reports of antisocial behaviour (petty theft, truancy, property destruction). The authors dismissed the argument that self-reports of criminal activity were, in this case, a less adequate measure than actual criminal records, since there was strong evidence for the validity of the scale employed. In light of the study by Olweus *et al.* (1980), it is notable that Scaramella and Brown (1978) reported that, while six out of seven aggressiveness items positively correlated with serum testosterone level in 14 male university hockey players, only one item, *response to threat*, reached significance.

There is general support for the notion that in humans testosterone may be more related to the feeling of anger than to the expression of anger. Social learning and cognitive over-ride may be the most critical factors in determining the expression of anger when anger is translated into aggressive criminal activity. In a study looking at the relation between PT and a number of personality inventories in 15 undergraduate males, a significant positive correlation was found between irritability (on the Buss–Durkee) and PT ($r = 0.73$). However, none of the other Buss–Durkee scales or the remaining inventories was significantly related to PT (Brown and Davis, 1975). Notably, more subjects above the median PT level than below reported aggressive feelings on the days that blood was drawn.

Kendenburg *et al.* (1973) examined the relationship between PT and reports of aggressive behaviour in 12 male inpatients on a psychiatric ward. PT levels were monitored weekly over an 8-week period. The investigators found that changes in PT level were correlated with observations of aggressive behaviour in eight patients ($r = 0.42$). For all 12 patients there was a non-significant correlation between mean PT levels and aggressive behaviour.

The results from several other studies on criminal populations have been far from convincing. Matthews (1979) examined 11 male prisoners with a history of violent crime and a matched sample of 11 detainees with no history of violent crime. There was no significant difference in PT level between the two groups. Mattsson *et al.* (1980) compared 40 male delinquent recidivists with a control group of normal adolescents on PT, aggressive behaviour, and personality variables. The mean PT level for the delinquent group (587 ng/100 ml) was non-significantly higher than the mean PT level for the control group (544 ng/100 ml). Among the delinquents, those who committed more violent offences had non-significantly higher PT levels than those who committed less violent offences. Mattsson *et al.* (1980) also noted that age of onset of delinquency was uncorrelated with PT levels.

Kreuz and Rose (1972) found that, while PT levels did not differ in fighting and non-fighting offenders (assessed according to the number of times placed in solitary confinement per year of incarceration), those prisoners with histories of more violent crimes in adolescence had significantly higher PT levels than prisoners without histories of adolescent violence. The investigators hypothesized that PT levels may constitute an important predisposing factor in the presence of other concomitant socio-environmental factors. Another study contrasted three groups of prisoners, 12 with histories of chronic physical aggressiveness, 12 who were 'socially dominant' but not physically aggressive, and 12 who were neither physically aggressive nor socially dominant (Ehrenkranz *et al.*, 1974). The physically aggressive prisoners had significantly higher PT levels than the other two groups, and the socially dominant prisoners had significantly higher PT levels than the third, non-aggressive and non-dominant, group. Perhaps most noteworthy was the *lack* of significant correlations between PT levels and *self*-reports on various inventories. This finding underscores the need for prior selection of subjects into groups based upon clinical/behavioural or criminal history criteria. In addition, one may note that the mean PT level for all 36 subjects in the Ehrenkrantz *et al.* study was similar to that reported by Kreuz and Rose (1972) (8.15 µg/ml vs 8.44 µg/ml). The range in the Ehrenkrantz *et al.* study was from $\bar{x} = 5.99$ µg/ml (non-aggressives) to $\bar{x} = 10.10$ µg/ml (aggressives), with the socially dominant prisoners falling in the middle ($\bar{x} = 8.36$ µg/ml). The range reported by Kruez and Rose was from 3.05 µg/ml to 15.35 µg/ml.

Mendelson and Mello's (1974) study, which looked at the effect of alcohol on testosterone in addicts, is a variant of the research just discussed. While the major finding of the study was the suppression of PT with chronic ethanol intake in eight of nine subjects, the investigators also reported *no* relationship between elevations in PT and violent behaviour in another sample of 42 alcohol addicts. All PT levels were checked during sobriety. According to the authors, 14 of the subjects (33 per cent) had abnormally high (>650 ng/100 ml) or low (<400 ng/100 ml) PT levels. Of those eight subjects who had high PT levels, two were least violent, two were moderately violent, and four were most violent. Of the four in the latter group, three had PT levels between 651 and 700 ng/100 ml and one had a PT level between 851 and 900 ng/100 ml. There were, however, two least violent subjects who had similarly high PT levels.

Murray *et al.* (1975) looked at endocrine changes after treatment in 12 male sex offenders. Three of the 12 subjects had elevated levels of testosterone and sex hormone-binding globulin (SHBG). In one study, tranquillizers (benperidol and chlorpromazine) were compared to a placebo. In a second study, ethynyl oestradiol and cyproterone acetate were compared. The tranquillizers produced no change in PT or luteinizing hormone (LH). Cyproterone acetate, the strongest known anti-androgen (Neumann, 1971), reduced levels of PT, LH, and follicle-stimulating hormone (FSH). While ethynyl oestradiol did not affect FSH, it produced a *rise* in PT (46 per cent), LH (49 per cent) and SHBG (120 per cent). The unexpected increase in PT and LH was attributed to the increase in SHBG, which produced a rise in bound, inactive testosterone. Cyproterone acetate did not affect SHBG. Despite the differing endocrine changes from the three active treatment conditions, all substances produced similar behavioural changes. In brief, the treatment conditions affected frequency of masturbation and self-ratings of frequency of sexual thoughts, while leaving unaffected both sexual attitudes (measured by the semantic differential) and plethysmographic erectile response to erotic visual stimuli.

Rada *et al.* (1976) looked at PT levels in 52 rapists and 12 child-molesters. The investigators rated the rapists according to the degree of violence during the offence, finding that the rapists judged to be the most violent had significantly higher mean PT levels than normals, child-molesters, and less violent rapists. The PT levels for these latter three groups were within normal limits: normals (mean 625 ng/100 ml), rapists (mean 610 ng/100 ml), child-molesters (mean 502 ng/100 ml). By contrast, the only rapist who murdered his victim had a PT level of 1236 ng/100 ml. The mean PT level for 'brutally violent' rapists was 853 ng/100 ml. Even the PT levels of these violent rapists, however, did not exceed normal limits. Mean rating scores on the Buss–Durkee Hostility Inventory for the rapists were significantly higher than the mean scores for normals. There was no correlation between the Buss–Durkee scores and PT levels.

Rada (1981) reported a follow-up study by himself and his colleagues in which they looked at PT, dehydrotestosterone, and LH in violent and non-violent sex offenders. Again, mean testosterone levels for rapists, child-molesters, and institutional controls were all within normal limits. While rapists in general had higher testosterone levels than child-molesters, violent child-molesters had the highest testosterone levels of all groups. In addition, the violent rapists had slightly *lower* testosterone levels than the non-violent rapists. Buss–Durkee scores again did not correlate with PT levels among the rapists, though younger child-molesters had higher hostility scores and higher PT levels than older child-molesters.

There are several important areas of sex hormone–behaviour interaction which, while not necessarily related to criminal acts, should be addressed. The following sections consider the effects of anti-androgenic substances on sexually deviant behaviour, the premenstrual syndrome, and the androgenic response to stress.

Androgen Depletion as an Intervention Strategy

The use of oestrogens to control sexually deviant behaviour is a comparatively old practice, dating back over 30 years (Golla and Hodge, 1949). During the 1960's a number of potent anti-androgenic substances came into experimental use (Lerner, 1964), including A-norprogesterone (Lerner *et al.*, 1960), cyproterone acetate (Neumann *et al.*, 1968) and chlormadinone acetate (Rocky and Neri, 1968). While cyproterone acetate is commonly used in Great Britain and elsewhere in Europe, it is not permissible to use it in the United States. The agent of choice in the States, since 1966, has been medroxyprogesterone acetate (MPA; Depo-Provera, Upjohn). Money *et al.* (1975) reported that the use of this steroid androgen antagonist, in combination with a programme of counselling, was beneficial in helping sex offenders regulate their behaviour. In five cases (out of 10) there was a remission of paraphiliac symptoms. Most of these paraphiliacs were, however, pedophiles and exhibitionists and not rapists. The investigators found that, while MPA had a potent effect on sexual behaviour (suppression of testicular androgen, suppression of erection and ejaculation, and a decrease in erotic imagery), it could not be concluded that the drug altered aggressiveness. This latter finding was based primarily upon the results of the administration of MPA to a comparison group of 13 XYY males who were non-sexual (robbery and destructiveness) offenders.

As previously noted, Murray *et al.* (1975) looked at the effects of tranquillizers and androgen antagonists in two groups of 12 male sexual offenders. In one study benperidol and chlorpromazine were compared with a placebo, and in another study ethynyl oestradiol and cyproterone acetate were compared with no treatment. While the tranquillizers had no effect on PT or LH, both hormones, as well as FSH, were reduced after administration of cyproterone acetate. Benperidol, cyproterone acetate, and ethynyl oestradiol all produced significant reductions in the self-rated frequency of sexual thoughts. The two hormones also reduced the frequency of masturbation and had a weak effect on the plethysmographic erectile response. Another report also concluded that benperidol, cyproterone acetate, and ethynyl oestradiol all produced similar behavioural changes (Bancroft *et al.*, 1974).

Spodak *et al.* (1978) reported that three out of six of their patients responded favourably to MPA. The three patients for whom there was apparently no recurrence of paraphiliac behaviour were two pedophiles and a sadist (a 42-year-old man involved in a 20-year-long sadomasochistic relationship with his wife). The three patients whose paraphiliac behaviour was unaffected by treatment were two pedophiles and an exhibitionist. The efficacy of MPA with respect to paraphiliac sex drive was certainly equivocal in this study. Curiously, one of the three cases in which the drug *did* prove efficacious involved the sadistic activities of a middle-aged man who beat his wife, shaved her head, and tied her in chains. The drug failed, however, to prove useful with three relatively non-violent offenders: a 27-year-old homosexual pedophile who engaged in frottage, a 52-year-old homosexual pedophile, and a 38-year-old exhibitionist.

A number of recent studies have reported on the use of MPA with sex offenders (e.g. Berlin and Coyle, 1981; Berlin and Meinecke, 1981; Gagne, 1981; Halleck, 1981). Berlin and Meinecke (1981) reported on 20 paraphiliac males treated with MPA. With the exception of two cases of sadomasochism, all other patients were pedophiliacs or exhibitionists, with one case of voyeurism and one case of transvestism. At the time of the report, 13 patients had completed or discontinued treatment. Of those 13, 10 relapsed less than 1 year after treatment. The three successes (no relapse 1 year after treatment) were all homosexual pedophiliacs. It should be pointed out that all relapses were treatment dropouts, whereas two of the three successes satisfactorily completed the treatment regimen.

Gagne (1981) reported on 48 male paraphiliacs who received MPA and milieu therapy for up to 12 months. Of the 48 patients, 27 were pedophiliacs, five were exhibitionists, four were compulsive masturbators, three were rapists and the remaining nine engaged in other offences (e.g. incest, voyeurism, transvestism, indecent assault, attempted rape). Despite the apparent heterogeneity of the sample, Gagne identified a number of common features: a history of hypersexuality manifested in frequent masturbation, multiple sex partners, inability to refrain from acting on deviant sexual thoughts, an abnormally high amount of sexual fantasies, and erotic dreams. In addition, all pedophiles had been introduced to sexual activity by an adult before they reached puberty. Gagne found that 40 of the 48 patients responded positively to treatment, all within 3 weeks. He reported a decrease in the urge to engage in deviant sexual behaviour and improved psychosocial functioning. While he stated that none of the 40 patients returned to their pre-treatment sexual behaviour after their testosterone levels restabilized, there was no indication of the length of follow-up. Unfortunately, the apparent absence of a control group in this study obviates any reliable conclusions that can be drawn from the data.

While the literature on chemical castration is important in elucidating the role of sex hormones in sexually aggressive behaviour, studies thus far have focused on samples of relatively non-aggressive pedophiles and exhibitionists. The results are reasonably consistent with respect to the treatment effects of MPA, and less consistent with respect to the post-treatment effects of an MPA regimen on recidivism. The effect of anti-androgenic medication on aggressiveness, however, cannot be deduced from this literature. One would surmise, if anything, that there were no direct effects. It may be, as Cooper (1981) suggested, that the reduction of PT functions primarily to alter the affect associated with the sex drive and secondarily to suppress hypothalamic releasing factors and pituitary gonadotrophins. Furthermore, as Rose (1978) pointed out, it would be helpful to have some idea whether reduced sexual interest was related in any systematic way to reduced circulating free testosterone.

Testosterone Response to Stress

A number of longitudinal studies have looked at PT levels in normal male humans. Kreuz et al. (1972) examined the relationship between PT levels and psychological stress in an officer candidate school. The investigators reported decreased levels of PT during the earlier, most stressful phase of the course. Kreuz et al. indicate that this is the first evidence associating psychological stress with suppressed levels of PT. Rose *et al.* (1969) had already presented data showing that soldiers in basic training who were anticipating Vietnam combat in the near future had lowered urine excretion of testosterone and other androgens. Hence, there is both direct and indirect evidence that psychological stress may suppress androgen levels. Notably, the depletion of testosterone reported by Rose *et al.* (1969) occurred along with an increase in adrenal cortical activity. This is consistent with Kling's (1975) suggestion that increased secretion of adrenal cortical hormones inhibits the secretion of LH, thereby inhibiting the secretion of testosterone from the testes. One would then expect that stress or anxiety states may be associated with a decrease in testosterone, and indeed this has been found to be the case (Kreuz *et al.*, 1972; Monden *et al.*, 1972).

Since it is commonly held that a psychopath is *less* likely to experience anxiety, particularly in regard to antisocial behaviour, it may be hypothesized that the psychopath has a decreased steroid production (e.g. 17-OHCS) and possibly increased secretion of testosterone. Ehrenkrantz *et al.* (1974) reported a relative absence of anxiety in their socially dominant inmates. In the Ehrenkrantz *et al.* study, physically violent offenders had significantly higher PT levels than less aggressive, socially dominant offenders. This again supports the hypothesis that the psychopath is a socially dominant, low-anxiety individual who engages in relatively non-aggressive antisocial behaviour. Furthermore, it follows from this chain of evidence that there exists a much more violent individual who is high in anxiety, albeit possibly low in PT. One would surmise that this latter violent individual is not androgenically motivated. High anxiety may be related to the suppression of impulses to aggress, surfacing in unpredictable, spontaneous expressions of violence. A more detailed explication of the possible aetiology for this high violence individual is provided in the summary statement at the end of this review.

Kling (1975) concludes in his review that

> the studies reported here seem to agree that a positive correlation exists between plasma levels of testosterone and dominance and aggressive behaviour in both human and non-human primate species; further, that this correlation may be present in both males and females (p. 318).

Importantly, Kling goes on to point out that 'none of the investigators appear to argue that the higher levels of testosterone are causal with respect to aggression' (p. 318). In other words, the testosterone level itself does not determine social rank, dominance, or aggressiveness, and plasma levels may fluctuate considerably with changes in dominance or aggression. Thus, while LH and testosterone are associated with aggressive behaviour, and while hormonally lowered circulating testosterone seems to reduce aggressive behaviour (Blumer, 1971), the relation between hormones and behaviour is unclear. It appears to be correlative but not causal.

One explanation is that testosterone may raise thresholds of excitation in the hypothalamus. This notion of increased sensitivity from neural facilitation has been articulated by Moyer (1971b): 'certain blood constituents act on the aggression brain circuits to increase their sensitivity with the result that they are more easily fired by the relevant stimuli' (p. 241). As Moyer points out, however, it is not clear whether changes in blood chemistry increase sensitivity directly, or whether the effect is indirect by altering neurotransmitters in key areas of the brain, such as the limbic system and ventral diencephalon, which in turn results in increased sensitivity of limbic and hypothalamic circuits.

The Premenstrual Syndrome

The 'premenstrual syndrome' has been described a number of times in the literature (Dalton, 1961, 1964; Greene and Dalton, 1953; Hamburg, 1966; Hamburg et al., 1968; Moos, 1968; Parlee, 1973). One of the cardinal features of this syndrome is irritability, deriving in part, from altered gonadal hormone levels, particularly the drop in progesterone—a hormone with known tranquillizing properties (Leshner, 1978). Thiessen (1976) noted that

> if the premenstrual cycle is divided into five phases that correspond to ovarian changes there is an obvious correlation between indices of negative affect (e.g., depression, irritability, jitteriness, tension, etc.) and the pattern of blood hormones. Negative affect is lowest during the follicular phase when estrogen levels are highest, and negative affect is highest when progesterone and estrogen levels are falling just prior to and during the initial phase of menstruation (p. 88).

In one study looking at mood change during the menstrual cycle in 15 married childless subjects, it was reported that anxiety and aggressive feelings peaked pre-menstrually and menstrually and reached a trough at mid-cycle, while self-ratings of pleasantness and sexual arousal peaked at mid-cycle (the phase of high oestrogen secretion) (Moos et al., 1969). Moyer (1971a) presented evidence suggesting that crimes of violence committed by women were related to their menstrual cycle. Sixty-two per cent of the violent crimes committed by 249 female prisoners occurred during the pre-menstrual week. Only 2 per cent of the crimes took place at the end of menstruation (Morton et al., 1953). In a female outpatient population with aggressive behaviour, it was reported that mean values for PT were normal in non-violent patients but significantly elevated in violent ones (Ehlers et al., 1980). Ehlers et al. also found that many of the violent patients reported increased 'emotionality' during their menses. Similar findings have even been noted in female rhesus monkeys, where the frequency of aggression and bite wounds is significantly increased prior to menstruation (Sassenrath et al., 1973).

Mayer and Wheeler (1982) reported the recent case of Sadie Smith, a 29-year-old British barmaid who had 20 or more convictions for arson, assault, and homicide. In 1981 she successfully avoided imprisonment for threatening the life of a police officer by attributing her behaviour to pre-menstrual tension. It was brought out in court that all of her offences occurred pre-menstrually. Furthermore, she claimed that she was 'a raging animal each month' unless she took progesterone. The role of pre-menstrual hormonal fluctuations as a catalyst for female aggression—not to mention its legitimacy as a legal defence due to diminished capacity—has generated considerable controversy.

Overview

Evidence documenting a relationship between plasma testosterone and aggression in criminal and non-criminal populations is inconclusive, with studies reporting both positive and negative findings (Doering *et al.*, 1975; Ehrenkrantz *et al.*, 1974; Kreuz and Rose, 1972; Rada *et al.*, 1976). It appears that the PT level in humans may be more related to the feeling of anger than to the actual expression of anger (Brown and Davis, 1975), with social learning and other cognitive over-ride mechanisms playing a critical role in determining the response. In this sense, PT may function to prime the pump but not to open the valve. This notion is further supported by the research on anti-androgenic therapy with sex offenders, where it has been suggested that the primary effect of PT reduction is to alter affect associated with the sex drive (Cooper, 1981). There seems to be more convincing evidence that altered gonadal hormone levels in women (particularly a drop in progesterone) results in negative affect (irritability, jitteriness, tension), as well as a disproportionate number of crimes of violence committed by women (Ehlers *et al.*, 1980; Morton *et al.*, 1953; Moyer, 1971a).

There is both direct and indirect evidence that psychological, social, and physical stress *lowers* PT levels (Kling, 1975). The stress-induced increase in adrenal cortical hormones inhibits the secretion of LH, which in turn inhibits the secretion of testosterone from the testes. Thus, there tends to be an inverse relation between the stress or anxiety level and the PT level, with heightened anxiety being associated with decreased PT (Kreuz *et al.*, 1972; Monden *et al.*, 1972). Since it is commonly reported that psychopaths are *less* likely to experience anxiety, it may be hypothesized that the psychopath has a decreased adrenal steroid output and an increased secretion of testosterone.

There are two periods during development when testosterone may be particularly influential with respect to aggressive behaviour. The first occurs *in utero*. The fact that male children are more aggressive than female children has been attributed to the presence of testosterone in males and its absence in females during a restricted period of *in utero* development (Simon, 1981). This author pointed out that one might examine this prospectively by correlating pre-natal hormone levels with post-natal behaviour. Like most prospective studies, this requires 15–20 years to accomplish.

The second period occurs during puberty, where there is a ten-fold increase in testosterone production (Brown, 1981). One might hypothesize that puberty should be related to the onset of, or increases in, antisocial behaviour among those disposed to engage in such behaviour. Konner (1982) reported that, in one study of male prison inmates, the higher the testosterone level the earlier the age of first arrest. Kreuz and Rose (1972) also found a significant correlation between the age of first occurrence of more violent or aggressive crimes and PT levels ($r = -0.65$). If the age-related changes in criminal behaviour can be tied to developmentally related changes in testosterone level, it would provide important correlative evidence implicating testosterone as a contributing factor.

Methodological Considerations

1. Generalizing from the abundant animal research to humans is problematic. First, few of the 188 primate species have been studied experimentally, and the experiments have used different measures of dominance and inter-male aggression (Dixson, 1980). Dixson further points out that while androgens have pronounced effects on sexual responses in adult male monkeys, the central effects upon aggression are much less important in monkeys than in rodents. Second, whatever applies to certain primate species is not mediated by the powerful impact of social learning in humans.

2. The use of personality inventories as dependent measures of hostility or aggression may be inappropriate to discriminate between the phenomenology of aggression, attitudes about aggression and, importantly, the latent potential for expressing aggression (Rada, 1981). A case in point is the Buss–Durkee Inventory which, as Olweus et al. (1980) pointed out, fails to relate significantly to PT levels in most studies that have used it. The generally poor association between self-reports of aggression and PT has been reported elsewhere (e.g. Kreuz and Rose, 1972; Meyer-Bahlburg et al., 1973, 1974). The only way to tap the aspect of human aggression that is influenced by androgens may be to select subjects who have reliably demonstrated aggressive, assertive, or competitive behaviour.

3. Most of the studies of human aggressive behaviour have been conducted on subjects who have demonstrable track records of antisocial behaviour or on subjects who are prosocial and relatively non-competitive (such as students). The former studies are important, though restricted to subjects who, by and large, come from a sociocultural background conducive to antisocial behaviour. As Kling (1975) pointed out, it is equally important to examine highly competitive non-criminal populations (along the lines of the Scaramella and Brown, 1978, study).

4. In general, it is not known what link in the causal chain of human aggression is occupied by testosterone. Does a high stable level of testosterone predispose to aggressive behaviour? Or do specific situations (such as provocation or threat, frustration, deprivation, isolation, etc.) precede and differentially provoke increased levels of testosterone? And what role does social learning play in the cognitive mediation of potentially stressful, testosterone-producing situations?

PITUITARY–ADRENAL CORTICAL HORMONES

Typically, androgens have been considered the only hormones important in aggression, since the effects of androgen manipulation tend to be more dramatic and more uniform across species of animal (Leshner, 1978). There is, however, an increasing interest in the role of hormones of the pituitary-adrenocortical axis on aggression (Bach-Y-Rita, 1975), in part because the adrenal cortex is a steroidogenic organ, in part because of the interplay of the two hormonal systems (gonadal and adrenocortical). While there is no direct evidence associating corticosteroids with sexual aggression, recent studies have implicated such hormones in non-sexual aggression (e.g. Bronson and Desjardins, 1971; Conner, 1972; Leshner, 1975, 1978).

Even here the experimental evidence is far from conclusive. Bronson and Desjardins (1971), Sigg (1969), and Sigg et al. (1966) found no evidence to support any *direct* relationship between adrenalectomy or ACTH manipulation and isolation-induced or spontaneous aggression, although it is reported that bilateral adrenalectomy reduces aggression by increasing ACTH secretion (Brain, 1971; Brain et al., 1971; Harding and Leshner, 1972; Leshner and Candland, 1973; Leshner et al., 1973).[1] Leshner (1975) concluded that

> high ACTH levels have been shown both to reduce aggressiveness and to increase fearfulness in the presence of a novel conspecific, while intermediate pituitary–adrenocortical hormone levels seem to predispose the animal to be more aggressive and less fearful (p. 228).

Importantly, it may well be the case that the real effects produced by adrenalectomy are not the result of tissue removal *per se*, but the consequent changes at target sites responsive to adrenocortical hormones (Harvey, 1974). Many stressors, including threat and aggression, have pronounced effects on adrenal stores of certain amines (Welch and Welch, 1971). These authors observed a 63 per cent elevation in adrenal epinephrine after ten days of fighting, dropping slightly to 56 per cent after 14 days. Clearly, there are extensive biochemical changes that occur in the brains of animals that experience aggression and defeat (Eleftheriou, 1971). Bronson and Desjardins (1971) found that in defeated mice plasma corticosterone levels peaked within 1 hour after fighting and remained elevated for 24 hours after defeat. The investigators concluded that

> these observations indicate that some aspect of the experience of defeat may continue to act on the hypothalamo–hypophyseal axis to elicit release of adrenocorticotrophic hormone for a considerable period of time after an attack actually has taken place (p. 53).

It appears that ACTH manipulation may differentially affect aggression depending on the duration of the change. The general notion that ACTH functions to decrease aggression holds only as a long-term effect, whereas short-term administration of ACTH has an excitatory effect on corticosterone secretion which increases aggression (Leshner, 1978). The decrease in aggression resulting from a chronic increase in adrenocortical activity may be the result of the extra-adrenal action of ACTH (Leshner, 1978). It is important to note in this connection that ACTH depresses gonadal secretion of testosterone.

Psychoendocrine research on the pituitary–adrenal cortical system was excellently reviewed by Mason (1968). Mason noted that with humans there are marked individual differences in psychoendocrine responses to an identical stimulus. Mason stated 'no matter how seemingly threatening or drastic the life situation, it cannot be assumed that all, or even most, subjects will experience substantial emotional arousal or distress' (p. 594). Given an emotionally arousing situation, the critical question for those *who evidence no hormonal response* is to determine if they were in fact aroused (but failed to evidence the expected physiological response) or if the situation was not salient in generating arousal. One could certainly envision both possibilities occurring. In the former case a real emotional response is not translated into a physiological response. In the latter case the most charged stimuli are filtered and fail to elicit any appreciable emotional response.

Mason found that 'studies with human subjects provide almost unanimous support for the conclusion that 17-OHCS levels sensitively reflect psychological influences' (Mason, 1968, p. 592). Pituitary–adrenal cortical activity increases during states of arousal or alerting, and the increase seems to be directly related to the intensity of the arousal. Mason went on to conclude that while 'the precise nature of the psychological correlates of 17-OHCS response is in need of further study.... **The effect of suppressed versus expressed anger** ... can be considered firmly established' (p. 592).

Important points pertaining to 17-OHCS were summarized by Mason (1968) as follows:

1. 17-OHCS levels are very sensitive to even relatively subtle psychological influences;

2. the acute sensitivity of 17-OHCS levels to the most subtle influences suggests that the central nervous system exerts a constant 'tonicity' upon these hormones.
3. increased levels of 17-OHCS reflect a rather amorphous or undifferentiated arousal state, not a highly specific one;
4. novelty, uncertainty, or unpredictability are all potent influences in producing 17-OHCS elevations;
5. intense emotional reactions with concomitant behavioural responses are associated with unusually marked increases in 17-OHCS;
6. psychological influences may function to raise *or* lower levels of pituitary-–adrenal cortical hormones; and
7. marked individual differences in pituitary–adrenal cortical response to any stimulus is a striking and consistent finding.

Rose (1969) proposed an extension of the psychoendocrine model to incorporate androgenic activity, forming the hypothalamic–pituitary–gonadal system. It was pointed out earlier in this review that testosterone may be suppressed following exposure to stressors or potential stressors. Given the wide range of 17-OHCS responses to stress, it would appear likely that there are important and noteworthy individual differences in the degree of testosterone suppression under stress. In sum, when considering the impact of physiological and psychological stressors, the assessment of androgen activity and pituitary–adrenal cortical activity cannot be viewed as two independent and unrelated systems. One might predict that the important hormone in this regard is not a glucocorticoid (such as 17-OHCS) but the polypeptide ACTH, which directly affects PT level. Thus, a chronic high level of ACTH may chronically suppress PT level, thereby reducing aggression. The glucocorticoids probably do not directly influence aggression but function more to control other aspects of the agonistic response, such as submission (Leshner, 1978).

A final parenthetic speculation comes from McEwen's (1972) statement that 'investigation of corticosterone uptake and binding by brain regions have provided us with a phenomenon, namely the intense concentration of this hormone in the hippocampus' (p. 48). Neuroendocrinological research has demonstrated that lesions in the hippocampus or the fornix (a bundle of fibres continuous with the fimbria emerging from the hippocampus and proceeding downward into the hypothalamus and mamillary body) tended to eliminate the normal diurnal variation of ACTH secretion (McEwen, 1972). Similarly, implantation of cortisone in the hippocampus was found to have the same effect (Slusher, 1966). The actual effect of hippocampal corticosteroid implantation seems to be the *enhancement* of basal and stress-induced ACTH secretion (McEwen, 1972). These effects are *opposite* to expectation since corticosteroids inhibit ACTH.

One explanation for this is that corticosteroids which act on the hippocampus, to inhibit a functionally inhibitory system concerned with blocking hypothalamic input, stimulate ACTH release (McEwen *et al.*, 1972). There are certainly other brain structures involved in ACTH release (e.g. amygdala, septum, hypothalamus, midbrain) that are also sensitive to adrenocortical 'feedback'. The amygdala, in particular, is of theoretical interest. Rubin *et al.* (1966) reported on five patients with intractable temporal-lobe epilepsy. Stimulation from chronic electrode implants in the basolateral amygdala produced increases in corticosteroids in plasma and urine. In fact, a 454 per cent increase in corticosteroid excretion was noted in the first-hour urine on the stimulation day compared with the control day. Rubin *et al.* further concluded that hippocampal stimulation produces decreases in plasma corticosteroids. Mason *et al.* (1961) also reported a marked decrease in 17-OHCS after 90 minutes of hippocampal stimulation. These findings are consistent with Smythies' (1970) conclusion that 'the amygdala is a moderately powerful centre for reward and punishment ... and it exerts powerful control over pituitary/adrenal function in an opposite direction to that exerted by the [hippocampus]' (p. 154).

In sum, the influence of pituitary–adrenal hormones seems to be indirect, possibly reverberative. These hormones may mediate aggressive responses by catalysing a chain of neurochemical events. It is not possible to separate cause from effect, in good measure because of complex neuroendocrine interactions (such as with the gonadal system).

CATECHOLAMINES

Catecholamine is a generic term which applies to all compounds possessing a catechol nucleus and an amine group. For all practical purposes the word refers to dopamine and its metabolic products—adrenaline and noradrenaline. Nerve stimulation (a propagated impulse) is required to release catecholamines from storage sites into the plasma (Sedvall *et al.*, 1968; Molinoff *et al.*, 1970). Mild stimulation increases tyrosine hydroxylase activity by releasing synthesized catecholamines, reducing enzymatic inhibition (Melmon, 1974). Intense or protracted stimulation increases synthesis of both tyrosine hydroxylase and dopamine beta-hydroxylase, resulting in a significant production of catecholamines (Molinoff *et al.*, 1970). One of the most common types of stimulation that has been investigated experimentally is stress. Melmon (1974) cited a host of studies to support his statement that 'when man or animals are subjected to extraordinary stresses (e.g. childbirth, burns, cold, hypoxia, immobilization, isolation, or physical exercise), the rate of synthesis of catecholamines increases greatly' (p. 295). Clearly, there are numerous varieties of stress that alter synthesis of catecholamines, including drugs and complex physical activities (e.g. aggression).

Weiss *et al.* (1975) looked at the effects of *chronic* exposure to stress (cold water or shock) on avoidance–escape behaviour and on norepinephrine in rats. The endogenous norepinephrine level in the hypothalamus and telencephalon was reduced by acute inescapable shock. Weiss *et al.* (1975) concluded, in reconciling their findings with the commonly held view associating stress with elevated catecholamine levels, that with repeated exposure to the stressor adaptation or habituation occurred in central noradrenergic systems. Whether such adaptation is stressor-specific, transitory, a 'learned' response or confined to relatively primitive responses remains to be seen, but it certainly prompts interesting speculation as to the long-term effect of chronic stress during childhood and adolescence. A question of some parsimony is whether the 'psychopath' is an individual whose noradrenergic system has ceased responding to stressors that ordinarily elicit responses in others. In this case the biological response may simply follow as one consequence of a highly stressed, abusive upbringing.

Obvious stressors are fear and aggression. Over 25 years ago Funkenstein (1955) theorized that fear and anxiety were conditions associated with increased adrenaline, while anger was associated with increased noradrenaline. One study in particular found support for Funkenstein's theory, discovering that aggressive behaviour in a laboratory setting (42 12–17-year-old boys) was positively correlated with methylnoradrenaline excretion (Ekkers, 1975). In this study, aggression was unrelated to methyladrenaline. Interestingly, Ekkers also reported a correlation between methyladrenaline/methylnoradrenaline excretion and a dimension, derived from psychoanalytic theory, of super-ego strength and drive strength (fear of being overwhelmed by one's impulses). Super-ego strength and drive strength were unrelated to the behavioural measure of aggression.

The relationship of bioamines to aggression was excellently reviewed by Welch and Welch (1971). These authors found that the rate of synthesis and turnover of brain amines was related to environmental stimulation, decreasing under conditions of isolation. In fact, they concluded that the tendency to fight was directly related to the time spent in isolation. While aggression is not characteristic of all isolated species, a more general reaction of hyperexcitability apparently is. It is the condition of hyperexcitability, particularly severe conflict or aggression, that produces an increase in bioamines. The intense stimulation of conflict or aggression accelerates the depletion of bioamines, presumably through neurotransmission. Welch and Welch (1971) reported reductions of 44 per cent–47 per cent of adrenaline after rage reactions in mice.

Two types of conditions of stimulation seem to modulate biosynthesis of catecholamines. Conditions of *stress*, including aggression, increase the rate of biosynthesis in response to an increased rate of release and turnover. If there is a *response* to the stressor (e.g. aggression), the rate of depletion increases. Conditions of *sensory deprivation*, including isolation, result in 'natural' states (e.g. aggression or hyperexcitability) which accelerate central and peripheral catecholamine metabolism.

In this regard, a number of studies have reported associations between increased catecholamines and 'hyperexcitability' in psychiatric patients. Nelson *et al.* (1966) found that elevated levels of metadrenaline and normetadrenaline were associated with agitated, unstable behavior in six psychiatric patients. Kunce *et al.* (1970) found elevated normetadrenaline levels to be associated with the 'neurotic triad' on the Minnesota Multiphasic Personality Inventory (hysteria, depression, hypochondriasis) in a sample of 44 psychiatric outpatients. Kunce *et al.* concluded that their 'clients with neurotic defence mechanisms may be more labile biochemically' (p. 293).

An important point made by Welch and Welch (1971) is that, in the *absence* of biosynthesis, stress produces *no* build-up of biogenic amines, nor is there necessarily an accelerated depletion rate. Under these circumstances, stress, even aggression, may actually decrease the depletion rate of amines following biosynthetic inhibition. Welch and Welch (1971) report on the lasting effects of brief daily fighting on the heart, the brain, and adrenal amine content. One such lasting effect seems to be elevation in brain and adrenal catecholamines. These changes are presumably adaptive; that is, the system has become accustomed to, hence anticipates, the stress-induced amine demand. If such a chronic state does indeed exist, it seems to represent the opposite condition from the one observed by Weiss *et al.* (1975), in which repeated exposure to stress reduced catecholamine levels.

SEROTONIN

Serotonin (5-hydroxytryptamine, or 5-HT) is found in high concentrations in blood platelets and, within the central nervous system, in the hypothalamus. In the synthetic chain, 5-hydroxytryptophan (5-HTP) is decarboxylated to yield 5-HT. A metabolite of serotonin, 5-hydroxyindoleacetic acid (5-HIAA), is excreted in the urine.

While the evidence relating serotonin to certain types of aggression is noteworthy (Welch and Welch, 1971; Conner *et al.*, 1973; Valzelli, 1977), what functional role serotonin plays in aggression is unclear. Welch and Welch (1971) reviewed early research with animals which associated *low levels* of brain serotonin with aggression. In addition, the potentiation of muricide (mouse killing) in rats with the administration of 5-HT biosynthesis inhibitors (parachlorophenylalanine or PCPA) has been reported by Karli *et al.* (1969) and Sheard (1969). Conner *et al.* (1973) found, however, that PCPA (or serotonergic mechanisms in general) had *no* effect on shock-induced fighting. This finding is not surprising and lends support to Moyer's (1968, 1971a,b,c) thesis that different brain mechanisms control different types of aggression.

Valzelli (1977) cited studies which suggest that lesioning the medial hypothalamus enhances aggression (defensive behaviour) while lesioning the lateral hypothalamus eliminates territorial aggression. Similarly, bilateral lesioning of the basal or central nuclei of the amygdala induces attack behaviour, while bilateral lesioning of the amygdala eliminates interspecific competitive aggression and muricide (Valzelli, 1977). Vergnes (1980) concluded that, while the serotonergic system in the amygdala is not necessarily implicated in the control of muricide, the amygdala *is* involved in the control of interspecies aggression by specific stimuli. Kostowski and Pucilowski (1980) found that serotonergic neurons of the dorsal raphe (midbrain raphe nuclei) are critically involved in muricidal behaviour in rats. Another structure, the septum, was examined by Potegal *et al.* (1980). These investigators reported that septal stimulation is synergistic with serotonergic activity. Specifically, Potegal *et al.* found that quipazine, a serotonergic agonist, lowers stimulation thresholds while metergoline, a serotonergic antagonist, raises them.

The biochemical interplay of various neurotransmitters was further explored by Vernikos-Danellis and Berger (1973). These authors concluded that there is evidence to support the interrelationship between brain 5-HT and the pituitary–adrenal cortical system. Specifically, they suggested that serotonin may mediate a negative feedback mechanism (with the hippocampus) which serves to regulate pituitary–adrenal function. Additionally, it is apparently the case that 5-HTP (5-hydroxytryptophan) *reduces* 24-hour excretion of 17-OHCS (Brodie *et al.*, 1973).

Weil-Malherbe and Szara (1971) concluded that

an absolute or relative preponderance of physiologically active brain catecholamines is correlated with alertness, aggressivity, improved performance, and increased motor activity, whereas an absolute or relative preponderance of active brain serotonin is correlated with sedation, anxiety, disorientation, and eventually, at higher levels of activity, with excitation, agitation, and convulsions (p. 25).

The specific effect of 5-HT on male sexual behaviour has been reviewed by Zitrin (1973). Most of this research has been carried out by the administration of PCPA. The most impressive effects of 5-HT depletion on male sexual behaviour are observed in the rat, where increased sexual excitement, increased mounting behaviour, and increased chasing/rolling over have been observed. Tagliamonte *et al.* (1969) reported compulsive sexual behaviour with PCPA alone and in combination with pargyline in rabbits as well as rats. Tagliamonte *et al.* noted that

brain serotonin inhibits sexual behavior in male rats. The increase in sexual excitement elicited by inhibition of monoamine oxidase suggests that the relative balance of serotonergic and noradrenergic tone in the brain may control sexual behavior in male animals (p. 1435).

Sheard (1969) observed a 'great increase' in sexual activity several hours after rats were injected with PCPA; 17–24 hours after injection he witnessed a 'pronounced increase in aggressive behavior' (muricide activity). Sheard reported a third phase of 'abnormal resting behavior' which overlapped and followed the aggressive activity. He concluded that serotonin pathways may exert an important inhibitory effect on sexual and aggressive behaviour, and that the site for this activity may be the amygdaloid complex.

Results of studies employing monkeys and humans have generally been negative; that is, PCPA treatment did not affect sexual behaviour. One study with humans did note other behavioural changes following PCPA treatment, such as depression, crying, anxiety, agitation, and irritability (Sjoerdsma et al., 1970).

Based primarily upon findings from animal research, there is presumptive evidence to conclude that:

1. *low* levels of serotonin may function to increase the likelihood of certain types of aggression;
2. some animal research associates *low* levels of serotonin with sexual excitement;
3. *high* levels of serotonin may produce anxiety and disorientation; and
4. stress increases the turnover of serotonin, though the absolute concentration of serotonin is usually not decreased and may in fact increase.

With respect to the last two points, Valzelli (1981) concluded that

> if emotional lability facilitates the emergence of anxiety and fear, and thus of irritability, probably serotonin is more directly involved than norepinephrine in the regulation of these affective components and in their possible aggression-promoting effect (p. 99).

Summary Remarks on Catecholamines and Serotonin

Of the catecholamines, noradrenaline in particular has been implicated in some forms of aggression, particularly those that Moyer (1968) refers to as irritable or spontaneous. Interventions with cats that are known to produce rage responses, such as decortication or stimulation of the amygdaloid nuclei or lateral hypothalamus, are accompanied by an increased turnover of noradrenaline with no parallel change in dopamine or serotonin (Sorenson and Gordon, 1975). In addition, in rats, chemical interventions which are known to increase the level of noradrenaline also produce spontaneous fighting (Sorenson and Gordon, 1975). By way of contrast are those studies involving animals intraventricularly injected with 6-hydroxydopamine (6-OHDA) (e.g. Eichelman and Thoa, 1973; Sorenson and Ellison, 1973; Sorenson and Gordon, 1975; Beleslin et al., 1980). Typically, 6-OHDA, which chronically depresses catecholamine levels, increases shock-elicited aggression. This syndrome of hyperreactivity to aversive stimuli, termed a 'rage syndrome' by Valzelli (1981), can be abolished with L-DOPA administration, as well as dopaminergic agonists.

There appears to be what might be described as two mirror-image phenomena, each of which is characterized by aggression but elicited by opposite types of input. The 6-OHDA-treated, catecholamine-deficient animal is hyperreactive to negative input and hyporeactive to positive input. The PCPA-treated, serotonin-deficient animal is hyperreactive to positive input, resulting, among other things, in hypersexuality. The PCPA-treated animal also appears hyporeactive to negative input (i.e. punishment) (Hartmann and Geller, 1971; Robichaud and Sledge, 1969; Stevens *et al.*, 1969).

The involvement of these two monoamines in human aggression has been supported by the work of Brown *et al.* (1979), who examined metabolites of serotonin (5-hydroxyindoleacetic acid, or 5-HIAA), norepinephrine (3-methoxy-4-hydroxyphenylglycol, or MHPG) and dopamine (homovanillic acid, or HVA) in the cerebrospinal fluid of 26 men with life histories of aggressive, violent, and impulsive behaviour. Aggression was found to be related to lower 5-HIAA and higher MHPG levels. In addition, all subjects with a prior history of at least one suicide attempt had significantly higher mean aggression scores, lower 5-HIAA, and higher MHPG levels than the 15 subjects with no such history. Brown *et al.* concluded that

> the significant negative correlation between the life history of aggressive behaviour and CSF 5-HIAA, and the significant positive correlation with CSF MHPG are in the directions predicted by the hypothesis that aggression in animals is related to serotonergic and catecholaminergic balance, i.e., decreased 5-HT and/or increased NE and DA, rather than simply to the functional level of either system independently (p. 141).

An interesting footnote to this animal research is the work of Eysenck, Gray and many others associating extreme extraversion and extreme neuroticism with criminal and antisocial behaviour (e.g. Eysenck, 1970; Passingham, 1972; Burgess, 1972; Shapland and Rushton, 1975). In an early study , Eysenck and Rachman (1965) reported that neurotic extraverted children evidenced such dominant behaviours as swearing, fighting, stealing, violence, rudeness, egocentricity, truancy, destructiveness, and lying. The theory behind the poor socialization and poor conditionability of these neurotic extraverts is that they habituate to stimulus cues very rapidly—so rapidly, in fact, that they often pay little attention to prior stimulation. Hence, response hierarchies fail to develop due to a lack of discrimination between stimulus cues.

It has also been predicted that the neurotic extravert is disposed to engage in risk-taking behaviour, evidences a higher than average sexual drive and, importantly, is hyporeactive to pain, and hyperreactive to pleasure, somewhat like a serotonin-deficient animal. Parenthetically, the conclusion of Tagliamonte *et al.* (1969), that an increase in sexual excitement is elicited by an inhibition of monoamine oxidase, has been echoed by Breakefield and her colleagues (Lewin, 1981). They associated lowered monoamine oxidase levels with 'excessive thrill-seeking', and Zuckerman (1979) found that lowered monoamine oxidase levels were correlated with high sensation seeking. These interesting speculations about the relationship of pain and pleasure to a personality dimension of introversion/extraversion have been discussed in detail by Gray (1970, 1971, 1972, 1978).

GENERAL SUMMARY

The preponderance of research on aggression involves animals (primarily rats, cats, and monkeys). Thus, while it is fair to surmise that much of what is already known about the pathogenesis of animal aggression is pertinent and instructive for understanding human aggression, facile generalizations must be avoided. The wealth of existent literature conveys, in its depth and diversity, the extraordinary complexity of the problem. In the human case it is virtually impossible to covary out the effect of psychological and environmental factors. Goldstein stated that

In regard to sexual hormones, the most convincing evidence would suggest that there are powerful learning and social factors that are related to the manner in which individuals learn to deal with emotional experiences associated with effects of hormones (Goldstein, 1974, p. 16).

Thus, not only may hormones importantly affect certain behaviours, but cognitive processes, as well as environmental influences, may initiate, attenuate, or modify hormonal output. In a compellingly simple conclusion, Brown and Davis (1975) found that 'testosterone in man may be related to feeling angry, but the translation of such feelings into behavior is highly dependent on other factors' (p. 87).

The important question posed by this review was whether the current state of knowledge permitted any reasonable conjectures about neurochemical contributions to sexual aggression. While it is obviously premature to draw any synthetic conclusions from the disparate array of data surveyed here, there is sufficient presumptive evidence to advance two different 'prototypes' of human aggressive behaviour that have import for sex offences. These prototypes are postulates set forth for heuristic purposes. It is not suggested that they are templates for behaviour; only frameworks from which to construct more sophisticated and elaborated theories. A neurochemical theory can neither substitute for, nor account for, the critical role of social learning.

The two prototypes that will be discussed possess high profiles in the literature. Blackburn (1974, 1975), Megargee (1966), and Petrie (1967) have all identified distinct personality types similar to the two presented here. In Megargee's (1966) well-known typology, the *overcontrolled* individual is overly inhibited in the expression of anger, tending to internalize it until the build-up culminates in an explosive act. As an offender, this individual would be expected to commit few, albeit very violent, crimes. The *undercontrolled* individual possesses few restraints, typically acting out quite often. As an offender, this individual would be expected to have a long criminal record, though not marked by extreme violence. This typology, particularly the overcontrolled type, has received considerable support (Blackburn, 1969a,b, 1974, 1975, 1979; Houts, 1970; Megargee, 1971, 1972, 1976; Molof, 1967; Staub, 1971; White *et al.*, 1973).

In a similar fashion, Monroe (1978) distinguished between 'pure' psychopaths and two groups of recidivist offenders characterized by high dyscontrol. The 'epileptoid dyscontrol' group evidenced high paroxysmal theta in the EEG and, presumably, a low threshold for neuronal discharge in the limbic region. The 'hysteroid dyscontrol' group evidenced low paroxysmal theta and a psychogenic aetiology. Williams (1969), who also distinguished between habitual aggressives and those who committed a solitary major crime of violence, found EEG abnormalities in 65 per cent of the first group and 24 per cent of the second group, compared with a base rate of 12 per cent in the general population. While both groups were equally abnormal with respect to theta activity, the habitual aggressives evidenced close to three times the percentage of abnormalities in the frontal and posterior regions as the solitary aggressives. Lorimer (1972) also identified two groups of violent individuals based upon EEG activity. One group had excess theta (6–8 Hz) while the other group had excess beta (30–40 Hz). While it is certainly not plausible to conclude that distinct subgroups of offenders can be isolated according to the EEG, it is legitimate to conclude that there are markedly different paths leading to aggressive behaviour and that at least two of those paths may have biological markers.

PSYCHOPATHIC AGGRESSION

The term 'psychopath' is used here reservedly. As a nosological entity it conjures up a variety of different meanings, including the occasional European reference to 'character neurosis'. In 1941 Cleckley determined that the 'psychopath is psychotic, not merely queer or perverse' (p. 257), while Preu (1944) concluded that 'the term psychopathic personality, as commonly understood, is useless in psychiatric research' (p. 936). The closest approximation to current diagnostic usage is the 'antisocial personality disorder' as described in the *Diagnostic and Statistical Manual* of the American Psychiatric Association (1980). For present purposes, a definition based upon Blackburn's (1974) extensive taxonomic studies employing the Lorr–McNair cluster analytic procedure (Lorr, 1966) is used.

Blackburn found that

it is possible to identify a class of antisocial individuals which is broadly consistent with the clinical concept of the psychopath, and which is characterized by a high degree of aggression, impulsivity, extrapunitive attitudes, extraversion, and undersocialization (1974, p. 26).

Blackburn's description is entirely consistent with Quay's (1965) statement that

The psychopath is almost universally characterized as highly impulsive, relatively refractory to the effects of experience in modifying his socially troublesome behavior, and lacking in the ability to delay gratification. His penchant for creating excitement for the moment without regard for later consequences seems almost unlimited. He is unable to tolerate routine and boredom. While he may engage in antisocial, even vicious, behavior his outbursts frequently appear to be motivated by little more than a need for thrills and excitement. His deficits in learning, in terms of both avoidance and approach responses, are clinically obvious and have recently been documented by experimental study (p. 180).

This same profile was described over 20 years ago by Karpman (1961):

Because the psychopath has no conflicts within and lacks long term goals, there is no accumulation of tension as there is in the neurotic. Tension rises quickly in the psychopath in response to instinctive urges, tension which is immediate in nature and which demands immediate release (p. 607).

In general, impulsivity, stimulation-seeking, low anxiety, poor socialization, and lack of affect are distinctive and cardinal features of the psychopath (Blackburn, 1969a,b, 1974). The apparent absence of even minimal anxiety in anxiety-inducing situations is particularly striking and well documented (Mednick et al., 1982). As Cleckley (1964) observed in the fourth edition of his book:

Regularly we find in him extraordinary poise.... Even under concrete circumstances that would for the ordinary person cause embarrassment, confusion, acute insecurity, or visible agitation, his relative serenity is likely to be noteworthy (p. 267).

This characteristic behavioural profile has been scrutinized with regards to putative evidence for biological roots of psychopathy (Eysenck (e.g. 1977); Feldman (1977); Fenz (1971); Hare (e.g. 1968, 1970, 1975a,b, 1978, Hare and Schalling, 1978); Jeffery (1979); Mawson and Mawson (1977); Mednick (e.g. 1974, Mednick and Christiansen, 1977, Mednick and Hutchings, 1978, Mednick et al., 1982); Quay (1965); Schachter (1971, Schachter and Latane, 1964); and Siddle (1977)). The following section reviews some of this evidence, with the aim of addressing the relevance of psychopathy for understanding sexual aggression.

A number of investigators have reported that psychopaths and psychopathic criminals are characterized by hyporeactivity of the autonomic nervous system (e.g. Hare, 1968; Lykken, 1957; Quay, 1965; Schmauk, 1970; Zuckerman, 1978) and, in particular, are electrodermally hyporesponsive. That is, psychopathic offenders, relative to non-psychopathic offenders, possess lower resting skin conductance levels, evidence smaller skin conductance responses to intense or aversive stimuli, and recover to baseline levels more slowly (Hare and Cox, 1978; Mednick et al., 1982). The finding of a particularly long recovery limb of the skin conductance response (SCR) has been the focus of considerable empirical and theoretical attention (e.g. Hare, 1978; Levander et al., 1980; Loeb and Mednick, 1977; Siddle et al., 1976). Siddle (1977) concluded that

> the results concerning SCR recovery and antisocial behavior appear to be quite consistent. Subjects who display antisocial behavior (psychopaths, adult criminals, and adolescent delinquents) also display significantly slower SCR recovery than do matched controls (pp. 206–7).

Mednick (1974) has reported data suggesting a possible genetic component:

> The finding on the heritability of EDRec [electrodermal recovery] and relating parents' criminality to slow EDRec in their children, certainly does not allow us to rule out the possibility that EDRec may be one of the genetically transmitted characteristics contributing to the heritability of psychopathy and criminality (p. 142).

While it is not certain how to interpret correctly an abnormally slow recovery rate (Edelberg and Muller, 1977) it has been suggested that lesions of the amygdala lead to a depression of adrenocortical steroid output, slower sodium reabsorption, and consequently a longer recovery time of the skin conductance response (Venables, 1974, 1975). A longer SCR recovery limb has also been associated with a closed attentional stance toward the environment, impaired avoidance, and rapid habituation (Mednick, 1974; Venables, 1974). Extending findings on adrenal steroids, the limbic system and skin conductance parameters to the behavioural character of the psychopath provides a tentative bridge connecting physiological anomalies with a cardinal feature of such individuals—poor conditionability or avoidance learning. The thesis advanced by Mednick (1970) extended the paradigm of the classically conditioned fear response to include, in the normal case, rapid dissipation of the anticipatory fear response so that inhibition will be rewarded with fear reduction. In other words, the impulse to engage in antisocial behaviour prompts anticipatory fear of punishment which inhibits the antisocial behaviour. The inhibition of the behaviour will be reinforced with fear reduction, thus increasing its probability of reoccurrence. Mednick (1974) proposed that the SCR recovery rate was a peripheral index of fear dissipation, and that the more serious and repetitive the antisocial behaviour, the slower the SCR recovery time.

The bridge connecting SCR recovery rate to avoidance learning again comes from the animal literature. Goddard (1964) reported that animals with lesions of the amygdala do poorly on virtually all known avoidance tasks. Subsequently, a number of studies demonstrated that, while it is impossible to establish a simple excitatory-conditioned galvanic skin response in amygdalectomized monkeys (Bagshaw and Coppock, 1968), such animals are normal and may even be superior with respect to habituation (Douglas and Pribram, 1969). Douglas (1972) provided an interesting discussion regarding the 'schizophrenic amygdala', reward–punishment and passive avoidance. For present purposes the theorized relationship can be simply described. Due to excessive internal inhibition an individual may habituate to stimulus cues so quickly that little attention is paid to prior stimuli.[2] As a result, response hierarchies fail to develop because discrimination between stimulus cues is lacking; that is, there is little or no discrimination between reward and punishment. Douglas (1972) argued that the solution to this problem is passive avoidance (i.e. behaviour is determined by alternative stimuli other than reward or punishment). The import for psychopathy is the possibility that a physiological condition may contribute to poor conditionability and hence poor socialization.

Not only is the amygdala an important centre for reward and punishment, it also exerts considerable control over pituitary-adrenal function (Smythies, 1970). In general, stimulation of the amygdala serves to elevate levels of corticosteroids while lesioning has the opposite effect. An Addison's model (chronic primary adrenocortical insufficiency) may be appropriate for shedding light on a number of signs and symptoms. *First*, a deficiency of aldosterone causes a decrease in serum sodium and an increase in potassium. As Venables (1974) suggested, this may provide some explanation for the slow recovery time of the SCR. *Second*, adrenocortical insufficiency is associated with a slowing of the electrical discharges in the electroencephalogram, an effect reversible with cortisol (Forsham, 1963a). While it is not conclusive that psychopaths are characterized by slow wave activity (Syndulko, 1978), many reports have pointed in that direction (Mednick *et al.*, 1982). *Third*, beginning with cholesterol there are a long series of enzymatic steps in the biosynthesis of the adrenal steroids. One might expect adrenocortical insufficiency to be associated with low serum cholesterol, and that condition has been reported in a large sample of offenders with antisocial personality (Virkkunen, 1979).

Fourth, the adrenal cortex secretes a number of androgenic compounds, including the 17-ketosteroids, androsterone, and 11-oxy derivatives. These compounds are, by and large, weak, with most testosterone coming from the male testicle. The adrenal cortex is, however, capable of synthesizing testosterone which has 40–60 times the androgenic activity of the 17-ketoster-oids (Forsham, 1963b). Conditions of congenital adrenal androgenic excess have in common a deficiency of cortisol (Forsham, 1963b). *Fifth*, the adrenogenital syndromes result from inhibition or blockade of one of the enzymes involved in the biosynthesis of the adrenal steroids. The most logical candidate is a prenatal adrenogenital syndrome produced by a block that prevents normal formation of 11-desoxycortisol and hence cortisol. The result is a deficiency of aldosterone, with concomitant sodium loss, and a marked increase in 17-ketosteroids due to a lack of cortisol inhibition of ACTH. The syndrome derives from a 'partial' lack of 21-hydroxylation. It is assumed that enough cortisol is produced to prevent marked adrenal cortical insufficiency.

Sixth, while it is not assumed that destructive atrophy of the adrenal cortex, which accounts for over half of the Addison's cases (Forsham, 1963b), is a factor here, it has been noted that an autoimmune disease may be responsible for this atrophy on some occasions (Forsham, 1963b). This is particularly interesting in light of recent reports relating excess testosterone to an increased risk of autoimmune disease in left-handed individuals (Marx, 1982). More specifically, Geschwind has suggested that excess testosterone, or increased sensitivity to testosterone, slows the development of the left hemisphere, resulting in an increased incidence of autoimmunity in left-handers by suppressing development of the thymus gland in the fetus (Marx, 1982). Whatever the chain of events may be, Geschwind sees a 'powerful association between testosterone and immunity', noting that genes which influence the development of autoimmunity may be related to, or even the same as, genes responsible for excess testosterone or testosterone sensitivity, which in turn may result in anomalous dominance (Marx, 1982). While there is some empirical evidence relating sinistrality and lateralization to psychopathy (e.g. Flor-Henry, 1979; Gabrielli and Mednick, 1980), wedding these data to the immune system, the gonadal system, and hemispheric development clearly rests on the fringe of metatheory.

Seventh, if a prenatal adrenogenital syndrome of the type described is an appropriate model for understanding psychopathic aggression, the 21-hydroxylase deficiency may result from an autosomal recessive gene (i.e. inheritance from both parents). Somewhat parenthetically, if such a recessive trait is rare (perhaps 1 in 50,000), one might expect a relatively high proportion of consanguinous parental matings. There does in fact appear to be support for a genetically transmitted biological predisposition to criminal behaviour, though interestingly there is little such support for a predisposition to 'violent' behaviour (Mednick *et al.*, 1982). This latter point underscores the premise that episodic (presumably more violent) aggression is less likely to be inherited than psychopathic aggression.

The functional significance of serotonin for psychopathy merits comment. Serotonin may provide negative feedback through the hippocampus which regulates pituitary–adrenal function (McEwen *et al.*, 1969). Since 5-HTP reduces 24-hour excretion of 17-OHCS (Brodie *et al.*, 1973), a relative preponderance of 5-HT in certain areas of the brain may suppress 17-OHCS. It is unlikely, however, that elevated 5-HT is operative in aggressive behaviour (as it may be in the case of marked depletion). Since stress functions to increase the turnover of serotonin, the frequent occurrence of stress-inducing activity may serve to depress chronically 17-OHCS. Furthermore, the increased rate of release of 5-HT may be expected to reduce the functional serotonin if there was not a compensatory increase in synthesis (Warburton, 1975). The most important points in this regard are the 5-HT pituitary–adrenal interrelationship, the high content of 5-HT in the hippocampus, the enhancement of the stress response by inhibitors of 5-HT synthesis, and the reduction of the stress response by 5-HT precursors (Vernikos-Danellis and Berger, 1973). In general, protracted and/or acute stress may function to lower biogenic amine levels (noradrenaline, dopamine, serotonin) in the brain. The intense nervous system response to engaging in aggressive or risk-taking behaviour elevates amine levels due to the inhibition of mitochondrial MAO (Welch and Welch, 1971).

While monoamine oxidase (MAO)[3] was not discussed separately in this review, there is some evidence to indicate that lowered MAO levels are associated with 'excessive thrill-seeking' (Lewin, 1981) and high 'sensation-seeking' (e.g. Murphy *et al.*, 1977; Schooler *et al.*, 1978; Zuckerman, 1979). Tagliamonte *et al.* (1969) related increased sexual excitement to inhibition of MAO. A related finding is that high PT levels recorded in male rhesus monkeys at the end of the mating season were associated with relatively low platelet MAO levels (Redmond *et al.*, 1976). While sensation-seeking may be related to low MAO levels, the evidence relating sensation-seeking (as assessed by the instrument of Zuckerman *et al.*, 1974) to psychopathy is less consistent. Studies with incarcerated criminals (Thorne, 1971) and clinical ratings of psychopathy (Blackburn, 1969a; Hare and Cox, 1978) revealed no relationship with sensation-seeking, while studies that classified criminals into primary and secondary psychopaths and 'normals' found that primary psychopaths were higher in sensation-seeking than either of the other two groups (Blackburn, 1978; Emmons and Webb, 1974).

In a study that looked at the relationship of sensation-seeking to androgens, it was discovered that the Dis (disinhibition) subscale of Zuckerman's test correlated with androgen level in a sample of 25 males ($r = 0.56, p<0.01$) and in another sample of 51 males and 7 females ($r = 0.36, p<0.01$) (Daitzman *et al.*, 1978). In a follow-up study, 40 normal male subjects were selected for extreme scores on the Dis subscale. It was found that high disinhibitors had significantly higher levels of testosterone, 17-beta-oestradiol and oestrone than did low disinhibitors (Daitzman and Zuckerman, 1980). The authors also reported that extraversion, sociability, self-acceptance, dominance, and activity were correlated positively with testosterone in males. Notably, hostility did not correlate significantly with testosterone.

In sum, the psychopath is a socially dominant, low-anxiety individual who engages in frequent but relatively non-violent antisocial behaviour. Bits of yet unintegrated evidence suggest that this individual may be (1) electrodermally hyporeactive, (2) adrenocortically deficient, (3) characterized by EEG slow wave activity, (4) androgenically excessive and/or hypersensitive, (5) serotonin-deficient, and (6) MAO-deficient. While the data culled from diverse investigations are understandably not confirmatory of a unitary biological model for psychopathic aggression, there is substantial corroborative evidence bolstering continued efforts to formulate such a model.

Two key features of the bio-behavioural composite of the psychopath pertain to sexual aggression. One such feature concerns the poor conditionability and hence poor socialization of the psychopath. Hare (1970) used the concept of response perseveration to explain how dominant response tendencies may not be inhibited by social restrictions or prohibitions in some people:

> If we assume that the effectiveness of such restrictions is dependent on the normal functioning of limbic inhibitory mechanisms, and if we further assume that under certain conditions these mechanisms malfunction in the psychopath, we would then predict that, given the urge, he would initiate and complete the act despite the restrictions. The clinical comment that the psychopath's behavior is impulsive and determined more by his immediate needs than by possible consequences could thus be interpreted in terms of the failure of the appropriate inhibitory mechanisms to function properly (p. 34).

Obviously, the tendency to engage in sexual behaviour increases when sexual drive is high. If there is no socially acceptable outlet, even the strongest sexual drive will be inhibited in a highly socialized individual. In an impulsive individual with weak internal restraints there is increased probability that the drive may be met without regard for social propriety. Thus, when impulsivity and poor socialization coexist with androgenic excess, the risk of the occurrence of sexual offences may increase. Impulsivity and poor socialization are obviously not traits unique to sexual offenders; in fact, one need not be an offender at all and can still be poorly socialized and impulsive. Thus, the determinants of sexual aggression for the psychopathic offender most likely rest with the complex nuances of development and opportunity, as well as the more generic characteristics of impulsivity, poor socialization, and gonadal hormones. The confluence of all of these factors during adolescence encourages the climacteric nature of that period for the onset of psychopathic antisocial behaviour.

EPISODIC AGGRESSION

Extensive research on a cluster of behaviours generally referred to as the 'episodic dyscontrol syndrome' (Bach-Y-Rita et al., 1971; Lion et al., 1968,

1969; Lion and Bach-Y-Rita, 1970; Lion, 1972; Mark and Ervin, 1970; Menninger, 1963; Monroe, 1970, 1976) provides a model for another type of aggression with potential relevance to sexual offences. Four principal behaviours define the episodic dyscontrol syndrome: (1) physical assault, (2) sexual assault and impulsive sexual behaviour, (3) a history of motor vehicle offences, and (4) dipsomania (pathological intoxication) with associated violence. There is a consensus that brain dysfunction contributes to this syndrome and that a limbic system problem is a good candidate. There is, however, no uniformity of opinion on the neuroanatomical substrates. A form of seizure-free temporal lobe epilepsy has been proposed as an analogue to episodic dyscontrol, but no uniform agreement exists here either. Using episodic dyscontrol as a model, another type of offence behaviour will be described and elaborated upon.

Andy and his colleagues (Andy, 1975; Andy et al., 1975) performed thalamotomies on six patients with 'hyperresponsiveness syndrome' (emotional instability, hyperactivity, aggression, agitation, nervousness, suicidal tendencies, anxiety, explosiveness, and hyperirritability). Lesions in the centre median nucleus of the thalamus produced marked improvement in five of the six patients. It was argued that this nucleus functions as a modulator of the excitatory state activated by perifornical septo-hypothalamic stimulation (Andy et al., 1975). In a similar investigation involving sex offenders (paedophilic homosexuals), Roeder et al. (1972) found that stereotaxic destruction of the non-dominant ventromedial hypothalamus had an 'excellent effect' in the first three of 10 cases without involving any hormonal changes. That is, there was no decrease in spermiogenesis and no change in the metabolites of the adrenocortical and gonadal steroids. Roeder et al. (1972) termed the ventromedial hypothalamus the 'sex-behaviour centre'.

From the animal literature one also notes that a lesion in the ventromedial nucleus of the hypothalamus turns ordinary placid cats into savage animals that will attack humans (Glusman et al., 1961; Kaelber et al., 1965; Wheatley, 1944). Similar results have been found with rats (Grossman, 1972; Panksepp, 1971).

Since the region designated by Roeder et al. (1972) as a sex behaviour centre coincides with sites postulated to be critical in certain types of aggression, there may be evidence for a pathophysiological basis to some sexual aggression. Furthermore, since sex hormone studies of aggressive and violent behaviour in humans have proved largely unrewarding, it is particularly noteworthy that destruction of this sex behaviour centre did not affect secretion of gonadal hormones (Roeder et al., 1972).

There is additional evidence to support the ventro- and postero-medial hypothalamus as being possible neuroanatomical sites for episodic aggression. Sano et al. (1972) reported that an unbalanced condition of two circuits with the dominance of the ergotropic circuit results in 'violent, aggressive, restless behaviours or rage' (p. 72). The region designated by Sano *et al*. (1972) as ergotropic was the postero-medial hypothalamus near the lateral wall of the third ventricle. Stimulation of this area produced tachycardia, a rise in blood pressure, and maximal pupillary dilation. It is again noteworthy that the ergotropic and trophotropic systems, originally described by W. R. Hess in the 1940s, are more or less antagonistic. Isaacson (1972) stated that

> Male sexual activity depends upon the trophotropic system's physiological prepara-tions for an erection, while the ejaculation of semen requires neural initiation of a sympathetic ergotropic origin (p. 514).

Ergotropic dominance might reduce the likelihood of erection, thus providing one explanation for those instances in which the sexual assault does not result in intercourse, often inciting the rapist to blame the victim for his inability to erect, resulting in greater violence towards the victim. This tentative explanation is obviously not intended to replace or compete with the powerful psychological factors that may also produce impotence.

Heath (1975) has also designated the same regions (the hippocampi and parts of the amygdala, periaqueductal sites in the mesencephalon, and the medial hypothalamus near the third ventricle) as sites for 'aversive emotional expression'. In sum, the role of central cholinergic mechanisms in facilitating episodic aggression is in the diffusion of acetylcholine to critical sites located near the walls of the third ventricle or the periaqueductal grey matter (Goldstein, 1974). The association of aversive reactions with cholinergic mechanisms has also been made by Stein (1969) and Stein *et al*. (1972).

In the previous section on psychopathic aggression, evidence from the animal literature addressing limbic involvement was introduced (Mednick, 1970; Venables, 1974). Venables hypothesized that lesions to the amygdala or hippocampus differentially affected avoidance behaviour as well as the recovery time of the skin conductance response. It was suggested that the psychopath appears to have impaired functioning of the amygdala, evidenced in terms of a slow recovery limb (of the SCR) and impaired avoidance behaviour. One might conjecture whether episodic aggression is characterized by deficits in hippocampal functioning, manifested as excessive 'openness' to the environment and active avoidance behaviour. Since the hippocampus has efferent control over sensory input, impairment causes a breakdown in gating and consequent 'openness' to the environment. Pursuant to the reasoning of Mednick and Venables, the episodic individual would be characterized as 'schizophrenic-like'.

There is a sizeable literature demonstrating that animals with hippocampal lesions act as if they lacked internal inhibition (e.g. Douglas, 1967; Kimble, 1968), spend less time in sleep due to failure to generate internal inhibition (e.g. Jarrard, 1968), and habituate more slowly than controls as a result of a deficit in response inhibition (e.g. Kimble, 1968; Jarrard and Korn, 1969; Leaton, 1965). In addition, it was pointed out by Venables (1974) that the relatively rapid recovery time of the SCR after hippocampal lesioning may result from chronic increases in ACTH, and hence elevated levels of adrenocortical hormones leading to faster sodium reabsorption. It was stated earlier in this section that Sano *et al.* (1972) related ergotropic dominance to 'violent, aggressive, restless behaviours or rage'. Isaacson (1972) suggested that 'the hippocampal influence upon the hypothalamus could be the inhibition of the ergotropic sysems in the posterior hypothalamus' (p. 514). With hippocampal impairment comes a failure to activate and in turn suppress the ergotropic system.

The lateral olfactory gyrus is continuous at its caudal extremity with the hippocampal gyrus. Together the two areas are called the pyriform lobe. The pyriform cortex includes the lateral olfactory stria, the limen insulae, the uncus and at least part of the parahippocampal gyrus. Lesioning in this area (the pyriform cortex) induces testosterone-dependent hypersexuality in male animals (Smythies, 1970), making it an important neuroendocrine centre. In a similar vein, it was pointed out by Ellison (1982) that animal research has consistently demonstrated 'that sexual behaviour is dramatically affected by manipulation of the medial preoptic area, the anterior hypothalamic nuclei, and the fibers of the median forebrain bundle' and that there is strong evidence 'to support the hypothesis that limbic structures have a regulatory effect' on the aforementioned areas (p. 508).

The physiological state hypothesized to be responsible for this episodic aggressive behaviour is one of chronic overactivation, a condition facilitated by cholinergic and catecholaminergic (particularly noradrenaline) mechanisms.[4] Since Carlton's (1963) proposal that acetylcholine and catecholamines interact in the control of behavioural arousal, research has generally supported the logical stance that, if arousal is mediated by catecholamines, acetylcholine— and perhaps serotonin—should suppress arousal by antagonizing the catecholamines (Mabry and Campbell, 1978).

A number of studies have reported associations between catecholaminergic activity and hyperexcitability, lability and agitation (e.g. Nelson *et al.*, 1966; Kunce *et al.*, 1970). This behavioural state undoubtedly reflects a chain of events involving hypothalamic stimulation of the adrenal medulla with the resulting sympathetic effects, such as an increase in peripheral vascular resistance and a rise in systolic and diastolic blood pressure. Paranthetically, it may be noted that episodic loss of control should have the salutary effect of temporarily reducing catecholamine stores. Such a reaction would appear even more 'explosive', if viewed against the background of a typically even-keeled, over-controlled demeanour.

A critical antecedent to this type of aggressive behaviour may be chronically high levels of 17-OHCS, reflecting a constant undifferentiated arousal state.

Behaviourally, such an individual would appear withdrawn, socially isolated, anxious, disorganized, and over-controlled. While novelty, unpredictability and 'risk' (all potent influences in elevating 17-OHCS) can be assiduously avoided, occasional intense emotional reactions (also associated with unusually marked elevations in 17-OHCS) cannot be avoided. One could hypothesize that it is more likely for there to be identifiable precipitating events associated with episodic aggression than with psychopathic aggression, and, furthermore, that it is more likely for those precipitating events to constitute a chronic aversive emotional state than the stimulation of thrill-seeking or periodic frustration.

It is hypothesized that the origin of the deficit lies in the limbic system, conceivably with hippocampal impairment or amygdaloid stimulation. Assuming that there is in fact a limbic-related condition of chronic primary adrenocortical excess, one might expect some Cushings-like side effects, such as high blood pressure, high blood glucose, a high red cell count, suppression of the inflammatory response with a resulting susceptibility to infections, and—tangentially—a high level of cholesterol. One might also expect that serial elevation in adrenal cortical hormones may function to suppress PT levels in this group of offenders.

In sum, the episodic aggressive type is a generally withdrawn, socially isolated, anxious, disorganized, and over-controlled individual. This undifferentiated or amorphous arousal state may, in part, be related to suppression of impulses to aggress, surfacing periodically in spontaneous and unpredictable expressions of violence. One would surmise, based upon Megargee's (1966, 1973) notions about the over-controlled offender, that such an individual would have a criminal record marked by relatively few offences, with a high degree of violence. Offences occur episodically as a form of release, a pressure valve letting off steam. Thus, while there may be long intervals between them, each episode is likely to be marked by violence.

When this form of human aggression takes on a sexual theme it is assumed that the biological substrates, if indeed any exist, are ergotropic (ventro- or postero-medial hypothalamus) and limbic (hippocampal). Valzelli (1981, p. 95) noted that neuroanatomical sites for sex-related aggression in humans include the anterior and ventromedial hypothalamus. The implication of the limbic system is based primarily upon extrapolation from animal research. It is not assumed that this condition is androgenically mediated, but more likely cholinergic and catecholaminergic (noradrenergic). With regard to these statements, Moss (1978) concluded that the 'complex interactions between neurons, hypothalamic peptides, and the catecholamines obviously are involved in the control of sexual activity' (p. 437). The most apparent feature of this condition, a chronic diffuse anxiety state, may be attributable to high levels of 17-OHCS. Chronically elevated levels of corticosteroids may be the result of amygdaloid stimulation or hippocampal impairment. While many of these conclusions are strictly suppositional and presumptive, evidence is accumulating that identifies common regions and neural circuitry in the elicitation of both sexual and aggressive behaviour.

CONCLUSION

Despite the foregoing observations and conclusions, any statement about the independent functioning of a single neurotransmitter is fatuous. Valzelli (1977) concluded with the following caveat:

> The change of a given neurotransmitter should be taken only as an indication that the entire machinery or region of the brain (serotonergic or catecholaminergic) subserved by this neurotransmitter is wrongly tuned. This incorrect tuning may involve the functioning of several different structures and circuitries thereby disrupting their reciprocal balance and leading to a series of disturbed behaviors rather than compromising selectively a single behavioral element. Therefore, to speak in terms of a single neurochemical transmitter or of a 'specific' neurochemistry as being responsible for aggressiveness or for any other behavioral element seems to be inappropriate and probably misleading, especially since aggressiveness is not a single entity (p. 125).

Thus, while there is abundant evidence to suggest a link between various types of aggression and fluctuations in blood chemistry (Moyer, 1968), identification of specific subsystems is obscured by the complex interactions between the adrenal cortex, the hypothalamus, the limbic system and the gonadal system.[5] Were it possible to sort out and identify the neural circuitry that underlies different aggressive behaviours, complex exogenous (cognitive and environmental) factors, which may alter the endogenous reaction, would still defy simple explanations. Focusing on one particular aspect of aggression, that which involves sexual assault, narrows somewhat the frame of reference by excluding all non-sexual aggression and including the presumably critical role of the gonadal system. Even here, however, it is obvious that exogenous factors are important and must be considered. Furthermore, it is apparent that the role of androgens in human aggression is neither direct nor obvious. The most compelling evidence to date underscores the powerful effect of social learning on the manner in which individuals cope with and react to the emotional experiences associated with hormonal changes. Thus, in either one of the postulated 'types' of human aggressive behaviour discussed in this review, social learning may serve to facilitate or inhibit the expression of the behaviour. Nevertheless, there remains convincing evidence to suggest that biological factors may have important influences on types of human sexual aggression.

ACKNOWLEDGEMENT

Preparation of this manuscript was supported by the National Institute of Mental Health (MH 32309), the National Institute of Justice

(82-IJ-CX-0058) and the Commonwealth of Massachusetts. The author wishes to acknowledge the thoughtful criticism and comments of Dr Terry Patterson and Dr Raymond Knight.

TECHNICAL APPENDIX

ACTH	adrenocorticotropin
CSF	cerebrospinal fluid
DA	dopamine
Dis	disinhibition
EDRec	electrodermal recovery rate
EEG	electroencephalogram
FSH	follicle-stimulating hormone
5-HIAA	5-hydroxyindoleacetic acid
5-HT	5-hydroxytryptamine
5-HTP	5-hydroxytryptophan
HVA	homovanillic acid
Hz	hertz
L-DOPA	L-dihydroxyphenylalanine
LH	luteinizing hormone
MAO	monoamine oxidase
MHPG	3-methoxy-4-hydroxyphenylglycol
MPA	medroxyprogesterone acetate
NE	noradrenaline
17-OHCS	17-hydroxycorticosteroids
6-OHDA	6-hydroxydopamine
PCPA	parachlorophenylalanine
PT	plasma testosterone
SCR	skin conductance response
SHBG	sex hormone-binding globulin

NOTES

1. Adrenalectomy effectively removes glucocorticoids (cortisol and cortisone) from circulation. Cortisol is the physiological inhibitor of adrenocorticotropic hormone (ACTH). A fall in cortisol produces a pituitary discharge of ACTH, which in turn stimulates the adrenal cortex to secrete 11-desoxycortisol (or compound S). Cortisol is then produced from 11-desoxycortisol by the enzyme 11-beta-hydroxy-lase. Most of the 17-hydroxycorticosteroids (17-OHCS) are derived from cortisol.
2. This statement is an extrapolation from data showing markedly slowed habituation with hippocampal lesions. The data in fact suggest that habituation is normal after amygdaloid lesions.
3. Since MAO is the inactivating enzyme that transforms noradrenaline and other monoamines into an aldehyde, one might expect inhibition of MAO activity to be accompanied by a rise in tissue levels of noradrenaline and serotonin. The

consequences of MAO inhibition are not the same in all species, and the question is obviously much more complex than can be adequately treated here. It has been reported, for instance, that MAO inhibition did not raise brain noradrenaline levels in the cat (Vogt, 1959). It has been pointed out by Wurtman (1966) that various endocrine conditions (e.g. hypothyroidism and marked hyperthyroidism) which depress MAO activity may result in significant changes in certain endogenous amines (e.g. serotonin and dopamine) that are better substrates for MAO than noradrenaline.

4. Obviously, positing an explanation for some presumed aberration in the rate of synthesis, release, or turnover of catecholamines is mere speculation. As Wurtman (1965) pointed out, 'it is not yet known which of the processes ... controls the rates at which catecholamines are synthesized ... or even whether a single process remains rate limiting under all physiologic circumstances' (p. 641).

5. An obvious example is the interrelationships between the hypothalamus, the anterior pituitary, and testosterone. Testosterone is produced only when the testes are stimulated by LH from the anterior pituitary gland. The secretion of LH is controlled by neurosecretory hormones from the hypothalamus. There is reciprocal inhibition of hypothalamic–anterior pituitary secretion of gonadotropin hormones by testosterone. That is, the introduction of testosterone inhibits the secretion of gonadotropins. Thus, it may be assumed that testosterone inhibits hypothalamic stimulation of the anterior pituitary gland. This inhibition has a marked effect on the production of LH. Normally, excess testosterone secretion inhibits LH secretion which in turn reduces secretion of testosterone. Just as LH is controlled by releasing factors from the hypothalamus, so is ACTH. Corticotropin releasing factor is carried from the hypothalamus to the anterior pituitary, where it induces secretion of ACTH, which in turn controls the secretion of the glucocorticoids (cortisol and corticosterone). Just as testosterone provides direct negative feedback to the hypothalamus, so does cortisol.

REFERENCES

American Psychiatric Association (1980) *Diagnostic and Statistical Manual: Mental Disorders*. Washington, DC: APA.

Andy, O. J. (1975) Thalamotomy for psychopathic behavior. *Southern Medical Journal*, **68**, 437–442.

Andy, O. J., Giurintano, L., Giurintano, S. and McDonald, T. (1975) Thalamic modulation of aggression. *Pavlovian Journal*, **10**, 85–101.

Bach-Y-Rita, G. (1975) Biological basis of aggressive behaviour: Clinical aspects. In H. J. Widroe (Ed.) *Human Behavior and Brain Function*. Springfield, Illinois: Charles C. Thomas.

Bach-Y-Rita, G., Lion, J. R., Climent, C. E. and Ervin, F. R. (1971) Episodic dyscontrol: a study of 130 violent patients. *American Journal of Psychiatry*, **127**, 1473-1478.

Bagshaw, M. H. and Coppock, H. W. (1968) Galvanic skin response conditioning deficit in amygdalectomized monkeys. *Experimental Neurology*, **20**, 188–196.

Bancroft, J. H. J., Tennent, T. G., Loucas, K. and Cass, J. (1974) Control of deviant sexual behaviour by drugs: behavioural effects of oestrogens and anti-androgens. *British Journal of Psychiatry*, **125**, 310–315.

Beleslin, D. B., Samardzic, R. and Stefanovic-Denic, K. (1980) '6-Hydroxydopamine and aggression in cats.' Paper given at Fourth Biennial Meeting of the International Society for Research on Aggression, The University of Groningen at Haren, The Netherlands. (Abstract in *Aggressive Behavior*, **6**, 249–277.)

Berlin, F. S. and Coyle, G. S. (1981) Sexual deviation syndromes. *Johns Hopkins Medical Journal*, **149**, 119–125.
Berlin, F. S. and Meinecke, C. F. (1981) Treatment of sex offenders with antiandrogenic medication: conceptualization, review of treatment modalities, and preliminary findings. *American Journal of Psychiatry*, **138**, 601–646.
Bernstein, I. S. (1970) Primate status hierarchies. In L. A. Rosenblum (Ed.) *Primate Behavior*, vol. 1, pp. 71–109. New York: Academic Press.
Bernstein, I. S., Rose, R. M., Gordon, T. P. and Grady, C. L. (1979) Agonistic rank, aggression, social context, and testosterone in male pigtail monkeys. *Aggressive Behavior*, **5**, 329–339.
Blackburn, R. (1969a) Sensation seeking, impulsivity, and psychopathic personality. *Journal of Consulting and Clinical Psychology*, **33**, 571–574.
Blackburn, R. (1969b) 'Personality patterns in homicide: A typological analysis of abnormal offenders.' Paper presented at the Fifth International Meeting of Forensic Sciences, Toronto, Canada.
Blackburn, R. (1974) 'Personality and the classification of psychopathic disorders.' Special Hospitals Research Report No. 10, Rampton Hospital, Retford, Notts, England.
Blackburn, R. (1975) An empirical classification of psychopathic personality. *British Journal of Psychiatry*, **127**, 456–460.
Blackburn, R. (1978) Electrodermal and cardiovascular correlates of psychopathy. In R. D. Hare and D. Schalling (Eds) *Psychopathic Behaviour: Approaches to Research*. New York: Wiley.
Blackburn, R. (1979) Cortical and autonomic arousal in primary and secondary psychopaths. *Psychophysiology*, **16**, 143–150.
Blumer, D. (1971) Das Sexualvehalten der Schlafenlappenepileptiker vor and nach Chirurgisher Behandlung. *Journal of Neuro-Visceral Relations*, Suppl. X: 469. (Cited in Kling, 1975.)
Brain, P. F. (1971) Some endocrine effects on fighting behavior in isolated male albino mice. *Journal of Endocrinology*, **51**, 18–19.
Brain, P. F., Nowell, N. W. and Wouters, A. (1971) Some relationships between adrenal function and the effectiveness of a period of isolation in inducing intermale aggression in albino mice. *Physiology and Behavior*, **6**, 27–29.
Brodie, H. K. H., Sack, R. and Siever, L. (1973) Clinical studies of L-5-hydroxytryptophan in depression. In J. Barchas and E. Usdin (Eds) *Serotonin and Behavior*, pp. 549–559. New York: Academic Press.
Bronson, F. H. and Desjardins, C. (1971) Steroid hormones and aggressive behaviour in mammals. In B. E. Eleftheriou and J. P. Scott (Eds) *Physiology of Aggression and Defeat*, pp. 43–63. New York: Plenum Press.
Brown, G. L., Ballenger, J. C., Minichiello, M. D. and Goodwin, F. K. (1979) Human aggression and its relationship to cerebrospinal fluid 5-hydroxyindoleacetic acid, 3-methoxy-4-hydroxyphenylglycol, and homovanillic acid. In M. Sandler (Ed) *Psychopharmacology of Aggression*, pp. 131–148. New York: Raven Press.
Brown, W. A. (1981) Testosterone and human behaviour. *International Journal of Mental Health*, **9**, 45–66.
Brown, W. A. and Davis, G. H. (1975) Serum testosterone and irritability in man. *Psychosomatic Medicine*, **37**, 87 (abstract).
Burgess, P. K. (1972) Eysenck's theory of criminality: a new approach. *British Journal of Criminology*, **12**, 74–82.
Carlton, P. L. (1963) Cholinergic mechanisms in the control of behavior by the brain. *Psychological review*, **70**, 19–39.
Cleckley, H. (1941) *The Mask of Sanity*. St. Louis: C. V. Mosby Co.

Cleckley, H. (1964) *The Mask of Sanity*. (4th edn.) St. Louis: C. V. Mosby Co.

Cochran, C. A. and Perachio, A. A. (1977) Dihydrotestosterone propionate effects on dominance and sexual behaviors in gonadectomized male and female rhesus monkeys. *Hormones and Behavior*, **8**, 175–187.

Conner, R. L. (1972) Hormones, biogenic amines and aggression. In S. Levine (Ed.) *Hormones and Behavior*, pp. 209–233. New York: Academic Press.

Conner, R. L., Stolk, J. M. and Levine, S. (1973) Effects of PCPA on fighting behavior and habituation of startle response in rats. In J. Barchas and E. Usdin (Eds) *Serotonin and Behavior*, pp. 325–333. New York: Academic Press.

Conner, R. L., Levine, S., Wertheim, G. A. and Cummer, J. F. (1969) Hormonal determinants of aggressive behavior. *Annals of the New York Academy of Sciences*, **159**, 760–776.

Cooper, A. J. (1981) A placebo-controlled trial of the antiandrogen cyproterone acetate in deviant hypersexuality. *Comprehensive Psychiatry*, **22**, 458–465.

Daitzman, R. and Zuckerman, M. (1980) Disinhibitory sensation-seeking, personality and gonadal hormones. *Personality and Individual Differences*, **1**, 103–110.

Daitzman, R. J., Zuckerman, M., Sammelwitz, P. H. and Ganjam, V. (1978) Sensation seeking and gonadal hormones. *Journal of Biosocial Science*, **10**, 401–408.

Dalton, K. (1961) Menstruation and Crime. *British Medical Journal*, **2**, 1752–1753.

Dalton, K. (1964) *The Premenstrual Syndrome*. Springfield, Illinois: Charles C. Thomas.

Dieckman, G. and Hassler, R. (1977) Treatment of sexual violence by stereotactic hypothalamotomy. In W. H. Sweet, S. Obrador and J. G. Martin-Rodriguez (Eds) *Neurosurgical Treatment in Psychiatry*. Baltimore: University Park Press.

Dixson, A. F. (1980) Androgens and aggressive behavior in primates; a review. *Aggressive Behavior*, **6**, 37–67.

Dixson, A. F. and Herbert, J. (1977) Testosterone, aggressive behavior and dominance rank in captive adult male talapoin monkeys (Miopithecus talapoin). *Physiology and Behavior*, **18**, 539-543.

Doering, C. H., Brodie, K. H., Kraemer, H. C., Moos, R. H., Becker, H. B. and Hamburg, D. A. (1975) Negative affect and plasma testosterone: a longitudinal human study. *Psychosomatic Medicine*, **37**, 484–491.

Douglas, R. J. (1967) The hippocampus and behavior. *Psychological Bulletin*, **67**, 416–442.

Douglas, R. J. (1972) Pavlovian conditioning and the brain. In R. A. Boakes and M. S. Halliday (Eds) *Inhibition and Learning*, pp. 529–553. New York: Academic Press.

Douglas, R. J. and Pribram, K. H. (1969) Distraction and habituation in monkeys with limbic lesions. *Journal of Comparative and Physiological Psychology*, **69**, 473–480.

Edelberg, R. and Muller, M. (1977) 'The status of the electrodermal recovery measure: a caveat.' Paper presented at the Annual Meeting of the Society for Psychophysiological Research, Philadelphia.

Ehlers, C. L., Rickler, K. C. and Hovey, J. E. (1980) 'Elevated plasma testosterone levels in a female out-patient population with aggressive behavior.' Paper given at Fourth Biennial Meeting of the International Society for Research on Aggression, University of Gronigen at Haren, The Netherlands. (Abstract in *Aggressive Behavior*, **6**, 249–277.)

Ehrenkranz, J., Bliss, E. and Sheard, M. H. (1974) Plasma testosterone: correlation with aggressive behaviour and social dominance in man. *Psychosomatic Medicine*, **36**, 469–475.

Eichelman, B. S. and Thoa, N. B. (1973) The aggressive monoamines. *Biological Psychiatry*, **6**, 143–164.

Ekkers, C. L. (1975) Catecholamine excretion, conscience function and aggressive behaviour. *Biological Psychology*, **3**, 15–30.

Eleftheriou, B. E. (1971) Effects of aggression and defeat on brain macromolecules. In B. E. Eleftheriou, and J. P. Scott (Eds.) *The Physiology of Aggression and Defeat*, pp. 65–90. New York: Plenum Press.

Ellison, J. M. (1982) Alterations of sexual behavior in temporal lobe epilepsy. *Psychosomatics*, **23**, 499–509.

Emmons, T. D. and Webb, W. W. (1974) Subjective correlates of emotional responsivity and stimulation seeking in psychopaths, normals and acting-out neurotics. *Journal of Consulting and Clinical Psychology*, **42**, 620–625.

Eysenck, H. J. (1970) *Crime and Personality*. (2nd edn.) London: Paladin.

Eysenck, H. (1977) *Crime and Personality*. (3rd edn.) London: Routledge and Kegan Paul.

Eysenck, H. J. and Rachman, S. (1965) *The Causes and Cures of Neurosis*. San Diego: R. R. Knapp.

Feldman, M. P. (1977) *Criminal Behaviour*. New York: Wiley.

Fenz, W. (1971) Heart rate responses to a stressor: a comparison between primary and secondary psychopaths and normal controls. *Journal of Experimental Research in Personality*, **5**, 7–13.

Flor-Henry, P. (1979) Laterality, shifts of cerebral dominance, sinistrality and psychosis. In J. Gruzelier and P. Flor-Henry (Eds) *Hemisphere Asymmetries of Function in Psychopathology*. Amsterdam: Elsevier.

Forsham, P. H. (1963a) The adrenal gland. *Clinical Symposia*, **15** (1), 3–21.

Forsham, P. H. (1963b) Abnormalities of the adrenal cortex. *Clinical Symposia*, **15** (2), 35–66.

Freud, S. (1966) *The Complete Introductory Lectures on Psychoanalysis* (Lect. XXXII). (Trans. J. Strachey). New York: W. W. Norton.

Funkenstein, D. (1955) The physiology of fear and anger. *Scientific American*, **192**, 74–80.

Gabrielli, W. F. and Mednick, S. A. (1980) Sinistrality and delinquency. *Journal of Abnormal Psychology*, **89**, 654–661.

Gagne, P. (1981) Treatment of sex offenders with medroxyprogesterone acetate. *American Journal of Psychiatry*, **138**, 644–646.

Glusman, M., Won, W., Burdock, E. I. and Ransohoff, J. (1961) Effects of midbrain lesions on 'savage' behavior induced by hypothalamic lesions in the cat. *Transactions of the American Neurological Association*, **86**, 216–218.

Goddard, G. V. (1964) Functions of the amygdala. *Psychological Bulletin*, **62**, 89–109.

Goldstein, M. (1974) Brain research and violent behavior. *Archives of Neurology*, **30**, 1–35.

Golla, F. L. and Hodge, R. S. (1949) Hormone treatment of sex offenders. *Lancet*, **1**, 1006–1007.

Gray, J. A. (1970) The psychophysiological basis of introversion–extraversion. *Behavior Research and Therapy*, **8**, 249–266.

Gray, J. A. (1971) *The Psychology of Fear and Stress*. New York: McGraw-Hill.

Gray, J. A. (1972) The psychophysiological nature of introversion-extraversion: a modification of Eysenck's theory. In V. D. Nebylitsyn and J. A. Gray (Eds) *Biological Bases of Individual Behavior*, pp. 182-205. New York: Academic Press.

Gray, J. A. (1978) The neuropsychology of anxiety. *British Journal of Psychology*, **69**, 417-434.

Green, R., Whalen, R. E., Butley, B. and Battie, C. (1972) Dominance hierarchy in squirrel monkeys: role of gonads and androgen on genital display and feeding order. *Folia Primatologica*, **18**, 185–195.

Greene, R. and Dalton, K. (1953) The premenstrual syndrome. *British Medical Journal*, **1**, 1007–1014.

Grossman, S. P. (1972) Aggression, avoidance and reaction to novel environments in female rats with ventromedial hypothalamic lesions. *Journal of Comparative and Physiological Psychology*, **78**, 274–283.

Halleck, S. L. (1981) The ethics of anti-androgen therapy. *American Journal of Psychiatry*, **138**, 642–643.

Hamburg, D. A. (1966) Effects of progesterone on behavior. In R. Levine (Ed.) *Endocrines and the Central Nervous System*. Baltimore: Williams and Wilkins.

Hamburg, D. A., Moos, R. H. and Yalom, I. D. (1968) Studies of distress in the menstrual cycle and the postpartum period. In R. P. Michael (Ed.) *Endocrinology and Human Behaviour*. London: Oxford University Press.

Harding, C. F. and Leshner, A. I. (1972) The effects of adrenalectomy on the aggressiveness of differently housed mice. *Physiology and Behavior*, **8**, 437–440.

Hare, R. D. (1968) Psychopathy, autonomic functioning, and the orienting response. *Journal of Abnormal Psychology Monograph Supplement*, **73**, 1–24.

Hare, R. D. (1970) *Psychopathy: Theory and Research*. New York: Wiley.

Hare, R. D. (1975a) Psychophysiological studies of psychopathy. In D. C. Fowles (Ed.) *Clinical Applications of Psychophysiology*. New York: Columbia University Press.

Hare, R. D. (1975b) Psychopathy. In P. H. Venables and M. J. Christie (Eds) *Research in Psychophysiology*. New York: Wiley.

Hare, R. D. (1978) Electrodermal and cardiovascular correlates of psychopathy. In R. D. Hare and D. Schalling (Eds) *Psychopathic Behaviour: Approaches to Research*, pp. 107–143. Chichester: Wiley.

Hare, R. D. and Cox, D. N. (1978) Clinical and empirical conceptions of psychopathy, and the selection of subjects for research. In R. D. Hare and D. Schalling (Eds) *Psychopathic Behaviour: Approaches to Research*. New York: Wiley.

Hare, R. D. and Schalling, D. (Eds) (1978) *Psychopathic Behaviour: Approaches to Research*. New York: Wiley.

Hartmann, R. J. and Geller, I. (1971) p-Chlorophenylalanine effects on a conditioned emotional response in rats. *Life Sciences*, **10**, 927–933.

Harvey, J. A. (1974) Physiological and pharmacological analysis of behavior. In R. E. Whalen (Ed.) *The Neuropsychology of Aggression*, pp. 125–147. New York: Plenum Press.

Heath, R. G. (1975) Brain function and behavior. I. Emotion and sensory phenomena in psychotic patients and in experimental animals. *Journal of Nervous and Mental Disease*, **160**, 159–175.

Henderson, H. (1981) Exploring the human sexual response. *Sexual Medicine Today*, April, 6–16.

Houts, M. (1970) *They Asked for Death*. New York: Cowles.

Isaacson, R. L. (1972) Neural systems of the limbic brain and behavioral inhibition. In R. A. Boakes and M. S. Halliday (Eds) *Inhibition and Learning*, pp. 497–528. New York: Academic Press.

Jarrard, L. E. (1968) Behavior of hippocampally lesioned rats in home cage and novel situations. *Physiology and Behavior*, **3**, 65–70.

Jarrard, L. E. and Korn, J. H. (1969) Effects of hippocampal lesions on heart rate during habituation and passive avoidance. *Communications in Behavioral Biology*, **3**, 141–150.

Jeffery, C. R. (1979) *Biology and Crime*. Beverly Hills, Calif: Sage.

Joslyn, W. D. (1973) Androgen-induced social dominance in infant female rhesus monkeys. *Journal of Child Psychology and Psychiatry*, **14**, 137–145.

Kaelber, W. W., Mitchell, C. L. and Way, J. S. (1965) Some sensory influences on savage behavior in cats. *American Journal of Physiology*, **209**, 866–870.

Karli, P., Vergnes, M. and Didiergeorges, F. (1969) Rat–mouse interspecific aggressive behaviour and its manipulation by brain ablations and by brain stimulation. In S. Garattini and E. B. Sigg (Eds) *Aggressive Behaviour*. Amsterdam: Excerpta Medica.

Karpman, B. (1961) The structure of neurosis: with special differentials between neurosis, psychosis, homosexuality, alcoholism, psychopathy and criminality. *Archives of Criminal Psychodynamics*, **4**, 599–646.

Kendenburg, D., Kendenburg, N. and Kling, A. (1973) 'An ethological study in a patient group.' Paper presented at the Annual Meeting of the American Psychiatric Association, Honolulu, Hawaii.

Keverne, E. B., Meller, R. E. and Martinez-Arias, A. M. (1978) Dominance aggression and sexual behaviour in social groups of talapoin monkeys. In D. J. Chivers and J. Herbert (Eds) *Recent Advances in Primatology*, vol. 1, pp. 533–547. London: Academic Press.

Kimble, D. P. (1968) The hippocampus and internal inhibition. *Psychological Bulletin*, **70**, 285–295.

Kinsey, A. C., Pomeroy, W. B. and Martin, C. E. (1948) *Sexual Behavior in the Human Male*. Philadelphia: W. B. Saunders.

Kling, A. (1975) Testosterone and aggressive behavior in man and non-human primates. In B. E. Eleftheriou and R. L. Sprott (Eds) *Hormonal Correlates of Behavior*, vol. 1, pp. 305–323. New York: Plenum Press.

Knight, R. A., Prentky, R. A., Schneider, B. and Rosenberg, R. (1983) Linear causal modelling of adaptation and criminal history in sexual offenders. In K. T. Van Dusen and S. A. Mednick (Eds) *Prospective Studies of Crime and Delinquency*, pp. 303–341. Boston: Kluwer-Nijhoff.

Konner, M. (1982) She and He. *Science 82*, September, 54–61.

Kostowski, W. and Pucilowski, O. (1980) 'Effects of stimulation of midbrain raphe nuclei on mouse-killing behavior in rats.' Paper given at Fourth Biennial Meeting of the International Society for Research on Aggression, University of Groningen at Haren, The Netherlands. (Abstract in *Aggressive Behavior*, **6**, 249–277.)

Kreuz, L. E. and Rose, R. M. (1972) Assessment of aggressive behavior and plasma testosterone in a young criminal population. *Psychosomatic Medicine*, **34**, 321–332.

Kreuz, L. E., Rose, R. M. and Jennings, R. J. (1972) Suppression of plasma testosterone levels and psychological stress. *Archives of General Psychiatry*, **26**, 479–482.

Kunce, J. T., Masuda, M. and Carter, T. E. (1970) MMPI scores, psychiatric disturbance and catecholamine metabolites. *Journal of Clinical Psychology*, **26**, 291–295.

Leaton, R. N. (1965) Exploratory behavior in rats with hippocampal lesions. *Journal of Comparative and Physiological Psychology*, **59**, 325–330.

Lerner, L. J. (1964) Hormone antagonists: inhibitors of specific activities of estrogen and androgen. *Recent Progress in Hormone Research*, vol. 20, pp. 435–490. New York: Academic Press.

Lerner, L. J., Bianchi, A. and Barman, A. (1960) A-Norprogesterone: an androgen antagonist. *Proceedings of the Society for Experimental Biology and Medicine*, **103**, 172–175.

Leshner, A. I. (1972) The adrenals and testes: two separate systems affecting aggressiveness. *Hormones*, **5**, 272–273.

Leshner, A. I. (1975) A model of hormones and agonistic behavior. *Physiology and Behavior*, **15**, 225–235.

Leshner, A. I. (1978) *An Introduction to Behavioral Endocrinology*. New York: Oxford University Press.

Leshner, A. I. and Candland, D. K. (1973) The hormonal basis of aggression. *New Scientist*, **57**, 126–128.

Leshner, A. I., Walker, W. A., Johnson, A. E., Kelling, J. S., Kreisler, S. J. and Svare, B. B. (1973) Pituitary adrenocortical activity and intermale aggressiveness in isolated mice. *Physiology and Behavior*, **11**, 705–711.

Levander, S. E., Schalling, D. S., Lidberg, L., Bartfai, A. and Lidberg, Y. (1980) Skin conductance recovery time and personality in a group of criminals. *Psychophysiology*, **17**, 105–111.

Lewin, R. (1981) Genetic link with human behavior causes stir. *Science*, **211**, 373.

Lion, J. R. (1972) *Evaluation and Management of the Violent Patient*. Springfield, Illinois: Charles C. Thomas.

Lion, J. R. and Bach-Y-Rita, G. (1970) Group psychotherapy with violent outpatients. *International Journal of Group Psychotherapy*, **20**, 185–191.

Lion, J. R., Bach-Y-Rita, G. and Ervin, F. R. (1968) The self-referred violent patient. *Journal of the American Medical Association*, **205**, 503–505.

Lion, J. R., Bach-Y-Rita, G. and Ervin, F. R. (1969) Enigmas of violence. *Science*, **164**, 1465.

Loeb, J. and Mednick, S. A. (1977) A prospective study of predictors of criminality: 3. Electrodermal response patterns. In S. A. Mednick and K. O. Christiansen (Eds) *Biosocial Bases of Criminal Behavior*. New York: Gardner Press.

Logan, F. A. (1971) Dominance and aggression. In H. D. Kimmel (Ed.) *Experimental Psychopathology*, pp. 185–201. New York: Academic Press.

Lorenz, K. (1966) *On Aggression*. New York: Harcourt, Brace, and World.

Lorimer, F. M. (1972) Violent behavior and the electroencephalogram. *Clinical Electroencephalography*, **3**, 193.

Lorr, M. (1966) Approaches to typing: a critique. In M. Lorr (Ed.) *Explorations in Typing Psychotics*. Oxford: Pergamon.

Lykken, D. T. (1957) A study of anxiety in the sociopathic personality. *Journal of Abnormal and Clinical Psychology*, **55**, 6–10.

Mabry, P. D. and Campbell, B. A. (1978) Cholinergic–monoaminergic interactions during ontogenesis. In L. L. Butcher (Ed.) *Cholinergic–Monoaminergic Interactions in the Brain*, pp. 257–270. New York: Academic Press.

MacLean, P. D. and Ploog, D. W. (1962) Cerebral representation of penile erection. *Journal of Neurophysiology*, **25**, 29–55.

Mark, V. H. and Ervin, F. R. (1970) *Violence and the Brain*. New York: Harper and Row.

Marx, J. L. (1982) Autoimmunity in left-handers. *Science*, **217**, 141–144.

Mason, J. W. (1968) A review of psychoendocrine research on the pituitary-adrenal cortical system. *Psychosomatic Medicine*, **10**, 567–607.

Mason, J. W., Nauta, W. J. H., Brady, J. V., Robinson, J. A. and Sachar, E. J. (1961) The role of limbic structures in the regulation of ACTH secretion. *Acta Neurovegativa*, **23**, 4–14.

Masters, W. H. and Johnson, V. E. (1966) *Human Sexual Response*. Boston: Little, Brown.

Matthews, R. (1979) Testosterone levels in aggressive offenders. In M. Sandler (Ed.) *Psychopharmacology of Aggression*. New York: Raven Press.

Mattsson, A., Schalling, D., Olweus, D., Low, H. and Svensson, J. (1980) Plasma testosterone, aggressive behavior, and personality dimensions in young male delinquents. *Journal of the American Academy of Child Psychiatry*, **19**, 476–490.

Mawson, A. R. and Mawson, C. D. (1977) Psychopathy and arousal: a new interpretation of the psychophysiological literature. *Biological Psychiatry*, **12**, 49–72.

Mayer, A. and Wheeler, M. (1982) *The Crocodile Man: A Case of Brain Chemistry and Criminal Violence*. Boston: Houghton Mifflin.

Mazur, A. (1976) Effects of testosterone on status in primate groups. *Folia Primatology*, **26**, 214–226.

McEwen, B. S. (1972) Steroid hormones and the chemistry of behavior. In J. L. McGaugh (Ed.) *The Chemistry of Mood, Motivation, and Memory*, pp. 41–59. New York: Plenum Press.

McEwen, B. S., Magnus, C. and Wallach, G. (1972) Soluble corticosterone-binding macromolecules extracted from rat brain. *Endocrinology*, **90**, 217–226.

McEwen, B. S., Weiss, J. M. and Schwartz, L. S. (1969) Uptake of corticosterone by rat brain and its concentration by certain limbic structures. *Brain Research*, **16**, 227–241.

Mednick, S. A. (1970) Breakdown in individuals at high risk for schizophrenia: possible predispositional perinatal factors. *Mental Hygiene*, **54**, 50–63.

Mednick, S. A. (1974) Electrodermal recovery and psychopathology. In S. A. Mednick, F. Schulsinger, J. Higgens and B. Bell (Eds) *Genetics, Environment and Psychopathology*. Amsterdam: North-Holland.

Mednick, S. A. and Christiansen, K. O. (1977) *Biosocial Bases of Criminal Behavior*. New York: Garner Press.

Mednick, S. A. and Hutchings, B. (1978) Genetic and psychophysiological factors in asocial behavior. *Journal of American Academy of Child Psychiatry*, **17**, 209-223.

Mednick, S. A., Pollock, V., Volavka, J. and Gabrielli, W. F. (1982) Biology and violence. In M. E. Wolfgang and N. A. Weiner (Eds) *Criminal Violence*, pp. 21-80. Beverly Hills, Calif: Sage.

Megargee, E. I. (1966) Undercontrolled and overcontrolled personality types in extreme antisocial aggression. *Psychological Monographs*, **80** (3, Whole No. 611).

Megargee, E. I. (1971) The role of inhibition in the assessment and understanding of violence. In J. L. Singer (Ed.) *The Control of Aggression and Violence: Cognitive and Physiological Factors*. New York: Academic Press.

Megargee, E. I. (1972) *The Psychology of Violence and Aggression*. Morristown, NJ: General Learning Press.

Megargee, E. I. (1973) Recent research on overcontrolled and undercontrolled personality patterns among violent offenders. *Social Symposium*, **9**, 37–50.

Megargee, E. I. (1976) The prediction of dangerous behavior. *Criminal Justice and Behavior*, **3**, 3–21.

Melmon, K. L. (1974) The adrenals, Part II. Catecholamines and the adrenal medulla. In R. H. Williams (Ed.) *Textbook of Endocrinology*. pp. 283–322. Philadelphia: W. B. Saunders.

Mendelson, J. H. and Mello, N. K. (1974) Alcohol, aggression and androgens. In S. H. Frazier (Ed.) *Aggression*, pp. 225–247. Baltimore: Williams and Wilkins.

Menninger, K. A. (1963) *The Vital Balance*. New York: Viking Press.

Meyer-Bahlburg, H. F. L., Boon, D. A., Sharma, M. and Edwards, J. A. (1973) Aggressiveness and testosterone measures in man. *Psychosomatic Medicine*, **35**, 453.

Meyer-Bahlburg, H. F. L., Nat, R., Boon, D. A., Sharma, M. and Edwards, J. A. (1974) Aggressiveness and testosterone measures in man. *Psychosomatic Medicine*, **36**, 269–274.

Mirsky, A. F. (1955) The influence of sex hormones on social behavior in monkeys. *Journal of Comparative and Physiological Psychology*, **48**, 327–335.

Molinoff, P. B., Brimijoin, S., Weinshilboum, R. and Axelrod, J. (1970) Neurally mediated increase in dopamine-beta-hydroxylase activity. *Proceedings of the National Academy of Sciences*, **66**, 453–458.

Molof, M. J. (1967) Differences between assaultive and nonassultive juvenile offenders in the California Youth Authority. Sacramento: California Youth Authority Research Report No. 51.

Monden, Y., Koshiyama, K., Tanaka, H., Mizutani, S., Aono, T., Hamanaka, Y., Uozumi, T. and Matsumoto, K. (1972) Influence of major surgical stress on plasma testosterone, plasma LH, and urinary steroids. *Acta Endocrinologica*, **69**, 542–552.

Money, J., Wiedeking, C., Walker, P., Migeon, C., Meyer, W. and Borgaonkar, D. (1975) 47, XYY and 46, XY males with antisocial and/or sex-offending behavior: antiandrogen therapy plus counselling. *Psychoneuroendocrinology*, **1**, 165–178.

Monroe, R. R. (1970) *Episodic Behavioral Disorders*. Cambridge, Mass.: Harvard University Press.

Monroe, R. R. (1976) Episodic sexual disorders. *Medical Aspects of Human Sexuality*, **10**, 50–64.

Monroe, R. R. (1978) The medical model in psychopathy and dyscontrol syndromes. In W. H. Reid (Ed.) *The Psychopath*. New York: Bruner/Mazel.

Monti, P. T., Brown, W. A. and Corriveau, D. P. (1977) Testosterone and components of aggressive and sexual behavior in man. *American Journal of Psychiatry*, **134**, 692–694.

Moos, R. H. (1968) The development of a menstrual distress questionnaire. *Psychosomatic Medicine*, **30**, 853–867.

Moos, R. H., Kopell, B. S., Melges, F. T., Yalom, I. D., Lunde, D. T., Clayton, R. B. and Hamburg, D. A. (1969) Fluctuations in symptoms and moods during the menstrual cycle. *Journal of Psychosomatic Research*, **13**, 37–44.

Morton, J. H., Addition, H., Addison, R. G., Hunt, L. and Sullivan, J. J. (1953) A clinical study of premenstrual tension. *American Journal of Obstetrics and Gynecology*, **65**, 1182-1191.

Moss, R. L. (1978) Effects of hypothalamic peptides on sex behavior in animal and man. In M. A. Lipton, A. DiMascio and K. F. Killam (Eds) *Psychopharmacology: A Generation of Progress*, pp. 431–440. New York: Raven Press.

Moyer, K. E. (1968) Kinds of aggression and their physiological basis. *Communications in Behavioral Biology*, **2**, 65–87.

Moyer, K. E. (1969) Internal impulses to aggression. *Transactions of the New York Academy of Sciences*, **31**, 104–114.

Moyer, K. E. (1971a) *The Physiology of Hostility*. Chicago: Markham.

Moyer, K. E. (1971b) A preliminary physiological model of aggressive behavior. In B. E. Eleftheriou and J. P. Scott (Eds) *The Physiology of Aggression and Defeat*, pp. 223–263. New York: Plenum Press.

Moyer, K. E. (1971c) The physiology of aggression and the implications for aggression control. In J. L. Singer (Ed.) *The Control of Aggression and Violence*, pp. 61–92. New York: Academic Press.

Murphy, D. L., Belmaker, R. H., Buchsbaum, M., Martin, N. F., Ciaranello, R. and Wyatt, R. J. (1977) Biogenic amine-related enzymes and personality variations in normals. *Psychological Medicine*, **7**, 149–157.

Murray, M. A. F., Bancroft, J. H. J., Anderson, D. C., Tennent, T. G. and Carr, P. J. (1975) Endocrine changes in male sexual deviants after treatment with anti-androgens, oestrogens or tranquillizers. *Journal of Endocrinology*, **67**, 179–188.

Nelson, G. M., Masuda, M. and Holmes, T. H. (1966) Correlation of behaviour and catecholamine metabolite excretion. *Psychosomatic Medicine*, **28**, 216–226.

Neumann, F. (1971) Use of cyproterone acetate in animal and clinical trials. *Gynaecological Investigations*, **2**, 150–179.

Neumann, F., Von Berswordt-Wallrabe, R., Elger, W. and Steinbeck, H. (1968) Activities of anti-androgens: experiments in prepubertal and pubertal animals and in foetuses. In J. Tamm (Ed.) *Testosterone*, pp. 134–143. Proceedings of the Work Shop Conference, Tremsbuettel. Stuttgart: Georg Thieme Verlag.

Olweus, D., Mattsson, A., Schalling, D. and Low, H. (1980) Testosterone, aggression, physical, and personality dimensions in normal adolescent males. *Psychosomatic Medicine*, **42**, 253–269.

Panksepp, J. (1971) Effects of hypothalamic lesions on mouse-killing and shock-induced fighting in rats. *Physiology and Behavior*, **6**, 311–316.

Parlee, M. B. (1973) The premenstrual syndrome. *Psychological Bulletin*, **80**, 454–465.

Passingham, R. E. (1972) Crime and personality: a review of Eysenck's theory. In V. D. Nebylitsyn and J. A. Gray (Eds) *Biological Bases of Individual Behaviour*. New York: Academic Press.

Persky, H., Smith, K. D. and Basu, G. K. (1971) Relation of psychologic measures of aggression and hostility to testosterone production in man. *Psychosomatic Medicine*, **33**, 265–277.

Petrie, A. (1967) *Individuality in Pain and Suffering*. Chicago: University of Chicago Press.

Potegal, M., Gibbons, J., Blau, A. and Ross, S. (1980) 'Serotonergic modification of muricide-inhibitory septal stimulation.' Paper given at Fourth Bienniel Meeting of the International Society for Research on Aggression, University of Groningen at Haren, The Netherlands. (Abstract in *Aggressive Behavior*, **6**, 249–277.)

Pradhan, S. N. (1975) Aggression and central neurotransmitters. In C. C. Pfeiffer and J. R. Smythies (Eds) *International Review of Neurobiology*, vol. 18, pp. 213–262. New York: Academic Press.

Preu, P. W. (1944) The concept of psychopathic personality. In J. McV. Hunt (Ed.) *Personality and the Behavior Disorders*, vol. 11, p. 936. New York: Ronald Press.

Quay, H. C. (1965) Psychopathic personality as pathological stimulation seeking. *American Journal of Psychiatry*, **122**, 180–183.

Rada, R. T. (1981) Plasma androgens and the sex offender. *Bulletin of the American Academy of Psychiatry and Law*, **8**, 456–464.

Rada, R. T., Kellner, R. and Winslow, W. W. (1976) Plasma testosterone and aggressive behavior. *Psychosomatics*, **17**, 138–142.

Rada, R. T., Laws, D. R. and Kellner, R. (1976) Plasma testosterone levels in the rapist. *Psychosomatic Medicine*, **38**, 257–268.

Rada, R. T., Laws, D. R., Kellner, R., Stivastava, L. and Peake, G. (1983) Plasma androgens in violent and non-violent sex offenders. *Bulletin of the American Academy of Psychiatry and Law*, **11**, 149–158.

Redmond, D. E., Baulu, J., Murphy, D. L., Loriaux, D. L., Zeigler, M. G. and Lake, C. R. (1976) The effects of testosterone on plasma and platelet monomine oxidase (MAO) and plasma dopamine-beta-hydroxylase (DBH) activities in the male rhesus monkey. *Psychosomatic Medicine*, **38**, 315–326.

Robichaud, R. C. and Sledge, K. L. (1969) The effects of p-chlorophenylalanine on experimentally induced conflict in the rat. *Life Sciences*, **8**, 965–969.

Rocky, S. and Neri, R. O. (1968) Comparative biological properties of SCH 12600: (6-chloro 4,6 pregnadien 16-methylene 17-alpha-ol-3,20-dione-17-acetate) and chlormadinone acetate. *Federation Proceedings*, **27**, 624. (Abstract No. 2300.)

Roeder, F., Orthner, J. and Muller, D. (1972) The stereotaxic treatment of pedophilic homosexuality and other sexual deviations. In E. Hitchcock, L. Laitinen and K. Vaernet (Eds) *Psychosurgery*. Springfield, Illinois: Charles C. Thomas.

Rose, R. M. (1969) Androgen responses to stress. I. Psychoendocrine relationships and assessment of androgen activity. *Psychosomatic Medicine*, **31**, 405–417.

Rose, R. M. (1975) Testosterone, aggression, and homosexuality: a review of the literature and implications for future research. In E. J. Sachar (Ed.) *Topics in Psychoendocrinology*, pp. 83–103. New York: Grune and Stratton.

Rose, R. M. (1978) Neuroendocrine correlates of sexual and aggressive behaviour in humans. In M. A. Lipton, A. DiMascio and K. F. Killam (Eds) *Psychopharmacology: A Generation of Progress*, pp. 541–552. New York: Raven Press.

Rose, R. M., Bernstein, I. S. and Gordon, T. P. (1975) Consequences of social conflict on plasma testosterone levels in rhesus monkeys. *Psychosomatic Medicine*, **37**, 5–61.

Rose, R. M., Bourne, P. G. and Poe, R. O. (1969) Androgen responses to stress, II. Excretion of testosterone, epitestosterone, androsterone and etiocholanolone during basic combat training and under threat of attack. *Psychosomatic Medicine*, **31**, 418–436.

Rose, R. M., Gordon, T. P. and Bernstein, I. S. (1972) Plasma testosterone levels in the male rhesus: influences of sexual and social stimuli. *Science*, **178**, 643–645.

Rose, R. M., Holaday, J. W. and Bernstein, I. S. (1971) Plasma testosterone dominance rank and aggressive behaviour. *Nature*, **231**, 366–368.

Rubin, R. T., Mandell, A. J. and Crandall, P. H. (1966) Corticosteroid responses to limbic stimulation in man: localization of stimulus sites. *Science*, **153**, 767–768.

Sano, K., Sekino, H. and Mayanagi, Y. (1972) Results of stimulation and destruction of the posterior hypothalamus in cases with violent aggressive, or restless behaviors. In E. Hitchcock, L. Laittinen and K. Vaernet (Eds) *Psychosurgery*, pp. 57–75. Springfield, Illinois: Charles C. Thomas.

Sassenrath, E. N., Rowell, T. E. and Hendrickx, A. G. (1973) Perimenstrual aggression in groups of female rhesus monkeys. *Journal of Reproduction and Fertility*, **34**, 509–511.

Scaramella, T. J. and Brown, W. A. (1978) Serum testosterone and aggressiveness in hockey players. *Psychosomatic Medicine*, **40**, 262–265.

Schachter, S. (1971) *Emotion, Obesity and Crime*. New York: Academic Press.

Schachter, S. and Latane, B. (1964) Crime, cognition and the autonomic nervous system. In M. R. Jones (Ed.) *Nebraska Symposium on Motivation*, pp. 221–275. Lincoln: University of Nebraska Press.

Schmauk, F. J. (1970) A study of the relationship between kinds of punishment, autonomic arousal, subjective anxiety and avoidance learning in the primary sociopath. *Journal of Abnormal Psychology*, **76**, 325–355.

Schooler, C., Zahn, T. P., Murphy, D. L. and Buchsbaum, M. S. (1978) Psychological correlates of monoamine oxidase activity in normals. *Journal of Nervous and Mental Disease*, **166**, 177–186.

Scott, J. P. (1971) Theoretical issues concerning the origin and causes of fighting. In B. E. Eleftheriou and J. P. Scott (Eds) *The Physiology of Aggression and Defeat*, pp. 11–41. New York: Plenum Press.

Sedvall, G. C., Weise, V. K. and Kopin, I. J. (1968) The rate of norepinephrine synthesis measured in vivo during short intervals: influence of adrenergic nerve impulse activity. *Journal of Pharmacology and Experimental Therapeutics*, **159**, 274–282.

Selmanoff, M. K., Goldman, B. D. and Ginsberg, B. E. (1977) Serum testosterone, agonistic behavior and dominance in inbred strains of mice. *Hormones and Behavior*, **8**, 107–119.

Shapland, J. and Rushton, J. P. (1975) Crime and personality: further evidence. *Bulletin of the British Psychological Society*, **28**, 66–67.

Sheard, M. H. (1969) The effect of p-chlorophenylalanine on behavior in rats: relation to brain serotonin and 5-hydroxyindoleacetic acid. *Brain Research*, **15**, 524.

Sheard, M. H. (1979) Testosterone and aggression. In M. Sandler (Ed.) *Psychopharmacology of Aggression*. New York: Raven Press.

Siddle, D. A. T. (1977) Electrodermal activity and psychopathy. In S. A. Mednick and K. O. Christiansen (Eds) *Biosocial Bases of Criminal Behavior*. New York: Gardner Press.

Siddle, D. A. T., Mednick, S., Nicol, A. R. and Foggitt, R. H. (1976) Skin conductance recovery in anti-social adolescents. *British Journal of Social and Clinical Psychology*, **15**, 425–428.

Sigg, E. B. (1969) Relationship of aggressive behaviour to adrenal and gonadal function in male mice. In S. Garattini and E. B. Sigg (Eds) *Aggressive Behaviour*, pp. 143–149. Amsterdam: Excerpta Medica.

Sigg, E. B., Day, C. and Colombo, C. (1966) Endocrine factors in isolation induced aggressiveness in rodents. *Endocrinology*, **78**, 679–684.

Simon, N. G. (1981) Hormones and human aggression: a comparative perspective. *International Journal of Mental Health*, **10**, 60–74.

Sjoerdsma, A., Lovenberg, W., Engelman, K., Carpenter, W. T., Jr, Wyatt, R. J. and Gessa, G. L. (1970) Serotonin now: clinical implications of inhibiting its synthesis with para-chlorophenylalanine. *Annals of Internal Medicine*, **73**, 607.

Slusher, M. A. (1966) Effects of cortisol implants in the brainstem and ventral hippocampus on diurnal corticosterone levels. *Experimental Brain Research*, **1**, 184–194.

Smith, M., Harris, P. J. and Strayer, F. F. (1977) Laboratory methods for the assessment of social dominance among captive squirrel monkeys. *Primates*, **18**, 966–984.

Smythies, J. R. (1970) *Brain Mechanisms and Behavior*. New York: Academic Press.

Sorenson, C. A. and Ellison, G. D. (1973) Non-linear changes in activity and emotional reactivity scores following central noradrenergic lesions in rats. *Psychopharmacologia*, **32**, 313–325.

Sorenson, C. A. and Gordon, M. (1975) Effects of 6-hydroxydopamine on shock-elicited aggression, emotionality and maternal behavior in female rats. *Pharmacology, Biochemistry and Behavior*, **3**, 331–335.

Spodak, M. K., Falck, Z. A. and Rappeport, J. R. (1978) The hormonal treatment of paraphiliacs with Depo-Provera. *Criminal Justice and Behavior*, **5**, 304–314.

Staub, E. (1971) *The Learning and Unlearning of Aggression: The Role of Anxiety, Empathy, Efficacy, and Prosocial Values*. New York: Academic Press.

Stein, L. (1969) Chemistry of purposive behavior. In J. T. Tapp (Ed.) *Reinforcement and Behavior*. New York: Academic Press.

Stein, L., Wise, C. D. and Berger, B. D. (1972) Noradrenergic reward mechanisms, recovery of function and schizophrenia. In J. L. McGaugh (Ed.) *The Chemistry of Mood, Motivation and Memory*, pp. 81–103. New York: Plenum Press.

Stevens, D. A., Fechter, L. D. and Resnick, O. (1969) The effects of p-chlorophenylalanine, a depleter of brain serotonin, on behavior: II, retardation of passive avoidance learning. *Life Sciences*, **8**, 379–385.

Syndulko, K. (1978) Electrocortical investigations of psychopathy. In R. D. Hare and D. Schalling (Eds) *Psychopathic Behaviour: Approaches to Research*, pp. 145–155. London: Wiley.

Tagliamonte, A., Tagliamonte, P., Gessa, G. L. and Brodie, B. B. (1969) Compulsive sexual activity induced by p-chlorophenylalanine in normal and pinealectomized male rats. *Science*, **166**, 1433–1435.

Thiessen, D. D. (1976) *The Evolution and Chemistry of Aggression*. Springfield, Illinois: Charles C. Thomas.

Thorne, G. L. (1971) The Sensation-Seeking Scale with deviant populations. *Journal of Consulting and Clinical Psychology*, **37**, 106–110.

Ulrich, J. (1938) The social hierarchy in albino mice. *Journal of Comparative Psychology*, **25**, 373-413.

Valzelli, L. (1977) About a 'specific' neurochemistry of aggressive behavior. In J. M. R. Delgado and F. V. DeFeudis (Eds) *Behavioral Neurochemistry*, pp. 113–132. New York: Spectrum.

Valzelli, L. (1981) *Psychobiology of Aggression and Violence*. New York: Raven Press.

Venables, P. H. (1974) The recovery limb of skin conductance response in 'high risk' research. In S. A. Mednick, F. Schulsinger, J. Higgins and B. Bell (Eds) *Genetics, Environment and Psychopathology*. Amsterdam: North-Holland.

Venables, P. H. (1975) Progress in psychophysiology: some applications in a field of abnormal psychology. In P. H. Venables and M. Christie (Eds) *Research in Psychophysiology*, pp.418–434. New York: Wiley.

Vergnes, M. (1980) 'Amygdaloid control over mouse-killing behavior in the rat.' Paper given at Fourth Biennial Meeting of the International Society for Research on Aggression, University of Groningen at Haren, The Netherlands. (Abstract in *Aggressive Behavior*, **6**, 249–277.)

Vernikos-Danellis, J. and Berger, P. A. (1973) Brain serotonin and the pituitary-adrenal system. In J. Barchas and E. Usdin (Eds) *Serotonin and Behavior*, pp. 173–177. New York: Academic Press.

Virkkunen, M. (1979) Serum cholesterol in antisocial personality. *Neuropsychobiology*, **5**, 27–30.

Vogt, M. (1959) Catecholamines in the brain. *Pharmacological Review*, **11**, 483–489.

Warburton, D. M. (1975) *Brain, Behaviour and Drugs*. London: Wiley.

Weil-Malherbe, H. and Szara, S. I. (1971) *The Biochemistry of Functional and Experimental Psychoses*. Springfield, Illinois: Charles C. Thomas.

Weiss, J. M., Glazer, H. I., Pohorecky, L. A., Brick, J. and Miller, N. E. (1975) Effects of chronic exposure to stressors on avoidance-escape behavior and on brain norepinephrine. *Psychosomatic Medicine*, **37**, 522–534.

Welch, A. S. and Welch, B. L. (1971) Isolation, reactivity and aggression: evidence for the involvement of brain catecholamines and serotonin. In B. E. Eleftheriou and J. P. Scott (Eds) *The Physiology of Aggression and Defeat*, pp. 91–142. New York: Plenum Press.

Whalen, R. E. (1966) Sexual Motivation. *Psychological Review*, **73**, 151–163.

Wheatley, M. D. (1944) The hypothalamus and affective behavior in cats: a study of the effects of experimental lesions with anatomic correlations. *Archives of Neurology and Psychiatry*, **52**, 296–316.

White, W. C., McAdoo, W. G. and Megargee, E. I. (1973) Personality factors associated with over- and under-controlled offenders. *Journal of Personality Assessment*, **37**, 473–478.

Williams, D. (1969) Neural factors related to habitual aggression. *Brain*, **92**, 503–520.

Wurtman, R. J. (1965) Catecholamines. *New England Journal of Medicine*, **273**, 637–646 and 746–753.

Wurtman, R. J. (1966) *Catecholamines*. Boston: Little, Brown.

Zitrin, A. (1973) Changes in brain serotonin level and male sexual behavior. In J. Barchas and E. Usdin (Eds) *Serotonin and Behavior*, pp. 365–370. New York: Academic Press.

Zuckerman, M. (1978) Sensation seeking and psychopathy. In R. D. Hare and D. Schalling (Eds) *Psychopathic Behavior: Approaches to Research*, pp. 165-185. New York: Wiley.

Zuckerman, M. (1979) *Sensation Seeking: Beyond the Optimal Level of Arousal*. Hillsdale, NJ: Erlbaum.

Zuckerman, M., Kolin, E. A., Price, L. and Zoob, I. (1964) Development of a Sensation Seeking Scale. *Journal of Consulting Psychology*, **28**, 477–482.

Aggression and Dangerousness
Edited by D. P. Farrington and J. Gunn
© 1985 John Wiley & Sons Ltd.

CHAPTER 3

Characteristics of Non-institutionalized Psychopaths

CATHY SPATZ WIDOM and JOSEPH P. NEWMAN

INTRODUCTION

In pursuing their lifestyle, psychopaths frequently engage in unethical, immoral, and/or criminal behaviour. Until recently, research on psychopaths has concentrated on adult male offenders incarcerated in penal institutions. However, researchers and clinicians have long recognized that psychopaths are not necessarily criminal (or incarcerated). This is particularly evident upon inspection of Cleckley's (1976) classic volume of case histories of psychopaths. To begin to remedy this limited research perspective, Widom (1977) proposed a methodology for studying non-institutionalized psychopaths. She argued that traditional theorizing and research on psychopaths was restricted by its focus on the criminal and perhaps unsuccessful psychopath. In that paper, data were presented demonstrating that non-institutionalized psychopaths could be identified, brought into the research laboratory, and tested.

The methodology was originally proposed to fill a void in the empirical literature. However, the larger goal of studying non-institutionalized psychopaths is to understand their characteristics, unconfounded by criminal and/or prisoner status, and to disentangle those attributes related to psychopathy and those related to criminality or antisocial behaviour (as defined by arrests and incarcerations). By relying solely on individuals labelled 'criminal' by justice agencies, we are implicitly incorporating decisions by police, courts, and others into the definition of a psychological construct. By studying non-institutionalized psychopaths, rather than institutionalized ones, the effects of institutionalization and labelling are minimized, research subjects represent a broader range of socioeconomic backgrounds, are less often minority individuals (who are typically overrepresented in prison populations), and may represent more successful psychopaths.

For such a methodology to be considered useful, its generalizability and replicability need to be demonstrated. The original research was carried out in

Boston. Is the methodology limited to particular geographic regions or large metropolitan areas? Or, does the usefulness of the methodology extend to a variety of geographic areas, including smaller, non-urban ones? Part I of this chapter describes a replication of Widom's (1977) initial study in a non-urban, midwest community. Part II compares four approaches to diagnosing or selecting psychopaths.

PART I: STUDYING NON-INSTITUTIONAL PSYCHOPATHS: ADVERTISING METHODOLOGY REPLICATION

Subjects and Recruitment

Forty subjects (24 males and 16 females) from Bloomington[1] and the surrounding community participated in the study. Following Widom (1977), the characteristics of the psychopath were delineated in a non-pejorative way and incorporated into a classified advertisement placed in the local newspaper. The advertisement read:

ARE YOU ADVENTUROUS?

Psychologist studying adventurous carefree people who've led exciting impulsive lives. If you're the kind of person who'd do almost anything for a dare, call 337-xxxx any time.

A 24-hour telephone answering service was utilized to receive calls. Operators recorded the respondent's name and telephone number, but did not provide information about the content of the study. Upon being contacted by the researchers, callers were told that the study would require approximately 2½–3 hours and that they would receive $10 for participating. Attempts were made to contact all respondents to arrange for interviews and testing.[2]

Procedure and Measures

When the subject arrived in the building, he/she was escorted to the interview and testing room and was asked to read and sign a consent form. The subject completed a personality inventory, a demographic and family background questionnaire, and a card task, and was interviewed. During the experimental session, subjects were asked to make six time estimations. The measures, interview, and behavioural tasks are described below.

Personality Inventory

Subjects first completed a personality inventory composed of the Lie, Depression, Psychopathic deviate, Hypomania, and Welsh Anxiety scales from the MMPI, the Socialization scale of the California Psychological Inventory (Gough, 1960), and the Extraversion Scale of the Eysenck

Personality Questionnaire (Eysenck and Eysenck, 1975). (For a discussion of the rationale for including these measures, see Widom, 1977).

Demographic Background Questionnaire

This questionnaire elicited information regarding school, job, military, psychiatric, legal, drug and alcohol history, socioeconomic background, and family history information including parents' education; occupation; mental and emotional health; and criminal, drug, and alcohol histories.

Personal Interview

Subjects were asked to describe themselves and how the advertisement applied to them. The interview protocol also included questions about school and job performance; personal relationships (family, friends, and sexual relations); adolescence; and adult behaviour, including criminal activities, hobbies, and physical health. With the permission of the subjects, the interviews were tape recorded.

Although the goal of this research was to replicate Widom's (1977) study as closely as possible, two additional *behavioural measures* were included. These measures are described below.

Passive-avoidance

Passive-avoidance learning is the ability to inhibit a response that previously resulted in punishment. Although a passive-avoidance deficit has been noted frequently among psychopaths (e.g. Lykken, 1957; Hare, 1970), Schmauk (1970) demonstrated that the deficit may be eliminated by using loss of reward in place of electric shock as punishment for avoidance errors.

In the present study, a task adapted from the work of Chesno and Kilmann (1976) was used to assess passive-avoidance. In contrast to the Lykken maze, the avoidance contingency in this task is explicit. In addition, to avoid punishment, subjects must inhibit a response that sometimes leads to a reward. Such a task would seem relevant to the circumstances of antisocial behaviour—where a person is tempted to act for personal gain but may also face negative consequences. Newman (1980) and Newman *et al.* (1984) demonstrated that psychopathic delinquents and extraverts exhibited a passive-avoidance deficit on this task even when loss of reward was the consequence of avoidance errors.

The passive-avoidance task is essentially a successive go/no-go discrimination. Subjects view a series of stimuli presented on file cards. The subject's task is to learn to respond when this leads to a reward (5 cents), and to inhibit responding when it leads to a loss of reward (loss of 5 cents). The series, composed of eight 2-digit numbers, is repeated ten times in a different order each time for a total of 80 trials. The 1 inch black vinyl numbers on file cards are displayed one at a time for a period of 2 seconds. Responses to four of the stimulus numbers are rewarded, while responses to the other four are punished. No reinforcement is provided on trials without a response. Subjects are expected to learn by trial-and-error when to respond and when not to respond.

Time Estimation

The second behavioural measure focuses on the limited time perspective that is thought to characterize psychopaths (e.g. Cleckley, 1976) and the inability to tolerate boredom (e.g. Zuckerman, 1974). Several studies have indicated a shorter time perspective among delinquents and psychopaths (e.g. Siegman, 1961; Friel and de Abovitz, 1968) and others have shown that psychopaths get bored more quickly than non-psychopaths during monotonous tasks (e.g. London and Monello, 1974). A series of time estimates was included in the design of the present study to assess, relatively unobtrusively, this phenomenon.

Time estimation was assessed by asking the subjects to estimate the time spent in various parts of the experiment. At the beginning of the study they were told that they would be asked to estimate how long was each segment of the study, and were asked to remove watches, if applicable. There were a total of *six* time estimations, corresponding to the four parts described previously (personality inventory, card task, background questionnaire, interview) plus two additional aspects of the design. The first four were thought to reflect time estimates of neutral events. For each of these, the actual time spent was recorded and subjects were asked for their estimates. For the two additional parts, actual time spent was controlled. In the *ice water* (or negative) condition (pseudo-cold pressor test), the subjects were told that they would be asked to hold their right hand in a bucket of ice water for as long as possible. At the appropriate time the experimenter picked up an empty bucket and left the room, telling the subject the experimenter would have to go and get the ice water. After 2 minutes the experimenter returned, apologized for the lack of ice water, blaming a malfunction, and asked the subject to estimate the amount of time the experimenter was away. The second (positive) condition was conducted in an analogous fashion and labelled *cash*. At the end of the study the experimenter totalled the amount of money earned by the subject ($10 plus the amount earned on the card task) and informed him or her that the experimenter would have to leave the room to get the money (cash). After 2 minutes the experimenter returned with the cash and asked the subject to estimate the time. This concluded the study and the subjects were then thanked, paid, and any questions they may have had were answered.

The sequence of tasks was identical for all subjects. The personality inventory was administered first, followed by the ice water condition, the card task, the background questionnaire, the interview, and finally, the cash payment.

Demographic and Background Characteristics

As an aid to assessing the success of this study as a replication, Table 1 presents a summary of selected demographic and background characteristics of the present sample, with data from the original sample for comparison.

The subjects generally represented the lower end of the occupational spectrum as defined by Hollingshead (1975) level 5 ($M = 5.14$, $s.d. = 2.12$, range 2–8). Of those employed, a wide range of occupations was represented: bartender, carpenter, self-employed contractor and tutor, house husband, delivery person, cook/manager, musician, property manager, waitress, home entertainment sales, behavioural clinician, surveyor's apprentice, computer technician, cook, factory worker, clerk, and social activist. Almost one-quarter (23.1 per cent) reported having collected unemployment benefits or welfare payments and almost half (46.2 per cent) reported having 'serious financial problems making it difficult to pay off debts or meet other financial responsibilities'. Five were currently unemployed.

Psychiatric Hospitalization and Treatment

Only 10.3 per cent ($n = 4$) of the sample reported that they had spent some time as an inpatient in a psychiatric hospital. However, 51.3 per cent ($n = 20$) reported that they had sought help for emotional problems. One in 10 had treatment for drug problems, 2.6 per cent for alcohol problems, and 23.1 per cent ($n = 9$) for behaviour problems. More than two-thirds of the sample ($n = 26$) reported having 'ever had depression' and one-third ($n = 11$) reported having made suicide attempts.

Sexuality

Homosexual experiences were reported by approximately one-third of the sample ($n = 13$), of whom three subjects were primarily homosexual.

During the interview the subjects were asked whether they had engaged in any unusual sexual behaviour. Almost half ($n = 18$) reported having participated in group sex, six reported having engaged in sadism/masochism or bondage, and a few were in pornographic movies or sex marathons or were watched by friends while engaging in sex.

Table 1   Characteristics of sample: Comparison with original Boston study

Characteristic	Present study ($n = 40^a$)	Widom (1977) ($n = 28$)
Age	$M = 25.15$	$M = 25.7$
	s.d. $= 6.83$	s.d. $= 5.1$
Education		
No high school degree	7.9%	7.1%
High school degree	15.8	32.1
Some college	60.5	21.4
College degree	10.5	32.1
Some graduate school	5.3	3.6
Marital status		
Single	65.0	75.0
Married	17.5	none
Divorced, separated, or widowed	17.5	25.0
Parental psychopathology		
Divorced, separated, or broken homes	27.5	28.5
Parental psychopathology	41.0	7.1
Alcoholism	25.6	17.8
Psychiatric hospitalization		
Hospitalization	10.3	21.4
Outpatient only	51.3	46.4
Suicide attempts	27.5	28.6
Arrest records		
Juvenile arrest	15.4	NA
Detained	NA	17.9
Adult arrest	33.3	64.3
Adult convictions	NA	17.9
At least one arrest	41.0	
Incarceration		
Juvenile	2.6	10.7
Adult	5.1	32.1
Either	7.7	42.8
Overnight	NA	14.3

Note: NA = Information not available

[a]   In some cases, information from one subject was not available. Thus, some percentages were calculated on the basis of an n of 39.

Antisocial Characteristics

More than three-quarters of the sample reported stealing as a child, and almost 40 per cent reported running away from home. Almost one-half reported that their teachers complained that their work was not up to their ability; this was not surprising, since almost one-third missed time from school through truancy. Suspensions from school were also fairly frequent (35.9 per cent), with one-third of these for fighting.

Heavy Drinking

A history of heavy drinking was reported by one-quarter of the sample, whereas 35.9 per cent reported having experienced blackouts, and 27.5 per cent reported that they had got drunk at least once a week. Only 5.1 per cent considered themselves alcoholic. The age of onset of heavy drinking in these subjects ranged from 7 to 21, with a mean age of 16.

Drug Usage

The subjects reported considerable drug usage, with multiple drug use common. One-quarter of the subjects reported having used heroin, and three reported heavy use of speed. Six limited their use to alcohol and marijuana and three people reported never using any drugs, including marijuana.

Criminal History

At the time of the study, 41 per cent of the group had been arrested at least once. Of those, only three had been incarcerated. The mean number of arrests for the entire sample was 1.1, with a range of 0–9 arrests. The arrests varied greatly and were for vagrancy, runaway, public intoxication, driving under the influence, probation violations, 'selling encyclopedias without a licence', trespassing, possession, shoplifting, forgery, criminal mischief, criminal recklessness, assault, battery on an officer, assault and battery, breaking and entering, armed robbery, burglary while soliciting, and attempted rape. Almost 60 per cent of the sample reported having two or more non-parking traffic violations.

Robins' Criteria

Table 2 presents data for these subjects using Robins' (1966) diagnostic criteria for sociopathy. Almost three-quarters of the sample (72.5 per cent) met Robins' minimal criteria, with the average number of characteristics for the sample being 7.62. Table 2 also presents the results from Widom's earlier study (1977) for comparative purposes.

Table 2   Robins' criteria for sociopathy

Characteristic	Present study ($n = 40$)		Widom (1977) ($n = 28$)	
Poor work history	57.5%	(23)	78.6%	(22)
Poor marital history				
Single	65.0	(26)	75.0	(21)
Divorced or separated	17.5	(7)	25.0	(7)
Excessive drugs	52.5	(21)	67.9	(19)
Heavy drinking	45.0	(18)	46.4	(13)
At least one arrest	40.0	(16)	67.9	(19)[a]
More than two arrests	17.5	(7)	28.6	(8)
Physical aggression	40.0	(16)	39.3	(11)
Sexual promiscuity or perversion	57.5	(23)	50.0	(14)
Impulsiveness	82.5	(33)	57.1	(16)[a]
School problems and truancy	47.5	(19)	42.9	(12)
Public financial care	25.0	(10)	17.9	(5)
Poor armed service	NA		NA	
Vagrancy (wanderlust)	37.5	(15)	46.4	(13)
Many somatic symptoms (>9)	20.0	(8)	NA	
Pathological lying	25.0	(10)	21.4	(6)
Lack of friends	47.5	(19)	28.6	(8)
Use of aliases	42.5	(17)	42.9	(12)
Lack of guilt	35.0	(14)	35.7	(10)
Reckless adolescence	45.0	(18)	35.7	(10)
Suicide attempts	27.5	(11)	32.1	(9)
With five or more characteristics (Robins' minimal criteria)	72.5	(29)	78.6	(22)
Mean number of characteristics	7.62		7.46	

Note: Numbers in parentheses indicate actual number in sample.
      NA = Information not available from interview data.

[a]   Chi square significant at less than 0.05 level.

Psychometric Characteristics of the Sample

Table 3 presents means and standard deviations for the sample on the personality scales. Simply for comparative purposes, Table 3 also includes scores from a sample of college students, the subjects in the original Widom study, and prison inmates. The college students were all attending a major university in the midwest at approximately the same time as the advertisement appeared in the newspaper.

A multivariate analysis of variance (MANOVA) using Wilks' lambda was performed to test for mean differences between personality scale scores of subjects in the present study and college students. The overall multivariate

Table 3 Personality scale scores: present sample and comparative groups

Scale	Present sample (n = 40)		Widom (1977) (n = 28)		College students (n = 241)		Prison inmates		
	M	s.d.	M	s.d.	M	s.d.	n	M	s.d.
Lie	3.87	1.98	3.21	2.44	3.71	1.67	32	4.25	2.03[e]
Depression	19.22	4.61	19.89	5.29	20.07	5.32			
Psychopathic deviate	22.52	4.67	23.32	6.06	19.09	4.83[b]	32	24.44	5.13[e]
Mania	25.47	4.68	23.39	4.10	20.73	4.95[b]			
Welsh Anxiety	14.60	7.59			15.50	8.33	32	11.03	9.67[e]
Socialization (CPI)	26.32	5.19	26.52	7.29	33.68	5.79[b]	177	27.76	6.03[c]
Extraversion (EPQ)	16.72	3.81			14.42	4.22[a]	1023	13.62	4.69[d]

[a] Comparison between present sample and college students, significance level 0.01.
[b] Comparison between present sample and college students, significance level 0.001.
[c] From Gough (1960).
[d] From Eysenck and Eysenck (1975).
[e] From Widom (1976).

$F(39,785) = 4.21, p <0.0001$. Significant univariate differences were found on: Psychopathic deviate ($F(3,277) = 7.61, p <0.001$), Mania ($F(3,277) = 13.08, p <0.001$), Socialization ($F(3,277) = 23.26, p <0.001$), and Extraversion ($F(3,277) = 3.85, p <0.01$). Subjects in the present study had significantly higher scores on Pd, Ma, and Ex, and lower scores on So than the college students. There were no significant differences between the two groups on the Welsh Anxiety, Depression, or Lie scales.

The present sample demonstrated personality, demographic, and social history characteristics frequently associated with the diagnosis of psychopathy. The methodology developed earlier in Boston, therefore, appears useful in a different geographic location. In demographic and background characteristics the present sample was quite similar to that in Widom's earlier study. The samples differed somewhat in level of education (a lower proportion of college graduates in the present sample), but primarily in terms of criminal history (fewer arrests and incarcerations in the present sample). Psychometric test scores available for both groups were remarkably similar.

In terms of Robins' criteria (Table 2), the samples are again similar overall, with the majority of both samples meeting the criteria for sociopathy. The original 1977 sample appeared more deviant with respect to work history, excessive drug usage, and at least one arrest, whereas the present sample was characterized by more impulsiveness and a higher rate of the characteristic 'lack of friends'. Of these discrepancies between the samples, only two were significant—arrests and impulsiveness.

Lower arrest and incarceration rates among the Bloomington subjects may, in part, be a product of the higher frequency of criminal activity in Boston than Bloomington (US Bureau of the Census, 1978) and differences in police styles in these different communities (Wilson, 1968). However, given the extensive similarities noted between the two samples, differences in arrests and incarcerations should not cause much concern, unless one includes criminal behaviour as a necessary component in the definition of psychopathy. Indeed, as mentioned earlier, one of the purposes of studying non-institutionalized psychopaths is to avoid dependence on the practices of criminal justice agencies for defining a psychological construct, which is implied by the inclusion of criminal history as a criterion for defining psychopathy. The usefulness of the method lies in being able to study psychopaths who have *not* necessarily been arrested or incarcerated.

Undoubtedly, changes in the recruitment procedure in the present study permitted the inclusion of more impulsive individuals. Previously, respondents were required to send brief biographies. In the present study potential respondents were able to call 'on the spur of the moment' at any hour of the day. This 'spur of the moment' calling is reflected in the large number of individuals who were no longer available at the original telephone number that they had provided (often because they had left town or had checked out of a motel).

However, the heterogeneity of this sample should not be ignored. By no means are all the participants in this study psychopaths, by any criteria. We have cast a broader 'net' with this method than limiting ourselves by utilizing incarcerated psychopaths. While the 'catch' here has been richer in some ways, the ones who got away, the 'no shows', those who could not be located or who had moved, may be a richer group still.[3]

Given that normative data are not available for the behavioural measures, as they are for the personality, demographic, and social history data, it would not be particularly informative to present these findings for the whole sample. Furthermore, since the subjects in the present study are a heterogeneous group, and not all meet criteria for psychopathy, Part II of this paper compares the subjects who meet the various criteria. The findings from the behavioural data are included in the context of this discussion.

PART II: COMPARISON OF APPROACHES
TO DIAGNOSING PSYCHOPATHS

In addition to the limitations of biased subject samples, considerable disagreement exists in the field as to the most appropriate diagnostic criteria for subject selection. How is the clinician or researcher to choose among them? From a practical perspective it is likely that existing approaches to conceptualizing and diagnosing the psychopath lead to different diagnostic practices. Some conceptions may include a broad range of criteria for inclusion, whereas others may define a narrower range and exclude many individuals. Hence, the choice of diagnostic system may affect the number and type of patients considered psychopathic as well as treatment decisions. For research purposes the use of a variety of subject-selection techniques by researchers presents serious problems in evaluating the results of research.

Furthermore, debates continue about the reliability and validity of the diagnosis of psychopathy. High levels of inter-rater reliability have been reported (Chesno and Kilmann, 1975; Dengerink and Bertilson, 1975; Hare and Quinn, 1971) as well as substantial agreement between scores on two rating scales (Ross and Hundleby, 1973; Heilbrun, 1979). On the other hand, low and non-significant correlations have been noted between composite ratings of psychopathy and scores on self-report inventories (Ross and Hundleby, 1973) and between behavioural correlates and MMPI code types associated with antisocial behaviour (Gynther et al., 1973). Hundleby and Ross (1977) found no substantial agreement among psychopathy scales that they felt could lead to a 'factor interpretation of the concept'.

Given the current state of affairs, a comparison and examination of the overlap between various diagnostic approaches is warranted. Although the selection of a particular diagnostic assessment technique may vary depending on the need of the clinician, researcher, and subject population, as well as on practical concerns such as time, money, and staff resources, diagnostic utility remains an empirical issue. Part II of this chapter compares four approaches to diagnosing or selecting psychopaths.

Several specific concerns form the basis of Part II. Different methods used to diagnose psychopaths may represent merely broader or narrower views of psychopathy, not necessarily identifying mutually exclusive subjects as psychopaths. Are some diagnostic criteria more inclusive than others? Do various approaches consider different kinds of individuals as psychopaths? What proportion of subjects are diagnosed psychopaths according to the various sets of criteria? Finally, what role does blatant antisocial behaviour (i.e. arrests and/or incarcerations) play in each of the four approaches?

Major diagnostic and assessment techniques differ in the extent to which they are based on descriptions of observed behaviour or on inferences from psychometric or psychophysiological data. Two general approaches to classification were selected for use here—one which focuses on clinical and behavioural checklists (based on interview data) and the other which utilizes psychometric test instruments to identify psychopaths.

Data from the same 40 subjects recruited for the study in Part I are used for this analysis, which thus includes personality, behavioural, demographic, and family background information, as well as information obtained from a semi-structured clinical interview. The interview protocol covered a variety of topics (school and job performance, personal relationships, adolescence, and adult behaviour) as well as questions about criminal activities, hobbies, and physical health. Specific questions were included from the SADS-L (Spitzer *et al.*, 1975) to permit the diagnosis of antisocial personality disorder. Interviews were tape-recorded with the subject's permission.

Self-report Inventories

Psychopathic Deviate (Pd) Scale of the MMPI

Of scales derived from self-report inventories, probably the most frequently used with psychopaths is the Pd scale of the MMPI. The Pd scale, empirically derived from responses of diagnosed male and female psychopaths, has been shown to have test–retest reliabilities ranging from 0.38 to 0.95 for different samples and intervals ranging up to 3 years (Dahlstrom *et al.*, 1975). It has also been shown to be useful in typologies of antisocial behaviour and to differentiate between psychopathic and non-psychopathic offenders in a variety of studies (Craddick, 1962; Dahlstrom *et al.*, 1972; Hare, 1970; Silver, 1963).

Using the Pd scale alone for classifying psychopaths is not generally recommended, since elevated Pd scale profiles have been found in behaviourally non-deviant groups (Hawk and Peterson, 1974). However, the extent to which such individuals share common psychological characteristics or predispositions for developing behaviour that is traditionally defined as psychopathic is as yet undetermined.

Socialization (So) Scale of California Psychological Inventory (CPI)

The So scale of the CPI was originally developed to test Gough's (1948) role-taking theory of psychopathy by comparing the responses of delinquents and non-delinquents. It was designed to assess the degree to which a person has internalized the rules, values, and conventions of society. With reliability ranging from 0.65 to 0.80 for intervals up to a year, the 'So scale is one of the best validated and most powerful personality scales available' for which an 'impressive array of data have accumulated demonstrating the concurrent, predictive, and construct validity of the scale' (Megargee, 1972).

The So scale has repeatedly been shown to discriminate delinquent groups from controls (Megargee, 1972) and psychopaths from controls (Widom, 1974) as well as to distinguish individuals along a socialization continuum (Gough, 1960). It is frequently used as an index of psychopathy by dividing subjects into high and low groups on the basis of their So scale score (where *low* scores on the So scale represent psychopathic or unsocialized individuals). Physiological correlates of subjects grouped according to their scores on the So scale have been found to be similar to those obtained when more extensive ratings of psychopathy are used (Hare and Cox, 1978).

Clinical and Behavioural Checklists Based on Interviews

Research Diagnostic Criteria (RDC)

The diagnostic criteria in the RDC were originally developed for use with a structured clinical interview in an attempt to increase reliability and validity in psychiatric diagnosis and to enable researchers to apply a consistent set of criteria for a variety of functional psychiatric disorders. The RDC criteria (Spitzer *et al.*, 1975) are primarily behavioural and include four indices of: early behavioural problems; poor academic and occupational performance; persistent antisocial behaviour; and a judgement of some evidence of impaired capacity to sustain lasting interpersonal relationships. In developing the RDC an explicit decision was made to have the direction of error avoid false positives.

Along with the criteria, a focused clinical interview guide and rating scale was designed specifically for eliciting information relating to the criteria. The SADS-L version was used here as recommended for situations when the researcher is primarily interested in diagnosing on the basis of lifetime occurrences. Thus, one important difference between the RDC criteria approach and the personality scale approach is that the former requires certain symptoms to be present before the age of 15, whereas the latter depends more strongly on the cross-sectional picture at the time of testing.

Robins' Criteria for Sociopathy

The criteria originally delineated by Robins (1966) incorporate a variety of life areas that provide support for a diagnosis of sociopathy. The 19 symptoms in adulthood cover work, education, military, psychiatric, and marital history as well as drug use and delinquent and criminal behaviours. Robins' criteria provide a measure of antisocial behaviour, but do not necessarily determine psychopathy in the clinical sense (cf. Cleckley, 1976).

In sum, four approaches to diagnosing psychopathy—two self-report inventories and two rating based on interviews—were compared in a sample of non-institutionalized individuals.

Independent diagnoses for each subject were made using each of the four sets of criteria. To meet Robins' criteria, subjects had to show evidence of at least six symptom characteristics. (Robins' minimal criteria for the diagnosis of sociopathy are five characteristics. However, given that 72.5 per cent of the sample met at least five criteria, the requirements were made slightly more stringent and still 62.5 per cent of the sample fulfilled them.)

Each subject was given a diagnosis according to the RDC, with scores ranging from 0 to 4, corresponding to the four individual criteria necessary for a diagnosis of antisocial personality disorder. Cohen's (1960) Kappa coefficient of reliability, which takes into account chance agreement, was used for the RDC diagnoses. Out of 38 decisions, in five cases the raters were off by one point, producing a Kappa coefficient of 82.8. Disagreements were settled by discussion. Only subjects meeting all four RDC criteria were diagnosed as psychopaths or antisocial personality disorder.

A median Socialization scale score of 26 was used as a cutoff (Hare, 1978), with subjects scoring 26 or below being labelled as psychopaths. For the Pd scale of the MMPI, a value of 26 was used as the cutoff point (representing a T-score of approximately 70, not K-corrected), such that subjects scoring 27 or above were labelled psychopaths.

A total of 27 (67.5 per cent) of the 40 subjects in the sample were classified as psychopaths (sociopaths, antisocial personality disorder) by *at least* one set of criteria. The RDC criteria were the most stringent, with only five subjects meeting the criteria. On the other hand, the largest group ($n = 25$) met Robins' criteria.

To assess the extent to which the different sets of criteria were just broader or narrower than each other or whether they included different subjects, comparisons were made of individuals considered psychopathic by each combination of two diagnostic systems. Table 4 presents this comparative

Table 4 Comparison of systems for diagnosing psychopathy (or antisocial personality disorders)

| Diagnostic criteria | n | Percentage of subjects[a] also considered psychopathic by the following systems | | | |
		Robins	So	Pd	RDC
Robins (1966) criteria	25	—	72	28	20
CPI So scale	20	90	—	35	20
MMPI Pd scale	8	87.5	87.5	—	25
Research diagnostic criteria (RDC)	5	100	80	40	—

[a] Total number of subjects = 40.

Table 5 Intercorrelations of four sets of criteria

| | | Questionnaire | | Interview |
		Pd	So[b]	Robins
Questionnaire	Pd	—		
	So	−0.779**	—	
Interview rating scales	Robins	0.457*	−0.637**	
	RDC[a]	0.433*	−0.568**	0.886**

[a] Correlations with RDC scores are based on an n of 38 since two subjects did not have a rating on the RDC.

[b] A negative correlation reflects the scoring of the Socialization scale, where the lower the So score, the less socialized the individual (and the more psychopathic).

Note: * p<0.01; ** p<0.001.

information. The RDC criteria group contained the largest proportion of subjects also considered psychopaths by the other methods. All subjects meeting the RDC criteria also met Robins' criteria, 80 per cent were also considered psychopathic by the So scale and 40 per cent by the Pd scale. On the other hand, using Robins', So or Pd scales as criteria, only 20–25 per cent of each group also met RDC criteria.

Table 5 presents a Pearson product–moment correlation matrix for the two sets of scores for each of the two different methods (self-report inventories and interview ratings). Total scores were used for the So and Pd scales. For Robins, each subject's score was the total number of symptoms recorded. For the RDC, scores ranged from 0 to 4, representing the four criteria utilized in the diagnosis of antisocial personality (SADS-L), so that persons who satisfied all four criteria were scored 4. If they satisfied none, they were scored 0.

As expected, the *intra-method* correlations (Pd with So, Robins with RDC) were highest. However, the important part of this analysis lies in the cross-method correlations (questionnaires with interview ratings), which should be substantial if they are measuring the same thing. The magnitudes of the correlations indicate that they are.

Table 6 illustrates the percentage of subjects arrested and the mean number of arrests for the sample divided into groups according to the four sets of criteria. The most lenient criterion, Robins', shows the smallest average number of arrests ($M = 1.64$, $s.d. = 2.78$). Of the subjects selected according to this criterion, only 56 per cent have had at least one arrest. On the other hand, the most exclusive of the criteria, the RDC, shows the largest (80 per cent) proportion of psychopaths having at least one arrest as an adult and the highest average number of arrests for the identified group ($M = 3.60$, $s.d. = 3.36$).

Table 6   Frequency of arrest in subjects diagnosed by each of the four approaches

	Diagnosis			
	Psychopaths		Non-psychopaths	
	Percentage at least one arrest	Mean number of arrests	Percentage at least one arrest	Mean number of arrests
RDC	80	3.60	36.4	0.71
Pd	75	2.25	31.2	0.78
So	65	2.00	15.0	0.15
Robins	56	1.64	6.7	0.13

Is blatant antisocial behaviour (i.e. arrests) a *necessary* component of criteria for diagnosing psychopaths? Although there are a few items referring to 'having had trouble with the law', one can still achieve either a high score on the Pd scale or a low score on the So scale (the two questionnaire methods) without endorsing such individual items.

To determine whether antisocial behaviour in the form of arrests is a necessary component for the other two criteria of psychopathy, the protocols of subjects meeting the criteria for sociopathy and antisocial personality disorder were examined and a determination was made as to whether subjects would still meet the criteria if the arrest variable was excluded. Specifically, for the RDC, the item in Section III—'been arrested (yes, if 3 or more serious arrests)'—was excluded, as were the symptoms 'at least one arrest' and 'greater than two arrests' from Robins' criteria. *Excluding* these specific items, all subjects previously classified as meeting the criteria for antisocial personality disorder and sociopathy continued to meet the criteria and to warrant such diagnosis.

Who are the subjects diagnosed according to the four sets of criteria? Subjects meeting the RDC criteria appear to come from families with more disturbed backgrounds (see Table 7). Across these family background characteristics, individuals identified by the RDC criteria reported the most frequent family pathology (i.e. mother and father as problem drinkers or alcoholics, erratic emotional state, family arrests and drug usage, and being hurt or beaten by parents).

Table 7   Reported incidence of family pathology for subjects meeting each set of diagnostic criteria (in percentages)

Characteristic	Robins (n = 25)	So (n = 20)	Pd (n = 8)	RDC (n = 5)
Mother problem drinker or alcoholic	8.3	5.3	0.0	20.0
Father problem drinker or alcoholic	29.1	21.0	25.0	60.0
Mother:				
Got along fine	21.7	21.1	12.5	0.0
Ups and downs	43.5	42.1	62.5	60.0
Treatment or hospitalization for nerves	34.7	36.8	25.0	40.0
Father:				
Got along fine	22.7	16.7	14.3	0.0
Ups and downs	63.6	72.2	57.1	80.0
Treatment for nerves or depression[a]	13.6	11.1	28.6	20.0
Family member ever arrested?[b]	12.5	15.8	12.5	40.0
Family member drug problem?[b]	41.7	47.4	50.0	80.0
Hurt by your parents?[c]	50.0	57.9	75.0	80.0
Beaten by parents?[d]	16.7	26.3	37.5	60.0

[a] None of the fathers was reported to be hospitalized for nerves.
[b] Defined as father or mother *and* brother or sister.
[c] Question: Were you ever injured, bruised, or hurt by your parents?
[d] Question: Did your parents ever beat you when you didn't deserve it?

Other results suggest that these findings represent more than simply exaggerated self-reporting of symptoms among those individuals diagnosed according to the RDC criteria. For example, as can be seen in Table 8, the RDC-diagnosed subjects had low lie scores on the personality inventory. As a group they were the oldest. Only one of the RDC-diagnosed subjects was less than 28, whereas 70 per cent of the So group, 75 per cent of the Pd group and 37.5 per cent of the Robins group were under 28. Although the best-educated, the RDC-diagnosed subjects had held the largest number of jobs, had most

Table 8   Personality and demographic characteristics of subjects meeting the four sets of diagnostic criteria

	Robins ($n = 25$)	So ($n = 20$)	Pd ($n = 8$)	RDC ($n = 5$)	Total sample ($n = 40$)
Demographic characteristic					
Age	25.33	24.47	26.37	29.80	25.15
Last grade school completed	13.83	13.39	12.37	14.80	13.71
Occupational level[a] (Hollingshead)	5.38	5.20	5.25	5.75	5.14
Percentage ever unemployed or on welfare	33.30	26.30	50.00	80.00	23.10
Mean number of jobs	12.31	10.72	14.50	26.50	10.11
Personality					
Lie (MMPI)	4.20	3.60	3.63	3.60	3.87
Depression	20.68	19.95	22.87	22.00	19.22
Psychopathic deviate (MMPI)	23.76	25.70	28.87	24.20	22.52
Mania	26.56	26.85	28.00	29.80	25.47
MacAndrews	26.72	28.10	29.37	30.00	25.87
Socialization (CPI)	24.04	22.20	21.37	22.00	26.32
Self-esteem (TSBI)	8.60	8.45	8.25	8.40	8.60
Anxiety (Welsh)	16.36	16.10	24.12[b]	20.80	14.60
Hostility	11.28	11.75	17.12[b]	15.60	9.82
Extraversion (EPQ)	16.44	16.50	15.50	19.00	16.72

[a] Hollingshead level 5 = skilled workers and level 6 = semi-skilled workers.
[b] Subjects *not* assigned to the high Pd group had substantially lower (less than half) Welsh anxiety ($M = 12.21$) and hostility scores ($M = 8.00$).

frequently been on welfare or been unemployed, and had the lowest reported occupational level.

As a check on the veracity of the subjects' scores, correlations were computed between personality variables, diagnostic category, and the Lie scale scores. These were found to be non-significant. RDC-defined subjects, although they reported the greatest number of arrests, family pathology, and personality pathology on some variables, did *not* simply over-endorse pathology across the board. Their Hollingshead scores were lower and their Lie scores were lower than subjects meeting other criteria. Their responding did not reflect acquiescence, nor did it represent a social desirability response set.

Performance on the *passive-avoidance* task was assessed through an analysis of the frequency of two types of errors: passive-avoidance (or commission) errors (failure to inhibit a punished response) and omission errors (failure to respond when appropriate to do so). Separate analyses for the behavioural data were conducted by dividing subjects on the basis of each of the diagnostic approaches (RDC, Robins, So, and Pd). Major differences between psychopaths and non-psychopaths were found only with the RDC criteria. Dividing the subjects on the basis of the other criteria yielded no significant differences on the behavioural tasks.[4]

An analysis of covariance was conducted, comparing the number of passive-avoidance (commission) errors among RDC-defined subjects ($n = 5$) and non-RDC-defined subjects, using anxiety as the covariate. The results of this analysis approached significance for groups ($F(1,37) = 3.51, p = 0.069$) but not for the covariate anxiety. As would be predicted for psychopaths, RDC subjects had more commission errors ($M = 16.4$, s.d. $= 5.3$) than non-RDC subjects ($M = 12.6$, s.d. $= 5.6$). A comparable analysis for omission errors was not significant for either the main effect or for the covariate.

Time Estimates

Ratios of estimated over actual time spent were computed for each of the six segments to control for individual differences in actual time spent. Table 9 presents the means and standard deviations of these ratios for the six estimates and the results of the analyses of covariance (with anxiety as the covariate). RDC subjects differed from non-RDC subjects on three of the six time estimates (personality inventory, card task, and cash), and the covariate anxiety was not significant. RDC-defined subjects generally *over*estimated time spent during the experiment, although they were just about accurate in two estimates (card task and interview).

The present study found some agreement among four approaches to diagnosing psychopaths. There is a wide range, with some criteria appearing very exclusive, and others appearing more lenient. Out of a sample of 40 subjects, only five were found to meet RDC criteria, whereas 25 were found to fulfil a somewhat more stringent criterion than Robins' (1966).

For general screening purposes (i.e. to obtain a broad sample), the researcher might want to utilize Robins' (1966) criteria. On the other hand, the RDC seems to be the most conservative of the four approaches. The RDC contained the largest proportion of subjects also considered psychopathic by the other criteria. In contrast, only 20–25 per cent of the subjects diagnosed as psychopaths according to Robins (1966), the Socialization scale, or the Psychopathic deviate scale of the MMPI, were also diagnosed as psychopaths by the RDC.

Choice of diagnostic criteria affects not only how many subjects are considered psychopaths or antisocial personality disorders, but also affects characteristics of groups of persons so defined. For example, the RDC criteria identify a small, select group of individuals who report the most family

Table 9   Estimated time ratios (estimated/actual time) for subjects grouped according to RDC criteria

	Subjects meeting RDC criteria for antisocial personality disorder ($n = 5$)		Subjects not meeting RDC criteria ($n = 35$)		F	Degrees of freedom	Significance
	M	s.d.	M	s.d.			
Personality Inventory	1.41	1.08	0.89	0.37	3.84	1,33	0.06
Ice	1.60	0.67	1.42	0.58			
Passive-avoidance task	0.98	0.26	1.32	0.51	4.42	1,33	0.04
Background questionnaire	1.21	0.48	1.06	0.43			
Interview	1.02	0.48	0.89	0.32			
Cash payment	1.97	0.81	1.27	0.69	4.18	1,32	0.05

pathology and the most extensive criminal history (as measured by number of arrests), yet they are also the oldest and best educated, but not necessarily successful in their occupations (i.e. they have the lowest Hollingshead scores). Thus, subjects meeting the RDC criteria appear to represent a homogeneous group of blatantly antisocial individuals—consistent with their diagnosis. Interestingly, individuals diagnosed as meeting the RDC criteria also performed differently on the behavioural task than did subjects not meeting the criteria. For these reasons, the RDC might provide a useful tool for researchers interested in examining genetic, physiological, or criminal factors.

Conclusions drawn about the relative breadth of the diagnostic approaches examined here should be limited in consideration of the sampling procedures used. That is, although the RDC was the most conservative within the non-institutionalized group of psychopaths identified here, we cannot conclude that the RDC will necessarily be the most conservative in other populations. For example, if the RDC were used in a prison setting where (by definition) people have engaged in criminal behaviour, we might expect the RDC with its emphasis on antisocial behaviour to be less conservative than the other criteria which place more emphasis on personality characteristics.

Although the RDC represents the most exclusive of the criteria compared here, it is not always possible for researchers to use rating scales based on official records and case histories; nor is it always possible to conduct extensive interviews with subjects. Would either of the questionnaire measures be acceptable as a substitute? What would researchers be losing? Of the subjects classified according to the Socialization scale of the CPI, only 20 per cent also met the RDC criteria for antisocial personality disorder. Of those identified by the Psychopathic deviate scale of the MMPI, only 25 per cent would be classified as antisocial personality disorder by the RDC. Future analyses might examine the usefulness of different cutoffs for the Pd and So scales. For the present, diagnosing or categorizing subjects simply on the basis of Pd or So scales apparently dilutes the phenomenon being studied.

Although Hundleby and Ross (1977) interpreted their findings as indicating no support for a factor interpretation of the concept of psychopathy, the results of the present study challenge that assertion. There was overlap among individuals meeting the four diagnostic criteria. However, additional research is planned to compare further the diagnostic utility of these and other approaches.

While the replication described in Part I was generally successful in identifying non-institutionalized psychopaths, only a fraction of the group met the RDC criteria for antisocial personality disorder. We have seen that a diagnosis of antisocial personality disorder according to the RDC criteria *by definition* depends very heavily on blatant antisocial behaviour. Of the total sample studied here, those subjects who met RDC criteria for antisocial personality disorder were also the ones who behaved most similarly to incarcerated psychopaths. That is, the behaviour of the most antisocial individuals in the present sample most closely resembled behavioural characteristics of their institutionalized counterparts, noted in previous research. Thus, we return to the original rationale for developing this methodology (Widom, 1977) to disentangle behaviour associated with criminality from that associated with psychopathy.

ACKNOWLEDGEMENTS

This research was supported by BRSG Grant S07 RR07031 awarded by the Biomedical Research Support Grant Program, Division of Research Resources, National Institutes of Health. The authors wish to thank Michael G. Maxfield for his comments on an earlier draft of this paper.

NOTES

1. Bloomington is a city of moderate size in south central Indiana. The 1980 population of Bloomington's SMSA (Standard Metropolitan Statistical Area) was 98,800, with 52,000 residing within the city.
2. Out of the 153 people who called the answering service in response to the advertisement, 40 became subjects, 60 people could not be reached (wrong number, phone disconnected, left town for the marines, doesn't live here any more, checked out of motel, no-one here by that name, etc.), 20 were never scheduled for appointments (not interested, too young, wanted course credit, 'never called', just visiting for a short time in town), and 33 were scheduled for testing but did not show up for the appointment or cancelled beforehand.
3. The authors wish to thank David T. Lykken for his comments on an earlier draft of this paper and particularly for suggesting the metaphor used here.
4. The failure of the Pd and So measures to differentiate the performance of subjects on the passive-avoidance card task was counter to prediction and contradicts results from previous work (e.g. Newman, 1980; Nathan, 1980). A possible explanation for this discrepancy may relate to the high level of impulsivity characteristic of this sample in general.

REFERENCES

Chesno, F. and Kilmann, P. (1975) Effects of stimulation intensity on sociopathic avoidance learning. *Journal of Abnormal Psychology*, **84**, 144–150.

Cleckley, H. (1976) *The Mask of Sanity*, (5th edn.) St. Louis: C. V. Mosby Co.

Cohen, J. A. (1960) A coefficient of agreement for nominal scales. *Educational and Psychological Measurement*, **20**, 37–46.

Craddick, R. (1962) Selection of psychopathic from non-psychopathic prisoners within a Canadian prison. *Psychological Reports*, **10**, 495–499.

Dahlstrom, W. G., Welsh, G. S. and Dahlstrom, L. E. (1972) *An MMPI Handbook*, vol. 1: *Clinical Interpretation*. Minneapolis: University of Minnesota Press.

Dahlstrom, W. G., Welsh, G. S. and Dahlstrom, L. E. (1975) *An MMPI Handbook*, vol. 2: *Research Applications*. Minneapolis: University of Minnesota Press.

Dengerink, H. A. and Bertilson, H. S. (1975) Psychopathy and physiological arousal in an aggressive task. *Psychophysiology*, **12**, 682–684.

Eysenck, H. J. and Eysenck, S. B. G. (1975) *Eysenck Personality Questionnaire (EPQ)*. San Diego, California: Educational and Industrial Testing Service.

Friel, C. M. and de Abovitz, F. S. (1968) Temporal orientation in the criminal psychopath. *Proceedings of the 76th Annual Convention of the American Psychological Association*, **3**, 485–486 (Summary).

Gough, H. G. (1948) A sociological theory of psychopathy. *American Journal of Sociology*, **53**, 359–366.

Gough, H. G. (1960) Theory and measurement of socialization. *Journal of Consulting Psychology*, **24**, 23–30.

Gynther, M. D., Altman, H. and Warbin, R. W. (1973) Behavioral correlates for the Minnesota Multiphasic Personality Inventory 4–9, 9–4 code types: a case of the emperor's new clothes? *Journal of Consulting and Clinical Psychology*, **40**, 259–263.

Hare, R. D. (1970) *Psychopathy: Theory and Research*. New York: John Wiley.

Hare, R. D. (1978) Electrodermal and cardiovascular correlates of psychopathy. In R. D. Hare and D. Schalling (Eds) *Psychopathic Behaviour: Approaches to Research*. Chichester, England: John Wiley.

Hare, R. D. and Cox, D. N. (1978) Clinical and empirical conceptions of psychopathy, and the selection of subjects for research. In R. D. Hare and D. Schalling (Eds) *Psychopathic Behaviour: Approaches to Research*. Chichester, England: John Wiley.

Hare, R. D. and Quinn, M. J. (1971) Psychopathy and autonomic conditioning. *Journal of Abnormal Psychology*, **77**, 223–235.

Hawk, S. S. and Peterson, R. A. (1974) Do MMPI psychopathic deviance scores reflect psychopathic deviancy or just deviance? *Journal of Personality Assessment*, **38**, 362–368.

Heilbrun, A. B. (1979) Psychopathy and violent crime. *Journal of Consulting and Clinical Psychology*, **47**, 509–516.

Hollingshead, A. B. (1975) 'Four factor index of social status'. Unpublished manuscript, Yale University, New Haven, Connecticut (working paper).

Hundleby, J. D. and Ross, B. E. (1977) Comparison of measures of psychopathy. *Journal of Consulting and Clinical Psychology*, **45**, 702–703.

London, H. and Monello, J. (1974) Cognitive manipulation of boredom. In H. London and R. E. Nesbitt (Eds) *Thought and Feeling: Cognitive Alteration of Feeling States*. Chicago: Aldine.

Lykken, D. T. (1957) A study of anxiety in the sociopathic personality. *Journal of Abnormal and Social Psychology*, **55**, 6–10.

Megargee, E. I. (1972) *California Psychological Inventory Handbook*. San Francisco: Jossey–Bass.

Nathan, S. (1980) Unpublished data, Indiana University.

Newman, J. P. (1980) The role of response perseveration in the learning deficits of psychopathic delinquents (Doctoral dissertation, Indiana University). *Dissertation Abstracts International*, **41**, 5012–5013 (University Microfilms No. 80–87, 995).

Newman, J. P., Widom, C. S. and Nathan, S. (1984) Passive-avoidance in syndromes of disinhibition: psychopathy and extraversion. *Journal of Personality and Social Psychology*, in press.

Robins, L. N. (1966) *Deviant Children Grown Up*. Baltimore: Williams and Wilkins.

Ross, B. and Hundleby, J. (1973) 'A comparison of measures of psychopathy on a prison sample'. Paper presented at the meeting of the American Psychological Association, Montreal.

Schmauk, F. J. (1970) Punishment, arousal, and avoidance learning in sociopaths. *Journal of Abnormal Psychology*, **76**, 325–335.

Siegman, A. W. (1961) Anxiety, impulse control, intelligence, and the estimation of time. *Journal of Clinical Psychology*, **18**, 101–105.

Silver, A. W. (1963) TAT and MMPI psychopathic deviate scale differences between delinquent and non-delinquent adolescents. *Journal of Consulting Psychology*, **27**, 370.

Spitzer, R. L., Endicott, J. and Robins, E. (1975) *Research Diagnostic Criteria*. New York: Biometrics Research, New York State Department of Mental Health.

US Bureau of the Census (1978) *County and City Data Book, 1977*. Washington, DC: US Government Printing Office.

Widom, C. S. (1974) Interpersonal conflict and cooperation in psychopaths (Doctoral dissertation, Brandeis University, 1973). *Dissertation Abstracts International*, **34**, 3480-B (University Microfilms, No. 73–32, 414).

Widom, C. S. (1977) A methodology for studying non-institutionalized psychopaths. *Journal of Consulting and Clinical Psychology*, **45**, 674–683.

Wilson, J. Q. (1968) *Varieties of Police Behavior*. New York: Atheneum.

Zuckerman, M. (1974) The sensation seeking motive. In B. A. Maher (Ed.) *Progress in Experimental Personality Research*, vol. 7, pp. 79–148. New York: Academic Press.

Aggression and Dangerousness
Edited by D. P. Farrington and J. Gunn
© 1985 John Wiley & Sons Ltd.

CHAPTER 4

Psychological and Physiological Characteristics of Personality-disordered Patients

GISLI H. GUDJONSSON and JOANNA C. ROBERTS

INTRODUCTION

The purpose of this chapter is to give an account of some of the research that the authors have carried out at the Henderson Hospital in Sutton, England. The chapter concentrates on psychological and physiological research findings, which are of particular relevance to patients with personality disorders. Since the Henderson was founded by Maxwell Jones during the 1950s a large number of studies and over 100 scientific papers have emerged, but the present chapter will mainly concentrate on previous studies which are relevant to the present research. Before reviewing the literature a brief description of the historical development and present-day functioning of the Henderson will be given.

THE HENDERSON HOSPITAL

Present-day View

The Henderson hospital is a 36-bed National Health Service inpatient unit administered by the South West Thames Regional Health Authority, but it is not bound to a restricted catchment area. The Henderson provides treatment for young adults with personality disorder (Whiteley et al., 1972) within a therapeutic community where emphasis is placed on a combination of sociotherapy and psychotherapy (Whiteley, 1980).

All treatment is conducted in groups, and there is no individual therapy or psychotropic medication. The 24-hour residential treatment is based on exploration of the 'here and now' interaction of the individuals within the social environment around them. There are a wide variety of groups, which include daily community meetings where all staff and residents meet; small psychotherapy groups; work groups; and several specialist groups such as psychodrama, role play, and art therapy. The patients, who are called residents within the Henderson, are encouraged to take an active part in the everyday running of the community and to hold a wide variety of community posts, ranging from menial jobs (e.g. as catering assistants) to positions of greater responsibility such as chairman of the community meeting.

The residents will often have a history of disturbed early family life, truancy from school, convictions for minor offences, and previous psychiatric admissions. The residents are not considered sufficiently disturbed or dangerous to warrant treatment in a Regional Secure Unit but are thought unlikely to benefit from prison or orthodox psychiatric hospital treatment. All residents must be willing to take part voluntarily and must be free to discontinue treatment and leave if they wish. Therefore, applicants are not accepted under compulsory sections of the Mental Health Act. Residents are expected to abide by the basic rules of the community and to participate in the treatment programme offered. If they consistently fail to comply with these basic requirements they may face the possibility of discharge by a vote of the community in which both staff and residents take part.

The Henderson is unusual in its selection of residents, in that before being accepted all applicants must attend a special Selection Group to see how they function in a group setting. The Selection Group consists of eight or nine senior Henderson residents of over 3 months standing, and five members of staff representing medical, nursing, and social work disciplines. One of the basic requirements for selection is to be able to express oneself verbally in groups, and applicants accepted tend to be of average intelligence or above. What is looked for is the potential for personality growth and the ability to accept criticism and confrontation without a dangerously violent or self-destructive response. For these reasons the Henderson does not accept applicants who are clearly subnormal in intelligence, brain-damaged, or psychotic.

Historical Development

A comprehensive review of the historical development of the Henderson was recently completed by Whiteley (1980) and only a brief account will be given here. The Henderson became established as an autonomous unit in 1959 when it was so named in honour of Professor D. K. Henderson, the author of '*Psychopathic States*' (Henderson, 1939). The unit had initially been set up in 1947 by the Ministry of Labour as an Industrial Rehabilitation Unit at Belmont Hospital. It was originally intended for chronically disabled neurotics who were unable to maintain a job, and patients diagnosed as suffering from character disorder or borderline psychotic illness. Experience during the Second World War had shown the potential of group work with social misfits and neurotics, which stimulated post-war developments in psychiatry.

Maxwell Jones' application of group- and community-oriented techniques to the new Belmont unit caused some friction within the rest of the hospital where orthodox treatment was paramount. Towards the mid-1950s the unit was gradually developing into two major areas of specialization: therapeutic community ideology and treatment for psychopaths or character disorders. By the late 1950s the direction of the unit, now called the Henderson Hospital, was firmly established, and the basic ideology of democratization, permissiveness, communalism, and reality confrontations (Rapoport, 1960) has remained fundamentally unchanged during the past three decades. There have, however, been many developments such as more sophisticated treatment techniques, a more specialist staff team, better living conditions, and more varied leisure facilities.

Past Research

It would not be possible to review adequately all the research carried out at the Henderson during the past three decades. During the early 1950s Maxwell Jones was under pressure from critics to document the value of his innovative therapeutic community techniques. He managed to get a grant from the Nuffield Foundation in 1954 for a research project which was under the direction of Robert Rapoport, an American social anthropologist. It had originally been planned to evaluate the effectiveness of therapeutic community treatment with psychopaths, but the study turned instead to focusing on the workings of a therapeutic community. This was because Rapoport and his research team (Rapoport, 1960) realized that no evaluative research could reveal success or otherwise of the treatment regime unless the process and individuals treated were more clearly defined.

Many research papers resulted from the work of Rapoport and his team, which was predominantly sociological in nature and contributed to the understanding of the dynamic processes operating within the therapeutic community (Rapoport, 1960; Manning and Rapoport, 1976). From a psychological point of view, one of Rapoport's important findings was that a therapeutic community treatment was not effective with all psychopaths, highlighting the importance of individual differences and appropriate selection of residents. Indeed, Rapoport considered that those with a weak ego-structure could be further damaged by the intensive social and interpersonal pressures commonly accompanying therapeutic community methods.

Given the importance of adequate classification of patients for evaluating treatment and for appropriate selection of patients, extensive investigation was carried out by O'Brien (1976). She reviewed over 300 admissions and concluded that the social history of patients showed several signs of social maladjustment of the kind generally attributed to persons diagnosed as psychopathic or personality-disordered (Robins, 1966). Some of the most salient findings related to the residents' previous work history and criminal record. The residents had generally been unemployed immediately prior to admission and many had had ten or more previous jobs (despite their youth) since leaving school. Very few had held any job for 2 or more years. Approximately two-thirds of the group had been convicted of at least one criminal offence prior to admission, and many had had previous psychiatric admissions.

Findings on the personality characteristics indicated several traits consistent with the diagnosis of psychopathic disorder, such as low ego strength, non-conformity and hostility. Other traits such as high trait anxiety and a tendency towards intro-punitiveness were not consistent with the conventional view of the 'primary' psychopath (Cleckley, 1976) and correspond with later work at the Henderson aimed at measuring guilt feelings and trait anxiety (Gudjonsson and Roberts, 1983).

Whiteley (1970) had earlier attempted to evaluate the effectiveness of treatment at the Henderson by following up 122 male discharged patients. Of the 87 patients with a previous criminal conviction 38 (43.6 per cent) were not reconvicted in 2 years, and of the 66 patients with a previous history of psychiatric hospital admission 38 (57.6 per cent) had no psychiatric re-admissions within a 2-year follow-up. Out of the total 122 discharges 72 (59.0 per cent) relapsed in the 2-year follow-up period, in that they either had a subsequent conviction or a further psychiatric hospital admission. The study looked at several social history factors that might be predictive of treatment outcome. Good outcome was found to relate to previous ability to achieve success in school, work, and interpersonal relationships, together with a capacity for emotional feeling and involvement. At a later stage Copas and Whiteley (1976) analysed the significant prognostic factors and validated a mathematically weighted prediction equation. A further follow-up study of 198 admissions demonstrated the importance of length of stay for outcome, with those residents staying over 165 days having a 66 per cent success rate in a 3-year follow-up as compared with a 27 per cent success rate for those staying 17 days or less (Brotherstone et al., 1982). A particular subgroup of patients was identified, labelled 'extrapunitive neurotic', which had the poorest treatment prognosis.

In a recent study Norris (1982) utilized repertory grids to measure changes in self-esteem, independence, and attitudes towards authority in 165 Henderson subjects. When the results were compared with those obtained for subjects in a detention centre and a hostel for social misfits, it was found that Henderson subjects, in contrast to the other groups, showed a substantial increase in self-esteem during treatment. It was concluded that the Henderson appeared to be achieving measurable benefit in improving self-concept.

Between 1978 and 1980 the authors carried out a number of studies into psychological and physiological attributes of patients admitted to the Henderson Hospital. Some of these studies are presented in this chapter under the following four headings: Personality characteristics, Aggressive behaviour and personality, Physiological characteristics and Feelings of guilt during transgressive behaviour.

THE PRESENT RESEARCH

Personality Characteristics

The authors investigated some personality characteristics of 24 males and 24 females admitted to the Henderson Hospital in 1979. The results were compared with those of 'normal' groups of 24 males and 24 females. These were drawn from a variety of occupations, both manual and professional, and were approached directly or through personal contacts. The tests administered were all relevant to the diagnosis of personality disorder. These were: The Eysenck Personality Inventory (EPI; Eysenck and Eysenck, 1964), the Gough Socialization Scale (Gough, 1960) and the Arrow-Dot Test (Dombrose and Slobin, 1958). It was hypothesized that the Henderson subjects would differ significantly from normals on all three tests. That is, they were expected to score low on Socialization and high on Impulsivity, Extraversion, and Neuroticism. The results are shown in Table 1. In order to evaluate the influences of sex and group (normals vs. Henderson) two-way analysis of variance (ANOVA) tests were performed on the data. A significant sex effect was noted on the Neuroticism factor only.

As predicted, the Henderson subjects were significantly less socialized than the normal subjects according to the Gough Socialization Scale, $F(1,92) =$

Table 1   Mean and standard deviation scores for the EPI, Gough Socialization Scale and Arrow-Dot test in four groups of subjects

TEST	Experimental groups							
	Normal males ($n = 24$)		Normal females ($n = 24$)		Henderson males ($n = 24$)		Henderson females ($n = 24$)	
	Mean	s.d.	Mean	s.d.	Mean	s.d.	Mean	s.d.
EPI								
Neuroticism	7.92	4.04	9.46	4.63	17.71	5.08	19.74	2.68
Extraversion	11.25	5.29	11.92	4.57	12.25	5.31	10.13	5.90
Lie	1.79	1.44	1.83	1.63	2.04	1.40	1.87	1.36
Gough So Scale	35.4	4.96	39.0	5.31	22.9	3.47	22.3	7.40
Arrow-Dot test								
Id	2.38	3.52	2.96	2.84	3.77	3.82	5.23	4.49
Ego	18.79	3.74	17.73	3.80	16.83	5.31	15.94	5.11
Superego	1.38	0.92	2.31	1.94	2.40	3.11	1.83	1.97

162.4, p <0.001. They also scored higher on Neuroticism, $F(1,92) = 134.2$, p <0.001, Arrow-Dot Id (impulsivity), $F(1,92) = 3.80$, p <0.05, and had poorer Ego Control, $F(1,92) = 3.46$, p <0.05. The prediction regarding Extraversion was not confirmed. The findings concur with those of Farrington *et al.* (1982), supporting the view that as far as the EPI is concerned only the Neuroticism scale can adequately discriminate between delinquent and non-delinquent groups. However, it is important to bear in mind that the EPI Extraversion score is made up of two major factors: impulsiveness and sociability (Eysenck and Eysenck, 1963). When the impulsiveness and sociability items were separated in 33 male and 24 female Henderson subjects they were found to be significantly more impulsive and significantly less sociable than normal subjects, even though they did not differ in their Extraversion scores (Gudjonsson and Roberts, 1981a).

This finding concurs with that of Schalling and Holmberg (1970) in their studies of psychopathic disorders, and it points to the need to separate the impulsiveness and sociability items of the EPI when studying delinquent groups. Alternatively, it might be better to use the Eysenck Personality Questionnaire (EPQ, Eysenck and Eysenck, 1975) as it gives a more refined Extraversion score than that obtained by the EPI. This is due to the fact that some of the EPI impulsiveness items relate to Psychoticism (P or tough-mindedness) rather than Extraversion when the EPQ is used.

Aggressive Behaviour and Personality

We also investigated the relationship between the frequency of aggressive behaviour of patients at the Henderson, and Socialization, Extraversion, and perceptual-motor rule breaking (Gudjonsson and Roberts, 1981a). Thirty-three males and 24 females, who had completed the Gough Socialization Scale, EPI, and the Arrow-Dot Test, were rated by two independent observers in regard to the frequency of aggressive behaviour during the initial part of their stay at the Henderson. The aim of the study was to investigate the potential of personality and perceptual-motor variables in predicting aggressive responding of personality-disordered males and females undergoing treatment in a therapeutic community. The study had the advantage of employing both personality-disordered males and females, but research with the latter group has not been well documented in the literature.

As a result of discussions with nursing and medical staff at the Henderson, the following questions were selected that seemed directly related to the type of aggressive behaviour observed in patients during their stay at the Henderson:

1. Does the resident fly off the handle?
2. Does the resident have violent verbal outbursts?
3. Does the resident have violent physical outbursts against people?

4. Does the resident have violent physical outbursts against objects?
5. Does the resident show self-mutilating behaviour?
6. Does the resident provoke anger in other people by active confrontation?
7. Does the resident provoke anger in people by withdrawing?

Each question was rated on a four-point frequency scale, labelled 'never', 'rarely', 'sometimes', and 'frequently'. A senior psychiatrist and a social worker who were well acquainted with the day-to-day behaviour of the residents rated each resident's overt aggression during his or her first 4–5 weeks at the Henderson. The Pearson correlation between the psychiatrist and social worker overall ratings for the 57 subjects was 0.82. The mean ratings for each of the seven questions were subsequently factor-analysed using a principal component analysis. It was not possible to do the analysis separately for males and females because of the rather small numbers, which is unfortunate in view of the findings of Edmunds and Kendrick (1980) that the sexes may differ in factor structure. However, a principal component analysis was carried out using sex as a variable and it was found that sex did not load significantly on the two factors (the loadings being 0.051 and 0.101 for factors one and two respectively). Two components had eigenvalues greater than unity and these were rotated by using the Varimax procedure.

The two questions 'Does the resident fly off the handle?' and 'Does the resident have violent verbal outbursts?' had high loadings (0.911 and 0.877 respectively) on component one. The first question referred to behaviour such as storming out of meetings, shouting, and screaming. The second question related to insults and verbal abuse. For both questions an important part of the behaviour was that the resident concerned could not be reasoned with. Two questions had significant loadings on component two. These were: 'Does the resident have violent physical outbursts against people?' and 'Does the resident have violent physical outbursts against objects?'. The loadings were 0.889 and 0.518 respectively for the two questions. The former question referred to physically hitting or threatening people whereas the latter referred to breaking windows, throwing crockery and furniture, and causing damage to property. The individual item inter-rater reliability for the four questions varied between 0.66 and 0.79 for males and 0.64 and 0.84 for females. The mean score for each component was used to correlate with the personality and perceptual-motor rule-breaking scores. Component one will be referred to as Verbal Aggression, and component two as Physical Aggression.

The Eysenck Personality Inventory (EPI), the Gough Socialization Scale and the Arrow-Dot Test were administered during the first 2 weeks and the observer-rated aggressiveness scale was completed for each subject by the two raters after the subject had been at the Henderson for at least 1 month. Verbal and Physical Aggression correlated significantly for both males and females. The correlations were 0.621 ($p < 0.001$) and 0.846 ($p < 0.001$) for males and females respectively. The difference between the two correlations as tested by the r-to-z transformations is not significant by a two-tailed test ($z = 1.80, p < 0.10$).

Table 2 gives the Pearson correlations between the psychometric measures and observer-rated aggression scores for males and females respectively. The results suggest that the ability of personality dimensions to predict the frequency of aggressive behaviour is different for male and female patients. Extraversion and lack of role-taking ability were significantly related to both Verbal and Physical Aggression in the female sample, but no such significant relationship was found for males. In fact, in males, Verbal Aggression did not correlate significantly with any of the personality scores. Physical Aggression, on the other hand, was related to Arrow-Dot Id and Ego scores, which is consistent with the findings of Davis (1974), who found some correlation between rated aggression and the performance on a psychomotor test. Thus perceptual-motor abilities may hold some promise in the study of individual differences in aggressive/violent responding, as indeed has been documented by Spellacy (1977, 1978) and Gudjonsson and Roberts (1981b).

Gudjonsson and Roberts (1981b) administered the Reitan Trail Making Test (Reitan, 1958) to 25 males and eight females at the Henderson who had been rated on the aggressiveness scale described earlier. Parts A and B of the Trail Making Test were found to correlate significantly with Physical Aggression ($r = 0.34, p < 0.05$ and $r = 0.59, p < 0.001$, respectively), whereas only Part B was found to correlate with Verbal Aggression ($r = 0.51, p < 0.001$). The long time difference between Parts A and B correlated significantly with both Verbal ($0.36, p < 0.05$) and Physical ($0.37, p < 0.05$) Aggression. The results suggest that poor planning and slowness in making a behavioural shift may be concomitants of aggressive behaviour.

Physiological Characteristics

Electrodermal reactivity of the Henderson subjects was recorded during an experiment designed to explore some of the psychological determinants of electrodermal responses to deception (Gudjonsson, 1982a). Pulse rate was concurrently recorded. The deceptive paradigms consisted of three guilty-knowledge card tasks that differed in the nature of the stimuli used and in the procedural instructions. There was also a general question task involving five neutral questions and two emotive/moral questions concerned with lying and stealing behaviour. After each task a number of self-report analogue scales (Bond and Lader, 1974) were administered in order to record the subjects' reaction to each task and the type of countermeasure they had used. There were four groups of 24 subjects, consisting of normal males and females and Henderson males and females.

Table 2 Pearson correlations between aggressiveness and personality scores

| | Personality measures | | | | | | |
| Aggressiveness measure | EPI Scores | | | Gough Scores | Arrow-Dot Scores | | |
	E	N	L	So	Id	Ego	Superego
Males ($n = 33$)							
Verbal Aggression	0.01	0.25	-0.10	-0.20	0.20	-0.12	-0.19
Physical Aggression	0.08	0.05	-0.10	-0.10	0.35*	-0.23	-0.02
Females ($n = 24$)							
Verbal Aggression	0.55**	-0.16	-0.22	-0.49**	0.38*	-0.40*	0.10
Physical Aggression	0.48**	-0.29	-0.21	-0.37*	0.37*	-0.39*	0.11

* $p < 0.05$; ** $p < 0.01$

This section reports on the differences between the Henderson subjects and normal controls with respect to tonic heart rate, electrodermal arousal, differential responsivity and concordance between electrodermal and self-report measures.

(i) Tonic Heart Rate

The pulse was recorded by means of a finger photoplethysmograph and the amplified signal was converted into beats per minute by counting the individual beats within each minute. The tonic heart rate was averaged for the whole experiment, which lasted for approximately 45 minutes. The mean heart rate levels recorded during the experiment for the four groups of subjects are shown in Table 3. The Henderson subjects exhibited significantly higher heart rate levels than the normal subjects, $F(1,92) = 12.6$, $p < 0.001$. Females were found to have higher heart rate levels than males, $F(1,92) = 6.1, p < 0.01$).

Table 3   Mean and standard deviation scores for tonic heart rate in the four groups of subjects

Group	n	Mean	s.d.
Normal males	24	72.9	11.5
Normal females	24	81.6	10.4
Henderson males	24	83.7	7.9
Henderson females	24	88.5	10.2

(ii) Electrodermal Arousal

The degree of electrodermal arousal experienced by the subjects during the experiment was recorded from tonic skin resistance level (SRL) and non-specific fluctuations in skin conductance (NSs). The former was measured immediately, prior to each stimulus, and averaged for each task, whereas the latter monitored any change free of artifact (movements, coughs, etc.) exceeding 0.5 kohms, scored in 7 and 8 second intervals preceding each stimulus for the card tasks and general question tasks respectively. NSs were counted in each period and a mean score was obtained for each subject on each task. The skin resistance response (SRR) to each stimulus was also recorded. This was taken as any response occurring between 1 and 4 seconds of stimulus presentation and exceeding 0.4 kohms. Tables 4 and 5 give the mean and standard deviation scores for SRL and NSs respectively. Two way ANOVAs revealed that the Henderson subjects exhibited significantly lower SRL on all tasks than the control groups. They generally also had greater numbers of NSs than normals. Therefore, the Henderson subjects were significantly more aroused electrodermally than the normal subjects.

(iii) Differential Responsivity

Differential responsivity on the three card tasks and the general questions task was calculated in the following way. The mean SRR magnitude value (of two trials) to each stimulus item was converted into logarithms to normalize the distributions, as they tended to be skewed. In order to avoid the log of zero, 1 was added to all the resistance values. Subsequently the log SRR difference between the critical and control items was calculated and a difference or a detectability score was obtained for each subject on each task.

Two-way ANOVA tests revealed no sex or group (normals vs. Henderson) effects on the three card tasks, but there was a significant group effect regarding differential responsivity on the general question task. The F ratios were 9.33 (1,92), $p < 0.01$ and 12.18 (1,92), $p < 0.001$ for the stealing and lying questions, respectively. Therefore, the Henderson subjects were relatively unreactive electrodermally when being interrogated about lying and stealing behaviour. Overall, there was no significant difference in responsivity between the card task and the general question task, although it is worth noting that the normal subjects gave particularly large differential responsivity on the general question, which was relatively more emotionally loaded, while the reverse was true of the Henderson groups.

The results suggest that the Henderson subjects were not particularly concerned, disturbed, or embarrassed by the fact that they were admitting or denying a socially condemned behaviour. It is tempting to conclude that this relates to their emotional and personality disturbance 'through failure to condition social approval or disapproval to antisocial conduct' (Eysenck and Eysenck, 1978). However, another possible explanation is that the Henderson subjects have accepted admitting lying and stealing as part of their everyday behaviour and have ceased to be disturbed by such admissions. In other words, they have become 'desensitized' to such socially condemned behaviour as lying and stealing. This may in turn have affected the way they reacted electrodermally to incriminating questions. Such a process of 'desensitization' may also apply to criminals in general, as the previous findings by Gudjonsson (1979) suggest.

(iv) Concordance between Electrodermal and Self-report Measures

It is a common phenomenon in stress research that individuals' self-reports of

Table 4 Mean and standard deviation scores for tonic skin resistance level (SRL) in the four groups of subjects

| Group | n | Task | | | | | | | |
| | | 1* | | 2* | | 3* | | 4* | |
		Mean	s.d.	Mean	s.d.	Mean	s.d.	Mean	s.d.
Normal males	24	163.8	96.3	156.3	86.7	159.2	84.4	157.4	91.7
Normal females	24	182.6	91.5	173.7	60.5	179.7	91.0	185.0	83.8
Henderson males	24	112.4	88.1	114.9	73.5	114.0	76.1	107.1	74.8
Henderson females	24	112.7	62.5	110.0	70.9	110.8	64.3	121.3	85.5

* Significant group effects:
Task 1: $F(1,92) = 12.07$, $p < 0.001$
Task 2: $F(1,92) = 10.71$, $p < 0.001$
Task 3: $F(1,92) = 10.97$, $p < 0.001$
Task 4: $F(1,92) = 11.02$, $p < 0.001$

Table 5 Mean and standard deviation scores for the number of spontaneous fluctuations in the four groups of subjects

Group	n	Task							
		1		2*		3*		4*	
		Mean	s.d.	Mean	s.d.	Mean	s.d.	Mean	s.d.
Normal males	24	6.67	6.06	4.92	4.76	8.08	5.96	8.21	6.37
Normal females	24	3.79	4.76	3.67	4.09	2.79	2.64	5.75	5.97
Henderson males	24	7.63	6.13	7.96	7.52	10.80	6.54	10.00	9.86
Henderson females	24	5.33	4.12	6.63	6.36	6.54	6.00	9.92	9.82

* Significant group effects:
  Task 2: $F(1,92) = 6.40, p < 0.01$.
  Task 3: $F(1,92) = 5.92, p < 0.01$.
  Task 4: $F(1,92) = 3.50, p < 0.01$.

anxiety and disturbance are frequently inconsistent with behavioural and physiological measures (Hodges, 1976). Several studies have demonstrated that self-perceptions are particularly inaccurate in people who have a defensive coping style (Weinstein et al., 1968; Weinberger et al., 1979). However, Gudjonsson (1981) found that both under- and over-reporting of subjective disturbance are related to defensiveness and trait anxiety. That is, subjects who report low subjective disturbance to emotionally loaded questions but react relatively strongly electrodermally tend to have high defensiveness (Lie) scores and low trait anxiety scores. On the other hand, subjects who have high trait anxiety and low defensiveness scores tend to amplify their disturbance. It is from the latter perspective that the authors took the view that the Henderson subjects would show greater discordance between self-report and electrodermal measures than normal subjects.

During the deception experiment quoted earlier (Gudjonsson, 1982a) the four groups of 24 subjects rated their subjective reactions to each task on a number of visual analogue scales. These related to the following: how tense the subjects felt during the experiment, how interested they were in the tasks, how challenged they felt by the tasks, how confident they felt during the tasks, how dishonest they felt about deceiving, how concerned they were about being detected, how much they tried to escape detection, and how successful they thought they were at beating the polygraph. On one of the four deception tasks (a general question task) they were also required to indicate how disturbing they had found each of the following seven questions:

1. Do you have brown eyes?
2. Are you sitting down now?
3. Do you ever steal things?
4. Are you wearing black shoes?
5. Do you ever tell lies?
6. Are you in England now?
7. Do you sometimes watch television?

The Pearson correlations between self-reported analogue scores and electrodermal parameters were, in general, low. However, in the case of normal males and females several meaningful and significant correlations emerged which were not noted in the Henderson groups. In fact, for the Henderson subjects there was almost no concordance between the self-report and electrodermal measures.

The relationship between skin resistance responses and self-reported emotional disturbance on the general question task is given for normal and Henderson females in Figures 1 and 2 respectively. The male scores were very similar to the results shown in Figures 1 and 2 and are therefore not

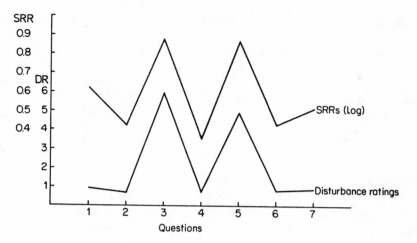

Figure 1 The relationship between differential responsivity and self-reported emotional disturbance among normal females

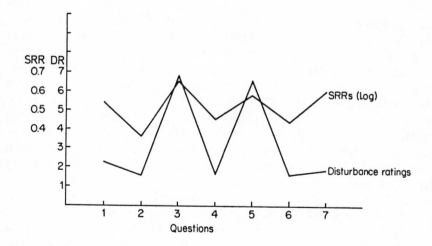

Figure 2 The relationship between differential responsivity and self-reported emotional disturbance among Henderson females

given. Correlation procedures were performed on the scores. Mean within-subject correlations were carried out and the coefficients for each group of subjects were averaged by the Fisher r–z transformation method (Gudjonsson, 1982b). These are shown in Table 6. The correlations were significant for both the normal groups, but not for the Henderson subjects. This gave

Table 6   Mean within-subject correlations between self-reported emotional disturbance and electrodermal responses

Group	n	z-value	r	d.f.
Normal males	24	0.85	0.69*	5
Normal females	24	0.91	0.72*	5
Henderson males	24	0.54	0.49	5
Henderson females	24	0.41	0.21	5

* $p < 0.05$.

further evidence for greater discordance between electrodermal and self-report measures in the Henderson subjects than in the normal subjects.

Feelings of Guilt During Transgressive Behaviour

Lack of remorse and shame are commonly regarded as basic characteristics of psychopaths (Cleckley, 1976). However, psychopaths have been shown empirically to endorse particularly high feelings of guilt (Foulds et al., 1960; Marks, 1965). Gudjonsson and Roberts (1983) suggest two possible reasons for high guilt in some psychopaths. The first is that the guilt is related to the high level of trait anxiety commonly seen in such people when they present themselves in psychiatric hospitals. Secondly, some psychopaths may have a low self-esteem which is reflected in a constant feeling of guilt, regardless of whether or not they are involved in antisocial behaviour. Gudjonsson and Roberts (1983) attempted to investigate the above hypotheses by administering a number of Semantic Differential scales to 32 Henderson males and 25 Henderson females as well as 'normal controls'. The scales related to the following concepts: *Myself as I am, Myself when I lie, Myself if I were to steal, Myself as I would like to be*, and *People who steal*. The Mosher Morality-Conscience Guilt Scale and the Eysenck Personality Inventory (EPI) were also administered.

The Henderson subjects scored significantly higher than the controls on the Mosher Guilt Scale, $F(1,101) = 4.26$, $p < 0.05$. The ratings of the Semantic Differential scales were factor-analysed. The factor structure that emerged after Varimax rotation corresponded to 'Evaluative', 'Potency', and 'Guilt' components. Wise–Foolish, Good–Bad, Fair–Unfair, Responsible–Irresponsible, Honest–Dishonest and Kind–Cruel all had significant loadings on the first (Evaluative) factor. Strong–Weak and Brave–Cowardly had highest loadings on factor two (Potency), although they also had some significant loadings on factor one. Remorseful–Unremorseful and Ashamed–Unashamed had significant loadings on factor three (Guilt).

Two-way analysis of variance tests showed that the Henderson subjects had significantly lower self-esteem than the normal subjects. This was noted on the

Evaluative, $F(1,101) = 42.1$ $p < 0.001$, Potency, $F(1,101) = 7.7, p < 0.01$, and Guilt, $F(1,101) = 41.7, p < 0.001$, components. There was no significant sex or interaction effect. No main effects were observed on the concept *Myself as I would like to be*. Profile comparisons were made by summing over individual scales for each of the three components, using the 'semantic formula' recommended by Osgood *et al.* (1957):

$$D = \sqrt{\Sigma(X - Y)^2}$$

that is, semantic distance (D) represents the overall difference between two profiles with regard to all the adjectives (scales) comprising each component. For example, if a subject gave profile scores of 6 and 5 on two scales on profile X and 1 and 2 on two scales of profile Y then the D between X and Y would be as follows:

$$D = \sqrt{(6 - 1)^2 + (5 - 2)^2} = 5.8$$

The following profile comparisons were made:

(a) *Myself as I am*   vs. *Myself as I would like to be*
(b) *Myself as I am*   vs. *Myself when/if I lie/steal*
(c) *Myself when/if I lie/steal* vs. *People who lie/steal*

The Henderson subjects were found to have significantly greater semantic distance between their self and ideal self than the normal subjects. The discrepancy was particularly great in regard to Evaluative, $F(1,101) = 59.8$, $p < 0.001$ and Guilt, $F(1,101) = 30.9$, $p < 0.001$ components. The normal subjects showed a very small discrepancy between their self and ideal self on the Guilt component. That is, they were, unlike the Henderson subjects, content with their general level of shame and guilt.

There was a similar discrepancy for all groups on the Evaluative and Potency components regarding *Myself as I am* vs. *Myself when/if I lie/steal*. However, unlike the normal subjects the Henderson ones showed significantly less change in their Guilt scores when transgressing, $F(1,101) = 10.0, p < 0.001$. In other words, the Henderson subjects reported that they were constantly feeling guilt regardless of whether or not they were involved in transgressive behaviour.

In general there was no marked discrepancy between the way the subjects rated themselves as compared with others when transgressing, except on the Guilt component, $F(1,101) = 5.6, p < 0.05$. Most subjects seemed to think that only they experienced guilt feelings during transgression.

The results from the study suggest that the Henderson subjects generally have a poor self-concept, which is reflected in a constant feeling of guilt, regardless of whether or not they are involved in antisocial behaviour. The normal subjects, on the other hand, only seemed to feel guilty when they violated some acceptable norms. Such findings may partly explain why guilt (typically viewed as the emotional component of conscience) fails to inhibit unacceptable behaviour in some psychopaths. That is, some psychopaths are constantly experiencing strong feelings of guilt which are not related specifically to situational transgressions but rather to a generalized poor self-concept and negative preoccupation.

DISCUSSION

The findings consistently confirm some of the conclusions of O'Brien (1976): patients admitted to the Henderson tend to exhibit very high levels of anxiety and have poorly socialized personality characteristics (i.e. low role-taking ability and high impulsiveness). They have poor self-concepts and report constant preoccupation with feelings of guilt. The Cleckley–Hare description (Cleckley, 1976; Hare, 1978) of the psychopath as lacking anxiety, affect, and guilt is not supported by the findings presented in this chapter. This suggests the relevance of the distinction between 'primary' and 'secondary' psychopaths (Karpman, 1947; Hare, 1975). In the case of the latter, antisocial behaviour is considered to be secondary to anxiety and emotional problems, which is consistent with the data for the Henderson subjects. It seems that the large majority of patients admitted to the Henderson fit the description of the secondary psychopath, and very few indeed could be classed as primary psychopaths. This finding is consistent with previous studies into hospitalized psychopaths (Foulds et al., 1960; Marks, 1965; Schalling, 1975; Holland et al., 1980). It may be that only secondary psychopaths endorse feelings of anxiety and guilt, and that these are the people one commonly sees in psychiatric hospitals.

The psychological and physiological characteristics of the Henderson patients have several implications for treatment. The combination of very high levels of anxiety, the lack of awareness of the discordance between subjective and electrodermal measures, and the high non-specific guilt levels underline the need not only to relieve the high anxiety levels which could interfere with the effectiveness of therapy, but also to concentrate on increasing emotional and bodily awareness and to encourage guilt and anxiety to be more situationally specific. The poor self-concept of many of the patients should also be taken into account and the enhancement of self-esteem seen as an important aim in treatment. This view would be consistent with the findings of Norris (1982), quoted earlier.

Treatment at the Henderson, with constant feedback on an individual's behaviour, the chance to take on graduated community posts, and a variety of other groups in which different modes of interaction can be practised, provides a good forum to work on these problems. The range could perhaps be extended to incorporate areas where the individual could become more bodily and socially aware, and better able to cope with stressful situations.

ACKNOWLEDGEMENT

The authors are grateful to Dr Stuart Whiteley, Medical Director of the Henderson Hospital, for his helpful comments concerning the manuscript and for allowing access to his patients.

REFERENCES

Bond, A. and Lader, M. (1974) The use of analogue scales in rating subjective feelings. *British Journal of Medical Psychology*, **47**, 211–218.

Brotherstone, J., Copas, J., O'Brien, M. and Whiteley, S. (1982) An examination of social, personality and behavioural factors, and their relationship to outcome for a group of personality disordered referrals to the Henderson Hospital. Unpublished manuscript.

Cleckley, H. (1976) *The Mask of Sanity*. (5th edn.) St. Louis, Mo.: C. V. Mosby Co.

Copas, J. and Whiteley, J. S. (1976) Predicting success in the treatment of psychopaths. *British Journal of Psychiatry*, **129**, 388–392.

Davis, W. M. (1974) Psychometric prediction of institutional adjustment: a validation study. *British Journal of Social and Clinical Psychology*, **13**, 269–276.

Dombrose, L. A. and Slobin, M. S. (1958) The IES Test. *Perceptual and Motor Skills*, **8**, 347–389 (Monogr. Suppl. 3–V8).

Edmunds, G. and Kendrick, D. C. (1980) *The Measurement of Human Aggressiveness*. Chichester: Ellis Harwood.

Eysenck, H. J. and Eysenck, S. B. G. (1964) *Manual of the Eysenck Personality Inventory*. London: University of London Press.

Eysenck, H. J. and Eysenck, S. B. G. (1975) *Manual of the Eysenck Personality Questionnaire (Junior and Adult)*. London: Hodder and Stoughton.

Eysenck, H. J. and Eysenck, S. B. G. (1978) Psychopathy, personality and genetics. In R. D. Hare and D. Schalling (Eds.) *Psychopathic Behaviour: Approaches to Research*, pp. 197–223. Chichester: Wiley.

Eysenck, S. B. G. and Eysenck, H. J. (1963) On the dual nature of extraversion. *British Journal of Social and Clinical Psychology*, **2**, 46–55.

Farrington, D. P., Biron, L. and LeBlanc, M. (1982) Personality and delinquency in London and Montreal. In J. Gunn and D. P. Farrington (Eds) *Abnormal Offenders, Delinquency, and the Criminal Justice System*, pp. 153–201. Chichester: Wiley.

Foulds, G. A., Caine, T. M. and Creasy, M. A. (1960) Aspects of extra- and intro-punitive expression in mental illness. *Journal of Mental Science*, **106**, 599–610.

Gough, H. G. (1960) Theory and measurement of socialisation. *Journal of Consulting Psychology*, **24**, 23–30.

Gudjonsson, G. H. (1979) Electrodermal responsivity in Icelandic criminals, clergymen and policemen. *British Journal of Social and Clinical Psychology*, **18**, 351–353.

Gudjonsson, G. H. (1981) Self reported emotional disturbance and its relation to electrodermal reactivity, defensiveness and trait anxiety. *Personality and Individual Differences*, **2**, 47–52.

Gudjonsson, G. H. (1982a) Some psychological determinants of electrodermal responses to deception. *Personality and Individual Differences*, **3**, 381–391.

Gudjonsson, G. H. (1982b) Electrodermal responsivity to interrogation questions and its relation to self-reported emotional disturbance. *Biological Psychology*, **14**, 213–218.

Gudjonsson, G. H. and Roberts, J. C. (1981a) The aggressive behaviour of personality disordered patients and its relation to personality and perceptual-motor perform-ance. *Current Psychological Research*, **2**, 101–109.

Gudjonsson, G. H. and Roberts, J. C. (1981b) Trail making scores as a prediction of aggressive behavior in personality disordered patients. *Perceptual and Motor Skills*, **52**, 413–414.

Gudjonsson, G. H. and Roberts, S. C. (1983) Guilt and self-concept in 'secondary psychopaths'. *Personality and Individual Differences*, **4**, 65–70.

Hare, R. (1975) Psychopathy. In P. H. Venables and M. J. Christie (Eds) *Research in Psychophysiology*, pp. 325–348. New York: Wiley.

Hare, R. D. (1978) Electrodermal and cardiovascular correlates of psychopathy. In R. D. Hare and D. Schalling (Eds) *Psychopathic Behaviour: Approaches to Research*, pp. 107–143. Chichester: Wiley.

Henderson, D. K. (1939) *Psychopathic States*. London: Chapman and Hall.

Hodges, W. F. (1976) The psychophysiology of anxiety. In M. Zuckerman and C. D. Spielberger (Eds) *Emotions and Anxiety: New Concepts, Methods and Applications*, pp. 175–194. New York: Halsted.

Holland, T. R., Levi, M. and Watson, G. (1980) Personality patterns among hospitalized vs. incarcerated psychopaths. *Journal of Clinical Psychology*, **36**, 826–832.

Karpman, B. (1947) Passive parasitic psychopathy: towards the personality structure and psychogenesis of idiopathic psychopathy (anethopathy). *Psychoanalysis Review*, **34**, 102–118, 198–222.

Manning, N. and Rapoport, R. (1976) Rejections and re-incorporation: a case study in social research utilisation. *Social Science and Medicine*, **10**, 459–468.

Marks, I. M. (1965) *Patterns of Meaning in Psychiatric Patients: Semantic Differential Responses in Obsessives and Psychopaths*. London: Oxford University Press.

Norris, M. (1982) Treatment outcome for patients at the Henderson Hospital therapeutic community during 1977–1981. Unpublished manuscript.

O'Brien, M. (1976) The diagnosis of psychopath: a study of some characteristics in personality and behaviour of 'psychopaths' referred for treatment to a therapeutic community. Unpublished Ph.D. thesis, University of London.

Osgood, C. E., Suci, G. J. and Tannenbaum, P. H. (1957) *The Measurement of Meaning*. Urbana Ill.: University of Illinois Press.

Rapoport, R. (1960) *Community as Doctor*. London: Tavistock.

Reitan, R. H. (1958) Validity of the Trail Making Test as an indicator of organic brain damage. *Perceptual and Motor Skills*, **8**, 271–276.

Robins, L. (1966) *Deviant Children Grow Up: A Sociological and Psychiatric Study of Sociopathic Personality*. Baltimore: Williams and Wilkins.

Schalling, D. (1975) 'Psychopathy and the psychophysiology of socialization'. Paper presented to NATO Advanced Study Institute on Psychopathic Behaviour, Les Arcs, France.

Schalling, D. and Holmberg, M. (1970) 'Extraversion in criminals and the dual nature of extraversion'. Reports from the Psychological Laboratories, the University of Stockholm, No. 306.

Spellacy, F. (1977) Neuropsychological differences between violent and non-violent adolescents. *Journal of Clinical Psychology*, **33**, 966–969.

Spellacy, F. (1978) Neuropsychological discrimination between violent and non-violent men. *Journal of Clinical Psychology*, **34**, 49–52.

Weinberger, D. A., Schwartz, G. E. and Davidson, R. J. (1979) Low-anxious, high anxious, and repressive coping styles: psychometric patterns and behavioral and physiological responses to stress. *Journal of Abnormal Psychology*, **88**, 369–380.

Weinstein, J., Averill, J., Opton, E. M. and Lazarus, R. S. (1968) Defensive styles and discrepancy between self-report and physiological indices of stress. *Journal of Personality and Social Psychology*, **10**, 406–413.

Whiteley, S. (1970) The response of psychopaths to a therapeutic community. *British Journal of Psychiatry*, **116**, 517–529.

Whiteley, J. S. (1980) The Henderson Hospital. *International Journal of Therapeutic Communities*, **1**, 38–58.

Whiteley, J. S., Briggs, D. and Turner, M. (1982) *Dealing with Deviants*. London: Hogarth Press.

Aggression and Dangerousness
Edited by D. P. Farrington and J. Gunn
© 1985 John Wiley & Sons Ltd.

CHAPTER 5

Jealousy, Pathological Jealousy, and Aggression

PAUL E. MULLEN and LARA H. MAACK

INTRODUCTION

Jealousy is a dangerous passion. Those at risk from the aggression engendered by jealousy are the partners and presumed loved ones. The rivals or supposed rivals are rarely those upon whom the violence of the jealous individual is vented. The romantic myths of jealous rivals duelling for the hand of the beloved are a long way from the reality of the domestic violence engendered by jealousy. This chapter sets out to discuss briefly the emotion of jealousy and in particular its pathological extensions, and to examine the direction, type, and degree of violence associated with it.

JEALOUSY AS A STATE OF MIND

Jealousy, like so many of the phenomena of mental life, is easier to recognize than to define or describe. The word itself shares a common origin with zeal from the Greek *zelos* implying ardour or fire, but it had gathered its modern connotations by the time of Descartes who described jealousy as a 'kind of fear related to a desire to preserve a possession'. Spinoza, however, illuminated and highlighted the anger towards the beloved in his definition:

> Anyone who imagines that the thing loved is joined to another than himself with the same or a faster bond of love, he will be affected with hatred towards the object loved and envy towards the other. This hatred towards an object loved, together with the envy of another, is called jealousy.

The hatred alloyed to love of the partner is placed at the very centre of Spinoza's concept of jealousy. This introduction of hatred and aggression towards the loved one in jealousy allows a distinction to be made in the erotic sphere between rivalry, envy and jealousy.

Rivalry

Rivalry refers to a situation where two or more individuals desire the love

103

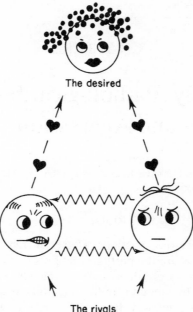

Figure 1   Rivalry: aggression between the rivals; affection for the desired

and affection of the same person. They share, or at least believe they share, the same intentions: those of desire and affection towards the loved one, and they experience themselves as being in competition. Aggression in this situation would be directed exclusively at the rival. The situation of rivalry is a common, if not a universal, experience in our society. When normal individuals confess to jealousy, they are in practice often referring to simple rivalry. The erotic entanglements of adolescence often show rivalry as a central element.

Envy

Envy can be conceptualized as of two types: that involving predominantly admiration and the desire to become like the envied person, and that where the desire is to deprive or destroy some attribute or possession of another. This corresponds to Aristotle's distinction between emulation and envy. Emulation would obviously not involve aggression towards either the rival or the admired partner of the rival. In destructive envy the wish would be to see the rival deprived of the envied relationship. The aggression in destructive envy is directed at the rival and would either not involve the admired partner or only as a by-product of the desire to deprive the rival. The aggression in envy is predominantly, if not exclusively, towards the rival.

The desired

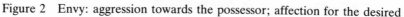

The envious

Figure 2   Envy: aggression towards the possessor; affection for the desired

Jealousy

Jealousy involves aggression directed at the partner as well as the rival. The loved one is also the object of anger in jealousy and the aggression is turned towards him or her as well as to the rival. Envy, in this context, is usually directed at the supposed relationship of others, whereas jealousy is of the individual's own partner.

A distinction has been made between jealousy and envy in the psychoanalytic literature based on the interpersonal situations in which they occur (Spielman, 1971). Envy is said to involve essentially a two-person situation, whereas jealousy invariably involves at least three persons (Sullivan, 1953). In this theoretical framework jealousy is often viewed as emerging later developmentally than envy (Klein, 1957). Envy is said to occur in a two-person relationship or in a relationship of the individual to a part object, and is characteristic of the pre-oedipal phase. Jealousy is derived from the three-person relationship of the oedipal phase. This does not distinguish between rivalry and jealousy, nor clearly from the adult who envies the loved one of another.

Jealousy has traditionally been regarded as one of the emotions. Emotions involve feelings about things and they accompany the mental events of perceiving, conceiving, or imagining, from which they are inseparable. Emotions involve not only feelings about something but a disposition to behave in a particular manner. Thus the emotion of affection is associated with a tendency to approach and behave pleasantly towards the object of that

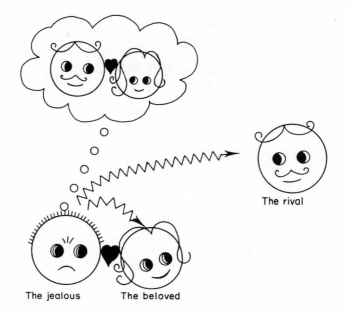

Figure 3   Jealousy: aggression towards the 'rival'; aggression and affection towards
the beloved

affection, just as the emotion of fear would predispose to recoiling or fleeing.
The concept of emotions as being irrational responses ungoverned by intent
and judgement is deeply ingrained in our thinking. In this culture the emotions
are placed at the opposite pole from reason. It can be argued, however, that
emotions involve judgements and are in many senses intentional acts
(Solomons, 1976). Emotions involve the experience of feelings such as
pleasure, anger, or embarrassment; they have an object in that they are about
something, they often involve a disposition to behave in a particular manner,
and finally, they embody judgements about and intentions towards the object
of the emotion.

The structure of jealousy can be outlined employing this model. Jealousy
involves the judgement that an act of infidelity has been committed by the
loved one who is the object of the emotion. This creates the experience of
painful feelings, such as a fear of loss and anger towards the partner, often
combined with a sense of humiliation and insecurity. The intentions generated
tend to be ambivalent with regard to the partner, involving both erotic and
possessive intent and angry and destructive intent. The behaviour predisposed
to is in line with these contradictory intentions in that it may involve both angry
and accusatory actions, as well as placatory and sexual approaches. The
experiences and behaviour associated with jealousy will vary according to the
personality structure, previous experience, and social and cultural expecta-

tions of the individual. Jealousy arises and expresses itself within the context of a relationship, and the partner is critical, not only in the invoking of the passion but in its subsequent development. Jealousy also involves anger towards or fear of the rival, though it is the feelings and intentions towards the partner which so often predominate to the virtual exclusion of those directed at the rival.

THE EXPERIENCE OF JEALOUSY
IN NORMAL INDIVIDUALS

Jealousy, as it is experienced in otherwise normal populations, has been the subject of relatively little systematic study. Tipton and his colleagues (1978) developed a self-report questionnaire to investigate jealousy, and subjected the responses from their 335 subjects to a factor analysis. From this analysis they extracted five dimensions. A factor involving the need for loyalty accounted for 35 per cent of the variance and a further 13 per cent was accounted for by the need for intimacy. Despondency and moodiness accounted for 9 per cent, with a lack of self-confidence close behind, and finally, a factor they identified with envy accounted for 7 per cent. Their sample was heavily weighted towards female respondents and this may well have accounted for the good showing of loyalty and intimacy and the poor performance of envy and the virtual absence of declared possessiveness and aggression. Employing a different jealousy self-report scale, Jaremko and Lindsey (1979) studied 80 subjects. They noted that high scores on their jealousy scale correlated with higher scores on ratings of anxiety and poor self-esteem.

SEX DIFFERENCES IN THE EXPERIENCE OF JEALOUSY

Jealousy, in the popular imagination, is often portrayed as a predominantly female emotion. Jones (1948) in his oft-quoted psychoanalytical study of jealousy, reported 'women are so much more prone to jealousy than men'. There is nothing approaching a serious epidemiological study of jealousy to which it is possible to turn for an answer as to sex incidence. What little evidence there is indicates that jealousy is actually rather less common in women. Gottschalk's study of jealousy in normal individuals found significant problems with sexual jealousy in 21 of 25 men but only 6 of 27 women (reported in Bohm, 1961). The various series of cases of morbid jealousy from Krafft-Ebing (1905) onward have usually reported an excess of males in their patient populations. Morbidly jealous males are reported to develop symptoms of jealousy not only more frequently but also significantly earlier in their relationships than women (Vauhkonen, 1968; Dominik, 1970).

Theodore Reik (1957) claimed there were sex differences both in the source of jealousy and in the subjective experience of jealousy. He suggested that men concentrated more on the sexual aspects of infidelity, whereas women were more concerned with the loss of relationship and security. Men, according to Reik, not infrequently torture themselves with vivid images of their partners engaged in sexual activity with the rival. Women, conversely, express more concern with the threat of loss and resultant insecurity, combined with the fears of the alienation of the partner's affections. Seeman (1979), in a detailed analysis of jealousy in five women, concluded that insecurity and lowered self-esteem were common factors in its precipitation. She also noted, however, an 'obsession with the details of the supposed infidelity, imagining the husband ridiculing personal attributes of the wife in front of the rival' and 'a constant theme of other people knowing and feeling sorry for the wife'. Clearly here status and position in the eyes of others, rather than the sexual activity itself, is highlighted.

A study of Teismann and Mosher (1978) of jealous conflict in 80 couples led them to conclude that 'men selected their issues of jealousy as sexual, while women selected jealous issues which involved a loss of time and attention'. They did not find, however, any sex differences in the patterns of verbal behaviour and the interpersonal strategies adopted. A sex difference in the response to experiencing jealousy was claimed by Bryson (Bryson 1977—reported in Jaremko and Lindsey, 1979). Males were said to respond to the experience of jealousy with anger, and women by attempts to make themselves more attractive to their partner.

Female jealousy tends, according to Tov-Ruach (1980) to be 'directed to matters of practical dependence ... and it is rare that female jealousy is strictly sexual'. This she contrasts with the male's more specific concern with sexual fidelity. The evidence adduced by the author for this contention rests on the, to her, apparently self-evident truths of psychoanalytic theories of psychosexual development and the social position of women in our society. The author points out that women are dependent on the male's attachment and attention for their well-being, and that social and economic differences help to explain some of the differences in the experience of and reactions to jealousy between the sexes.

The question of sex differences in the experiences and behaviour associated with jealousy will be returned to in the section of this chapter dealing with aggression and violence.

PATHOLOGICAL EXTENSIONS OF JEALOUSY

The paucity of systematic studies on jealousy in otherwise normal individuals leaves enormous gaps in our knowledge of the nature, frequency, and variability of this phenomenon. The available studies of jealousy draw largely, if not exclusively, on highly selected groups of psychiatric patients or mentally abnormal offenders. The approach of attempting to illuminate the nature of a normal phenomenon by study of its pathological extensions is a time-honoured one in medicine. The difficulty in this situation is how to draw a distinction between the normal and the morbid.

Krafft-Ebing (1905) made the distinction on the basis of the presence of delusions which, interestingly, he classified as two types. If the lawful wife was believed to be deceiving the patient, it was a 'delusion of marital infidelity', but, if it was a mistress, the term 'delusion of jealousy' was to be applied. Mowat (1966), in his excellent monograph, also determined the presence of morbid jealousy on the basis of delusions of infidelity. The problem of employing the presence or absence of delusion as the yardstick of the pathological is firstly that it is overly narrow and restrictive. Secondly, it is dependent on the definition of delusion. Krafft-Ebing employs delusion in the sense of a false belief of morbid origin. This creates no problems for him as he confines morbid jealousy to the effects of chronic alcohol intoxication. Though in alcoholism he recognizes pathoplastic features in terms of deteriorating sexual and interpersonal relationships, he clearly views the emergence of delusion as based on organic brain disorder. The problems begin when it is simply a truth or falsity of the belief in infidelity that is seen as the touchstone of the definition. Retterstøl (1967) drew his line between the normal and the pathologically jealous solely on the basis of the 'actual facts'.

The first problem with the 'actual facts' is that they may be just as obscure to the physician as they are to the patient. Ødegaard (1968) routinely advised separation in his morbidly jealous patients. He has, as a result, been able to note the frequency with which the wives of his patients subsequently marry or become sexually involved with the subjects of their ex-husbands' 'delusions'. Another problem is that patients with bizarre beliefs about the supposed sexual exploits of their partners, who offer as evidence the most extraordinary of extraneous happenings, and whose convictions clearly have a morbid origin, may nevertheless be correct in their central hypothesis about the partner's extramural activities. A patient of ours had the infidelity of his spouse conclusively revealed to him one Christmas Eve when he noted that the lights on the Christmas tree in his window flashed in synchrony with the lights on the tree in his neighbour's window. The actual affair between his wife and this particular neighbour was irrelevant to the delusional nature of his belief of infidelity. Thus the truth or falsity of the beliefs may be a shaky basis for the distinction between pathological and normal, even if the facts are available.

Todd and his colleagues (1971) employed the absence of reasonable grounds for suspicion as a criterion of abnormality, but added that jealous reactions, justified or not by the evidence, were abnormal if they were of such intensity as to render the person dangerously aggressive. This has the advantage of taking account of the patient's reactions and way of responding, but the concentration on dangerous aggression is perhaps overly restrictive and would lead to very considerable problems if applied in the forensic field. Todd (1978), in a later paper, made this clear when he said 'psychiatrists are concerned with sexual jealousy stemming from delusion and not with an excessive reaction'. In the situation of the courtroom, a psychiatrist who proposed that an accused person, who had acted in a dangerously aggressive way as a result of jealousy, was therefore abnormal mentally, could create difficulties.

This is exemplified by one of our recent homicide cases. The accused was a somewhat shy young man who was unusually emotionally dependent upon his wife who was some years older than he. He discovered the wife's liaison with another man, and when threats to kill himself or her failed to persuade her to give up the relationship, he carefully planned and carried out a murderous assault on her and her lover. This man had grown to adulthood in Southern Italy and his social attitudes were those of his birthplace rather than those of the smart middle-class suburb in North London where his wife had grown up and in which they both now resided. He was distressed and threatened by the wife's infidelity, but his actions, though undoubtedly dangerously aggressive, in no way arose from abnormality of mind. Should such a man's jealousy be considered morbid, or is it not preferable to see his jealousy as understandable culturally and personally, and the actions stemming from it as criminal?

Shepherd (1961) makes a similar but less restrictive distinction when he says 'a person's jealousy may be considered abnormal as much by virtue of the facility and intensity with which they react as by the abnormal quality of their reactions'. Langfeldt (1961, 1962) also suggests intensified normal reactions based on psychologically understandable foundations should be considered as giving rise to a morbid form of jealousy. Vauhkonen (1968) considered any jealous reaction pathological where the reaction was sufficiently strong or prolonged to necessitate psychiatric care. Boranga (1981) suggests jealousy 'remains within the bounds of normality as long as it expresses a situation of conflict which the individual is capable of controlling and overcoming in the evolution of his personality'. Lagache (1947) suggested that it was the personality and character traits of the jealous individual which distinguished between the normal and abnormal jealous reactions. These types of distinction, as Shepherd recognized, leave the borderline between morbid jealousy and the normal, understandably jealous individual, arbitrary and poorly defined.

The study of clinical material shows the shallowness and inadequacy of most attempts to separate so-called 'normal' from so-called 'pathological' jealousy. The truth or falsity of the suspicions will not do as a distinction. Equally the intensity of the response, both in terms of the distress and the behaviour elicited, makes an uncertain ground for a clear distinction. Cases of suicide or murder as a response to supposed or actual infidelity are within the experience of most psychiatrists with an interest in the forensic field. But without knowing more about the nature of the individual, his vulnerabilities, ethical and religious convictions, the way he habitually deals with anger and frustration, the meaning and significance of this particular spouse or partner to him, and the nature of their previous relationship, could any of us say that the resort to such terrible violence unequivocally indicated psychiatric pathology? Only the most mechanistic approach allows such an equation.

If the distinction is allowed to revolve around the presence of delusions of infidelity, quite apart from the practical problem of their definition, a large number—probably the majority of cases currently seen and treated as morbid jealousy—would be excluded. A patient of ours confines his wife to the house during his absence by locks and bars. He follows her whenever she leaves. He checks on all visitors. He ruminates continually when away from her on what could happen in his absence. He, however, does not believe his wife has been unfaithful to him. He does not even believe she wishes to be unfaithful. He simply doubts that she or any woman can be certain of resisting temptation, and his aim in life is to prevent her virtue being tried. No delusions of infidelity are there, but the jealousy is surely pathological.

Jealousy is not a simple emotion and this holds equally for its morbid developments. There is a complex interaction between feelings, beliefs, and actions. It is not surprising that, with such a concatenation of phenomena, boundaries and distinctions are as difficult to draw as they are to maintain.

Jealousy, it was postulated earlier in this chapter, has a structure in that it involves judgements, feelings, intentions and behaviour directed towards the partner. The pathologies of jealousy can involve one or more of these aspects or axes of emotion. Thus the judgement that an act of infidelity has occurred may be pathological in that it is based on a morbid belief such as a delusion. The associated feelings may be evoked with abnormal facility or manifest with increased intensity. The intentions may be unusual both in their content and the degree of their ambivalence. The behaviour may be abnormally violent, may involve extensive checking and cross-questioning, or may conversely demonstrate unusual tolerance or even active complicity with the infidelity (Pinta, 1978). The nature of the relationship in which the jealousy arises, and the judgements made by the jealous individual of his rights and prerogatives within the relationship, may also be abnormal.

This approach to jealousy would allow judgement of whether an abnormality exists in the particular case to be made along each of the parameters. To take a rather unusual example, one of our cases was troubled by the insistent and intrusive thought that his wife was being unfaithful to him. He believed the suspicion to be ungrounded and unfair, but it constantly recurred, and despite his resistance to it he was plagued for many hours each day by the unwanted suspicion. He developed a ritual to try and assuage his fears which involved the performance of complex mental arithmetic which he felt, if he performed it correctly, would in some magical way preserve his wife's fidelity. Though recognising the absurdity and irrationality of his ruminations, he still felt compelled to carry them out. He was distressed and fearful in association with these obsessional ruminations, but they did not affect his intentions and behaviour to his partner, nor did he even attempt to question her or check on her fidelity. Here the abnormality was confined to the obsessive doubt involving the patient's judgement of the partner's fidelity. More commonly, several or all the parameters are affected to a greater or lesser degree, though often in only one aspect is there a gross deviation.

CLASSIFICATIONS OF PATHOLOGICAL JEALOUSY

The two most influential classificatory systems of pathological jealousy have been those suggested by Freud (1922) and Jaspers (1910).

Freud (1922) described three forms of jealousy: competitive, projected, and delusional. The classification arises, as do the distinctions between normal and pathological variants, from the mental mechanisms postulated to underlie the phenomena. Competitive jealousy is considered by Freud to be universal, but he writes:

> Although we may call it normal, this jealousy is by no means completely rational, that is, derived from the actual situation, proportionate to the real circumstances and under the complete control of the conscious ego, for it is rooted deep in the unconscious, it is a continuation of the earliest stirrings of the child's affective life and it originates in the Oedipus complex.

Competitive jealousy in Freud's system is indistinguishable from simple rivalry. Projected jealousy is derived in both men and women either from their own actual or fantasied unfaithfulness. It is, writes Freud, 'a matter of everyday experience that fidelity is only maintained in the face of continual temptation'. Relief from these temptations and their attendant guilt is achieved by projecting the impulses on to the partner. Jealousy that arises from projection has, Freud (1922) writes, an 'almost delusional character', but is still amenable to correction through exposing the unconscious fantasies of personal infidelity.

Delusional jealousy is Freud's third level. It also takes root from the repressed impulses to infidelity, but the object in these cases is the same sex as the subject. Delusional jealousy, states Freud, represents 'acidulated homosexuality and rightly takes its position among the classical forms of paranoia'.

The projective mechanisms postulated by Freud are impossible to exclude as the basis for jealousy, but equally they are difficult to establish in all but a minority of cases. The speculations about delusional jealousy being the overt manifestations of repressed and therefore unconscious homosexual impulses are even more problematic. Overt homosexual fantasies may accompany jealousy and practising homosexuals may exhibit delusions of infidelity, though presumably this is not a theoretical problem if you find it possible to accept the assertion of Lagache (1950) that overt homosexual behaviour can be a defence against unconscious homosexual impulses. Freud's view that delusional jealousy is a 'classical form of paranoia' still survives to be enshrined in DSM III (1980) under the term 'conjugal paranoia' to be classified under Paranoia (297.10). This is despite the lack of any empirical evidence to connect the content of a delusion with any particular diagnostic entity with a common natural history or outcome and in fact considerable evidence suggesting the reverse (Retterstøl, 1970; Kendler, 1980).

Freud's two postulates on jealousy do, however, provide an insight into the mental mechanisms of some jealous subjects. There is often a barely disguised homosexual content to many of the fantasies of our jealous patients. The identification of the jealous subject with his partner in the intercourse fantasies is not infrequently painfully obvious. The choice of rival, particularly in delusions of infidelity, often reflects a choice of dominant and envied, if not desired, figures in the jealous person's own life rather than in the partner's life. In our own case material the jealous subjects frequently expressed the belief that the rival was one of their own siblings or occasionally one of their partner's relatives, thus giving overt expression to incest fantasies. The use of jealous fantasies and mutual confession as a sexual titillation in otherwise normal individuals may also have their origins in part in the identification with the partner and consequent gratification of homosexual wishes. Similarly, with the projection of actual or fantasied infidelity into the partner, everyday clinical practice offers a host of examples even if introspection fails to convince.

Jaspers (1910) recognised four variants of jealousy. First, psychological or normal jealousy, the characteristics of which he left undefined. Secondly, pathological jealousy where the individual is assailed by intense doubts and suspicions about the partner's fidelity on the basis of no, or inadequate, grounds. In these cases it was suggested the patient recognized the suspicions to be either poorly founded or excessive, but at times the subject might be overwhelmed by them, only later to regain insight into their exaggerated or morbid nature. The third type was jealousy with non-systematized delusions, which was characterized by true delusions of infidelity which fluctuated in intensity, to some extent according to changes in the patient's circumstances or state of mind. These delusions could totally dominate the patient's mental life but at other times could recede into the background, though never to the extent that they were clearly recognized by the patient as morbid or unfounded. Finally, the fourth type was jealousy with systematized delusions, which was characterized by an extensive system of delusional ideas around the central core of the delusion of infidelity. In this situation the jealousy dominated the mental life and the system developed by gradual accretion and elaboration. Jaspers made further division into process and developmental jealousy. This division only applies to the fourth type of systematized delusions of infidelity.

The various classifications employed in European psychiatry following Jaspers, such as those of Lagache (1947) Ey (1950) and Vauhkonen (1968), appear to the authors to revolve largely around the themes, firstly of whether the jealousy is reactive, secondly whether it can be understood developmentally in relationship to the patient's personality structure, and finally if it is part of or symptomatic of some underlying process. The simplest classification so far proposed is that of Cobb (1979) in which he divided jealousy into normal, neurotic, and psychotic. Simplicity would seem to be its only virtue. The most alliterative is that of Mooney (1965) with Excessive, Obsessive, and Delusional types.

Table 1 presents a basic clinical classification incorporating divisions into the reactive, the developmental, and the symptomatic. Reactive Jealousy differs from the jealousy of the commonality by virtue of the abnormal personality structure of the individual which exaggerates aspects of the jealousy. Developmental Jealousy is primarily related to a disorder of personality, but the situations which may sensitize such an individual to the provocation of jealousy can include other mental disorders. Thus, in Developmental Jealousy, a personality vulnerable to develop jealousy may be sensitized by a depressive illness in the context of which some minor provocation may set off jealousy. The types of personality which have been described in this context include those lacking the ability to trust others, those hypersensitive to slights and reverses, the superficially arrogant and self-assured who harbour deep personal insecurity, the litigious, and those with heightened tendencies to self-reference (Kretschmer, 1952). In theory, Symptomatic Jealousy is explained entirely by the causal pathology; however, there may be some contribution from previous experience, with the relationship and personality not immediately apparent. There is obviously some overlap between the three categories.

This classification does not give sufficient weight, as it stands, to the ways in which the individual's previous experiences may act to sensitize him to jealous reactions. In several of our cases a sensitizing previous experience has seemed of critical importance. In one case the man had shown no tendency to jealousy in his first marriage but his wife had left him for another man. This apparently came as a complete shock to him and he had a period of some months of significant depression following the loss. He remarried some 6 years later to his ex-wife's younger sister, and it was in this second marriage that he became increasingly suspicious and developed a heightened sensitivity to any possibility of infidelity. The second marriage ended tragically when he stabbed his wife to death at a party when she refused to stop dancing with another man. The other perspective absent from this clinical classification is the cultural and social. Jealousy may well be encouraged and sanctioned in some cultures more than others, and this may well determine the threshold for its emergence in the Reactive and Developmental types.

PATHOLOGICAL JEALOUSY AND MENTAL DISORDER

The extensive literature on pathological jealousy and its relationship to mental disorder has so far had little influence on those responsible for the official

Table 1   A clinical classificatory system for pathological jealousy

	Reactive	Developmental	Symptomatic
Necessary conditions	1. A provoking event; always understandably related to fears of infidelity. 2. A situation and/or relationship which maintains the jealousy. 3. A personality structure which accentuated aspects of the jealousy.	1. A disorder of personality usually predisposing to oversensitivity and feelings of persecution as well as jealousy. 2. A provoking event which may or may not easily be related by others to fears of infidelity. 3. A situation, relationship, or change in the mood state of the jealous individual which perpetuates the jealousy.	1. An underlying disorder which forms the necessary and sufficient cause for what is a true symptom of jealousy.
Course	Dependent on the nature and course of the supposed or actual infidelity, the relationship between the partners and the type of reactions in terms of behaviour and feelings engendered.	Tends to be of exacerbations and remissions. The predisposition to jealousy is life-long and a variety of events in the environment, relationship, or individual may rekindle it.	That of the underlying pathological cause.

classifactory system of the International Classification of Diseases or the Diagnostic and Statistical Manual of the American Psychiatric Association. These systems only allow jealousy the status of a symptom of some other primary diagnosis.

In Table 2 the diagnoses attached to 138 cases of morbid jealousy treated at the Maudsley and Bethlem Hospitals in the years 1967–1980 are listed. Taken at face value this confirms the nature of morbid jealousy as a symptom which

Table 2   Diagnoses made in 138 patients exhibiting pathological jealousy

Alcoholism (including alcoholic psychosis			*Paranoid states*		
	Total	15	Paranoia		10
			Involutional paraphrenia		1
			Unspecified		1
				Total	12
Personality disorders			*Other psychoses*		
Paranoid		40	Acute paranoid reaction		2
Obsessional		2	Psychosis unspecified		1
Hysterical		2			
Explosive		1		*Total*	3
Schizoid		1			
Sociopathic		1			
Other or unspecified		9			
	Total	56			
Depression			*Other conditions*		
Depressive neurosis		21	Alzheimer's disease		1
Affective psychosis		53	Friedreich's ataxia		1
	Total	74	Mental retardation (unspecified)		3
			Multiple sclerosis		1
			Huntington's chorea		1
Drug abuse			Psychosis associated with		
Dependence		4	other cerebral conditions		13
With associated psychosis		1			
	Total	5		*Total*	20
Schizophrenia					
Unspecified type		7			
Paranoid type		8			
	Total	15			

Note: Seen at the Bethlem and Maudsley Hospital between 1967 and 1980. The criteria of ICD 8 are employed. One hundred and thirty-eight primary and 62 associated disorders are listed.

may be the outward manifestation of a wide range of mental disorders. Closer inspection of this case material revealed, however, that those classified under paranoid personality disorder and paranoid states had in the main only evidence of jealousy and its manifestations. Thus some 52 cases could have been classified under pathological or morbid jealousy if such an entity existed in the eighth revision of the International Classification of Diseases (1968). In fact, 17 cases were so classified by psychiatrists in resistance to or ignorance of the rules, only to be redesignated paranoid personality disorder by the records clerk.

Abnormal mental phenomena are, in accordance with the dictates of the traditions inherited from the nineteenth-century nosologists, regarded as symptoms indicative of underlying disease entities. The problems of this approach, when applied to abnormalities of mental state, have been recently discussed (Mullen, 1984). The situation with jealousy and its pathological extensions clearly illustrates the difficulties produced by rigid adherence to this theoretical stance. It necessitates, in some situations, relegating to the status of mere symptoms the only observable phenomena. Psychiatrists may have become immured from the theoretical difficulties of explaining the observable in terms of the unknown and unknowable, but this practice in the situation of pathological jealousy may obscure more than it illuminates.

Another interesting and ambiguous quality of jealousy as a symptom is illustrated by one of our cases where delusions of infidelity emerged in the context of two entirely separate mental disorders. The patient, on the first occasion, presented with delusions about his wife's infidelity in the context of extensive delusions of reference (largely, though not exclusively, concerned with his wife's adultery), auditory hallucinations, and passivity experiences. The diagnosis was of a schizophrenic illness which gradually resolved on phenothiazines over some months. The second presentation, 8 years later, was with Creutzfeld–Jacob disease, but again the delusions of infidelity emerged in association with the organic pathology. On this occasion there were no other associated abnormalities of mental state.

The pain and despair associated with the experience of jealousy is on occasion associated with, or may precipitate, a depressive syndrome. In our series no less than 74 cases were given a diagnosis of a depressive disorder. In many of these cases, particularly those diagnosed as depressive neurosis, it would appear that the affective symptomatology emerged after the jealousy. A detailed analysis of these 138 cases revealed 33 had indulged in seriously self-destructive behaviour in the 6-month period immediately prior to their admission, and one killed herself while an inpatient (Table 3).

PATHOLOGICAL JEALOUSY AND THE RELATIONSHIP

The relegation of pathological jealousy to the role of symptom has had, as one of its by-products, the concentration on the mental events or postulated brain

Table 3   Patterns of self-destructive behaviour

	Males	Females	Total
Suicide	0	1	1
Self-poisoning	9	9	18
Other serious attempts at suicide	5	2	7
Severe self-inflicted injuries (largely cutting and slashing)	3	4	7
Totals	17	16	33

Note: In 138 cases of pathological jealousy treated at the Bethlem and Maudsley Hospital between 1967 and 1980. Only those acts committed in the 6 months prior to admission or during the index admission itself are listed.

changes in the afflicted individual to the virtual exclusion of the interpersonal aspects. Jealousy, however, only exists in relationships, even if they be fantasied ones, and may often best be regarded as the disorder of a system rather than the disorder of an individual. It is, of course, arguable that as one moves from so-called normal to pathological jealousy, so one moves from the pathology of a relationship to individual pathology. It is, nevertheless, remarkable how few studies there are of the relationships in which pathological jealousy has occurred.

Shepherd (1961) noted the importance of interpersonal relations particularly in 'the neurotics' in his series, and stated

the interplay of both partners therefore entered into and modified the symptoms and the manifestations to such a degree that the significance of the phenomena in an individual case could not be assessed without an understanding of the relationship between them.

Turbott (1981) described a case where the spouse intervened to prevent the husband's treatment and maintain the jealousy. The emergence of morbid jealousy in the husbands of patients successfully treated for agoraphobia (Hafner, 1979) also suggests a role for complementary psychopathology in such couples. Vauhkonen (1968) provides a study of the marital relationships of pathologically jealous subjects. He reported that nearly half of the spouses of morbidly jealous patients had evidence for significant disorders of personality. The wives of jealous husbands were reported as showing histrionic traits of character, whereas the husbands of the female patients were said to be of a passive dependent personality. In several case studies, wives of jealous husbands emerge as somewhat flamboyant personalities, and amongst our own cases provocative and flirtatious behaviour has been a prominent feature of the behaviour of several of the wives.

Vauhkonen (1968) also provides the most extensive data available on the sexual relationships of this group of patients. He reports that 32 of the 37 wives of jealous patients gave a history of severe sexual dysfunction in the form of anorgasmia and frigidity. The husbands of the female patients were not, however, reported as exhibiting a greater than normal level of sexual dysfunction. The sexual function of the patients themselves did not differ significantly, in this study, from a normal population.

Theories of the genesis of delusion abound, but one view of possible relevance here is that paranoia takes its origin not in abnormal experiences of, or in beliefs about, the world, but in the failure or disintegration of the relationship with others. According to this theory the breakdown or failure to develop trust in others creates the over-sensitivity, self-reference, and ultimately delusions. In the relationship of love there often rapidly develops an intense sense of mutual identification, an absorption into each other. Once committed to love there is an immense investment in the love of the other for oneself. If this is not, or cannot be, trusted, then it must be tested and checked. For the subject afflicted by intense self-doubt and self-denigration, the other's love must be doubted, if not totally rejected. It becomes not merely suspect but a lie. Here may be a road to suspicion, to obsessive doubt, and to delusion. The passion of love moves faster that the relationship of reason and may thus destroy reason itself.

The American philosopher, Jerome Neu (1980), attempts to place jealousy clearly in the context of loving relationships and as a consequence of the exclusivity of love. For Neu, in jealousy there is always a person involved, for it can never be the loss of a possession which is central, but only the loss of the love and affection that a person can bestow. This turns on its head the more recently fashionable view of jealousy which sees it as deriving from the belief that others are only objects to be possessed. Jealousy, he argues, exists between people and is about the personal relationship, simply because it is only other people who have the power to respond to our desires.

The way in which jealousy is dealt with in a relationship, and the way its emergence is responded to by the partners, can clearly on occasion be critical to the development of pathological jealousy. The individuals experiencing jealousy may seek, and where possible accept, reassurance whilst trying to control and overcome the emotion. The individuals consumed by the passion of jealousy may not seek reassurance but evidence which will confirm the infidelity. They may reject all reassurance, and seek only to demonstrate the extent and totality of the betrayal. Conversely, though the jealous individual may look for reassurance, his partner may deny that comfort, either because they cannot give it or because of their own needs to escalate the tension. Interpersonal disputes can be escalated or alleviated according to the responses of the protagonists. Jealousy is an interpersonal conflict that easily becomes an escalating dispute. Accusation followed by denial leads to further accusations.

Accusation followed by admission leads to rage, distress, and even more extensive accusations. The partner may equally inflame and escalate the situation by provocative or ambivalent statements and behaviour; two people are involved, either or both of whom may be fulfilling unadmitted needs in the increasing conflict. Normal individuals seek to bring this interaction to a rapid solution; the pathological may seek to prolong it.

JEALOUSY AND AGGRESSION

Spinoza's definition of jealousy put hatred towards the loved one as a central characteristic. The behaviour of jealous subjects amply confirms the presence of this feature. The anger and aggression are vented in so-called normal as well as pathological jealousy far more frequently upon the partner than on the actual or supposed rival.

Mowat (1966), in his study of 71 patients with morbid jealousy who had killed, noted that the victims were almost exclusively the partners, with the supposed rival killed in only five of the cases. Ruin (1933) reported on 17 cases of homicidal jealousy, all of whom were male, and in 14 of these the victim was the partner. Lagache (1947) reported on 18 homicidal attacks in his series of pathologically jealous patients, all of whom were male and 14 of whom killed their wives. Psarska's (1970) series of jealous homicides were all male and the victims were, with one exception, their female partners. Podolsky (1961) also reported two male cases of homicide where pathological jealousy was the motive—in both cases the perpetrators were male and the wives were killed.

The aggression towards the partner in jealousy does not only manifest in the extreme form of homicide, or more usually in this context gynocide, but in every level of interpersonal violence. Two-thirds of the women at a refuge for battered wives reported that their husbands were excessively jealous and that this was the motivation for the repeated assaults (Gayford, 1975, 1979). In this group of women only a minority admitted to any grounds for the husband's suspicions.

Violence in both word and deed has been noted in most series of pathologically jealous subjects. A detailed account of the extent and direction of the aggressive behaviour in this group of patients is, however, lacking. The information bearing on this question, from the studies already cited, largely derives from a group who have been studied following committing a homicide or other serious assault, and does not necessarily reflect the type or pattern of aggression to be found more generally in such patients.

In an attempt to answer these questions a detailed analysis was carried out of the records of 138 patients admitted to the Maudsley and Bethlem Hospitals between 1967 and 1980 who had been diagnosed as exhibiting pathological jealousy (Maack and Mullen, in preparation). This group is clearly a highly selected one in terms of referral. There were only six cases of the 138 which were referred primarily because of a violent incident. None was referred from the courts and none was awaiting trial on any offence at the time of the index admission. Only three of the men and one of the women had a history of criminal convictions as adults and in only two of these, both men, did the convictions involve a crime of violence. In only one case was there an assault on a member of staff during the admission of sufficient seriousness to be recorded.

The records were analysed for evidence of aggression—towards both the partner, and the supposed rival, or rivals—and for any aggressive or violent behaviour or fantasies towards others. The grounds for this analysis were the histories recorded from the patient, and in all cases one or more independent informants, usually including the partner. The period chosen for inclusion was the 6 months immediately prior to admission and the period of the index admission itself. This cohort was selected solely on the criterion of the presence of pathological jealousy. However, in 111 cases there was a clear history of either threatening or actually perpetrating physical violence on their partners (Table 4).

Table 4   Acts of aggression committed against partners

	Males		Females	
No history obtained of threats or acts of violence	13	(15%)	14	(27%)
Threats of intent to injure or kill	20	(24%)	13	(24%)
Indirect evidence of aggression	4	(5%)	3	(6%)
Acts of physical violence	48	(56%)	23	(43%)
Totals	85		53	

Note: By 138 cases of pathological jealousy. Only acts committed in the 6 months prior to admission are included. Each patient is only counted once in the highest category of aggression reached. Those committing actual violence had usually also threatened violence.

Threats to kill or maim the partner were made by 20 of the male patients and 13 of the female. Six of the men and two of the women accompanied their threats by brandishing a knife, a further nine men underlined their threats by waving blunt weapons such as pokers, and one man pointed a gun at his wife whilst threatening to kill her. In seven cases there was indirect evidence of aggression. Two of the wives had separated from their jealous husbands because of what they termed their violence, without further details. Two reported being terrified of the husband's violence or, as one termed it, his 'aggressive paranoia', but no details of actual assaults were given. Three of the male spouses reported that their wives were aggressive and violent, without further elaboration.

Assaults of one type or another were inflicted by 48 of the men and 23 of the women upon their partners. The seriousness of these attacks, both in terms of the violence intended and the damage actually perpetrated, varied widely. No actual homicides occurred within this cohort. However, 10 men gave a history of attempting to strangle their wives, and it would appear from both partners' accounts that the attacks were potentially homicidal. One man attempted to kill his wife by coal-gas poisoning, and five other male patients gave accounts of attacks on their partners, three with knives, which they said had a homicidal intent. One woman planned to kill her husband and went as far as purchasing rat poison but did not put the plan into action. The pattern of assault in many cases was of repeated attacks involving hitting, punching, and kicking the partner. Three women attacked their husbands by clawing and scratching at their faces. Ten male and two female patients slashed their partners with knives. Nine men and two women struck their partners with blunt instruments, and four of the men inflicted fractures on their wives. The physical violence was accompanied by the deliberate damage and destruction of personal and treasured possessions by four of the women and 10 of the men.

This horrifying catalogue of the verbal and physical abuse of their partners by these patients exhibiting pathological jealousy was not accompanied by any comparable level of aggressive activity toward the real or supposed rivals (Table 5). Four of the male patients threatened their rivals with violence or death, underlining the threat in one case by brandishing a knife, and in another a club. Three men attacked their supposed rival, in one incident employing a knife. Four women attacked their supposed rival, in one incident employing a knife. One of these ladies managed to assault no less than 20 other women she believed her husband to be having affairs with. Two male patients entertained extensive fantasies about killing the supposed rival, and one female patient indulged in fantasies of physically beating the rival.

Table 5   Acts of aggression towards the actual or supposed rival

	Males		Females	
No history obtained of threats or acts of violence	78	(91%)	49	(92%)
Threats of intent to injure or kill	4	(5%)	0	
Acts of physical violence	3	(4%)	4	(8%)
Totals	85		53	

Note: In 138 cases of pathological jealousy. Only acts committed in the 6 months prior to admission are included.

The pattern of aggression in this group of patients clearly supports the hypothesis that aggression in pathological jealousy is directed predominantly at the partner and not at the rival. It is possible, as the supposed rivals were not interviewed, that the acts of aggression towards them are under-reported. However, the patients, by and large, made little attempt to conceal the history of aggression towards the partner which might on the face of it be more obviously an area for shame and concealment. Criminal charges might also have been expected to have occurred more frequently had the rivals been the object of the aggression in the manner and with the frequency with which the partners were abused. There are few data available on the level of violence amongst the population attending or admitted to psychiatric hospitals. Post and his colleagues (1980) questioned 60 consecutive male patients for evidence of domestic violence, and report that some 25 per cent gave a history of battering their partners. The level and severity of domestic violence in our cohort of pathologically jealous subjects is clearly far higher than this.

The role of jealousy and its pathological extensions in domestic violence is not exhausted by an account of the attacks on the partner. The violence in these partnerships may be vented upon the one who is jealous. Three of the women in the series mentioned above were regularly and severely battered by their husbands, usually in response to accusations of infidelity, and similarly one of the male patients was beaten by his wife. The situation is illustrated by one of our cases not included in this series who subjected her husband to repeated accusations of infidelity. The husband responded for the first few years of marriage with denials and attempts to placate his jealous wife, but following one particularly intense episode of accusation and cross-questioning he struck her. A pattern soon developed where the husband responded to the accusations by hitting and beating his wife. In this case the beatings became increasingly systematic and vicious. In joint interviews the sadistic gratification obtained by the husband from the violence was revealed, and fortunately the pattern of violence stopped, but not before the wife had sustained several fractures.

Jealousy is the ideal solution for the closet sadomasochist. The sadistic elements can be indulged by the attacks on the partner and the masochistic by the pain of betrayal and loss. Ankles (1939) noted the frequency of sadomasochistic motivations and fantasies in subjects with so-called normal jealousy. The fantasies accompanying jealousy have been little studied, but both Schmideberg (1953) and Seeman (1979) noted in their female patients sadomasochistic fantasies and the intentional use of visions of their spouse in sexual activity with the rival as a masturbatory fantasy. In several of our male patients, sexual excitement and masturbation was the accompaniment of fantasies of the partner with the rival. Some patients indulged in vivid fantasies of their partner being raped and abused by the supposed rival.

Children may become enmeshed both directly and indirectly in the jealousy afflicting their parents. Seidenberg (1967) suggested that jealousy may be excited by the wife's attention towards their child. She suggests that in modern society where jealousy of one's own child is intolerable, it may be displaced onto the more acceptable belief in the intrusion of another adult, even a fantasied one. Jealousy, as well as being displaced from the child, may be directed at the child. The child may be seen as evidence of the infidelity in that it is the rival's child and may, as a result, be the victim of aggression. In the series of 138 cases, six of the male patients were violent towards their young children, one making a potentially murderous attack. One man entertained sadistic and murderous fantasies towards his child, though never acted upon them.

A case not included in the series illustrates this interaction. The patient was a man in his early twenties who, though overly dependent on his wife, had not shown any overt jealousy until her first pregnancy. He then began accusing her of having a sexual relationship with the obstetrician, both in her initial prenatal contacts and right up to and including the confinement. Following the wife returning home with the child, his jealousy became centred on the child. He was not only jealous of the child's relationship with the wife but believed the child wilfully annoyed and frustrated him. This ended tragically with him killing the infant when it was 6 weeks old.

CONCLUSION

Jealousy has as its core the elements of anger and aggression towards the partner. This is as true of so-called normal jealousy as it is of the pathological extensions. An attempt has been made in this chapter to clarify the concept of jealousy and to provide a clinical framework for understanding and classifying its pathologies. Jealousy occurs in relationships and, in all but the clearest cases of Symptomatic Jealousy, it cannot be understood in isolation from this context. The degree of violence documented in our series of patients underlines the dangerousness of this passion to the sufferer and the loved one. In its less florid manifestations amongst those of us not so overtly disturbed, it still remains a distressing and disruptive emotion; 'a creeping skeleton around the frozen marriage bed' (Blake, 1793).

REFERENCES

American Psychiatric Association (1980) *Diagnostic and Statistical Manual of Mental Disorders (DSM III)*. Washington, DC: APA.
Ankles, T. M. (1939) *A Study of Jealousy as Differentiation from Envy*. London: A. H. Stockwell.
Blake, W. (1793) Visions of the Daughters of Albion. Reprinted in G. Keynes (Ed.) *Complete Writings*. Oxford: Oxford University Press, 1972.

Bohm, E. (1961) Jealousy. In A. Ellis (Ed.) *The Encyclopedia of Sexual Behavior*. New York: The Corsano Co.

Boranga, G. (1981) 'On the psychogenesis of jealousy—paranoic psychosis'. Unpublished thesis, Royal Australian and New Zealand College of Psychiatrists.

Cobb, J. (1979) Morbid jealousy. *British Journal of Hospital Medicine*, 21, 511–518.

Descartes, R. (1953) *Œuvres et Lettres*. Paris: Bibliotheque de la Plelade Gallimard.

Dominik, M. (1970) Pathological jealousy in delusional syndromes. *Acta Medica Polona*, 11, 267–280.

Ey, H. (1950) Jealousie Morbide. In *Etudes Psychiatriques*, vol. 2. Paris: Desclée de Brouwer et Cie.

Freud, S. (1922) *Some Neurotic Mechanisms in Jealousy, Paranoia and Homosexuality*. Standard edition (Ed. J. Strachey), XVIII, 221–232. London: Hogarth Press, 1955.

Gayford, J. J. (1975) Wife battering; a preliminary survey of 100 cases. *British Medical Journal*, 1, 194–197.

Gayford, J. J. (1979) Battered wives. *British Journal of Hospital Medicine*, 22, 496–503.

Hafner, R. J. (1979) Agoraphobic women married to abnormally jealous men. *British Journal of Medical Psychology*, 52, 99–104.

International Statistical Classification of Diseases (1968). *A Glossary of Mental Disorders*. London: HMSO.

Jaremko, M. E. and Lindsey, R. (1979) Stress-coping abilities of individuals high and low in jealousy. *Psychological Reports*, 44, 547–553.

Jaspers, K. (1910) Eifersuchtswahn. *Zeitschrift für die gesamte Neurologie und Psychiatrie*, 1, 567–637.

Jones, E. (1948) Jealousy. In *Papers on Psycho-analysis*, pp. 325–340. London: Bailliére Tindall and Cox.

Kendler, K. S. (1980) Are there delusions specific for paranoid disorders vs schizophrenia? *Schizophrenia Bulletin*, 6, 1–3.

Klein, M. (1957) *Envy and Gratitude*. London: Tavistock.

Krafft-Ebing, R. von (1905) *Text Book of Insanity*, pp. 513–514 (trans. C. G. Chaddock). Philadelphia: F. A. Davis.

Kretschmer, E. (1952) *A Textbook of Medical Psychology* (trans. E. B. Strauss). London: Hogarth Press.

Lagache, D. (1947) *La Jalousie Amoureuse*. Paris: Presses Universitaires de France.

Lagache, D. (1950) Homosexuality and jealousy. *International Journal of Psychoanalysis*, 31, 24–31.

Langfeldt, G. (1961) The erotic jealousy syndrome: a clinical study. *Acta Psychiatrica Scandinavica Supplements 151*.

Langfeldt, G. (1962) The erotic jealousy syndrome. *Journal of Neuro-Psychiatry*, 3, 317–321.

Maack, L. H. and Mullen, P. E. (in preparation) The morbidly jealous and their loved ones: on aggression in morbidly jealous patients. Unpublished paper.

Mooney, H. (1965) Pathologic jealousy and psychochemotherapy. *British Journal of Psychiatry*, 111, 1023–1042.

Mowat, R. R. (1966) *Morbid Jealousy and Murder*. London: Tavistock.

Mullen, P. E. (1984) Introduction to descriptive psychopathology. In P. McGuffin and M. Shanks (Eds) *Scientific Principles of Psychopathology*. London: Academic Press.

Neu, J. (1980) Jealous thoughts. In A. O. Rorty (Ed.) *Explaining Emotions* pp. 425–464. Berkeley: University of California Press.

Ødegaard, J. (1968) Interaksjonen Mellom Partnerne ved de Patologiske Sjalusireaksjoner. *Nordisk Psykiatrisk Tidsskrift*, 22, 314–319.

Pinta, E. R. (1978) Pathological tolerance. *American Journal of Psychiatry*, **135**, 698–701.

Podolsky, E. (1961) Jealousy as a motive in homicide. *Disorders of the Nervous System*, **22**, 438–441.

Post, R. D. *et al*. (1980) A preliminary report on the prevalence of domestic violence among psychiatric inpatients. *American Journal of Psychiatry*, **137**, 974–975.

Psarska, A. D. (1970) Jealousy factor in homicide in forensic psychiatric material. *Polish Medical Journal*, **9**, 1504–1510.

Reik, T. (1957) *Of Love and Lust*. New York: Grove Press.

Retterstøl, N. (1967) Jealousy—paranoic psychosis: a personal follow-up study. *Acta Psychiatrica Scandinavica*, **43**, 75–107.

Retterstøl, N. (1970) *Prognosis in Paranoid Psychosis*. Springfield, Illinois: Charles C. Thomas.

Ruin, R. (1933) *La Jalousie Homicide*. Thèse, Université de Paris.

Schmideberg, M. (1953) Some aspects of jealousy and of feeling hurt. *Psychoanalytic Review*, **40**, 1–16.

Seeman, M. V. (1979) Pathological jealousy. *Psychiatry*, **42**, 351–361.

Seidenberg, R. (1967) Fidelity and jealousy: socio-cultural considerations. *Psychoanalytic Review*, **54**, 583–608.

Shepherd, M. (1961) Morbid jealousy: some clinical and social aspects of a psychiatric symptom. *Journal of Mental Science*, **107**, 687–753.

Solomons, R. C. (1976) *The Passions*. New York: Doubleday-Anchor.

Spielman, M. D. (1971) Envy and jealousy: an attempt at classification. *Psychoanalytic Quarterly*, **40**, 59–82.

Spinoza, B. (1948) *Ethics*. London: Dent.

Sullivan, H. S. (1953) *The Interpersonal Theory of Psychiatry*. New York: W. W. Norton.

Teismann, M. W. and Mosher, D. L. (1978) Jealous conflict in dating couples. *Psychological Reports*, **42**, 1211–1216.

Tipton, R. M., Benedictson, C. S., Mahoney, J. and Hartnett, J. J. (1978) Development of a scale for assessment of jealousy. *Psychological Reports*, **42**, 1217–1218.

Todd, J. (1978) The jealous patient. *The Practitioner*, **220**, 229–233.

Todd, J., Mackie, J. R. M. and Dewhurst, K. (1971) Real or imaginary hypophallism: a cause of inferiority feelings and morbid sexual jealousy. *British Journal of Psychiatry*, **119**, 315–318.

Tov-Ruach, L. (1980) Jealousy, attention and loss. In A. O. Rorty (Ed.) *Explaining Emotions* pp. 465–488. Berkeley: University of California Press.

Turbott, J. (1981) Morbid jealousy, an unusual presentation with the reciprocal appearance of psychopathology in either spouse. *Australia and New Zealand Journal of Psychiatry*, **15**, 164-167.

Vauhkonen, K. (1968) On the pathogenesis of morbid jealousy. *Acta Psychiatrica Scandinavica Supplements 202*.

Aggression and Dangerousness
Edited by D. P. Farrington and J. Gunn
© 1985 John Wiley & Sons Ltd.

CHAPTER 6

The Psychodynamics of Borderline Personality

PATRICK L. G. GALLWEY

In forensic psychiatry one sees cases that do not fit at all easily into the established diagnostic categories so that very general terms such as 'personality disorder', 'psychopathic disorder', 'atypical such-and-such' are in common usage. These terms, although very loose, nevertheless do represent some differentiation between those patients who are amenable to psychiatric treatment within the ordinary framework of general psychiatry and those in which the question of treatment response is very much more uncertain and depends upon a number of factors, not least among which will be the availability of a good psychotherapist. Many psychiatrists doubtful of the value of psychotherapy will exclude, as far as possible, those cases which they do not feel fall reasonably within the sphere of influence of established psychiatric practice and confine themselves to those who are clearly mentally ill or diagnosable within familiar parameters of neurotic illness. As a forensic psychiatrist it is almost impossible to practise in this way if one is concerned with more than simple assessment in the narrowest sense and want to develop, improve, and discover ways of responding to these atypical and difficult cases.

In order to decide what cases one can help, and in what way, one needs something more than the existing very broad categorization between illness and personality disorder, or at least some simple nosology which will have heuristic value for treatment possibilities and guidance with management. One of the difficulties with many psychotherapeutic models is that they are far too complex for general use or mask their lack of practical value with esoteric terminology which may, in fact, only restate the problem in another language. It is also no use if one gives as the definition of a condition something that cannot be ascertained within the framework in which one is employing the terminology. Because of the complexity of psychiatric cases and the elusiveness of the data on which one hopes to base diagnosis and treatment it is inevitable that practical psychopathological descriptions have to be rather general. Any psychodynamic models for immediate use connected with these general descriptions must take account of the lack of precision, but nevertheless must have some empirical specificity as well.

One of the most demanding examples in this regard are offender patients who appear to have a psychotic parameter to their disturbance which may, or may not, have entered directly into the offending behaviour and for which the direct evidence is either transient or very elusive amongst a plethora of disturbed emotions and destructive behaviour. Such cases are very common amongst those referred by non-medical agencies, such as the Probation Service or the Courts, who pick up the strangeness within their client's mental life and, feeling that they are dealing with something irrational which suggests mental illness, quite rightly refer them for a psychiatric opinion. Very frequently no direct evidence for what worried the observer can be discovered at interview, and all too often such referrals are written off as not suffering from a psychiatric condition and, very possibly, simulating mental illness for their own manipulative ends. Consequently, no further involvement is offered.

Quite often the disturbance of which those referring the patient had become aware may occur in one particular set of circumstances, or within one set of interpersonal relationships. Almost all workers who are engaged consistently with offenders know that many whose maladjusted behaviour appears to be purely hedonistic or antisocial in some simple sense are very actively disturbed in some episodic or cleverly concealed way so that it is hard to investigate the disturbance or its connection with the maladjustment. In others the episodes of disturbance are more floridly psychotic, and may parallel the major mental illnesses, but pursue an atypical course. It is, for instance, difficult to be involved for very long with disturbed offenders without admitting the reality of functional schizophreniform reactions in which there can be indications of first-rank symptomatology but which fail to show the expected course of an established illness.

There are therefore a whole range of conditions, from elusive suggestions of a psychotic process to open manifestations of atypical mental illness, which in line with the need to give rather general descriptions that effectively distinguish such cases from the established categories, are frequently called borderline states, borderline patients and even borderline personalities. Since the terms cover a wide variety of different conditions with the single common characteristic that they have an affinity with another set of conditions more accurately defined (the mental illnesses) but with much uncertainty about the extent or content of any intersection, then it is inappropriate to describe such a heterogeneous group as constituting a 'syndrome' or even a 'condition', as is sometimes done. This does not mean, of course, that one should not try to find sub-sets which do contain some uniformity within the general set of such loosely gathered cases, and it would be comforting to think that one could turn to the literature of the borderline patient to discover some help in this direction.

Unfortunately the situation has become increasingly confused and, although much of the abundant literature on the subject is interesting, informative, and sometimes helpful, there is also an enormous muddle which has grown around the use of the term. Before offering a psychodynamic model which I think can be used to make some practical, clinical differentiations within this heterogeneous group it is necessary to look at some features of the confusion surrounding the use of the term.

THE BORDERLINE ISSUE

It is puzzling why so many authors appear to feel that there must be a single condition to which this term properly refers. Many case studies, often interesting in their own right, nevertheless speak as if they had discovered the defining characteristics of a single condition and that what is true for one patient, or a group of similar patients, is likely to apply necessarily to others who have been similarly designated by someone else. In the excellent examinations of the topic by such authors as Gunderson and Singer (1975) or Perry and Klerman (1978), which demonstrate well the very wide use of the term, the authors nevertheless clearly find it difficult to accept their own findings and offer new sets of criteria for the 'diagnosis' or urge more research to discover its correct use. In his excellent short account of the development of the term Chessick (1965) describes very lucidly its various usages, both clinical and psychoanalytic, but persists in referring to 'the condition'.

It is true that historically the term has often been linked to particular issues or attempts to establish a new psychiatric disease category such as latent schizophrenia or pseudo-neurotic schizophrenia. Its more recent popular general use and widening scope almost certainly results from a greater exposure of psychiatrists to groups of patients suffering from different kinds of disturbance than have been traditionally referred for professional opinion. The growth of forensic psychiatry is a case in point. This widening scope of the use of the term has been accompanied by an inability to tolerate the fact that a name can be used for the purposes of broad identification, and this contradiction seems to have particularly affected the Americans. It is odd that a professional group who would not dream of using, say, 'bisexuality' as a diagnostic category should have been engaged in a determined endeavour to make an entity out of a perfectly respectable and useful general descriptive label.

This endeavour has now resulted in the DSM III (1980) including a Borderline Personality Disorder in its classification of personality disorders. The recommended criteria for making the diagnosis were obtained by the factor analysis of a large number of cases in which the term had been used and represent, therefore, a common denominator of factors relevant to the group selected for the factor analysis. As a reflection no doubt of the popularity of the term as a quasi-diagnosis in America (see Perry and Klerman, 1978) these criteria no longer contain reference to psychotic symptomatology as definitive.

Instead there are a number of other personality types listed that contain a clearer connection with psychotic disorders such as 'schizotypal', 'paranoid', or 'narcissistic personality' disorders. All of these can be used to complement 'borderline personality disorder' which is said to be frequently associated with other personality disorders. It is difficult to imagine how anything useful can come out of this artificially created diagnostic category. Any groups of patients within the original total sample who, in fact, shared a common more specific psychopathology have had their undiscovered common disability defined out, and there now exists a psuedo-condition which can be treated as a definable entity so that spurious comparisons can be made and research conducted with multiplication of the basic error.

It is true that there are a number of works on borderline patients which discuss a range of conditions. Kernberg (1975) and Stone (1980) both use a wide scope for the term and suggest hypotheses in relation to unitary factors underlying their different clinical types, and Grinker et al. (1968) have offered a categorization of sub-groups based on a careful evaluation of a selected series. Such works are of much potential value but are of only limited use to the general clinician because they are complicated and their immediate clinical relevance somewhat uncertain. This also applies to a great deal of the psychoanalytical literature on the subject, which is very substantial.

The term 'borderline' has in psychoanalysis become bound up with the concept of narcissism, for which there are a number of definitions and a number of different competing theories. Frequently both terms are used quite loosely, and they usually mean that some aspect of a patient is felt to have some more or less well-defined link with the psychopathology of the psychosis. Psychoanalytic theories of psychosis, and of the part psychotic mechanisms play in the problems of personality and neurosis have been well developed particularly in Britain in the so-called British School of Psychoanalysis following Fairbairn, Winnicott, and Klein, and in America Kernberg and Kohut are in the vanguard of contemporary theorists. Some of the more important international papers on the borderline group of conditions within the psychoanalytic setting are now available in collected forms (see Le Boit and Capponi, 1979).

It is possible, therefore, for the psychoanalytical psychotherapist to approach the treatment of cases which might not at one time have been considered suitable for psychotherapy because of indications of psychotic disturbance within their histories or presenting symptomatology. Part of the problem for the general psychiatrist is to use the psychoanalytic developments in clinical practice, in terms of either categorization into broad groups for practical purposes such as designing treatments or making referrals for psychotherapy. Many of the concepts connected with such patients' disturbances are derived within the special setting of psychoanalysis and are not necessarily obtainable, or usable, outside it.

There is a further, much less respectable stumbling block to the use of psychoanalytic literature for the understanding of these groups of patients, and that is the idiosyncratic way in which some analysts use their terminology. This is very well illustrated in the much-quoted paper by Stern (1938) that gave popularity to the term 'borderline patient'. In this paper he discusses patients who, as part of a range of symptoms, became very angry and disturbed when difficulties in psychoanalytic work were encountered and he calls this a tendency to 'negative therapeutic reaction'. He gives other criteria which identify the characteristics of his particular group which he calls 'the borderline group of neuroses'.

The term 'negative therapeutic reaction' was originally coined by Freud to describe his observation that some of his patients appeared to have become worse directly after a successful phase of treatment. They showed a negative reaction to positive progress and this paradox, he felt, was essentially connected with an unconscious sense of guilt which produced a moral masochism making it impossible for them, out of guilt, to take advantage of anything which made them feel better. Later psychoanalytical theorists noted the importance of the negative therapeutic reaction as an expression of anti-developmental impulses, particularly in its relationship to psychotic processes (see Rosenfeld, 1970) and, by extension, to a whole group of conditions designated as 'borderline'. Clearly Stern means something different by 'negative therapeutic reaction' from this other group of writers because he is using it to describe patients who become excessively upset in connection with difficult experiences. Of course this discrepancy is likely to be missed by many trying to compare different psychoanalytic papers on the subject.

Stern's cases are very different from, say, Deutsch's group of 'as-if' patients described in her 1945 paper, and very popularly quoted in the literature on the borderline issue without the difference from Stern's group being noted. Deutsch described her patients as seeming to be depersonalized without their being aware of it. She used the term 'as-if' personality to highlight the artificiality of their sense of normality which, according to Deutsch, can nevertheless be discerned as lacking in emotional depth. This deficiency emerged in treatment as a profound disturbance of personal identity which Deutsch believed might have relevance to schizophrenia, and she described them as being schizoid. Her cases were not given to aggressive outbursts or florid behavioural disturbances. They were rather shy and passive, although inclined to criminality or bad behaviour because of their openness to suggestibility and a tendency to quick concrete identification with external figures.

I do not wish to discuss the technical psychoanalytic relevance of Deutsch's paper, but the concept of the 'as-if' personality has proved meaningful for many clinicians and the concept of artificially based personalities, giving a false impression of normality, has been developed by Winnicott (1955). Many authors who have written on cases which have been designated as 'borderline' have mentioned the paradox of individuals who are achievers or socially well adapted but who have episodes of disturbance which seem quite out of character with their everyday personalities (see Knight, 1953; Chessick, 1965; Kernberg, 1975). The potential for these severe bouts of disturbance seems incompatible with the way they present, and certainly with the immediate appraisal of their life histories and achievements. Sometimes it remains contradictory even when one looks more closely at their life histories and one finds patients who are unquestionably successful, talented, and have areas of adaptation and development quite at variance with the emergence of sudden, severe psychotic level illness.

I want to take this paradoxical characteristic as a focus of interest and suggest two broad categories of individual who present with dual personalities in which a false self or pseudo-normal ego is in dynamic balance with a more pathologically disordered area of the self. I am hoping to show that the two categories can be fairly readily clinically differentiated, have different aetiologies and different prognoses, provide different problems for treatment and management, and are well represented among offender patients. I am not attempting to claim that these groups represent the main body of patients for which the term 'borderline' is generally used, or indeed that the terms should be reserved for these particular groups. I shall provide psychodynamic models which I hope have practical value and on which further research into the reality of my two broad subgroups might be based.

TWO TYPES OF DUAL PERSONALITIES

Knight (1953) describes a situation in which the ego of patients he classifies as 'borderline' seems to occupy two positions. He borrows Freud's metaphor of the deployment of military forces to illustrate the concept of regression to fixation points and applies this to his observations on the dual ego-functioning of this group of borderline patients. One position he described as a forward holding position which might contain within its scope certain neurotic symptoms. The other position is occupied by the major part of the ego which he described as being in a state of regression and more severely disordered. He discussed the implications of his model for treatment and for diagnosis. He suggested that clinicians who conduct a superficial examination will take the forward holding position as representing the patient's problem and would, of course, be overtaken by the unexpectedness of the more hidden regressed part of the ego.

Although Knight's model is somewhat over-reliant on metaphor and not properly worked out in structural terms, nevertheless it does emphasize that, if one is to understand this group of patients who present as relatively normal but are harbouring a more grave disturbance, then it is necessary to take into account the duality of personality structure. As much attention seems to be paid to the capacity for adaptation in the presence of grave disturbance as to the disturbance itself. It is the balance, and loss of balance, between these two areas which is crucial in shaping the patient's presentation. I think two broad categories of dual personality structure can be distinguished:

Type A: Those with concealed ego deficiences resulting from early prolonged infantile deprivation; and
Type B: Those with schizoid encapsulation of destructive impulses.

Type A — Clinical and Theoretical Considerations

A psychodynamic model based on the general hypothesis of a false personality organization covering an essential hollowness of properly developed ego resources produced by deprivation must take into account the nature of the ego deficiencies, the specific effects of deprivation, and conceptualize in more detail how the false self is constructed. The study of effects of infantile deprivation within both social and psychoanalytic frames of reference has been pioneered by Spitz (1965) and Bowlby (1971). However the influence of their findings and formulations on the main body of psychoanalytic development has not been very great. In fact the specific effects of severe infantile deprivation have never played a large part in psychoanalytic theories. Freud made no distinction between the deprivation of need and the frustration of instinct; many later psychoanalytic theories have tended to reflect this original bias and, although in Fairburn's structural model psychopathology is purely reactive, nevertheless the most convincing techniques rely on the analysis of frustration and instinctual conflict. I offer here a compressed account of my own conceptualization, based on clinical observations and heavily reliant on the work of others.

I am concerned particularly with the effects of early deprivation within the mother/child relationship on the inchoate ego, which produces widespread permanent disability in the capacity to develop progressive psychological independence. I suggest these effects will include as continuing problems:

1. A deformed sense of identity with disturbances in body image and feelings of depersonalization which, during periods of stress, lead to a collapse of psychological containment or an organized sense of self.
2. A poverty of defences against emotional turbulence produced by internal or external factors which, together with (1), give rise to escalating anxiety and incontinence of impulse control instead of adaptive responses.
3. A reduced capacity to manage appropriate separation experiences from figures of dependence giving clinging, excessive ambivalence and violent jealousy.

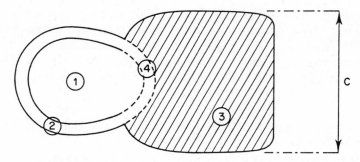

Figure 1 False self-personality organization, type A: 1 = disorganized core;
2 = 'eggshell' ego; 3 = fetishistic or host object identification (area of pseudo-ego
organization); 4 = unrealized ego potential; C = presenting personality

4. A continual sense of sensual starvation and profound loss with hopeless
   feelings of poverty and unworthiness accompanied by a deep sense of having
   been cheated. The general depressive tone to the affective basis of the
   personality is complicated by primitive feelings of revenge.

These basic areas of deficiency are more or less coped with and reacted against by
various mechanisms and strategies, many of which are poorly understood and
need much further study, but which, when well developed, produce a
functioning ego which, like a brittle eggshell, clothes and disguises the essential
hollowness of proper personality foundations (see Fig. 1). I would list the
following reaction formations to the specific problems outlined above as
important basic psychological strategies in the construction of such a brittle ego:

1. Artificial support of the self by the use of primitive fantasies of
   possessing or controlling the object. When total this can lead to a disguised
   parasitic reliance on a host structure. When less complete such fantasies are
   supported in infancy and childhood by various forms of self-stimulation
   giving rise, in later life, to a reliance on the use of objects in a fetishistic
   manner or a preoccupation with body, exhibitionism, and in-group rituals of
   various kinds. Women have an advantage over men here by being more able
   to use their bodies directly, together with socially based encouragement to
   corporal idealization, to support the fantasy of actually being the early
   nurturing objects in idealized form. This is probably one reason why sexual
   perversions, most forms of criminal behaviour, and a general over-reliance
   on domineering modes of conduct are so much more common in men who
   have further to go in sustaining their conviction of successfully identifying
   with or dominating prototypic ideal maternal objects.
2. A reduced capacity to develop psychologically based buffers against conflict
   is a serious problem. Anxiety is poorly controlled and a tendency to
   nightmare and excessive paranoid fantasy formation in childhood leads in

later life to a deficiency in a mobile repertoire of unconscious fantasies able to modify emotional turbulence. This, in turn, leads to attempts to replace these with behavioural equivalents. Such 'acting out' behaviour is usually interpersonally destructive, socially unacceptable, and manipulative.

3. Intolerance of separation experiences is partly overcome by endeavouring to reverse the problem. This may be achieved largely in fantasy, leading to a variety of inversions in the perception of dependency needs, including perversion formations. Less omnipotently based strategies can be expressed in adulthood by promiscuity and reliance on various forms of seductive behaviour, so that the persons are compelled to prove continually that others require them rather than the other way round. The problem of interpersonal clinging can cause avoidance of emotional involvement altogether, leading to social isolation.

4. The emotional hunger and underlying sense of poverty give a vulnerability to sensation-seeking, drug and alcohol abuse, grandiosity, and 'manic' flight from misery often only sustainable by continual exploitative behaviour and short-term satisfactions. Because the aggression connected with the vengeful feelings cannot find legitimate expression, this may lead to a compliant, passive, even masochistic relationship with others, or be organized into some habitual expression of cruelty; when mixed with (1) it leads to violent attacks on the self.

The false self which is constructed from a mixture of such defensive reactions and the psychopathology underlying it can give rise to an openly disturbed personality or, when the deprivation is not too great and the defensive reaction well balanced, to a very convincing pseudo-normality. From the point of view of delinquent behaviour, antisocial conduct can be connected with expressions of the basic psychopathology or a feature of the defensive organization itself. Deprived and inadequate personalities with very poor defensive organizations abound in forensic psychiatry and within the penal system, and make up the bulk of habitual offenders (see West, 1963; Griffiths and Rundle, 1976).

Such poorly defended personalities have a clear tendency to collapse in the face of almost any hazard or frustration, are usually unable to sustain an independent existence, show frequent bouts of self-destructiveness, are almost continually manipulative and self-preoccupied, and are generally poorly contained individuals. The group which I am attempting to identify will be less clearly collapsed and their maladjustment may be associated with their defensive personality organization, in which case it may show more contained well-directed features. Much crime which appears to be consciously motivated by a need for material gain has less obvious psychological determinants connected with the avoidance of anxiety and negotiation of specific internal emotional crises not directly connected to the material circumstances of the individual. In endeavouring to identify patients with this type of personality organization it is important to try and distinguish phenomena which are connected with the defensive aspect of the personality and those which are connected with its collapse. I find the four areas of ego disability, listed above, taken in conjunction with the four suggested general defensive reactions, a useful guide in trying to orientate one's clinical judgement in this regard.

Such cases may also give a history of an early, usually fairly discreet, failure in the continuity or adequacy of the early nurturing environment although this is sometimes elusive. When a patient's mother was temporarily disturbed, say with a substantial puerperal depression, this fact may have been kept from the patient and minimized by the family. Early separation as an event is of less consequence for the infant's development than other circumstances surrounding it. The infant's prior physical and emotional state, the quality of care during the separation and the way the reunion was managed are some of the factors which may be impossible to evaluate many years later. It may be necessary to dig rather persistently for early problems connected with developmental hurdles and usually denial of developmental difficulties is supported by apparent adequacy of achievement which can reassure everyone, including the patients, that they have managed to grow out of their difficulties. These difficulties emerge from time to time and a detailed examination of the circumstances, emotional and factual, which characterize these episodes will help in building up a picture of the way the two areas of personality are balanced and the specific features of each.

Many authorities have given lists of symptoms and symptom complexes as defining characteristics of borderline patients, but the pattern of failure or success in overcoming problems, together with a history of early deprivation, is more important with this group than an attempt to list a constellation of defining symptoms. Equally, no one type of offending is necessarily associated with either aspect of the personality, but severe offending, including homicide, particularly homicide connected with excessive escalation of jealousy under the thread of impending loss, can most certainly occur as a manifestation of defensive ego collapse. Sometimes the more impulsive or violent behaviour can be as much a desperate attempt to establish some supportive link with an object of over-dependency as an expression of pure destructiveness.

Often, tragically for the individual, the environment does not live up to expectations, is too harsh, or actually evokes the very difficulties from which the individual is attempting to escape. One sees cases then where there is a steady worsening in the overall condition as the individual is passed from institution to institution, often getting further away from the kind of experiences which might have called a halt to the steady deterioration. Indeed institutions are probably the worst environment for such individuals from the point of view of positive change, since they have general characteristics which make them particularly meaningful to the individual's basic pathology. They often encourage resourceless parasitic dependency, increase confusion of identity, and frequently respond to crises by imposing protracted periods of isolation, thereby reproducing the type of experience from which the individual's difficulties have originated. The essential deprivation and emptiness of these patients gives a marked depressive component to the episodes of disturbance. On the other hand the hollowness of the organized part of the personality and the profound lack of proper psychological defences against stress (and particularly when there is heavy reliance on an omnipotent fantasy of confusion with other objects) may mean that such patients develop open confusional states in which frank paranoid delusions and occasionally hallucinations may mimic schizophrenia.[1] These psychotic reactions can occur when the environment is felt to become excessively harsh, or when there is a threat of the removal of the supportive framework; for instance prior to release from prison when reliance on the total institution has become psychologically critical.

These psychotic reactions may result in such cases being transferred to hospital as suffering from schizophrenia. Often when they arrive the condition settles as quickly as it developed, and this may be interpreted as the person simulating mental illness in order to prolong some form of comfortable institutional protection. Indeed there might be something in this formulation but the profundity of the need is missed, together with the reality of the psychosis. The same sort of disguised resourcelessness with a false self-relying on parasitism with a host structure can occur within families, schools, commercial and caring institutions, and certainly the uniformed services. It is in fact such pseudo-normality achieved by the use of an alter-ego which makes it so hard for these individuals to mobilize the appropriate concern in others for the genuineness of their disturbance.

When the fantasy of concrete identification with the environment that is supporting them is working well, then they are capable of a level of functioning which does not suggest the degree of potential disturbance and the magnitude of the area of hollowness. When things start to go wrong, and the institution or relationships on whom they are relying shifts in a way that makes it impossible for the fantasy to be continued, then one of the first responses is to attempt to impose direct control by some form of pressure. This is interpreted by institutional environments as 'manipulation'. In a sense, of course, this is right, but the manipulation which the observers believe they are perceiving is of a kind which suggests some trivial, demanding, rather spoilt insistence on getting their own way. The response is to say 'I must demonstrate that I am not prepared to be manipulated'. This inevitably leads to a clash in which the collapsing individual resorts to further more desperate efforts to push the environment back into a shape which he feels he can use to hold up his sense of descent into resourcelessness.

As well as pressures to control the environment, the sudden emergence of disorganized infantile feelings in a violent and aggressive way, combined with the characteristic escalation of ubiquitous paranoid reactions, make such individuals seem extremely intimidating and frightening, so that others' reactions to them during such crises can be very over-militant and confronting. In institutions these confrontations can become long-drawn-out affairs with increasing disturbance, responded to with an increase in sanctions and with resolution becoming more and more remote. Phrases such as 'refusing to be manipulated' and 'teaching such people a lesson' represent very well the underlying discrepancy in the environmental response due to a combination of anxiety and mystification in many institutions and groups who attempt the care and management of potentially collapsed and very disturbed individuals. In the management of such cases it is of prime importance to encourage a flexibility of response and to stimulate interest and enquiry into the particular characteristics of the individual's personality organization and specific vulnerabilities. This can be very difficult, and perhaps impossible, in settings where the formal more traditional attitudes have become part of the institutional mores.

Psychological treatment of this group of cases depends upon a more profound understanding and particularly on identifying the nature of reliance on an external structure for the maintenance of ego integrity. As pointed out above, a willingness to go along with the pressure from the patient, at least a bit of the way, an ability to avoid unnecessary confrontations, and a readiness to be used as an alter-ego, especially during periods of assessment and the establishment of more accurate treatment programmes, are essential. The combination of emotional deprivation, and the need for an object to hold them together, renders such individuals capable of only a limited response to chemotherapy even when open psychotic symptoms are present. The usual pitfall is to over-medicate with detrimental effects on the non-psychotic areas of ego resourcefulness. The excessively violent, possessive, and jealous reactions in relation to helpful figures, who have become idealized and incorporated in the patient's ego, can be very discouraging, as they will be most present when a good therapeutic alliance appears to have been established. Continuity of team members is very important, and changes of one group of personnel to another produce symptomatic relapse or behavioural crises. On the other hand, to encourage reliance on a number of people will obviate the problem of a single individual being intolerably and parasitically overburdened with the inevitable crises and flare-ups during holidays and weekends, or when attempting to relate to other patients.

Individual psychodynamic psychotherapy is usually contraindicated in such cases because of the concrete dependent transference and the underlying profound physical deprivation. A decision in this regard will depend upon the experience of the psychotherapist and his capacity to manage this type of problem within the psychotherapeutic setting and, of course, the extent and degree of the deprivation and the fragility of the 'false self'. Where the original trauma was fairly discrete and other environmental and constitutional factors more positive, particularly where other strategies than the parasitic exploitation of a host object play a part in maintaining the pseudo-normality, then individual transference-based psychotherapy can be very worthwhile. It may offer the patient by far the best chance of fundamental resolution of these long-standing difficulties. However any experience of being taken on, encouraged to become deeply attached, and then terminated suddenly may be catastrophic to patients who have managed to keep themselves going by avoiding precisely that type of hazard, which no amount of interpreting in the short term can possibly alleviate. These patients also find the group situation very difficult because of their problems of jealousy although, if these can be understood and managed, then regular long-term groups can provide valuable, legitimate support within the context of the patient's needs. The added advantage is that the more understanding situation may allow for some areas of greater personal coherence to come to the fore. No patients of this kind are entirely reliant upon external structures for their coherence, since otherwise they would not have survived.

The indication of some areas of independent functions can lead to the design of programmes aimed at the development of such nascent potential. The development of interpersonal skills by methods of psychological encouragement and training can be of great value in these cases and can help to strengthen the defensive ego structure. These treatments work best when the individuals have been helped to overcome their fear that they can only live through other people and that, by taking some initiative on their own behalf, they are not in fact walking towards abandonment and the threat of disintegration. Here the therapeutic structure, working temporarily as a host structure, should hold the situation in equilibrium for long enough for these areas of potential to become manifest and for a sense of confidence within the individual to begin to emerge. The biggest problem in maintaining this is the development of a negative environmental stance and the inevitable ambivalence of the individual to the holding structure which is characterized by idealization on the one hand and hostility and mistrust on the other. Such individuals often feel trapped, as indeed psychologically they are, and frequently struggle to get free from the very thing upon which they are relying. Typically they show both claustrophobic and agoraphobic anxieties. The struggle to get free accompanies a struggle to cling, and these contradictory impulses give rise to episodes of confusion and unpredictable crises.

An understanding of these contradictory impulses provides the key to understanding individual cases which, as a result, become much less confusing to the members of the holding structure and this usually paves the way for a return to a therapeutic alliance. In trying to help such individuals outside the institutional setting the same rules apply. In the counselling and support of individuals involved in the same psychodynamic set-up, it is just as important to try to move them towards a more confident utilization of their own resources and provide plenty of opportunities to talk through problems of management with those holding the patient, whether that be family, spouse, or professional workers.

Type B — General Considerations

Type B are not 'false self' personalities at all in Winnicott's sense, since the part of the ego in the 'forward holding position' is not a defensive organization in the same way as described in Type A. These are individuals who really do have a coherent area of ego functioning in their own right but who maintain it by operating a functional independence from more actively disturbed areas of their personality. Provided they are able to maintain this split organization within their personalities and, although they may suffer from certain problems and symptom complexes as a result (see below), nevertheless within the framework of this equilibrium they can be surprisingly successful with varying degrees of personal fulfilment and satisfaction.

The difference between the forensic and non-forensic cases seems to be in the way the split between the two areas of function breaks down. In the case of those who become offender-patients the 'ego-dystonic' impulses are discharged into the environment resulting in some catastrophic social behaviour. In the other, non-forensic group, the breakdown of the split threatens or actually disrupts the main body of the ego so that, very often, via an increase in projective mechanisms, paranoid psychotic episodes result, with social collapse, rather than social offending. Although I am making this distinction for the purposes of clarification, the situation may not be so fixed. Bizarre behaviour and psychotic symptoms may be interchangeable or both present in varying degrees during disturbed episodes. The identification of this category of borderline patients depends upon understanding the consequences of split ego organizations.

The Non-forensic Type B Cases — Clinical Considerations

These are frequently discovered incidentally. They often present for treatment, as Knight (1953) has pointed out, for problems which are a feature of the non-disturbed parts of their personality such as ordinary neurotic symptoms. Sometimes they may present for treatment of a sexual perversion, a psychosomatic illness, or with a more elusive request for help, such as some sense of emptiness or meaninglessness in their lives. Unless one goes into things very carefully before accepting the patient for treatment in psychotherapy then one can be in for a shock. What appeared to be a psychotherapy with promise of helpful movement turns out to be entirely static with the sort of superior stonewalling and inaccessibility first described by Abraham (1919), or there emerges a very much more psychotic situation. Strong paranoid feelings and fantasies, sometimes near-delusional, start to be expressed, an initially well-disguised grandiosity can give way to incoherence and confusion within the sessions, or the patient's communications take on some form of concrete symbolization reminiscent of schizophrenic thinking or manic grandiosity. Often as the history and life circumstances of the patient emerge in treatment it becomes clear that one should have taken longer in assessment before accepting the patient into treatment. Long-standing paranoid feelings or episodes of collapse emerge in the history, and any successful attempt at understanding or sign of improvement is often followed by sharp, bewildering, negative therapeutic reactions with a possibility of more open symptoms of a psychotic state.

It sometimes happens that patients of this kind refer themselves for treatment when they feel the organization of their psychodynamic set-up becoming unstable, in which case there should be evidence for this if one takes a careful history with particular regard to life events leading up to the referral for treatment. General psychiatrists may have cases referred for the same reason, and are perhaps less likely to look at the non-symptomatic areas of the patient's life in such detail before initiating symptomatic treatment. These cases form part of that group who do not respond to psycho-pharmacological treatments or other general psychiatric therapies in the way one would expect from taking their symptoms at their face value. Often their incipient paranoia becomes rationalized into running battles and long-standing negative confrontations with clinical teams, and they are generally experienced as very difficult, unrewarding, unresponsive cases. Sometimes the non-forensic cases are referred because of the episodic psychotic breakdowns which reflect a collapse in the split psychodynamic organization. These episodes may be triggered by some clear evidence of stress, such as bereavement or, more often, from a blow to self-esteem, such as a disappointment at work, failure in an examination, or some highly personal grievance that can be very difficult to understand. Sometimes the trigger is very obscure and indeed such patients may break down in the face of an improving situation when they get accepted for a job, get promotion, or get married, and this kind of paradoxical precipitant for severe episodic disturbance can altogether mask the reactive nature of the problem. These cases differentiate from schizophrenia on the basis of previous episodes without personality deterioration, the atypical presentation, and the patchy response to neuroleptics.

In the other less obviously disturbed cases, diagnosis rests upon being aware that the presenting personality of the individual may not appear frankly abnormal and extra weight has to be given to particular factors. There may be paranoia and grandiosity, with or without obsessionalism, or admissions of clandestine pathological activity, such as a well-organized perversion. But often, especially where the psychodynamic organization is maintained via a collusive relationship or within psychogenic physical handicap, then the personality can appear well within normal limits and, because of the lifestyle and personal achievement, the basic severity of the psychopathological organization may be easily missed. Within collusive relationships the less sick partner can present for treatment because he, or she, has been unable to maintain pressures from the pathological side of a long-standing unconscious collusion. These types of cases are the bane of marital therapists; because of the very profound nature of the collusive arrangement they do not respond well to counselling and can be very confusing within any therapeutic situation.

The Forensic Type B Cases — Clinical Considerations

Amongst offender–patients this type of encapsulated split organization was described by Williams (1964) in the treatment of sexual murders. It is more widely represented by a proportion of individuals who commit offences which would appear to be out of context with their personalities and life histories. The offending has bizarre, violent, and quasi-sexual features. The disturbed episodes in which the behaviour occurs are self-limiting, sometimes rapidly, and ritualization is a common factor. Even where there has been more than one episode no overall personality deterioration can be detected; in fact very often the individuals appear to have a remarkable capacity to reinstate themselves in their life situation so that this capacity for achievement and recovery highlights the paradox of their disturbed behaviour. There is a general feeling of some profound primitive confusion having overtaken an otherwise reasonably adjusted individual but it would be rare to detect active psychotic symptoms or signs at examination.

Sometimes the individuals may be described as behaving strangely for a period before the offence and themselves may report a change, often very rapid, in their mental experiences; features of depersonalization or feelings of detachment and unreality are a constant feature. Sometimes amnesia, either total or partial, is reported and this is more often the case when the behaviour is catastrophically violent or homicidal. These individuals show the same rough groupings which characterize the non-forensic cases although psychosomatic cases do seem, in my experience, to be protected from severe behavioural breakdowns. Paranoid or obsessional features may emerge which appear to have been compatible with a reasonable degree of social adaptation prior to the offence and, where there have been previous offences, to have been compatible with an apparently satisfactory rehabilitation. Others may have a veiled sense of superiority, grandiosity, or self-absorption which suggests a great deal of narcissistic self-regard and is a warning of a more substantial propensity for paranoia. In others careful assessment reveals problems such as a sexual perversion, features of behaviour eccentricity, or a non-habitual delinquency which, although apparently compatible with a reasonable overall social adaptation and even successful heterosexual relations nevertheless do indicate that the primitive pathology has become organized, giving the individual a double lifestyle. In these cases the puzzle is why an apparently stable area of disturbance, such as a well-organized and perhaps common type of sexual perversion, should break down into open, malicious, violent, or bizarre behaviour and just as quickly disappear with the reinstatement of the *status quo*. In these cases the sexual perversion does not escalate progressively and the violent or sadistic aspects of the episodes are not necessarily directly suggested by the habitual perversion with which one assumes they are connected.

There is a final sub-group in which it proves impossible in ordinary clinical assessment to identify any psychopathology which one could satisfactorily link with the offending behaviour. The individuals may be rather passive or shy, but not to such a degree that they are socially crippled. They may have neurotic symptoms but nothing which would suggest or explain the profundity or strangeness of the catastrophic behaviour. In this group, because the pathological behaviour is so atypical, an organic aetiology is often suspected and, even when investigations reveal no evidence of this, some constitutional abnormality is usually put forward to explain the aberrant behaviour.

Precisely because all these sub-groups show personality capacities of a positive kind, and particularly when they lack psychopathic traits or antisocial tendencies in their normal phase, they will often manage well in custodial settings. This is always provided the environment does not clash with their psychopathological collusive arrangement, in which case their behaviour may deteriorate or they may become more openly psychotic. The sexually perverse and the apparently normal groups generally adapt well to the demands of such institutions, and do not raise staff anxieties or cause disciplinary worries. Typically any psychotherapy they are offered is very cursory. Their attitude to their own criminal behaviour is usually that of convincing disownership or confident rationalization. They may appear well motivated and, because they present so little pathology in their everyday patterns of relating, most therapists are seduced into a sense of reassurance. Since there is very little to pursue in the way of manifest pathology, treatment remains supportive, un-explorative, and completely ineffectual. If there are discernible aberrant features within the personality, some measure of progress can be made according to the prominence of the personality disability. Schizoid personalities may become rather more outgoing or the paranoid features may become less prominent, so that some sense of progression can be identified on which to base recommendations for release or termination of treatment. Where the personality appears more normal these cases really present the most difficult problem for prediction and recommendation.

If offending recurs it often happens after a successful period of rehabilitation and against a background of apparently improving social and psychological adjustment. The cases are important because of the gravity of the offending, and also because of the good overall personality features which, taken at their face value, suggest a good prognosis for general rehabilitation or psychological treatments. The difficulty is to relate the manifest episodic pathology to any psychotherapeutic procedure in a meaningful or effective way. The elusiveness of psychopathological equivalents in the personality, and the encapsulated disturbance, reduce psychotherapeutic activity to intellectual discussions. Even skilled therapists may lose their capacity to do direct work with relevant emotions, and many therapists seem to lack an adequate psychodynamic model on which to base their work with such patients.

Type B — Theoretical Model

I find the following psychodynamic theoretical model useful in conceptualizing the psychopathology of this group of borderline patients, and I think it has a degree of consistency and relevance to the empirical facts. It is a modification and simplification of highly developed psychoanalytic theories and is based upon the hypothesis of ego splitting developed by Fairbairn (1940) and Klein (1946). It also includes the concept of impulses which are incompatible with ego integration and normal functioning (see Klein, 1957; Bion, 1956, 1959). The theory of splitting differs fundamentally from the traditional linear psychoanalytic model of the mind. In the classical model ego dystonic conflicts are repressed into the main core of the unconscious with a failure in repression giving rise to symptoms modified by the particular characteristics of progressive zones of development, any resultant contemporary symptom being a reflection of an evolutionary change in symptom form through successive layers of ego development. More primitive areas of conflict can only be uncovered or produced if the more recently developed ego functions are lost, making regression a *sine qua non* for the emergence of primitive level pathology in any direct way.

Figure 2 illustrates the linear model diagrammatically. Figure 3 illustrates a model based on a stabilized (encapsulated) split ego organization where primitive pathology can be expressed without regression of the developed ego functions. I shall use a notation developed by Bion (1962) and derived directly from his psychoanalytic writings but used here in a very much simplified and somewhat altered form. α-Function is that part of ego function which assimilates basic drives, emotional conflicts, and traumatic experiences so that they do not dominate consciousness and disrupt the continual fine adaptation of ego organization to contemporary needs. This is achieved by the transformation and distribution of such strong psychic stuff into various modes of mental activity. It provides a background tone of meaning to existence and creates more specialized mental functions from the various types of thinking to dreaming. Minor α-dysfunctions will produce such symptoms as ruminative thinking, nightmares, persecutory ideas, maladapted behaviour such as

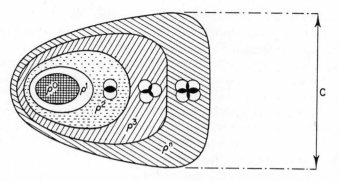

Figure 2 Neurotic personality organization (classical model): p^0 = reservoir of polymorphous instinctual drives; p^1 = primary repressive ego; p^2– p^n = developmental phases; ● = phase-linked symptoms; C = personality type

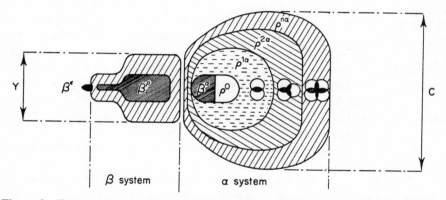

Figure 3 False self-personality organization (type B); β^p = β-elements in β-system; β^ε = discharging element; Y = type of β- system organization; β^α = β-elements in α-system; p^0 = object-related drives; $p^{1\alpha-n\alpha}$ = phase-linked α-function; ● = phase-linked symptoms; C = presenting personality

obsessionalism, and impulsive behaviour. Psychotic symptomatology results from major disruption to α-function. β-Elements in Bion's formulations are ego dystonic, incapable of assimilation by α-function, unable to link together to form organized psychic structures, and can only be dealt with by evacuation (projection).

I am suggesting a less complete situation where α-function can manage β-elements up to a certain point and where β-elements can be organized under special conditions into a separate system. The main body of the ego (the α-system) is freed from the threat of malignant impulses (β-elements) which would be incompatible with its coherence. It manages a functional independence from these impulses, which develop their own organization (the β-system) more or less completely, giving rise to a split bimodal organization. Relatively normal ego development can then ensue within the α-system and the extent to which functional independence of this healthy system is incomplete will be the extent to which a leakage of β-elements occurs into the system which are partly 'metabolized' by α-function. These, together with conflicts arising in the α-system, create zonally determined symptom formation (α-symptoms) in much the same way as in the classical model. Symptoms arising from partly metabolized β-elements would be obsessive–compulsive symptoms, depressive and paranoid ideation, violent or persecutory nightmares, and a whole series of non-specific malfunctions compatible with an overall α-system integration and adaptability but having a psychotic flavour.

The split off β-elements are organized in a different manner giving rise to a system (the β-system) which is socially or interpersonally dystonic to a greater or lesser degree, sometimes only manageable within a pathological collusion. The β-system may acquire some quite elaborate functions for itself and be organized into a double-life activity, such as a clandestine perversion or delinquent activity. It may, through omnipotent fantasy, become projected into another object producing, where there is collusive participation on the part of the other object or groups of objects, a disguised paranoid grandiosity (narcissism) of one kind or another. Where collusive interpersonal participation is not a feature, then a more active paranoid way of perceiving certain life events will result. Sometimes there appears to be very little projection into environmental objects, the split area remaining an un-owned area of psychic activity giving experiences of a mystic or quasi-mystic variety, sometimes perhaps amounting to episodic atypical hallucinosis or an habitual paranoid point of view.

This produces a schizoid personality in which encapsulation is only weak. Chronic exacerbating psychosomatic illness can be explained by conceptualizing the β-elements as becoming somatized, thereby removing unacceptable feelings and fantasies from the psychic systems altogether with a resultant impoverishment of the capacity for imagination and the expression of feelings in words, a phenomenon which has come to be described as 'alexithymia' (see Nemiah and Sifneos, 1970). The way the β-system is organized can change from time to time, producing a change in symptomatology. The organization of the equilibrium between the two systems can break down so that severe disturbances of one kind or another result. I have suggested above that, where β-elements are discharged excessively into the α-system by a process of breakdown in the split between the two systems, there is a crisis within the person's normal personality structure with an escalation of psychological symptoms and psychomotor disability. Where breakdown in the split is severe enough and the elements overburden the α-function, then ego disorganization ensues with confusional states, feelings of depersonalization, hallucinations, paranoid beliefs, and increasing psychomotor disturbance. As α-function fails the α-system increasingly resorts to evacuation of β-elements by projection, giving more florid psychotic symptoms including the development of frank paranoid delusions and hallucinations.

In the forensic cases the split between the two systems remains intact but the organization of the β-system fails, giving rise to behavioural outbursts including irrational, violent, criminal behaviour due to the 'naked' discharge of β-elements into the environment. Within the hypothesis it also follows that, where the β-elements are discharged into the α-system causing disruption and disorganization, then both the speed of development of dysfunction and the speed of recovery will be slower due to the partial metabolization and 'detoxification' of the β-elements by the α-function than when the discharge has been through a breakdown in the β-system leaving the α-system intact to deal with the perceived consequences of the catastrophe with the help of such defences as rationalization, denial, or amnesia. In the forensic type B cases the β-elements appear to take over on a temporary basis producing uncontrolled, bizarre, violent behaviour and an alteration in the sense of reality and experience of the self which these individuals consistently describe.[2]

All those who manage their functional independence on the basis of such encapsulated splits do it at the price of certain areas of their emotional life and personal identity. Where the β-elements represent violent, possibly homicidal feelings, the individuals will tend to be passive, shy, and somewhat unassertive; where the β-elements have more sadistic characteristics and are perhaps organized into a sexual perversion then the personalities are more likely to present as affable, perhaps somewhat obsessional, often excessively obliging individuals. In other words the personality characteristics of the main body of the ego (the α-system) will reflect the converse of the split off β-system when the two systems are more completely functionally separate, as with a well-organized perversion or psychosomatization. This phenomenon is less clear when there are psychopathological collusions which absorb β-elements into the activity of environmental objects and systems; in this case the α-system is likely to experience and express the quality of the collusive arrangements.

Assessment will depend upon trying to get some reasonable picture of the reality of the two systems to distinguish the α-symptoms from expressions of β-system activity and any 'leaking' β-elements such as apparently unmotivated impulsive behaviour or out-of-context jarring in social relations. Careful history-taking and precise observation may suggest the factors which produce a breakdown in the equilibrium between the two systems. This breakdown may be the result of an increase in β-element activity as a result of specific types of stimulation or individual vulnerability or an alteration in the way the β-system has been maintained. In my experience in forensic cases the β-elements are often 'undigested' memories or primitive images built of experiences connected with being terrorized or exposed to excessive pain or brutality through non-accidental injury or other early environmental abuses. Such traumata, however, do not seem to have produced overall inhibition of ego development, as in the Type A 'false self' personalities, but have been contained enough to be organized into a defensive system built upon this type of splitting.

It seems helpful to include in the hypothesis that an anti-developmental congenital factor producing an innate reservoir of β-elements plays an important part in the genesis of ego splitting in non-traumatized cases.[3] This might also represent the common factor between this particular type of borderline patient and those who develop schizophrenia; the capacity to maintain such a malignant area of the personality in a split-off state by organizing a β-system, and the capacity to reorganize the two separate systems after a breakdown in the splitting, depends finally on the prevalence of a more positive constitutional characteristic poorly represented in schizophrenia. A strong capacity for α-functioning would be an inherited variable together with positive factors within the environment encouraging the development of a healthy ego, so enhancing the potential of the α-system including its capacity to organize the splitting.

This briefly stated hypothesis is reasonably compatible with neurological and biochemical theories of schizophrenia. It is suggested that this model is an adequate hypothetical conceptualization of the psychodynamics of this group of borderline cases and increases the possibility of distinguishing them from other groups and of making some assessment of the nature and gravity of their disturbance. I have found it of practical value, not only in longer-term psychoanalytic work, but in attempting brief transference based psychotherapy as well (Gallwey, 1978).

The most difficult cases appear to be those in which the system has its organization within the patient's self as with somatization or well-stabilized perversion formation. In these cases the gathering of the relevant emotions, fantasies, and conflicts within the transference is very difficult indeed. More schizoid individuals, and those with collusive set-ups, have β-systems more available to transference techniques and offer individuals with well-developed α-systems a very much better opportunity for analytic psychotherapy. From the behavioural psychotherapy point of view, and speaking hypothetically, with some slight support from experience, such psychotherapy should concentrate on the relief of α-symptoms which should strengthen α-function, thereby making it possible for the α-system to absorb more β-elements and strengthen the split between the two systems. It should be remembered that many individuals, in some much more minimal way, run their lives without breakdown or catastrophe by operating such mechanisms. Although the price is inevitably some degree of impoverishment of the personality in terms of emotional fulfilment, and although many stress-related problems appear to be connected with maintenance of such a split, it does seem to be a common primitive mechanism for overcoming serious early conflict and adverse experience. Direct attempts to treat the system with behavioural psychotherapeutic methods can also be valuable where there are areas of malfunction or weakness, not connected with the main psychopathology.

There may be areas of deprivation in the defensive systems of the kind found in Type A, such as a lack of social skills and other problems deriving from over-dependency and inadequacy which may yield to direct methods of learning. On the other hand, direct methods aimed at the β-system are altogether more uncertain, partly due to the fact that the β-system by definition is very hidden and inaccessible. The system is also incapable of learning from experience and has a functional independence from the part of the mind that is capable of such learning (i.e. the α-system).

In my experience attempts to suppress directly the β-system or β-elements with aversion techniques or covert conditioning in perversions associated with this particular psychopathological set-up (not all perversions) does produce a worsening in the total organization of the individual. The two systems are by nature antithetical, and attempts to force the one upon the other will risk a collapse in the total organization and equilibrium resulting in psychological crises or behavioural catastrophes. However the number of cases I have seen in which such attempts have been made is not very large. The nature of my practice makes it more likely that I see the failures and, since the psychodynamic model is essentially the result of psychoanalytic experience and thinking, its usefulness to behavioural psychologists is an open question.

Whether some controlled leakage of β-elements into a consensual environment can be encouraged is also of uncertain value. This, in theory, should prevent sudden breakdowns of the β-system with catastrophic uncontrolled discharge which, as postulated, lie behind the episodic offending of this group. However there is always a danger in the use of systematic hypothetical models of this kind that one loses sight of the more real and immediate personality characteristics of a capacity for affection, anger, and contact with the world as central indicators of healthy adjustment. I have treated, in psychotherapy, several patients with sexual deviant problems; some associated with episodic criminal behaviour. They report a marked diminution in affectionate feelings when they had been encouraged to involve their partners in their sexually perverse needs at the behest of marital therapists or in an attempt to dispense with the 'double life' activity contingent upon supporting a perversion and a family.

Some controlled leakage of β-elements may already go on, and is tolerated by some environments, or even catered for by others. For instance, minor sexual assaults on public transport, particularly tube trains, are a common form of tolerated sexual crime, or prostitutes who cater for clients with such normally socially dystonic types of behaviour as sadistic acts or obscenity. Pornographic literature and films presumably encourage the absorption of β-elements by providing a ready-made framework for a β-system and supporting the α-system by stimulating the α-function (manufactured daydreaming). The danger would seem to be to encourage an addictive reliance upon such artificial aids which hypothetically could make matters worse if they, for some reason, cease to become available. Also hypothetically such addictive reliance could discourage spontaneous natural α-function and thereby the central strength of the overall personality. An 'atrophy of mis-use' in α-function might also enhance the shifting of the balance away from the more socially syntonic areas of the α-system with a deterioration in the individual's general life adjustment, ethical stance, and creative enjoyment of others. This would be in contradistinction to the enhancement of α-function by richer forms of artistic experience and in treatment by use of occupational therapy, art therapy, drama, and so on.

SUMMARY AND CONCLUSION

I have attempted to describe in broad terms two different types of case which may earn the label 'borderline patient', both being liable to episodes of psychosis and/or pathological aggression:

Type B, a schizoid type, have the best immediate prognosis but tend to relapse unexpectedly. They are difficult to treat supportively although they may seem easier because of their capacity to revive well-functioning areas of their personality.

Type A are ego deficient and seem more difficult because of their dependency needs but, on the other hand, their disturbance is readily available for psychological therapeutic endeavours.

Choice of approach may depend upon available skills, but it is important always to bear in mind that the interpretive psychotherapies are most indicated where the individual is intelligent, capable of working with abstract conceptualizations, conveys a psychodynamic organization in which it can be envisaged that the relevant area of pathology can be gathered within the transference without the demands on the therapist becoming impossible, and exists in an environment which can be reasonably expected to remain supportive during periods of readjustment and possible crisis. The psychodynamic models for these two groups of borderline patients are offered, for what they are worth. They are meant to be used to help distinguish these two broad categories of patients liable to episodic psychotic level disturbance and to provide working models for, at least, the initial organization of psychotherapeutic procedures. Closer acquaintance with patients will produce spontaneous interpersonal approaches and areas of individual difference which are simply not covered by the somewhat systematized nature of these models.

ACKNOWLEDGEMENT

The author wishes to thank Dr Murray Jackson of the Maudsley Hospital for his help with this chapter.

NOTES

1. In terms of the model of ego functions developed later this would be represented as a weak α-system unable to sustain either α-function or organize a split β-system.
2. The nature of the threat to the ego posed by the β-elements can be judged by the nature of the catastrophic behaviour and, in particular, by what the violence does physically and mentally to any victim.
3. In Melanie Klein's theories primitive envy is such a factor, having a close affinity to Freud's 'death instinct'. Klein felt it was responsible for individual variations in susceptibility to mental illness as an extra-environmental factor.

REFERENCES

Abraham, K. (1919) A particular form of neurotic resistance against the psychoanalytic method. In J. D. Sutherland (Ed.) *Selected Papers of Karl Abraham*. London: Hogarth, 1968.

Bion, W. R. (1956) Development of schizophrenic thought. *International Journal of Psychoanalysis*, **37**, 344–346.

Bion, W. R. (1959) Attacks on linking. *International Journal of Psychoanalysis*, **40**, 308–315.

Bion, W. R. (1962) *Learning from Experience*. London: Heinemann.

Bowlby, J. (1971) *Attachment and Loss*. London: Pelican.

Chessick, R. D. (1965) The Borderline Patient. In S. Arieti (Ed.) *American Handbook of Psychiatry*. New York: Basic Books.

Deutsch, H. (1945) Some forms of emotional disturbance and their relation to schizophrenia. *Psychoanalytic Quarterly*, **11**, 301–321.

DSM III (1980) *Diagnostic and Statistical Manual of the American Psychiatric Association*.

Fairbairn, W. R. D. (1940) *Psycho-Analytic Studies of the Personality*. London: Tavistock.

Gallwey, P. L. G. (1978) Transference utilization in aim-restricted psychotherapy. *British Journal of Medical Psychology*, **51**, 225–234.

Griffiths, A. W. and Rundle, A. T. (1976) A survey of male prisoners: some aspects of family background. *British Journal of Criminology*, **16**, 352–366.

Grinker, R. A., Werble, B. and Dryer, R. C. (1968) *The Borderline Syndrome*. New York: Basic Books.

Gunderson, J. G. and Singer, H. T. (1975) Borderline and schizophrenic patients—a comparative study. *American Journal of Psychiatry*, **132**, 1–10.

Kernberg, O. (1975) *The Borderline Conditions and Pathological Narcissism*. New York: Aronson.

Klein, M. (1946) Notes on schizoid mechanisms. In M. R. Kahn (Ed.) *Collected Works*, vol. III, pp. 1–24. London: Hogarth.

Klein, M. (1957) Envy and gratitude. In M. R. Kahn (Ed.) *Collected Works*, vol. III, pp. 176–235. London: Hogarth.

Knight, R. (1953) Borderline patients. *Bulletin of the Menninger Clinic*, **19**, 1–12.

Le Boit, J. and Capponi, A. (1979) (Eds) *Advances in Psychotherapy of the Borderline Patient*. London: Jason Aronson.

Nemiah, J. C. and Sifneos, P. E. (1970) Affect and fantasy in patients with psychosomatic disorders. In O. W. Hill (Ed.) *Modern Trends in Psychosomatic Medicine*. London: Butterworth.

Perry, R. C. and Klerman, C. L. (1978) The borderline patient: a comparative analysis of four sets of diagnostic criteria. *Archives of General Psychiatry*, **25**, 141–150.

Rosenfeld, H. (1970) Negative therapeutic reaction. *Bulletin of the Menninger Clinic*, **34**, 189–192.

Spitz, R. A. (1965) *The First Year of Life*. New York: International University Press.

Stern, A. (1938) Psychoanalytic investigation of and therapy in the borderline group of neuroses. *Psychoanalytic Quarterly*, **7**, 467–489.

Stone, M. H. (1980) *The Borderline Syndromes*. London: McGraw-Hill.

West, D. J. (1963) *The Habitual Prisoner*. London: Macmillan.

Williams, A. H. (1964) Psychopathology and treatment of sexual murderers. In I. Rosen (Ed.) *Psychology and Treatment of Sexual Deviation*. London: Oxford University Press.

Winnicott, D. (1955) Clinical varieties of transference. In M. R. Kahn (Ed.) *Through Paediatrics to Psychoanalysis*. London: Hogarth.

PART 2
THE MANAGEMENT OF
DANGEROUS PATIENTS

CHAPTER 7

Dangerousness and the Mental Health Review Tribunal

DAVID HEPWORTH

INTRODUCTION[1]

Legislation concerned with the mentally disordered in England and Wales, as typified by the Mental Health Act (1959), intended that decisions about detention or release from detention should be made by the holders of particular offices, to whom were assigned the responsibility and authority to make decisions in accord with prescribed procedures. This formally prescribed decision process was designed to ensure that an individual considered mentally disordered was only required to accept treatment in an institution against his will through the application of fair and impersonal rules and authority. The present research (Hepworth, 1982a) was concerned with the decision process as it operated in practice within the socio-legal framework established to deal with the restraint and release of mentally disordered men and women considered a danger to themselves and others.

The mental health review tribunal (explained later) was chosen as an important example of a formally prescribed decision process. The research demonstrated that the ways in which the decisions were made could not be explained solely on the basis of the formalized rules. The tribunal members found themselves faced with situations where the rules and criteria were inadequate. The rules assumed a reasonable certainty and agreement in regard to clinical diagnosis and prognosis, when in fact either or both could be absent. The evidence upon which decisions were made about the likely future behaviour of the individual could be inadequate. The tribunal members could be restrained in their 'duty to discharge' by treatment or rehabilitative considerations. They might consider that the individual's recovery and improved behaviour were dependent on social factors beyond his or their control.

The research orientation questioned the traditional model of judicial decision-making which suggested that the only significant variables affecting decisions were those externally visible 'facts' available in official records. It was assumed that the formally prescribed rules and procedures would be insufficient to study and explain the decision process in practice, because of the social nature of the concept of 'danger' (Hepworth, 1982b) and anomalies and dilemmas with which the decision-makers were faced. The study focused not only on the facts of the cases being considered by the tribunals but also on how the members perceived the facts. It also considered the dilemmas and conflicts facing tribunal members and the anomalies in rules and powers which might lead them to innovatory action.

LEGAL DETENTION OF THE MENTALLY DISORDERED IN ENGLAND AND WALES[1]

The assumption of the mental health legislation is that, with very few exceptions, men and women should be offered and receive psychiatric treatment and care with the same legal informality and on the same voluntary basis as they would receive medical treatment or professional help for any other disability or illness. The exceptions, where detention or compulsion are sanctioned, are not justified by the existence or diagnosis of mental disorder in itself. The justification for enforcing treatment against the will of the individual is related to the harm which has happened or is likely to happen to the person or others as a result of the disorder or as a consequence of not enforcing treatment.

For an individual to be required to enter a psychiatric hospital or a hospital for the mentally handicapped, for observation or long-term treatment, three conditions must be satisfied (Mental Health Act 1959, section 26):

1. The individual must be suffering from 'mental disorder of a nature or disability which warrants the detention of the patient in a hospital',
2. Informal (voluntary) admission or other means of dealing with the situation must be inappropriate,
3. The detention must be necessary 'in the interests of the person's health or safety or for the protection of other persons'.

The first point has to be assessed by two medical practitioners (only one in an emergency) and the others assessed in cooperation with the relatives of the individual and/or the responsible social worker, either of whom is required to make the actual application for admission to hospital. It is fundamental to the intention of mental health legislation in England and Wales that an individual should become a voluntary patient as soon as possible. More often than not, compulsory admissions for short periods of observation (Mental Health Act 1959, sections 25 and 29) are not followed by continued compulsory treatment. In deciding to release a person from compulsory treatment the decision-makers are not required to show that the person does not need further psychiatric treatment. They are required to decide whether, regardless of the severity of the mental disorder and the need for treatment, it is necessary to enforce treatment or detention to prevent harm to the individual or others. Periodically, the responsible medical officer is required to justify the renewal of detention by the application of similar criteria to those which justified the initial admission. This officer has a duty to discharge the detaining order if he does not consider that the criteria are satisfied.

In contrast with the above civil proceedings, when dealing with criminal offenders the criteria for justifying detention in a psychiatric hospital are more detailed. The court has to be satisfied on medical evidence of a specific mental disorder, and has to be:

> of the opinion, having regard to all the circumstances including the nature of the offence and the character and antecedents of the offender, and to the other available methods of dealing with him, that the most suitable method of disposing with the case is by means of an order (Mental Health Act 1959, section 60).

In respect of court orders under section 60, the responsible medical officer has the same requirement to renew detention and the same authority to discharge the order. The court can make the offender subject to further restrictions on discharge if:

> it appears to the court, having regard to the nature of the offence, the antecedents of the offender and the risk of his committing further offences if set at large, it is necessary for the protection of the public so to do (Mental Health Act 1959, section 65).

The main effect of the further restrictions is the requirement that the Home Secretary should approve any movement from the hospital.

For the Department of Health and Social Security to agree to the admission of people subject to detention under the Mental Health Act 1959 to one of the special security hospitals provided by central government, such as Rampton Hospital, they have to be satisfied that they:

> in the opinion of the Secretary of State require treatment under conditions of special security on account of their dangerous, violent or criminal propensities (Mental Health Act 1959, section 97).

Release from a special hospital is authorized in the same way as from any other psychiatric hospital, depending on the nature of the detaining order. If the person is subject to further restrictions on discharge under section 65, the responsible medical officer in the special hospital is required to obtain the approval of the Home Secretary for release. Otherwise, release from detention is within the authority of the responsible medical officer.

MENTAL HEALTH REVIEW TRIBUNAL

The mental health review tribunal is a body completely independent of the hospital within which the individual is detained. The tribunal is required to consider applications for discharge from the detained person or nearest relative, and to give advice to the Home Secretary in regard to patients detained further under section 65. In effect, the mental health review tribunal process is a form of 'appeal' against the detaining authority. The tribunal, comprising a legal chairman and medical and lay members, is required to review whether the conditions are satisfied for unrestricted patients to be detained. If they consider any of the conditions not to be satisfied, it is their duty to discharge the detaining order.

THE ASSESSMENT OF 'DANGER TO SELF AND OTHERS'

The general research aim was to examine the process by which the mental health review tribunal decided on the 'dangerousness' of the person before them as a basis for their judgement about release or continued detention. The methods of data collection adopted for 150 tribunal hearings held at Rampton Hospital during 1977 and 1978 were systematic observation of the hearings, structured interviewing of the legal chairmen, and structured examination of written records of the socio-demographic characteristics of the patients.

From the examination of literature and previous research it was assumed that an adequate definition of the concept of 'dangerous' would need to include reference to the 'threat and anxiety' experienced by others in regard to the 'risk of physical violence or assault' from an 'individual' whose behaviour was judged to be 'impulsive and/or unpredictable' and likely to react inappropriately or incongruously in response to certain aspects of a particular 'social situation' (Hepworth, 1982b).

MODEL OF DECISION-MAKING ABOUT 'DANGER TO SELF AND OTHERS'

Although the constitution, procedures, and powers of the mental health review tribunal were formally prescribed by legislation and rules, the decision-making of the tribunal was found to be a far more complex process (Hepworth, 1983). The more complete model of decision-making in regard to mentally disordered people considered a 'danger to self and others' appeared to involve various stages or subsidiary decision processes:

(a) an assessment of the risk and the need for continued detention on the basis of objective evidence;

(b) a more subjective and emotional response to the person and the anxiety and threat aroused by the 'danger';

(c) an evaluation of the rehabilitative facilities required to provide the control and care necessary in the interests of the patient's health or safety or for the protection of other persons;

(d) the process of dealing with restraints and difficulties in regard to obtaining information about the necessary rehabilitative resources; and

(e) the process of dealing with doubt about the need for continued detention and determining the 'benefit of the doubt'.

Although the model was developed and discussed within the five stages, at least ten distinct subsidiary decision processes were identified:

(a) An assessment of the risk to others and the need for continued detention on the basis of objective evidence

At this initial stage the decision-makers were primarily concerned with evidence of continued risk of physical harm or assault to others and continued lack of self-control and socially responsible behaviour. There were two distinct processes during this primary stage, one of which did not involve completely the whole decision-making team:

1. *'Clinical' decision process.* Determination of the mental disorder by the medical member.
2. *'Objective' decision process about risk to others.* Assessment of objective evidence of the risk of further physical harm or assault to people generally or to specific potential victims.

This stage is presented diagrammatically (Figure 1) to illustrate the interrelationship between the 'clinical' and 'objective' assessment of risk. The clinical assessment of mental disorder was separate and distinct in various ways. Whether the individual was 'suffering from mental disorder of a nature or disability which warranted the detention of the patient in a hospital' was one of the distinct statutory questions requiring an answer from the tribunal. As perhaps would be expected, the research findings demonstrated that the diagnosis, treatment, and prognosis of the mental disorder of the patient was the prime concern of the medical member of the tribunal. There was a separate supplementary medical decision process, with the medical conclusions normally accepted by the other members.

Quite apart from being an issue in itself, it was clear that evidence of continued mental disorder was used as a guide in assessing the degree of risk. It appeared to be used in assessing the extent to which the individual continued to be 'impulsive and unpredictable' and therefore 'dangerous'. The medical opinion of the mental state of the person tended to be accepted with other evidence of his social stability and self-control as an aspect of the objective

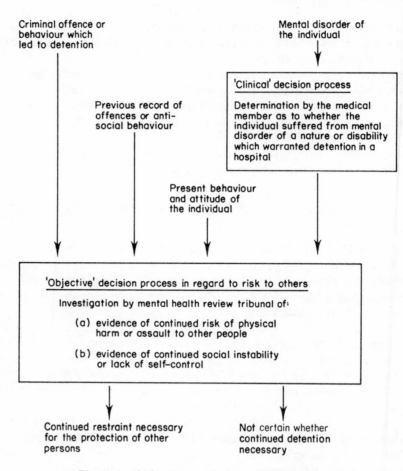

Figure 1   Objective assessment of risk to others

assessment of the risk to others. One of the highly significant research findings was a negative correlation between tribunal judgements in favour of release and mental disorder being perceived by the tribunal as the most influential evidence.

It was evident that, in addition to the mental disorder as judged mainly by the medical member, there were other factors which were influential in determining the risk and tending to be influences against release: the immediate offence or behaviour which led to the current detention, the previous record of offences and antisocial behaviour, and the present behaviour and attitude of the individual.

The nature and severity of the offence was probably the major factor in determining the need for the initial detention; but its importance subsequently was a matter of interaction with other factors. Where an offence had been relatively minor there would be less pressure on other factors to justify release or bring continued detention into question. Where the offence had involved more serious physical violence or sexual behaviour there would be greater emphasis on the need for clear evidence of clinical improvement, personality stability, and maturation. The severity of the offence was perhaps the major factor in determining whether the decision-makers would lean towards the welfare and liberty of the individual or the protection of others and restraint of the individual. There was likely to have been an interaction between the offence and other factors identified as positively associated with tribunal judgements in favour of release: the age of the individual and the length of stay in the hospital.

Attempts to predict future criminal or dangerous behaviour on the basis of objective 'facts' have tended to depend on the previous criminal record. Predictive measures such as the Legal Dangerousness Scale devised by Cocozza and Steadman (1974) have a seductive attraction. Cocozza and Steadman found that 30.6 per cent (11 individuals) of their released patients aged less than 50 years and with a high legal dangerousness score based on criminal history subsequently engaged in dangerous behaviour, in contrast with only 4.8 per cent (three individuals) aged 50 and over with low scores. Yet these statistics served to illustrate the problem of false positives emphasized by workers such as Meehl and Rosen (1955) and Megargee (1976). While most of the patients who engaged in dangerous behaviour were under the age of 50 and had relatively serious criminal backgrounds, the majority of the patients who satisfied these criteria did not display any subsequent assaultive behaviour.

Although the tribunal members were not applying such standard measurements in their approach to assessing the objective evidence, their deliberations illustrated the process by which false positives could accumulate. It was clear that in practice this early stage of the decision process was concerned with the issue of whether or not the individual continued to be a risk and required restraint. Normally, the conclusion of the objective assessment of the risk to others was a judgement that detention continued to be necessary or no definite decision or advice to release. In other words, this stage was simply a first hurdle for the individual. A definite decision would be in favour of continued detention; doubt about the need for continued restraint would be dealt with by progressing to a further stage of the decision process rather than by making a judgement in favour of release. Even though as a group the people considered by the tribunal to require continued detention on the basis of objective evidence were more likely to commit further dangerous acts if in a position to do so, already the numbers of false positives were beginning to accumulate. At each stage the definite decision was in support of continued detention with uncertainty normally resulting in progressing to the next stage of the decision process.

*(b)   A more subjective and emotional response to the person and to the anxiety
       and threat aroused by the 'danger'*

Where there was uncertainty about the risk to others and the continued need
for restraint on the basis of an objective assessment of the risk from the
individual, this appeared to be resolved through a more subjective response to
the 'personality' of the individual and the 'threat and anxiety' aspect of 'danger'.

3.   *'Subjective' decision process about risk to others.* An intuitive and
     emotional response to the individual, assessing the extent to which he was
     still impulsive and unpredictable, arousing threat and anxiety in others.

This stage is presented diagrammatically (Figure 2) to illustrate the central
importance of the personality of the patient as perceived and experienced by the
tribunal members or other decision-makers in determining the assessment of the
'danger' and of the need or otherwise for continued detention.

The research findings about the evidence on which the tribunal based their
judgements concluded that the one over-riding factor to the tribunal was the
personality of the patient. It was the one main influence in comparison with other

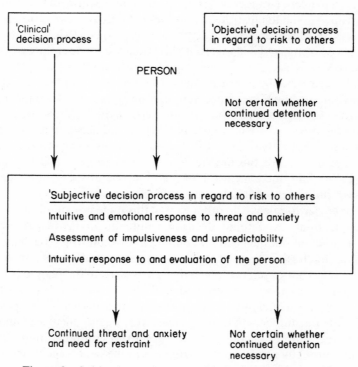

Figure 2   Subjective response to the danger and the person

factors; and it overlapped with, and incorporated aspects of, other factors. It overlapped both with more objective considerations such as offences and observable behaviour, and with less tangible variables such as subjective feelings and intuition. As other factors were acknowledged in their own right, when the tribunal acknowledged the predominant influence of the personality they were reacting on a more intuitive and emotional level in their impressions of the person before them. An intuitive sympathy and trust would counteract the threat and anxiety which was an inherent aspect of 'danger'. An emotion of warmth and confidence towards the person could reverse the labelling process which had determined the 'personality' to be 'dangerous'.

This 'gut-reaction' to the person was reminiscent of the emphasis of Sturup (1968) on the consensus of intuitive feeling towards the patient and the need for satisfactory emotional contact before he could effectively evaluate the person or be optimistic about treatment or rehabilitation. The influence of intuition and 'gut-feelings' on the tribunal was evident and tended to be in favour of release (in contrast with the decision when this influence was not acknowledged). It was shown that 'risk' factors such as offences and mental disorder tended to be negatively associated with judgements in favour of release when they were acknowledged as the main influences. Therefore some decisions or advice in favour of continued detention would have been determined at the earlier stage of the objective decision process before the subjective reactions to the person came to the fore.

Despite 'subjective feelings and intuition' being positively associated with judgements in favour of release, it appeared that this stage of the subjective decision process was still primarily concerned with determining whether or not continued detention was necessary. It was a further hurdle for the individual. A definite decision would tend to be in favour of continued detention; sufficient trust and sympathy to overcome the 'anxiety and threat' would simply lead to a further stage rather than directly to a judgement to release. When the tribunal remained doubtful about the need for continued detention (and perhaps disposed to decide or advise release), there were still further implications of release to be considered before a final conclusion was reached.

(c) An evaluation of the rehabilitative facilities required to provide the control and care necessary in the interests of the patient's health or safety or for the protection of other persons

Having not determined that continued detention was necessary on the basis of the objective and subjective assessment of the risk to others, the tribunal directed attention to rehabilitative considerations. The evidence on which the tribunal based their judgements demonstrated that *'parens patriae'* welfare considerations came to the fore once the question of risk had been assessed on the 'danger' factors of evidence. Having survived the first two primary hurdles it had to be shown that the necessary control was available for the protection of others and/or care was available for the health or safety of the individual. The 'protection of other persons' and the 'health or safety of the patient' appeared to receive separate attention:

4. *'Control' decision process.* Assessment of the controls necessary for the protection of others and the risk involved in release when those controls were not available.
5. *'Care' decision process.* Assessment of the care required for the health and safety of the individual and the risk to the person in being released without those care facilities.

This stage is presented diagrammatically (Figure 3) to illustrate that uncertainty about continued detention on the basis of objective and subjective assessment of the person led to consideration of factors external to the individual. Although the factors considered as possibly necessary for care or control were similar (continued health care, community residential and/or other rehabilitative facilities, and/or family support), 'protection of other persons' and 'the patient's health or safety' were separate considerations with distinct starting-points.

At the core of the assessment of the controls necessary for the protection of others and the risk involved in release without those controls was the very nature of 'dangerousness'. There was evidence in the perception of 'dangerousness' by the mental health review tribunal that they acknowledged 'danger' as being to some extent related to the social situation within which it was likely to appear. Their assessment was concerned with the 'probability of this or that sort of damaging behaviour occurring in this or that expected environment' (Scott, 1977) and 'avoiding the dangerous situation' (Sturup, 1968).

The difficulties experienced by the tribunal in obtaining evidence about control and/or care resources appeared to be centred on the non-availability or inadequency of reports rather than the non-availability of witnesses. It appeared to be 'information' they were lacking and not necessarily 'people' as a source of that information. Whilst the crisis in the decision process arising from these difficulties did appear to affect primarily the 'patient's health or safety' and issues around the question of whether 'the patient should continue to be detained', there was separate concern about the risk to others without support and control outside the special hospital. The tribunal expressed concern about their inability to 'test out' the good progress and the risk to others through a direct community discharge as opposed to transfer to a hospital in the home area.

The predominant concern about the anomalies in the tribunal's rules and powers was their inability to ensure continued hospital care on a voluntary basis for someone no longer considered to require maximum security care but

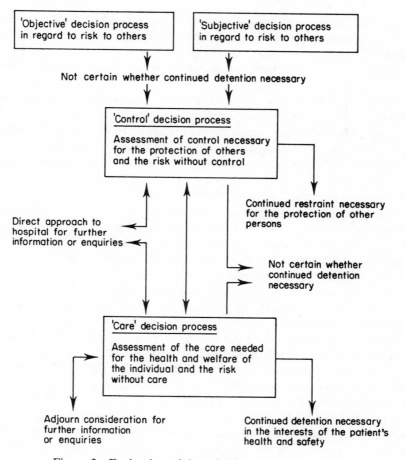

Figure 3   Evaluation of the rehabilitative requirements

vulnerable to relapse if discharged directly into the community. Although this problem primarily affected applications, it was experienced occasionally in respect of references when the hospital had already exhausted its own attempts to arrange transfer to another hospital. The tribunal would be aware that their own advice would be unlikely to achieve the movement any sooner. In respect of applications, where they had no authority to recommend transfer, adjournments and other actions were used to support or influence the hospital in making such arrangements.

The 'control' decision process was resolved either by deciding against release because of the non-availability of the resources necessary to minimize the risk, or by continuing to consider release with a view to relying on less tangible reassurances of support or taking the risk of discharging the order without such assurances. The duty was to discharge if detention was no longer considered necessary; yet they could be restrained in their 'duty to discharge' by the apparent need for continued health care or other rehabilitative support. The option of continued voluntary care was not available in the secure hospital and there could be uncertainty about the health service or other provision in the home area.

The focus of the 'care' decision process was on the rehabilitative or residential resources considered necessary for the welfare and protection of the individual, beyond simply satisfying the 'patient's health and safety' criteria required to justify continued detention. Particularly during this stage, the tribunal was faced with dilemmas where the practical choices available to them were inadequate and with anomalies where their rules and powers were insufficient to the task. Their rules and procedures were insufficient to enable direct communication with national health service hospitals or ensure adequate information from the local health and community services. Their powers did not allow them to order transfer to another hospital or ensure necessary rehabilitative resources in the community. When they did determine to continue the detention at this stage, they justified it in 'the interest of the patient's health or safety'. Yet sometimes the decision was reached in the absence of any more satisfactory alternative. Given such alternatives, they would perhaps not have chosen to continue the compulsory care.

This stage was yet a further hurdle for the patients which did not normally result in a definite decision to discharge the order. In fact this stage or subsidiary decision process did not normally result in a definite decision either way: to discharge or to continue the detention. Of 72 applications (the remaining hearings being concerned with references from the Home Secretary), the tribunal made a final decision to continue the detention of only 32 (44.4 per cent), with a decision simply to reclassify the mental disorder in one other case. At least some of these would have fallen at the previous hurdles in their deliberations. Only nine of the applications (12.5 per cent) within the research sample resulted in a definite decision to discharge the order. A high proportion of the applications (30; 41.7 per cent) were adjourned 'for the information to be obtained in such manner as they may direct or for the applicant or any other person concerned to produce the information' (Mental Health Review Tribunal Rules 1960, Rule 26:1). The use of the right to adjourn was determined mainly at this 'care' stage of the decision process.

The use of adjournment was the primary evidence of innovatory action designed to overcome the dilemmas and anomalies with which tribunal members were faced, thus satisfying Lemert's criteria for revolutionary change in law in response to crises in the legal decision process (Lemert, 1970). Various innovations and new departures in the use of their power to adjourn were identified (Hepworth, 1983):

(i) using adjournment as a means of exercising a 'watching brief' as opposed to obtaining further information;

  (ii) attempting to influence the hospital team into a course of action not available to the tribunal;

  (iii) attempting to negotiate the health care provision in the home area through direct contact or indirect influence;

  (iv) seeking to influence, through direct contact with the hospital team or Department of Health and Social Security, further clinical assessment or treatment whilst still in hospital; and

  (v) 'forcing the issue' through delayed discharge, making clear their intention to discharge the order after a given period.

Many of these actions went beyond the tribunal's limited powers to discharge or continue the detention or adjourn for further information. It was evident that the tribunal would have exercised a power of delayed discharge (if it had been available) on at least as many occasions as the order was discharged. This supported the conclusion of the Review of the Mental Health Act 1959 (HMSO, 1978) that the powers of the tribunal should be extended to provide this authority.

It was at this stage of evaluating the rehabilitative facilities that it became most evident that serious anomalies and dilemmas were experienced primarily in relation to the narrow 'discharge-or-not' power in response to applications. 'Welfare and protection' considerations came into conflict with the more narrow framework designed to emphasize 'justice and fairness'. External restraints and difficulties imposed upon members' deliberations made it necessary for them to go beyond their prescribed committee 'receiving information' approach to deal directly with external resources and/or seek to influence the provision of these resources.

(d) The process of dealing with restraints and difficulties in regard to obtaining information about the necessary rehabilitative resources

Having not determined that continued detention was necessary because of the need for control and/or care which was unlikely to be available, the tribunal appeared to focus more determined attention on ensuring or seeking to influence the provision of rehabilitative resources to enable the individual to leave the secure hospital. They tended to focus on distinct areas of care and support:

  6. *'Hospital care' decision process.* Seeking to support or initiate hospital plans for transfer to National Health Service care and/or undertake direct investigations into health care provision.

  7. *'Community services' decision process.* Investigations into community residential or other support services considered necessary for rehabilitation.

  8. *'Family support' decision process.* Assessment of the availability of family

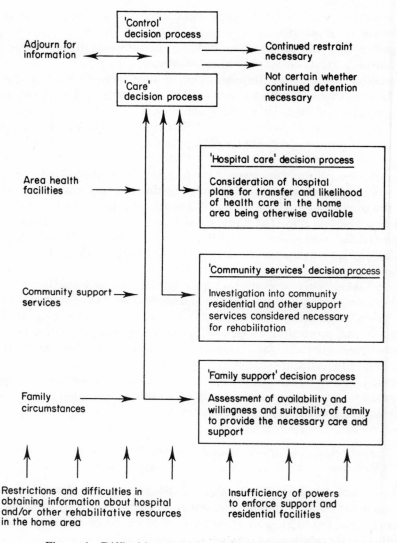

Figure 4   Difficulties meeting rehabilitative requirements

members and their willingness and suitability to provide the necessary care and support.

This stage is presented diagrammatically (Figure 4) to illustrate that enquiries into health care, community services, and the family were distinct and subsidiary to the 'control' and 'care' decision processes which they were serving. They tended to take the form of 'cul-de-sacs' in that the tribunal did not have the power to enforce the provision of any resource or to negotiate with any certainty a formal agreement with external agencies, the family, or the patient. In their report to the Home Secretary tribunal members could only advise, with no certainty that their advice would be accepted or that the rehabilitative resources would be provided. In response to applications they could only discharge the order with no means of ensuring care and/or support, nor of ensuring that the patient would cooperate with any specific rehabilitative intentions on the part of the tribunal. Even if they had obtained reliable information on the availability of such factors as accommodation in a community hostel and decided to discharge on that understanding, it was inherent in the discharge of the detaining order that the individual could not be required to comply with the residential arrangements.

Dilemmas in regard to the need for continued hospital care were observed and acknowledged in a substantial proportion of the hearings. The unsatisfactory choice with applications was between continuing the detention, thus not reflecting their view that the patient was ready for progress, or discharging the order with the risk to the patient or others if the necessary care and support facilities were not provided. This dilemma could arise even when the hospital team were in support of transfer to an open National Health Service psychiatric hospital. The tribunal members would face a situation where exhaustive enquiries by the hospital and the Department of Health and Social Security into alternative hospital care had been unsuccessful. In advice to the Home Secretary they could recommend transfer, knowing that this had already been approved on the recommendation of the responsible medical officer. In response to applications, their powers were insufficient to influence the provision of informal hospital care elsewhere. Therefore, they found the need to resort to the various innovatory actions identified above. About half the adjournments were acknowledged by the chairmen to be related to the need for continued hospital care.

There were similar dilemmas and anomalies in respect of community support services, although the problem did not arise as often. Tribunal members were faced with the same restrictions whereby they were unable to ensure that the necessary rehabilitative resources were available to support the patient on discharge. There was particular concern about community residential care. As with health care, the decision process in respect of the community support services involved an assessment of the services which were needed to support discharge from hospital, the likelihood of the hospital team arranging this or it being provided in some other way, and the risks to the individual and/or others of discharge without these support facilities being available. Although the right to adjourn was intended as a means of obtaining further information, it was used in practice in attempts to influence the provision of services through the hospital. The authority to subpoena the presence of a representative of the community services (Mental Health Review Tribunal Rules 14:1) was not exercised despite the serious dilemmas faced by the tribunal. The 'information' was sought through the hospital and sometimes expressed explicitly in terms of 'placement in the event of discharge when the tribunal reconvenes'.

The involvement of members of the family in the hearing, and information about the family circumstances, influenced tribunal decisions. There was a significant association between the attendance of family members and decisions or advice to discharge, with a tendency to advise transfer rather than discharge when the family were not involved. The tribunal members were more inclined to adjourn consideration of cases when the family were not represented at the hearing. The availability of reports on family circumstances was similarly associated with decisions and adjournments. Despite the importance of these reports, it was not evident that obtaining information about the family was considered to present serious difficulties at many of the hearings. Yet references to difficulties arising from the absence of family witnesses were observed on more occasions than in respect of the absence of representatives of hospital or community representatives. This was despite family members being present at about half of the hearings compared to very few attended by hospital or community witnesses. In other words, whilst the tribunal members sought information about health and community support services, they wanted to see and meet the family face to face.

Therefore, the family factor illustrated that it was not only in response to the patient that the tribunal members could be influenced on an interpersonal and subjective level. Also the presence of family members to express their commitment to supporting the patient on discharge appeared greatly to reassure the tribunal. The insufficiency of tribunal rules and powers did not present serious problems in relation to the family. The various dilemmas were more concerned with family stability and attitudes: the willingness but doubtful ability of the family to cope with the responsibility, the mixed attitudes of family members to the offences and the individual, and the worry that the family might cover up any further offending.

These subsidiary decision processes, concerned with evaluating hospital care, community services, and family support considerations, were 'cul-de-sacs' in the total tribunal process which were very important in respect of applications for discharge. Having established that the need for continued detention was doubtful on the basis of objective and subjective assessments of the risk to others, issues of care and control came to the fore. Having determined that continued detention was not likely to be justified given the availability and acceptance by the individual of necessary support and safeguards, the decision-makers focused on the rehabilitative resources available. Crises in the decision process at this stage mainly concerned applications, as advice to the Home Secretary in response to references could specify rehabilitative arrangements considered necessary. While these conditions on release could be the cause of serious delay in the acceptance of tribunal advice, more immediate dilemmas and conflicts arose from the limited 'discharge or not' powers in response to applications.

(e) The process of dealing with doubt about the need for continued detention and determining the 'benefit of the doubt'

A complete model of the decision process about the assessment of 'danger to self or others' would include an ultimate stage which was concerned with dealing with the doubt about the need for continued detention. A definite conclusion at an earlier stage would have determined in favour of continued restraint. Doubt about this would have accumulated during the various stages until eventually the residue of doubt about continued detention of the individuals who had survived the earlier hurdles became the focus of attention:

9. *'Doubt' decision process.* Clarifying the nature of any serious doubt in respect of continued detention or the requirements to justify release.
10. *'Benefit of doubt' decision process.* Determining the 'benefit of doubt' in response to the person in favour of continued detention or release.

This ultimate stage was presented diagrammatically (Figure 5) to illustrate that the implications of the nature of 'danger', the limitations of objective assessment, the uncertainties of subjective responses to the person, and all the doubts about the need for control and/or care culminated in the need to give the benefit of the doubt in favour of the liberty of the individual or the protection of others.

'Doubt' was an invariable component of a decision to release a serious mentally abnormal offender. If doubt had been resolved earlier, it would have been in favour of continued detention. The doubt did not arise from a single source, nor was it a straightforward factor. Doubt was associated with:

(i) the impulsive and unpredictable nature of 'danger';
(ii) the inadequacy and non-availability of objective information;
(iii) the insufficiency of tribunal rules and powers;
(iv) the uncertainties inherent in the subjective response to the dangerous individual; and
(v) uncertainties about rehabilitative provision and social support.

'Doubt' and 'risk' were closely related concepts. It was evident that doubt was resolved through a process of determining whether or not to 'take the risk'. The research evidence was that, having not determined the need for continued detention earlier, the 'benefit of the doubt' at this final stage was likely to favour the individual and his or her release from detention.

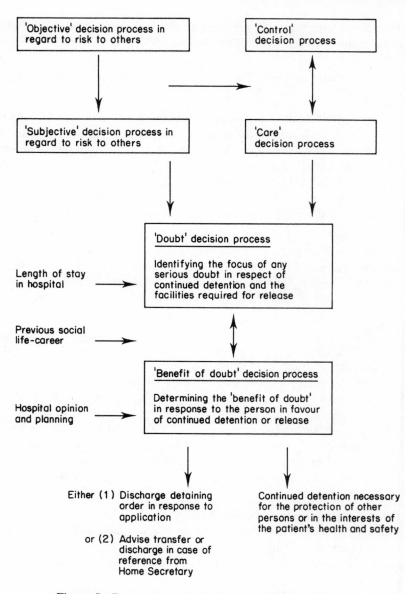

Figure 5   Determination of doubt and 'benefit of doubt'

ADVICE TO THE HOME SECRETARY (REFERENCES)

Whilst doubt was still a component of any judgement in favour of release in response to references from the Home Secretary, the influence of potential for crisis was not as immediate or acute as when considering applications for discharge from men and women who did not require the approval of the Home Secretary. As the tribunal members did not have the power to order the release of an individual referred by the Home Secretary, they were able to recommend the need for specified care or support or safeguards without the same immediate concern for the availability of such care, support, or safeguards.

The crises which did arise in response to references related mainly to the tribunal members choosing to extend their interest and involvement beyond the strictly advisory role. They would sometimes seek to influence the practical implementation of their judgements beyond their advisory role through the use of adjournments and direct approaches to health agencies.

Although it is reasonable to generalize from the tribunal decision process to other bodies concerned with assessing people identified as mentally abnormal and dangerous, there are certain practical implications from the research findings about references:

(i) the roles and responsibilities of the mental health review tribunal were so distinct and different in response to references and applications that it brought into question that one body was required to fulfil such distinct roles without clearer separation of the activities;

(ii) as even their 'advisory' judgements about the 'dangerous' individual involved the important subjective reaction to the person, this questioned the effectiveness of other advisory bodies without the same face-to-face contact with the individual concerned; and

(iii) similarly, it seemed undesirable that so many of the ultimate decisions in regard to the initial detention and release of mentally abnormal offenders were made by people in government agencies with no direct involvement with the person.

It was possible that the distinct roles of the tribunal created difficulties more through confusion in the minds of other people than in the decision process of the tribunal itself. Tribunal members appeared to be aware of the unrealistic expectations of them in their advice to the Home Secretary, as patients and others looked to them to exercise an authority they did not have. Conversely, the unlimited discretion to advise the Home Secretary may have contributed to an expectation from such people as relatives that the tribunal had the authority or influence to arrange transfer to hospital care nearer home of patients who were not further restricted by the Home Secretary.

In addition to receiving the advice of the mental health review tribunal, the Home Office is able to refer a mentally abnormal offender for assessment by the Aarvold Advisory Board (Aarvold, 1973). This is a central body advising the Home Office on a national basis (as opposed to the regionally based tribunals). Although both are advisory, the tribunal and the board have distinct emphases. Whilst the tribunal is primarily concerned with protecting the individual from unjustified detention, the Aarvold Board was established as a further safeguard for the protection of the public. As a central body which does not normally call witnesses, the Aarvold Board is dependent on the written evidence of others. Without the same face-to-face contact with the individual, it is required to make a judgement about the dangerousness of the person. In fact, the Aarvold Board found difficulty in fulfilling its task without that face-to-face contact, and it developed the practice of arranging for one of its members to visit people detained in special hospitals before their cases were considered.

It is likely that where the detaining authority, such as the Home Office, relies on the advice of others, there is an excessive emphasis on a strictly 'objective' approach to its own decision-making. The Home Office tend to deny the more subjective response to the danger. The denial of the 'doubt' and 'risk' inherent in dealing with a 'dangerous individual' could be reflected in an emphasis on requiring the absolute confidence of the decision-makers advising release. As the distance between the individual and the ultimate decision-makers widens, it appears inevitable that greater caution would prevail and that the proportion of false positives would increase.

A MORE COMPLETE MODEL OF DECISION-MAKING ABOUT 'DANGEROUS' PEOPLE

A stimulus–response or input–output model of behaviour would be consistent with viewing the decision process of the mental health review tribunal simply in terms of its formally prescribed rules and procedures and powers. Within a formal structural approach the tribunal would be seen to process the input of facts about the person and his circumstances and respond with the decision appropriate to those facts and the prescribed powers of the tribunal. Although the research did identify a significant correlation between some facts (e.g. age, previous hospital care) and tribunal decisions, the decision process in practice was far more complex. There was the need to take account of the 'human process' and the way the 'facts' were perceived by the decision-makers (see Hogarth, 1971, in respect of judicial decision-making by magistrates). There was the need to incorporate into the more complete model the conflicts, dilemmas and crises when the prescribed framework was inadequate to the task (see Lemert, 1970, in regard to changes in the juvenile court procedures in California).

The complete decision process of the mental health review tribunal developed through the research is shown in Figure 6. It is likely that this same presentation could apply to other decision processes about mentally disordered and dangerous individuals. The members of the various disciplines within the hospital team have more opportunity for direct contact with the individual and with his planned rehabilitation. Yet all the subsidiary decision processes apply

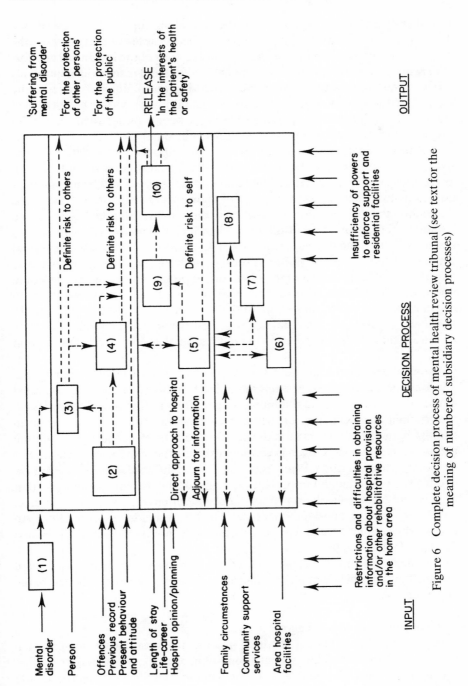

Figure 6   Complete decision process of mental health review tribunal (see text for the meaning of numbered subsidiary decision processes)

as well as the external restraints and difficulties about support facilities outside the hospital. In contrast with an appellate body, decision-makers with the direct primary responsibility for the care and control of the individual are able to deal directly with rehabilitative support facilities and maintain a continuous review assessment without the same need to adjourn. In other words, the aspects of the model concerned with 'direct approach to the hospital' and 'adjourn for information' applies to appellate bodies rather than the bodies with direct responsibility for the 'dangerous individual'.

The mental health review tribunals arose from the recommendations of the Royal Commission on the Law relating to Mental Illness and Mental Deficiency (Percy, 1957). In recommending that there should be an independent body to review the use of compulsory powers of admission and continued detention, the Commission advised that the tribunal should 'consider the patient's mental condition at the time when it considers the application, and decide whether the type of care which has been provided by the use of compulsory powers is the most appropriate to his present needs, or whether any alternative form of care might be more appropriate, or whether he could not be discharged from care altogether'. This appeared to assume an ability to organize or require the movement of the individual to less restrictive care. In the actual legislation the mental health review tribunal had only the authority to 'direct that the patient be discharged' (Mental Health Act 1959, section 123).

The inability of the tribunal (or the hospital authorities) to require the provision of rehabilitative or alternative care facilities to enable the individual to move to a less restricted situation brought into question the effectiveness of the tribunal as a safeguard of the liberty of the individual. There was often conflict between considerations of welfare, protection, and justice, when the tribunal was reluctant to exercise its duty to discharge without the assurance of support facilities. Tribunal members used their right to adjourn in attempts to resolve their conflict and to protect the rights of the patient. It was clear that they would have used the power of a delayed discharge by a given date, as envisaged in new legislation (Mental Health Amendment Act 1982), to resolve the conflict if that means of protecting the liberty of the individual had been available to them.

The new legislation (Mental Health Amendment Act 1982) extended section 123 to require that before determining whether to direct the discharge of a patient:

the tribunal shall have regard:
(a)   to the likelihood of medical treatment alleviating or preventing a deterioration of the patient's condition; and
(b)   in the case of a patient suffering from mental illness or severe mental impairment, to the likelihood of the patient, if discharged, being able

to care for himself, to obtain the care he needs or to guard himself against serious exploitation.

This requirement is reminiscent of the recommendations of the Percy Commission (1957). Yet it simply reflects the approach of the tribunal as it has developed in practice in response to the original limited power to discharge the order. It does not resolve the dilemmas of the tribunal in seeking to exercise their duty to discharge if the prescribed criteria are satisfied. The tribunal will have no greater authority to ensure the provision of facilities for 'preventing a deterioration of the patient's condition' or 'to obtain the care he needs or to guard himself against serious exploitation'.

Even the extended power to 'direct the discharge of a patient on a future date' (Mental Health Amendment Act 1982, section 39:3) served simply to regularize the innovatory use of the power to adjourn as a means of a delayed discharge. The delay would still be in the hope of facilities being made available without the means of ensuring their provision.

The more complete model of decision-making (summarised in Figure 6), which was developed from the research findings, could apply to some extent to any social situation where the 'danger' associated with an individual was being assessed. It is presented as relevant primarily to the assessment of men and women who have previously been identified as 'dangerous' in the sense of:

1. objective evidence of serious offences or behaviour involving the risk of physical harm or sexual assault,
2. serious 'threat and anxiety' about the individual on the part of others, and
3. a considered decision to restrain the person for the protection of other persons.

The more complete model was based on what happened in practice, and is not presented in itself as a prescription for the planned assessment of a dangerous individual. Yet, from the findings of the research project, it is proposed that any process of assessment of the 'dangerous individual' should deliberately acknowledge the distinct aspects of this human process:

1. the assessment of risk on the basis of objective evidence,
2. the evaluation of the subjective response to the individual,
3. the assessment of rehabilitative needs,
4. the investigation of rehabilitative support, and
5. determination of the benefit of the doubt.

A framework for the assessment of 'danger to self and others' or of the 'dangerous individual' is presented as an appendix to this chapter. This framework was based on the implications for the process of assessing 'danger' arising from the findings of the research project and the more complete model of decision-making. It has not been tested in any systematic practical situation and is presented simply as a useful guide for approaching the assessment of a 'dangerous individual'.

The framework made no attempt to apportion different responsibilities to the various disciplines and parties involved in the care and rehabilitation of people identified as dangerous. Certain aspects of the assessment process were traditionally expected of specific professionals such as psychiatrists, psychologists, social workers, and educationalists. Yet the framework was presented as a guide to the human process of a group of individuals with the prescribed responsibility of assessing another individual previously defined as dangerous. The members of the group are left to apportion their own allocation of responsibilities. It served to emphasize that, after all the professional expertise and skill had been applied, the process was essentially 'human' requiring a personal response by the decision-makers to the 'dangerous individual'.

NOTE

1. Mental health legislation in England and Wales was reformed and consolidated into the Mental Health Act 1983 after this research was completed. The general principles have not changed radically, but it should be noted that the summary of the legal framework here relates to the legislation at the time of the research in 1977–78.

REFERENCES

Aarvold, C. (1973) *Report of the Review of Procedures for the Discharge of Psychiatric Patients Subject to Restrictions*, London: HMSO.

Cocozza, J. J. and Steadman, H. J. (1974) Some refinements in the measurement and prediction of dangerous behavior. *American Journal of Psychiatry*, **131**, 1012–1014.

Hepworth, D. R. (1982a) Assessment of 'danger to self and others'. Unpublished Ph.D. thesis, University of Nottingham.

Hepworth, D. R. (1982b) The influence of the concept of danger on the assessment of danger to self and others. *Medicine, Science and the Law*, **22**, 245–254.

Hepworth, D. R. (1983) The decision process of the mental health review tribunal (Two parts). *Medicine, Science and the Law*, **23**, 131–141 and 171–182.

Hogarth, J. (1971) *Sentencing as a Human Process*. Toronto: Toronto University Press.

Lemert, E. (1970) *Social Action and Legal Change*, Chicago: Aldine.

Meehl, P. E. and Rosen, A. (1955) Antecedent probability and the efficiency of psychometric signs. *Psychological Bulletin*, **52**, 194–216.

Megargee, E. I. (1976) Prediction of dangerous behavior. *Criminal Justice and Behavior*, **3**, 3–21.

Mental Health Act 1959. London: HMSO.

Mental Health (Amendment) Act 1982. London: HMSO.

Mental Health Act 1983. London: HMSO.

Mental Health Review Tribunal Rules (1960). London: HMSO (S.I. 1960, No. 1139).

Percy, Baron E. S. Campbell (1957) *Royal Commission on the Law relating to Mental Illness and Mental Deficiency*, London: HMSO.

Review of the Mental Health Act 1959 (1978). London: HMSO.

Scott, P. D. (1977) Assessing dangerousness in criminals. *British Journal of Psychiatry*, **131**, 127–142.

Steadman, H. J. and Cocozza, J. J. (1973) The criminally insane patient: who gets out?'. *Social Psychiatry*, **8**, 230–238.

Steadman, H. J. and Cocozza, J. J. (1974) *Careers of the Criminally Insane*. Lexington: Heath.

Sturup, G. K. (1968) Will this man be dangerous? In H. R. Rollin (Ed.) *The Mentally Abnormal Offender*. London: Churchill.

APPENDIX:
FRAMEWORK FOR THE ASSESSMENT OF THE 'DANGEROUS INDIVIDUAL'

Stage One: Assessment of Risk on Basis of Objective Evidence

1. A careful distinction should be made between objective onsiderations and the more subjective evaluation of the person, the offence and the situation.

   The decision-makers should aim to:
   (a) clarify the extent to which continued restraint of the individual was justified on the basis of observable facts and verified information; and
   (b) ensure that such objective facts and information were not used inappropriately to justify a more subjective 'anxiety and threat' arising from the reactions of the decision-makers to the person.

2. The objective assessment of the risk to others should be based on:
   (a) the nature and severity of the offences and/or behaviour which led to the current detention;
   (b) the previous record of offences and/or antisocial behaviour,
   (c) the 'dangerous situation' and/or circumstances within which the offences and/or behaviour occurred and the 'triggers' in the situation;
   (d) the present social performance and achievements compared to previous social achievements and social life-career;
   (e) the present attitudes of the individual towards the past behaviour and future responsibilities;
   (f) clinical assessment of the 'psychiatric' condition of the person, as a contribution to the previous 'dangerous' behaviour and with regard to future clinical prognosis.

3. In respect of the particular 'dangerous individual' the decision-makers should seek to identify clearly the nature of the risk associated with the individual and the potential victims at risk.

4. A decision should be reached whether the risk to the potential victims on the basis of the objective evidence was sufficient to justify the continued restraint of the individual.

5. Whether or not the decision-makers were certain of the need for continued detention, they should seek to identify:
   (a) the aspects of the objective assessment where the factual information was insufficient and further investigation was desirable;

(b) the nature and focus of any 'doubt' about the need for continued detention on the basis of the objective evidence;

(c) the nature of any continuing 'risks' from the individual which required further attention, regardless of whether they were sufficient to justify continued detention or not.

Stage Two: Evaluation of Subjective Response to Individual

6. If the need for continued restraint was in doubt through the assessment of the risk on the basis of objective evidence, there should be a studied evaluation of the subjective responses and perceptions of the decision-makers and others towards the individual, and the prospect of release from detention.

7. The 'subjective' evaluation should be based on:

(a) the extent to which the decision-makers and others continued to experience 'threat and anxiety' within their relationship with the individual or in response to face-to-face interaction with him;

(b) the extent to which the decision-makers and others experienced feelings of sympathy and confidence in the individual and were able to perceive him as a person to be trusted;

(c) an attempt to identify the cause of the anxiety of others and the nature of the threat feared by others;

(d) an attempt to identify the justification for the feeling of confidence and the willingness to trust the person with social responsibilities again;

(e) evidence of the formation of, or potential for, constructive emotional relationships with the decision-makers and/or other significant people which could be used to help the person regain his self-respect and a responsible place back in society.

8. A decision should be reached whether the 'threat and anxiety' which others continued to experience in response to the individual, in support of the objective evidence of the risk to others, was sufficient to justify continued restraint.

9. Whether or not the decision-makers were certain of the need for continued detention, they should seek to identify:

(a) the aspects of the subjective evaluation which were restricted by insufficient information and/or experience of the individual;

(b) the nature and focus of any 'doubt' about the need for continued detention on the basis of the subjective evaluation;

(c) the nature of any continuing 'risks' from the individual in respect of his relationships with others and the opportunities available or to be created for the formation of the constructive emotional relationships necessary for rehabilitation.

Stage Three: Assessment of Rehabilitative Needs

10. If the need for continued restraint was in doubt through the assessment of the risk on the basis of objective evidence and subjective evaluation, there should be an examination of the rehabilitative considerations necessary for the release from detention and resettlement of the individual into open society.

11. The assessment of the rehabilitative needs of the individual and for the protection of others should be based on:

(a) an assessment of the ability of the individual to live an independent social life in the community without serious self-neglect or exploitation by others;

(b) an assessment of the social controls considered necessary for the protection of others in any potentially 'dangerous situation';

(c) clinical assessment of the further medical and psychiatric treatment and support required before and/or following release from detention;

(d) an assessment of further social training and educational needs;

(e) an assessment of the need for 'half-way' residential rehabilitation and/or continued social work support to the resettlement into open society;

(f) an assessment of family circumstances and relationships with the individual;

(g) an assessment of formed or potential constructive emotional relationships with support agencies and others in open society.

12. A decision should be reached as to whether the further help and support available, or likely to be available, to meet the specific care and control needs of the individual was sufficient to justify release from detention.

13. The decision-makers should seek to identify:

(a) the aspects of the care and control needs of the individual and the support facilities available in response to those needs which required further investigation before a decision can be finalized;

(b) the nature and focus of any 'doubt' about the care and control required in support of release from detention;

(c) the nature of any continuing 'risks' to the individual or others in respect of the need for continued care and/or control.

Stage Four: Preliminary Determination of 'Benefit of the Doubt'

14. Before the decision-makers responsible for the restraint of the individual could proceed to negotiating a rehabilitative release plan with the individual and the various support facilities, they were required normally to reach a preliminary decision in regard to the justification for release. If the need for continued detention remained in doubt on the basis of objective evidence and subjective evaluation and examination of rehabilitative considerations, this preliminary decision should be based on an examination of the areas of doubt.

15. The preliminary determination of the 'benefit of the doubt' should be based on an examination of:

(a) the nature and focus of any 'doubt' about the need for continued detention on the basis of the objective evidence;

(b) the nature and focus of any 'doubt' about the need for continued detention on the basis of the subjective evaluation;

(c) the nature and focus of any 'doubt' about the care and control required in support of release from detention;

(d) the availability of the further information identified as desirable in respect of the objective assessment and the subjective evaluation and the care and/or control needs;

(e) length of stay in detention in relation to the offences and/or behaviour which led to the detention;

(f) the confidence and 'trust' expressed in the individual by others with whom he had a significant relationship;

(g) the emotional responses of the decision-makers to the individual.

16. A decision should be reached as to whether, taking into account the areas of doubt which were inevitable because of the nature of 'danger' and the insufficiency of information, the 'benefit of the doubt' should be given in favour of the individual and release from detention.

Stage Five: Investigation of Rehabilitative Support

17. If the decision-makers were inclined to give the 'benefit of the doubt' in favour of release from detention, there should be an examination through direct involvement of the care and support available or which could be negotiated to aid the successful resettlement of the individual into open society.
18. The development of the plan to rehabilitate the particular 'dangerous individual' into open society should be based on:
    (a) investigation into the further information identified as desirable in respect of the objective assessment and the subjective evaluation and the care and/or control needs;
    (b) the nature of any continuing 'risks' from the individual which required further attention;
    (c) the nature of any continuing 'risks' from the individual in respect of his relationships with others;
    (d) the nature of any continuing 'risks' to the individual or others in respect of the need for continued care and/or control;
    (e) investigation into continued health care provision in open society;
    (f) investigation into community residential or other support services considered necessary for rehabilitation;
    (g) assessment of the availability of family and their willingness and suitability to provide care and support;
    (h) the opportunities available or to be created for the formation of the constructive emotional relationships necessary for rehabilitation.
19. A decision should be reached as to whether the care and support available and/or negotiated as part of the rehabilitative plan was sufficient to justify release from detention.
20. The decision-makers should seek to identify:
    (a) the aspects of rehabilitative support considered essential to the rehabilitative release plan but which are unavailable or uncertain;
    (b) the aspects of the desired rehabilitative support which are unavailable or uncertain yet not considered essential;
    (c) the resistances from health or community services and/or family which could put at risk the rehabilitation of the individual.

Stage Six: Ultimate Determination of 'Benefit of Doubt'

21. As 'doubt' was an invariable component of a decision to release a 'dangerous individual' and 'benefit of the doubt' was inherent in the acceptance of the individual as a 'person' to be returned to society, the final stage of assessing whether the individual should continue to be restrained as 'dangerous' should involve the acknowledgement of the areas of doubt and the subjective trust and sympathy of the decision-makers towards the individual.
22. The final decision should be based on:
    (a) the nature and focus of any remaining 'doubt' about the need for continued detention in respect of the objective assessment and the subjective evaluation and the care and/or control needs;
    (b) the nature of any continuing 'risks' from the individual on the basis of objective evidence and subjective evaluation and the need for continued care and/or control;
    (c) the aspects of the rehabilitative support plan which were unavailable or uncertain;

(d) length of stay in detention in relation to the offences and/or behaviour which led to the detention;

(e) the confidence and 'trust' expressed by significant others with whom the individual had formed or had the potential to form constructive emotional relationships;

(f) the emotional responses of the decision-makers to the individual.

23. A decision should be reached as to whether, despite the remaining 'doubts' and continuing 'risks', the 'benefit of the doubt' should be determined in favour of the individual and the implementation of the rehabilitative release plan.

24. As the areas of doubt and continuing 'risks' had been identified as clearly as possible, once the decision to support release was determined, the emphasis in the 'constructive emotional relationship' with the individual should be on the 'trust and confidence' in him as a 'person' inherent in the 'benefit of the doubt' and 'taking the risk'. This was important to the rehabilitative prognosis as a positive aspect of the 'equation' which had determined that release was justified.

Aggression and Dangerousness
Edited by D. P. Farrington and J. Gunn
© 1985 John Wiley & Sons Ltd.

CHAPTER 8

Security in a Local
Mental Hospital

MICHAEL CARNEY and JANE GARNER

INTRODUCTION

Three interrelated problems continue to preoccupy psychiatrists involved with the problems of security in our hospitals:

1. what to do with mentally abnormal offenders;
2. the management of violence in our hospitals; and
3. security in local general and psychiatric hospitals.

The interim Butler (1974) and Glancy (1974) reports recommending the establishment of a regional secure unit (RSU) in each health region are largely unimplemented. By 1980, none had been opened, but the Wessex Unit was far advanced. However, most of the English regions had not progressed beyond the planning stage (Knight, 1980). Some regions had provided interim secure units, notably Liverpool (Rainhill), Manchester, and Wessex (Knowle). The Rainhill unit has been described (Higgins, 1981). However, there is no consensus as to where to site RSUs, or indeed, whether they are needed at all. Price (1976) recommended that these units be sited in prisons. Bluglass (1978) put forward several alternative modes of caring for behaviourally disturbed psychiatric patients: a revival of the crisis management aspect of the ordinary psychiatric hospital's role without necessarily returning to the era of the locked-door mentality; continuing the present policy of developing RSUs but with an expansion of their role to accommodate the whole gamut of dangerous patients; more special hospitals; and siting RSUs within prisons. However, conditions in special hospitals have been criticized following disclosures about Rampton in a television programme (Editorial, *British Medical Journal*, 1980; Editorial, *Lancet*, 1980). Another cause for concern is the difficulty experienced by people working in the special hospitals in persuading psychiatric hospitals to take patients no longer in need of their special facilities (Dell, 1980). Indeed, Tennent *et al.* (1980) showed that only 35 per cent of a cohort of

185

special hospital admissions had been discharged or transferred elsewhere within 5 years of admission. From a different standpoint, Robertson and Gibbens (1980) complained of the declining number of patients transferred under section 72 of the Mental Health Act 1959 from prisons to hospitals, especially mental handicap hospitals.

The management of violence in our hospitals, though of great importance to hospital staff, has been strangely neglected in the British literature. An exception is the work of Fottrell (1980) who studied the incidence of intentional behaviour disturbance, such as assault, in two mental hospitals and a district general hospital psychiatric unit over a period of a year. Three degrees of violence were distinguished according to the degree of injury inflicted: no injury; bruising or laceration; and more serious injury. The details of each incident were recorded by a nurse, after briefing from the investigator. A great deal of violence was recorded, mainly in the first category (minor). More serious injury was rare. Most patients were non-violent and violence was most common during the daytime, on acute admission wards, and among women as compared with men. The most frequent associated disorder was schizophrenia. The inference was that most disturbed patients can be dealt with readily at the local level by relatively simple measures. McPhail (1978) looked at the various incidents which disrupted the smooth running of a general hospital psychiatric ward. He classified them as absences, refusals, aggression, self-harm, disturbing others, and incidents requiring staff control measures. By these criteria, 201 of 518 patients admitted over a 6-month period were found to have been involved in one or more incidents; many in several incidents. Younger patients and those staying longer in hospital were most likely to have been involved. However, specific staff control measures or transfer out of the unit were rarely required, and it was felt that episodes of difficult behaviour, though common, could normally be contained within the general hospital.

This view was supported by the report of the Royal College of Psychiatrists (1980), which stressed the need for secure facilities at all levels of the hospital service, from national to local. On the other hand, with the therapeutic revolution in psychiatry in the 1950s and 1960s, most locked doors have been opened, and many psychiatric hospitals are without a locked ward. Hospitals have also become increasingly reluctant to accept patients with known propensities for violence. Though fairly precise information is available about the provision (or lack of it) of RSUs (report of the Royal College of Psychiatrists, 1980), relatively little is known of more local secure facilities, with some exceptions (see below). However, there has been a report (Higgins, 1981) on an interim secure unit for the Liverpool region. The first 4 years' operation of a locked ward of 14 beds, sited in Rainhill Psychiatric Hospital, was described. The staff of this unit also gave a forensic service to local hospitals, prisons, and the community. Of 78 patients referred from these sources, 39 were admitted. All had committed dangerous acts and were legally detained. Forty per cent were women and most were schizophrenics. Only seven stayed for more than a year. Discharged patients were followed up by the unit team or by the local catchment area psychiatric service. The author reckoned that the number of occupied beds had settled at around 12 for this population of 1 million. The regime of the unit largely depended upon a policy of using a graded system of parole, more freedom being awarded for better behaviour, and consequently their seclusion room was very seldom required.

Coinciding with the translation of much acute work from traditional psychiatric hospitals to open district general hospital units and the increasing reluctance of hospital staff to cope with violence—probably on account of their lack of training and experience in this field—there has become apparent a real need for the development of local secure psychiatric facilities.

Reports of such units however, have been sparse, and their place in the range of secure facilities is uncertain. Woodside *et al.* (1976) described a local secure unit in Edinburgh, founded in 1974. Sited in a psychiatric hospital, it took referrals from the police, special hospitals, courts, and from the other wards of the hospital. It was staffed with 16 to 18 nurses, a part-time medical registrar, and a few hours of consultant time. It was intended to be a short-stay unit for behaviourally disturbed mentally disordered persons. One hundred patients were admitted over the first 8 months, 92 being discharged or transferred elsewhere. Half were psychotic and 29 per cent psychopathic. Many were alcoholic. Carney and Nolan (1978) described a small unit in Shenley Psychiatric Hospital, again founded in 1974. It gave a more clearly defined short-stay crisis management service to the local (Brent and Harrow) hospitals than the Edinburgh unit, and achieved a greater turnover of patients. However, the forensic element was much less, and fewer alcoholic and psychopathic patients were taken in. Eighty to 90 per cent were schizophrenic, compared with 25 per cent in the Edinburgh unit. Moreover, in this unit there was a clear policy of returning patients to originating wards when the unit staff judged behaviour disturbance to have abated. Staff levels were similar and about 50 per cent of the patients in each unit were legally detained. Both units differed from the Liverpool interim secure unit in having a local rather than a regional role and in having a smaller forensic component. However, there is a marked lack of follow-up information on people leaving these units.

There is also an absence of publications comparing British and North American practice in dealing with these problems. Whereas British literature has concentrated on the setting up and organizing of secure institutions for patients with behaviour problems, American writers seem more concerned with teaching and research as a means of improving staff morale in secure units (Knesper, 1978) and with training staff in techniques of restraining disturbed patients (including mechanical restraints). Thus, Wilson (1976) commented on the absence of adequate guidance for nursing staff on the control of disturbed behaviour, and described how a hospital committee was set up to initiate an appropriate training programme. An audio-visual aid package was produced and it was claimed that, in the subsequent 2 years, the number of violent incidents in the hospital, resulting in injuries to hospital staff and staff man-hours lost thereby, decreased substantially. Phillips (1977) recommended the use of mechanical restraints for certain violent patients, under careful supervision by senior nursing and medical staff.

This chapter describes our further experience in the Shenley Hospital local unit; the fate, 4 years on, of a cohort of longer-stay patients residing in the unit in 1978; and a 3-month prospective follow-up study of 40 short-stay patients taken in as a crisis management measure in 1982.

HISTORICAL

Shenley Hospital served a population of 523,000 in north-west London when the security unit began in May 1974. A 30-bed locked male ward of static population related only to the Harrow division of the hospital. It developed into a 48-bed unit of two locked wards with a considerable turnover of patients of both sexes (Carney and Nolan, 1978). Though, in theory, it served all of Shenley Hospital before 1974, in fact there was only one non-Harrow division patient in the ward when one of us (Carney) set up the unit in the ward. Subsequently it enlarged its role to serve all of Shenley Hospital and its catchment area district general hospital units—Northwick Park and Central Middlesex Hospitals. From August 1976, females were taken in. The policy of the unit from its inception was to assist open psychiatric wards in the management of behaviourally disturbed psychiatric patients. Consequently, arrangements for taking these patients have been flexible and informal, so that a place is always available when required. At the beginning it was doubted if the unit could accommodate the considerable expansion of patient numbers generated by this relaxed approach, or whether it could change from a purely custodial role to the active one demanded by its ever-increasing workload. Its role in the management of mentally abnormal offenders or personality-disordered patients was also uncertain. However, since May 1974 the unit has never been without a bed when needed. Table 1 shows that the vast majority of patients have been temporary.

THE SETTING

The two wards, each containing 24 beds, were intended to provide differing levels of security. The less secure one accommodates those patients who are occasionally or unpredictably harmful (e.g. committing sexual assaults or attacks on property), or who abscond from hospital and commit social indiscretions such as micturating in public places or endangering themselves, for example, by sleeping rough on frosty nights. The other ward, with a greater

Table 1 Bed complement and movement of patients in and out of the security unit

Year	No. of beds	Temporarily nursed-in	Admitted to the unit	Total movements in	Discharged	Deaths	Total movements out
1974/75	30	60	11	67	16	1	70
1975/76	30	66	18	72	8	2	73
1976/77	48	M 81 } 106 F 25	M 5 } 16 F 11	122	23	0	98
1977/78	48	M 182 } 276 F 94	M 6 } 11 F 5	280	17	0	281
1978/79	48	M 142 } 226 F 84	M 2 } 4 F 2	230	4	1	232
1979/80	48	M 142 } 246 F 104	M 14 } 19 F 5	249	25	0	249
1980/81	48	M 120 } 193 F 73	M 15 } 23 F 8	216	25	0	219
1981/82	48	M 130 } 227 F 97	M 14 } 25 F 11	233	15	0	225

ratio of nurses to patients, provides a greater level of security for patients with acute short-term behaviour disturbance, accompanying mental illness, and those continuously harmful to themselves and others over longer periods. Furthermore, in 1978 a closed basement activities area, under the two wards and communicating with them, was commissioned. There, physical and occupational activities are available for the eight to ten patients unable to leave the unit. However, most patients move in and out of the unit to hospital occupational therapy and social facilities under lesser degrees of supervision.

STAFFING

During the day there are nine nurses of both sexes. A consultant psychiatrist attends for two sessions, and a senior registrar and another doctor attend on a half-time basis. Occupational therapists, a remedial gymnast, social workers, and a psychologist come as required.

TRAINING

As pointed out by Woodside *et al.* (1976) a local security unit with a high turnover of acute psychiatric patients is an ideal training ground for psychiatric trainees. Since its inception the unit has been included in the senior registrar (joint London University/Shenley Hospital appointments) training programme. Medical students and student psychiatric and general nurses also attend.

POLICY

This has been to give help as required. From the outset, weekly meetings of the several disciplines involved were held, at which working arrangements were decided. These policies were then discussed and usually accepted by the Senior Clinical Committee of Shenley Hospital. Any difficulty in operating the unit which could not be settled on the spot was referred to this committee. However, though this 'complaints procedure' was quite often used in the early days, over recent years it has seldom been needed.

Most patients come to the unit as a temporary measure, at the instigation of the appropriate nursing officer or medical officer, while remaining on the nominal roll of the ward or hospital of origin. Their beds are kept for them until a definitive decision about disposal is made. They return to the relevant ward or unit when the crisis unit staff judge the behaviour disturbance to have subsided. In addition, a few patients are formally admitted to the unit, either directly after an approach in writing from the patient's consultant to the consultant in charge of the unit, or after a period of temporary residence and assessment in the unit, if they have shown by their behaviour that they cannot remain safely on open wards for any reasonable length of time.

It can be seen, therefore, that all patients are screened in the hospital first; none are taken direct from the community or from other institutions. Their characteristics will thus depend upon the sort of patients taken into the parent hospitals.

THERAPEUTIC MILIEU

The calming influence of the unit depends on three factors: the reassurance engendered in patients by the secure surroundings and the high nurse/patient ratio; physical activity; and the use of drugs and, where appropriate, ECT. The staff on the unit work as teams and the methods of dealing with aggression (Carney and Nolan, 1979) in general and in respect of each patient are worked out at ward meetings. Emphasis is placed on prevention. Causes of disturbance are analysed and an appropriate approach formulated. Individual nurses with a particular rapport with certain patients are encouraged to try to modify their behaviour to prevent violence occurring. However, when major violence seems imminent, the unit staff assemble as a team under a preappointed leader (usually a senior nurse) and work to a prearranged plan, understood by all the members. The propensities of particularly violent individuals are known and in the event of an incident this knowledge is clearly important in deciding on a strategy of management. If the patient is known to attack property, then intervention is delayed until just past the peak of aggression, but if he is known to attack people then intervention occurs as soon as practicable (i.e. when sufficient nurses assemble). Devices of mechanical restraint are not used, and there is no padded cell. However, disturbed individuals may be secluded in one of two side rooms, protected for patients' safety. Patients are encouraged to vent their aggression in a controlled way by physical activity—by gymnastic equipment, outdoor ball games on an adjacent pitch, rowing machines, punchballs, static bicycles, jogging machines—or even by the destruction of old worthless articles such as magazines.

A supportive environment of this kind inevitably encourages undue dependence. We try to avoid this by returning the patient to his ward when quiet, and before he is unduly attached to the unit. Hobbies, painting, modelling, and craftwork are encouraged, and we try to reproduce normal work situations in collaboration with the nursing officers involved in rehabilitation and employment, and with the occupational therapists, to assess physical skills, perseverance, concentration, and time-keeping. Courses of study may be carried on in a quiet room. Group meetings take place within each ward, weekly, for patients admitted to the ward. No attempt is made to institute any kind of formal group therapy because so many paranoid individuals find it threatening, but discussions are carried on to involve patients in their own care, disseminate information, prevent withdrawal and isolation, and maintain social awareness and responsibility.

THE PATIENTS

Table 2(a) shows that on 27 May 1982 the 22 admitted patients (7 females and 15 males) ranged in age from 22 to 66 years (mean 47.4 years), and had been in Shenley Hospital for an average of 21.2 years (range 1 month to 42 years). Table 2(b) shows that there were also 11 temporarily transferred patients (2 females and 9 males). On this date, 8 patients were detained under the Mental Health Act 1959—4 under section 26, 2 under section 71, 1 under section 72, and 1 under section 30. Schizophrenia (20) was the commonest diagnosis, and 2 others had schizophreniform psychoses. Eighteen were violent and dangerous to themselves or others, in particular to special groups like women and children. Four also had epileptic fits. Of 5 manic-depressives, 4 were temporarily transferred and 2 admitted to the ward. Three patients had organic brain deterioration and 3 personality disorders.

The numbers of patients taken into the unit annually have risen steadily over the 8 years, particularly in 1977/78 when there was a rise of 130 per cent over the previous year (Table 1). Overall, the intake increased by 248 per cent from 1974/75 until 1981/82, and this was almost entirely accounted for by the rise in temporarily transferred patients. Most patients came from Shenley itself (Brent and Harrow divisions), only a few originating from the district general hospital psychiatric units, but this latter element has gradually increased over more recent years.

The numbers of admitted patients have remained fairly static over the years. In Table 1 the numbers of temporary transfers and admissions exceed the 'total movements' into the unit because some patients were only admitted after being temporarily resident. The three deaths included two suicides. The 'admitted' figures include four patients taken from Broadmoor in exchange for four patients sent there from the unit (included in 'discharges'). The increase in temporarily transferred patients was complemented by a decrease in the time they stayed in the unit, from a mean of 20.6 days (range 1–115 days) in 1974/75 to 3 days (range 1–21 days) in 1981/82. In the last 5 years most patients came from Brent, some from Harrow, and a few from other hospitals. Since 1974 the proportion of patients emanating from the Harrow division declined (though their numbers actually rose) while the proportion coming from the Brent division increased to 68 per cent in 1981/82. Harrow is a fairly stable middle-class borough, whereas Brent is a working-class area with a large immigrant population and considerable social problems. Though we did not have exact data, the increase in the Brent intake to the unit seemed to be partly due to short-term psychosis among patients of West Indian origin.

Over the whole period more than 70 per cent of the patients were psychotic. Relatively few suffered from manic-depressive illness, personality disorders, alcoholism, epilepsy, subnormality, or other conditions. Patients who acted out or manipulated the hospital environment did even less well in a locked ward than in an open one, as their antisocial traits were reinforced by the greater attention they received from the enhanced concentration of nurses. The patients with personality disorder did not stay for very long.

During each year, approximately 25 per cent of the temporarily transferred patients had more than one spell in the unit. For example, 270 spells in 1977/78 were accounted for by 186 patients. In each year around 50 per cent of the patients taken into the unit were under a section of the Mental Health Act. A considerable number came under section 136 (taken to a place of safety by a police constable), for example 21 (9 per cent of the total intake of the unit) in 1981/82. In that year (the latest for which we have figures), 23 patients (10 per cent) were taken in under section 29, 45 (20 per cent) under section 25, 16 (7 per cent) under section 26, 15 (7 per cent) under section 60, 65 or 71, and 3 (1 per cent) under section 30. In all, 123 patients (54 per cent) were taken in under sections of the Mental Health Act.

PROSPECTIVE COHORT FOLLOW-UP

On 1 August 1978 there were 34 patients admitted to the unit (21 males and 13 females). Their characteristics are shown in Table 3. On 1 August 1982, the outcome of this cohort is shown in Table 4. Thus, of the original 34, only 35 per cent were still in the unit and 53 per cent were discharged into the community or to open wards.

Did any variable predict those who stayed and those who went out? The mean age of the 18 discharged patients (26.1 years) was lower than that of the 12 who stayed (43.7 years; $t = 4.89$; $p<0.001$). The discharged patients' stay in Shenley was also shorter (2.5 years; range 1–4, compared with 15.7 years; range 1–36). Did the number of incidents in which they were involved in 1978 predict the outcome over the next 4 years? 'Incidents' of violence or bad behaviour were operationally defined as those sufficiently noteworthy to be recorded in the incident report book. It was found that the mean number of incidents per patient who stayed in (5.8) was not markedly different from that of those who were discharged (6.7). Sex, however, was more clearly related to outcome. Thus, after 4 years, five females and one male had been discharged. On the other hand, as many as 20 males were either dead, still in hospital, or transferred to Broadmoor, compared with nine females ($\chi^2 = 4.17$; $p < 0.05$).

Were those remaining in the unit more ill than the patients who had left? Those remaining in hospital were assessed by an adaptation of a rating scale (Carney and Sheffield, 1973). Nine symptoms—hallucinations, delusions,

Table 2 (a)   Admitted patients

Patient no.	Sex	Status	Age	Length of stay* (years)	Date of admission to ward	Diagnostic formulation
1	Male	Informal	36	8	18 Apr. 1978	Borderline subnormal, epileptic, paranoid psychosis, history of violence.
2	Male	Informal	31	5	10 Feb. 1978	Schizophrenic, violent.
3	Male	Informal	57	37	9 July 1981	Schizophrenic, violent.
4	Male	Informal	39	23	18 Oct. 1959	Schizophrenic, history of violence.
5	Male	Informal	61	34	7 Nov. 1951	Schizophrenic, history of violence, absconds.
6	Male	Informal	34	10	17 Oct. 1974	Schizophrenic, absconds.
7	Male	Informal	43	14	5 Oct. 1981	Schizophrenic, violent.
8	Male	Section 26	22	1	12 Feb. 1982	Schizophrenic, absconds.

	Sex	Status	Age		Date	Diagnosis
9	Female	Informal	61	1 month	5 May 1982	Personality disorder, violent.
10	Male	Section 26	53	14	5 Nov. 1981	Schizophrenic, danger to children.
11	Male	Informal	59	38	17 Aug. 1978	Schizophrenic, danger to women.
12	Male	Informal	66	40	6 Mar. 1980	Schizophrenic, violent.
13	Male	Informal	59	35	16 Aug. 1976	Schizophrenic.
14	Male	Informal	60	4	16 Nov. 1981	Schizophrenic, offence against children.
15	Male	Informal	60	42	29 Jan. 1982	Schizophrenic.
16	Male	Informal	35	17	24 Mar. 1980	Schizophrenic, epileptic, offence against women.
17	Female	Section 71	61	11	10 July 1981	Schizophrenic.
18	Female	Informal	23	4	7 Sept. 1981	Personality disorder, self-mutilation.
19	Female	Section 26	53	21	19 Aug. 1980	Manic depressive.
20	Female	Informal	61	23	16 Aug. 1976	Schizophrenic.
21	Female	Informal	58	4	7 Sept. 1981	Personality disorder, post leucotomy epileptic.
22	Female	Informal	43	7	23 May 1979	Huntington's chorea, wanders abroad unsupervised.

*In Shenley Hospital

Table 2 (b)   Temporary residents

Patient no.	Sex	Status	Age	Date of admission to hospital	Date of admission to ward	Diagnostic formulation
23	Male	Informal	51	29 Mar. 1982	7 June 1982	Manic depressive, ? frontal lobe damage.
24	Male	Informal	39	19 Apr. 1982	26 July 1982	Paranoid schizophrenic, violent.
25	Male	Section 72	40	26 May 1967	18 July 1982	Schizophrenic, alcoholic.
26	Male	Informal	29	16 May 1982	19 July 1982	Manic depressive.
27	Male	Informal	18	23 May 1982	17 July 1982	Three grand mal fits, hypomanic.
28	Male	Section 26	32	28 Oct. 1981	25 July 1982	Psychotic, assaulted women.
29	Female	Section 30	39	21 May 1982	22 July 1982	Mania.
30	Female	Informal	77	20 Nov. 1944	26 July 1982	Senile dementia.
31	Male	Informal	47	11 June 1951	18 Aug. 1980	Schizophrenic, wanderer, fire risk.
32	Male	Informal	61	8 Dec. 1970	24 Aug. 1981	Brain-damaged, ex-boxer, 'punch-drunk'. Directs traffic at gate.
33	Male	Section 71	46	3 May 1976	7 July 1982	Paranoid schizophrenic, assaulted people.

Table 3 Characteristics of 34 patients in the unit on 1 August 1978

Sex		Mean age in years (range)	Length of stay in years (range)*	Diagnosis			
Male	Female			Schizophrenia and psychosis	Manic-depressive	Epilepsy	Subnormality
21	13	40(23–61)	11.9(1–34)	30	1	2	1

*In Shenley Hospital

Table 4   Outcome 4 years later, of 34 patients in unit on 1 August 1978

	Male	Female	Total
Still in unit	9	3	12
On open wards	8	4	12
Discharged	1	5	6
Dead	2	1	3
Transferred to Broadmoor	0	1	1

depression, elated mood, aggressive behaviour, non-aggressive behaviour disturbance, apathy, and social withdrawal—were rated on a 4-point scale (none = 0; mild = 1; moderate = 2; severe = 3) and the individual symptom scores summed to give an overall score for each patient. The mean score was 10, suggesting that these patients were still fairly disturbed and not in hospital on accommodation grounds alone! The patients on open wards, however, had lower symptom scores (8.5) than those remaining in the unit (11.5). This suggests that, not surprisingly, the more disturbed patients stayed in the unit.

SECLUSION AND VIOLENCE

Did the total number of seclusions differ between those who stayed and those who left. One of the most stable and objective criteria of violence was the level of seclusion. Seclusion in the unit was strictly supervised by both nursing and medical staff, and each occasion was recorded in the seclusion book. The mean number of seclusions for those 25 patients who were discharged or transferred at any time was compared with those who stayed in the ward throughout the 48 months. Not surprisingly, those who stayed in had a greater number of seclusions (16.2) than those who left (5.2). However, when this mean was related to months spent in the unit (i.e. the number of seclusions per patient per month) there was no difference (0.03) between those who left (excluding deaths and Broadmoor) and those who stayed full-time. Thus the intensity of violence warranting seclusion appears to bear no relation to outcome. However, these figures somewhat misrepresent the situation. Only five of the nine who stayed were secluded at any time, suggesting that these patients were a very disturbed sub-group. The other four remained because their *potential* for violence was so great. Thus one, when given freedom, would wreck cars, and another would commit sexual assaults.

Did the sexes differ in respect to levels of violence (and incidents of seclusion)? Previous evidence (Carney and Nolan, 1978) suggested that females were more violent than males. However, though the females spent a *shorter* mean time in the unit (19.8 months) than the males (28 months), the numbers of seclusions per month per patient for men and for women was the same. (0.03) Why then did women stay for shorter periods than men? Again the answer may be the greater potential for violence among men than among women.

Did the experience of being in locked wards itself influence the propensity for behaviour disturbance among this cohort? In order to investigate this, the mean number of seclusions for each patient for each 3-month period of the 4 years was calculated. Although there was a tendency towards more seclusion in the first and last years, in general there was no consistent trend. Thus the experience of being locked up itself was not associated with a reduction in behaviour disturbance as measured by the incidence of seclusion.

PROSPECTIVE STUDY OF TEMPORARILY TRANSFERRED PATIENTS

All short-stay patients taken into the unit between 24 May and 24 July 1982 (2 months) were assessed prospectively. There were 40 patients (22 male and 18 female). Their characteristics are shown in Table 5. They were appreciably younger than the admitted patients, and the proportion of females was greater, though males still outnumbered females. Over 75 per cent had had previous psychiatric admissions and 50 per cent had been in the unit before. The incident which provoked transfer to the crisis unit was in the vast majority of cases (36) concerned with violence—violence against others, against themselves, against property, or the threat of violence. In 26 of these patients the violence was facilitated by features of the patient's illness (e.g. voices telling them to do it, or a suspicious mood). One patient committed his act under the influence of alcohol. Over seventy per cent of these patients were schizophrenic or acute psychotics and the remainder had affective psychoses (six) or personality disorder (four). One was an elderly dement who was transferred in error.

With regard to management, 25 had medical measures including ECT (two) and spells in seclusion (11). Fifteen had milieu therapy alone. The modal length of stay was 3 days, but the mean was 5.4 days due to a few patients who stayed considerably longer (range 1–21 days). All were returned to the ward or hospital of origin, none being transferred elsewhere. Forty per cent were detained under the Mental Health Act, eight under part 4 sections, five under part 5 sections, and three under section 136.

Previous reports (Carney and Nolan, 1978) had suggested that violence was slightly commoner in females. To test this hypothesis, violence and violent tendencies were rated as follows: threats = 1; violence against property = 2; violence against persons without injury = 3; violence against persons with mild injuries = 4; violence against persons with moderate or severe injuries = 5. The mean scores of males and females were the same (1.7). Thus there was no evidence that the sexes differed in this respect.

Table 5   Characteristics of 40 temporarily transferred patients, May–July 1982

Sex		Age (range)			Diagnosis			
Male	Female	Mean	Mode	Median	Schizophrenia and psychosis	Affective psychosis	Personality disorder	Dementia
22	18	37.9(19–77)	30	30.4	29	6	4	1

DISCUSSION

It is evident that this local secure unit had three primary functions. The most important function, and that for which the vast majority of patients passed through the unit each year, was to act as a short-term facility for the control of the behaviourally disturbed and mentally ill patients of Shenley Hospital and the other hospitals in its catchment area. Its second function was to offer custody to the chronic mentally ill who were continuously or intermittently too dangerous to be looked after on an open ward. Thirdly, it took in some mentally abnormal offenders. These functions will be discussed in greater detail below.

This unit differs from other units mentioned in the Introduction in taking in no patients direct from the community or from non-medical institutions such as prisons or courts. Patients are all screened by open psychiatric wards first, though some section 136 admissions came direct to the unit on a temporary basis while remaining on the books of the ward or hospital of origin. Another point of difference was that patients with neurosis, personality problems, and alcoholism were largely screened out, so that nearly all the unit's patients were psychotic. Though, by virtue of its two locked wards, the unit offered a moderate degree of security, this was limited because of its relatively small floor area and the restricted recreational exercise/rehabilitative facilities available to patients too disturbed to be allowed out. This was because the parent hospital's resources were limited and had to be shared with all the other wards and units. Thus, the highest risk and the most chronic types of security problem patient could not be accommodated. The very small number of such patients were either not taken in or transferred to a special hospital. Neither did it offer a special forensic outpatient or assessment service, in contrast to the standard regional secure unit or the interim secure unit described by Higgins (1981). However, though this may suggest a limited role, the unit dealt with practically all the behaviour disturbance in the area psychiatric units and hospitals which was too severe to be accommodated by these units. Indeed virtually all the violent behaviour in area hospitals was dealt with locally, usually with the assistance of the crisis unit. Thus, our experience coincides with that of the recommendations of the Royal College of Psychiatrists (1980) and the findings of McPhail (1978) and Fottrell (1980) that violence in mentally ill patients can be dealt with on the spot.

The widespread feeling that units and hospitals should handle more of their disturbed patients—a function which they have tended to abdicate—is supported by our experience. Furthermore, by coping with these patients locally, our crisis unit was able to return them to their wards of origin once the behaviour disturbance had passed, without encouraging institutionalization or separating them from their local areas. If the few patients going to special hospitals are discounted, this suggests that a special role for regional secure units is questionable (Editorial, *British Medical Journal*, 1979). It may well be that resources earmarked for these would be better deployed in enhancing local units on the one hand and improving the special hospitals on the other.

Though there seemed to be an excess of disturbed psychotic inpatients from the Brent district, the local population is not markedly different from that of other urban areas of the country, so our conclusions may be of fairly general relevance. On the other hand, problems of access in rural areas emphasize the need for several smaller units than this one, or for possibly multi-tiered arrangements like that of South-East Thames; small local units feeding into a larger, more centralized facility. The South-East Thames plan visualises a four-tiered structure: community and outpatient facilities feed 15-bed units in psychiatric hospitals, which in turn relate to a centralized purpose-built 30-bed unit in a teaching hospital which in turn is linked to a special hospital.

The unit has never been without an empty bed from the time it opened and, as far as we are aware, no-one has ever been turned away for this reason. Patients are transferred back when the behaviour disturbance has subsided. The unit had a very considerable turnover in patients, which rapidly increased after its inception, reaching a peak in 1978. Since then demand, as measured by turnover, has levelled off. It may be that this means that the demand and the resources available to deal with it are roughly in equilibrium. The vast rise during the early years was achieved by a commensurate shortening of the mean length of stay in the unit from 20 days in 1974 to 2 days in 1978 (the figure which roughly prevails at the present time). This meant a lot of extra work for the staff, which was accommodated with relatively little extra allocation of resources.

At any given time, most of the places in the unit are occupied by long-stay admitted patients, and the short-stay temporarily transferred patients occupy a small proportion of the beds. To a large extent this is due to the much longer time that the admitted patients spend in the unit, but it is a mistake to regard the longer-term admitted patients as constituting a static population (see below). Most of the unit's patients pass through the small number of beds occupied by temporarily transferred patients. The prospective survey makes it clear that much of the behaviour disturbance necessitating this transfer was triggered off by features of the psychosis itself, such as delusions and hallucinations. Even so, the behaviour patterns seen in these short-stay transfers to the unit were reminiscent of those described by Weaver *et al.* (1978); for example, destructive behaviour designed to attract staff attention or lead to tangible rewards, such as shouting or window-smashing when lots of staff are around. Another example was the little epidemics or fashions in behaviour disturbance, such as crockery-breaking. Again, another pattern was behaviour disturbance designed to increase the patient's sense of security. Thus, many patients needed the presence of nurses around them to reassure them, and one even contrived to put himself into the secluded room, presumably to feel even more secure than he had been in the closed unit!

A striking feature of the short-stay patients prospectively surveyed was that all returned to their own wards after a brief calming spell in the unit, and perhaps a change in medication. None was admitted to the unit. However, the unit evidently had no remedies for psychopathic or personality disordered people. We found that the extra attention given to these patients merely exacerbated their outbursts, particularly when these were apparently designed to gain notice. Thus, a deterioration in behaviour seemed to take place. Fortunately, most of these were screened out by the method of selection. Disturbed adolescents, children under 16, and disturbed elderly dements were also excluded by virtue of the unit's policy and that of the catchment area hospitals.

Despite the slow turnover of the longer-stay admitted patients, there was some movement among these patients, over half of the cohort studied having been discharged or moved to open wards during the period of 4 years. This was a considerable achievement when it is recalled that, lacking a follow-up service of its own, the unit had no direct links with the community but had to work through other wards and services. These were nearly always, perhaps understandably, reluctant to take on these patients. As the years went by it became apparent that the only way to get one of these patients out was in exchange for a disturbed patient who needed to be admitted to the unit—a marked contrast to the flexibility conferred by the temporary transfer arrangement. On the other hand, the Rainhill interim secure unit (Higgins, 1981) had much greater success in discharging its patients into the community, but these were evidently not chronic inpatients like those of the present study, and the Rainhill unit had the benefit of follow-up facilities.

The division of the admitted patients by virtue of behaviour disturbance into those who caused most of the disturbance and who for this reason were kept in the secure facility, and those who were there because of their *potential* for violence, was of considerable interest. This latter sub-group of patients constituted a great problem because it was never possible to say with certainty that their potential for violence had abated. Possibly these patients could be housed in the regional secure unit, but in our experience even these responded to personally tailored programmes of reward and rehabilitation.

In order to achieve our very flexible temporary transfer policy, a great deal of goodwill and understanding from the consultants and other staff was required. This was achieved initially by careful planning and discussion at the local psychiatric advisory committee, of which all the consultants were members, and which other senior staff could attend. These discussions were imbued with a sense of purpose by the need to get the facility operational. Most aspects of unit policy were agreed before the unit opened and, for the most part, have been adhered to ever since. Occasionally breaches of the policy would need to be discussed at this committee, but usually the arrangements have worked smoothly. Time thus spent in preliminary discussion was never wasted and paid dividends in terms of cooperation and understanding once the unit opened. We also have got cooperation because most of the temporary transfer decisions were inspired by the nursing staff who, aware of the advantages of keeping free access to the unit, readily took back their patients once the crisis had passed. It is noteworthy that, during several industrial disputes since the unit opened, this free access to the unit has not been impeded.

This unit differed from those described in the Introduction in offering not a catchment area but a hospital service. Nearly all the patients transferred out of the unit were followed up by their own general psychiatric services. Neither did it offer a specifically forensic assessment service, inpatient or outpatient. Nevertheless, the assessment of *all* patients continued during their time in the unit. We found that good prognostic pointers among our admitted patients were younger age, shorter time in hospital, and female sex. Surprisingly, a record of violent behaviour and of any seclusions did not of itself prevent transfer out of the unit and was not obviously associated with the amount of time an inpatient spent in locked rather than open wards.

In respect of the third important aspect of its work, the forensic side, the unit served as a crisis control centre for the mentally ill, irrespective of legal status, rather than as a reception centre for mentally abnormal offenders. No special barriers were put up against legally detained patients, or those from the courts. (Since the unit opened, half of its patients were legally detained.) Nevertheless, we got relatively few offenders, perhaps because few were taken into the local hospitals. On the other hand, the record of Shenley Hospital in admitting patients under sections 60 and 65 compares well with other psychiatric hospitals (DHSS statistics, 1979). Throughout the 8 years there has been no RSU in the North-West Thames region, and the unit at St. Bernard's Hospital has yet to start and will probably take several further years to complete. However, the need for such a unit is not altogether clear.

An alternative proposal was the setting up of a number of sub-regional units at psychiatric hospitals, including Shenley. It was planned to designate six beds in the present unit as a forensic sub-unit for mentally abnormal offenders, domiciled within Brent and Harrow. When located in prison or special hospitals, these would be visited and assessed by our local unit team, consisting of doctors, nurses, and other professionals. It was proposed that these personnel would be separate from, and additional to, the existing staff. It was anticipated that patients with a reasonable chance of responding to treatment would be taken in, but that those in need of more security than the unit could offer—psychopaths, the mentally handicapped, the elderly, and those likely to stay for more than a year—would be excluded. This scheme had the advantages of offering a local forensic service to local patients and keeping them in touch with their homes and local facilities.

The Royal College report (1980) has also suggested such a variation on the national model. Perhaps, inevitably, local conditions determine the precise shape of each region's forensic service, sparsely inhabited areas concentrating on several small dispersed units and conurbations on larger centralized units. It is doubtful whether special forensic psychiatrists in such small local units would be more cost-effective than general psychiatrists with a forensic interest. Though concentrations of forensic expertise in some special centres are desirable, the economic argument for dividing up the forensic 'budget' among a number of generalists is persuasive. It is also arguable that the premature withdrawal of general psychiatrists precipitated the present crisis of communication between general psychiatric hospitals on the one hand and special hospitals on the other (Dell, 1980; Robertson and Gibbens, 1980).

There was a certain amount of contact with Broadmoor, a few patients being sent there for behavioural reasons. Very physically strong, aggressive, paranoid individuals, unresponsive to tranquillizing drugs, especially with some training in or experience of unarmed combat, are not readily controllable by hospital nurses. The nursing unions presently object to the introduction of police into wards to help deal with these patients. Moreover, the locked area in those hospitals fortunate enough to retain locked wards is seldom large enough to allow adequate exercise and rehabilitation over the longer term. For such patients adequate security under these conditions demands virtually continual use of the seclusion room—in itself undesirable. These patients can only be cared for in special hospitals. We found a ready response from Broadmoor, possibly because special attempts were made to foster mutual understanding, for example by reciprocal visits of staff.

A unit such as ours, with a large turnover of patients, must have an enhanced complement of nurses of both sexes (when there are patients of both sexes). These nurses should not be withdrawn to make up deficiencies elsewhere in the hospital. Inadequate numbers of nurses will cause a unit to degenerate into a place of merely custodial function. In general, it is an advantage if the nursing staff are enthusiastic volunteers rather than 'pressed' individuals posted to the unit. This does not preclude the inclusion of the unit in nursing training schemes or the introduction of students to it (provided the nurses are there as learners and not to replace more senior staff). Broome et al. (1979) argued that nurses working in a security unit have to exchange their traditional caring role for a contractor–client-orientated one in keeping with the behaviour modification techniques which may be employed. Our approach, however, was eclectic and our nurses seemed to find no great contradiction between traditional and behaviour-conditioning aspects of their work. Thus our nurses wore traditional uniforms and seemed not to be confused by conflicts between these roles. Morale has remained high, especially when the charge nurse exerted team leadership and each nurse felt secure in his place in the team.

As Knesper (1978), on the basis of the United States experience, found, teaching and research are potent attractions to work in mental hospitals. We have thus willingly participated in such programmes (see below). On the other hand, contrary to the United States experience mentioned earlier, we have not needed to use mechanical restraints. Indeed, we long since abandoned these, with the exception of the seclusion room, successor to the padded cell. We believe that team training of ward nurses in the anticipation and correct management of violence, together with the judicious use of drugs, make such methods redundant. We also believe that giving the patients useful employment and plenty of physical exercise has a prophylactic effect by defusing violence.

When the unit took women in 1976 it was hoped that they would have a calming effect on the aggressive males already there. This hope was not entirely realized, since the number of violent incidents apparently increased. This was largely attributable to the females, but not significantly so (Carney and Nolan, 1978). The reasons for this were obscure, but Fottrell (1980) reported a similar finding. However, the results of the surveys reported above do not confirm this initial impression. Integration between the sexes has conferred other benefits on the ward—the 'civilizing' effects of the presence of women, the more normal social environment, and the greater range of recreational and occupational pursuits thus afforded. Moreover, the crop of sexual misdemeanours, feared by some, has not materialized.

A unit serving a defined catchment area, for which the patients are selected on the basis of disturbed behaviour accompanying mental illness too severe for open wards to manage, offers almost unique opportunities for research into these aspects of psychiatry which for reasons discussed above are no longer seen in our psychiatric hospitals. It is noteworthy that in the South-East Thames region unit it is proposed to encourage research activities and incorporate links with the teaching establishment as a means of improving morale. Our unit has a very large turnover of patients, so that very many are available to study. There is also the advantage of the geographical situation of the unit in its own locality affording opportunities for follow-up when patients leave hospital. In units such as this one, serving a population of mixed ethnic and cultural composition, the genesis of mental illness in different groups can be more readily investigated in a controlled environment.

CONCLUSIONS

Where should local security units be ideally situated? Few district general hospitals are large enough to have space, beds, or indeed demand, for such a unit. Floor space has to be ample to contain patients locked within it for several days, and to provide the facilities needed to occupy them and absorb their aggression. At best a district general hospital can provide a secluded or 'blow-up' room for very short-term use. It usually does not have sufficient appropriately experienced staff to manage such a unit.

The mental hospital, on the other hand, usually has more space and staff, and may serve two or three district general hospitals as well as its own patients. Moreover, with the development of district general hospital units, and the removal of much of the acute work to them, psychiatric hospitals are threatened with low morale and redundancy, unless specialized jobs which they are better fitted to do than district general hospitals are identified. Bluglass (1978) suggested that the traditional psychiatric hospital has always coped with these patients, and this may now be the appropriate place to do this job. Our experience suggests that very few of these patients need to transfer to RSUs or special hospitals. Small local units were also recommended by the Royal College of Psychiatrists. However, if the psychiatric hospitals are to take on the job of providing security and crisis management (i.e. a more controlling role than presently is usual), there needs to be a reversal of present attitudes which tend to reject control and restriction. There may need to be a slowing down, or even a reversal, of the process of opening locked wards and instead a restoration of the security role of the psychiatric hospital. It is highly unlikely that regional secure units will ever be able to cope with more than a tiny fraction of this function, and the whole trend of current philosophy and planning has been away from incorporating this function within the prison service. We believe that our kind of enlightened local secure/crisis unit provides part of the answer.

ACKNOWLEDGEMENTS

We wish to acknowledge the help given by the following: Dr Brian Robinson and Dr George Echenique, Mr P. A. Nolan, Mrs Margaret Williams, and Miss Mylene Dixon (for secretarial assistance).

REFERENCES

Bluglass, R. (1978) Regional secure units and the interim security for psychiatric patients. *British Medical Journal*, 1, 489–493.

Broome, A. K., Weaver, S. M. and Kat, J. B. (1979) Long-term behaviour problems in psychiatric hospitals. *Nursing Times*, 75, 493–495.

Carney, M. W. P. and Nolan, P. A. (1978) Area security unit in a psychiatric hospital. *British Medical Journal*, 1, 27–28.

Carney, M. W. P. and Nolan, P. A. (1979) Psychiatric hospital security unit and the management of the disturbed patient. *Nursing Times*, 75, 1896–1899.

Carney, M. W. P. and Sheffield, B. F. (1973) The long-term maintenance treatment of schizophrenic out-patients with depot flupenthixol. *Current Medical Research and Opinion*, 1, 423–426.

Dell, S. (1980) Transfer of special hospital patients to the NHS. *British Journal of Psychiatry*, 136, 222–234.

Department of Health and Social Security (1974) *Working Party on Security in National Health Service Psychiatric Hospitals, Revised Report*. London: DHSS (the Glancy Report).

Department of Health and Social Security (1979) *Inpatient Statistics for the Mental Health Enquiry for England*. (DHSS Statistical and Research Report Series).

Editorial (1979) *British Medical Journal*, **2**, 1585–1586.

Editorial (1980) *British Medical Journal*, **2**, 1446.

Editorial (1980) *Lancet*, **2**, 1171–1172.

Fottrell, E. (1980) A study of violent behaviour among patients in psychiatric hospitals. *British Journal of Psychiatry*, **136**, 216–221.

Higgins, J. (1981) Four years' experience of an interim secure unit. *British Medical Journal*, **282**, 889–893.

Home Office, Department of Health and Social Security (1974) *Interim Report of the Committee on Mentally Abnormal Offenders*. London: HMSO, Cmnd. 5698 (the Interim Butler Report).

Knesper, D. J. (1978) Psychiatric manpower for state mental hospitals. *Archives of General Psychiatry*, **35**, 19–24.

Knight, L. (1980) Which way to regional secure units? *Community Care*, **299**, 24–26.

McPhail, N. I. (1978) Behaviour disturbances in a general hospital psychiatric unit. *Health Bulletin*, **36**, 79–88.

Montgomery, C. (1976) A programme for the prevention and management of disturbed behaviour. *Dimensions in Health Care*, **53**, 28–29.

Phillips, N. (1977) Safety and physical restraint. *Dimensions in Health Care*, **54**, 12–15.

Price, J. H. (1976) Security units for dangerous and difficult patients. *British Medical Journal*, **2**, 756.

Robertson, G. and Gibbens, T. C. N. (1980) Transfers from prisons to psychiatric hospitals under section 72 of the 1959 Mental Health Act. *British Medical Journal*, **280**, 1263–1264.

Royal College of Psychiatrists (1980) *Secure Facilities for Psychiatric Patients: A Comprehensive Policy*. London: Royal College of Psychiatrists.

Tennent, G., Parker, E., McGrath, P. and Street, D. (1980) Male admissions to the English special hospital 1961–1965: a demographic survey. *British Journal of Psychiatry*, **136**, 181–190.

Weaver, S. N., Broome, A. K. and Kat, B. J. B. (1978) Some patterns of disturbed behaviour in a closed ward environment. *Journal of Advanced Nursing*, **3**, 251–263.

Wilson, J. G. (1976) *Hospital and Community Psychiatry*, **27**, 724–727.

Woodside, N., Harrow, A., Basson, J. V. and Affleck, J. W. (1976) Experiment in managing sociopathic behaviour disorders. *British Medical Journal*, **2**, 1056–1059.

Aggression and Dangerousness
Edited by D. P. Farrington and J. Gunn
© 1985 John Wiley & Sons Ltd.

CHAPTER 9

The Impact of Deinstitutionalization

RONALD ROESCH and STEPHEN L. GOLDING

Attempts to reform any system typically involve the implementation of a vast number of changes. Changes in one system often have both intended and unintended consequences on programmes and policies within the system as well as on other interrelated systems. The deinstitutionalization movement, for example, has had widespread effects not only in mental hospitals and community mental health centres, but also in the criminal justice and welfare systems. Thus, changes in civil commitment and hospital release practices that occurred as part of the deinstitutionalization movement also resulted in changes in the manner in which the police, the courts, and social welfare agencies dealt with persons with mental health problems.

Although this chapter deals with the deinstitutionalization movement in the United States, it should be pointed out that many other countries have been involved in much the same process. The changes in other countries, of course, have occurred under different political and ideological climates and no doubt there are important variations that should be examined (see Goldman *et al.*, 1983b, for a review). The interested reader may want to review the process of deinstitutionalization in other countries, including Great Britain (Bennett and Morris, 1983), Canada (Barnes and Toews, 1983; Richman and Harris, 1983), Italy (Mosher, 1983), Latin America (Leon, 1983), Nigeria (Odejide *et al.*, 1983), the Soviet Union (Volovik and Zachepitskii, 1983), and Switzerland (Siegenthaler, 1983).

It is no surprise, of course, to those who have worked in either the legal or mental health systems, that both systems have a remarkable capacity to accommodate various reform attempts. While more empirical substantiation is needed (as will be discussed later) it is a widely shared belief that the legal and mental health systems are often quite successful in subverting reform. For example, some would argue that the pre-trial criminal justice system now receives many individuals who in the past would have been civilly committed. Because of changes in the commitment laws, police officers often arrest mentally ill persons, perhaps charging them with only minor crimes. The criminal justice system may view these individuals as in need of mental health treatment and may resort to other means for achieving that end. Thus, a lawyer may raise questions about a defendant's competency to stand trial, not out of any real concern for competency but as a means to get the defendant into treatment (Roesch and Golding, 1980).

However plausible this scenario, empirically minded readers will want to know what research support exists for it. Along with others, we wish to examine not the effect of any single programme but rather the overall impact of large-scale reform attempts. Bachrach and Lamb (1982) make this distinction in their chapter on the impact of deinstitutionalization: 'Whereas traditional evaluation asks, "How well does this program work?" impact evaluation asks "What effect does the totality of existing programs have on meeting the needs of the target population of chronically disabled persons?"' (p. 146). It is a purpose of this chapter to provide a review of some of the system-wide effects of legal interventions with mental health populations.

Another reason for writing this chapter is our belief that many of these unintended or unknown consequences of reform are quite predictable and hence potentially avoidable. We believe that many legal/mental health reforms have failed or have been subverted because the changes are often made in a vacuum with relevant parties not communicating with each other. Many of the problems created as a result of the deinstitutionalization movement were due to the fact that statutory changes were made with little consideration of the clinical realities and needs of the target population. In a provocative paper, Stone (1982) has recently addressed the issue of legal reform from the conceptual vantage-point of a leading authority in forensic psychiatry. He concludes that, however well-intended, the legal–psychiatric reforms of the last decade have 'increased the risk of violence to the public by the dangerously mental ill' (p. 11), decreased the quality of care and of life for mental patients, 'forced the psychiatrist into the role of policeman' (p. 12), deprived many patients of effective treatments, and driven the most capable mental health professionals 'out of the kitchen' because they are fed up with continual legal suits and accusations.

Lest the reader think we are focusing our attack on legal reformers, we should make it clear that the mental health system has also contributed to the problem. Our purpose, however, is not to lay blame on either system. Rather, it is our intention to learn from the past attempts at reform, to ascertain what we could do differently in future attempts to get changes adopted that better meet the needs of the target population. We believe that the psychological/attitudinal causes for failure or misdirection of reformist intervention are reasonably clear. Professionals who are engaged in evaluation research, programme planning, and system interventions (regardless of content area) are well aware of 'deterioration effects', 'trickle-down effects', 'unintended consequences', and the like. Indeed, the need for a reformer to consider such effects has been recognized since Machiavelli, who was not saying anything particularly novel even in the sixteenth century. However, when we step from academia to the 'streets', a certain set of cognitive and affective changes seem to take place that have, we believe, a dramatic impact on the nature of the ultimate systems-effects of the intervention. Based upon our understanding of the literature on the fate of reforms in the civil commitment arena, we believe that reformists need to guard against the following (non-exhaustive) set of errors:

1. *Failure to 'take the role of the other'*. In planning interventions, we believe that most reformers fail to consider how the various actors in the system (e.g. police, jail physicians, emergency room personnel, defence and prosecution lawyers, psychiatrists, judges, etc.) will accommodate to the reform in a role-consistent manner.

2. *Failure to appreciate the 'orders of change'*. While Seidman (1978, 1983) and Watzlawick *et al.* (1974) have analysed change in social systems from the perspective of first-order and second-order change, few reformers seem to take the message to heart. As a result, the target system reacts much like an amoeba when prodded—it withdraws one pseudopod and creates (extends) another. In a parallel fashion, changes in the legal procedure for civil commitment that fail to recognize the legitimate clinical concerns of the actors may result in an increased use and possible abuse of fitness evaluations and commitments. Civil commitment is a multifaceted societal reaction to a complex set of moral, behavioural, economic, legal, and psychological problems, and attempts at first-order change are, at a minimum, ineffective, and at a maximum, destructive.

3. *Misattribution of evil*. By definition, reformers tend to be a moralistic group whose great strength is to see, and react to, the world in terms of good and evil. The seductive error, however, is to see the other actors in the system as tainted by maliciousness. While this may be a natural human tendency, it potentially inhibits reformist interventions because it creates adversarial reactions and leads to a misapprehension of how others in the system will react to the change. As elaborated later, we prefer to analyse systems by the ascription of normal motivations to the actors. Thus, we think that most professionals are simply trying to do a reasonable job within their understanding of their role. We will argue that more effective change can take place by assuming such normative role functioning in trying to institute system interventions than by assuming the actors to have malicious, evil, or unusually selfish motivations.

4. *Failure to understand (as much as possible) the history of the target system*. It is sobering to consider the ultimate impact of many prior reform attempts. *Example:* Dorothea Dix, reformer *par excellence*, helped to eliminate the tragic abuse of the mentally ill in local asylums by creating centralized, modern, and efficient state mental hospitals. A century later, centralization and bureaucracy are seen as primary reasons for neglect and the growth of

destructive institutions. *Example:* reformers upset over the apparent misuse of the insanity plea argue either for its abolition or for the adoption of a plea for a verdict of 'guilty but mentally ill' without appreciating why an abolition attempt failed 70 years ago (see *State* v. *Strasburg*, 1910) or what happened to the 1883 Trial of Lunatics Act in England. This Act provided for a guilty but mentally ill verdict but faded into functional oblivion because it violated the entire philosophical and moral structure of both civil and criminal jurisprudence. It was replaced, ultimately, by a diminished responsibility plea in 1957 (Homicide Act, England, 1957). Similarly, Guy's (1869) work on the non-abuse of the insanity defence, and his analysis of reasons for the public's misunderstanding of the defence, remains buried except in the most scholarly of publications (Smith, 1981).

A BRIEF HISTORY OF CIVIL COMMITMENT REFORM

No area of mental health–legal reform reflects the problems inherent in evaluating the ultimate impact of such interventions better than attempts to reform civil commitment procedures. We will not present a comprehensive history of the movement (see, e.g., Wexler, 1983; Note, *Harvard Law Review*, 1974) but rather will try to highlight critical issues that were raised, and the data upon which the arguments were based.

It is generally acknowledged that the first significant reforms in civil commitment procedures were, at the federal level, Judge Sprecher's articulate, if controversial, reasoning in *Lessard* v. *Schmidt* (1972) and, at the state level, California's passage of the Lanterman–Petris–Short Act (LPS). *Lessard* was a class action suit that bounced between the Federal District Court and the United States Supreme Court on jurisdictional grounds, and was never reviewed by that higher court on substantive grounds.

While many attempts at reform of civil commitment procedures had been made prior to 1970, there was little progress (with the exception of California's Lanterman–Petris–Short Act, which was an isolated change) until the United States Supreme Court decided two juvenile cases, *Gault* and *Winship*. In these cases the court made it clear that civil procedures, justified on a *parens patriae* basis, would be subject to criminal due process standards if a significant deprivation of liberty were a possible outcome. Specifically, the court held that

civil labels and good intentions do not themselves obviate the need for criminal due process safeguards ... where the issue—whether the child will be found to the 'delinquent' and subjected to the loss of his liberty for years—is comparable in seriousness to a felony prosecution (*In re Winship*, 1970, pp. 365–366).

Two years later the court made it clear in an adult commitment case that it meant its statement to apply to all *parens patriae* commitments, not just those of children. In *Humphrey* v. *Cady*, 1972, the court stated that commitment standards must take into account that the person's 'potential for doing harm, to himself or to others, is *great enough to justify such a massive curtailment of liberty*' (p. 509, italics added). This trilogy gave reformers the opening needed to bring both the substantive and procedural aspects under due process scrutiny. Given the easily documented abuses (Hiday, 1977; Lipsitt, 1980), the various courts and legislatures reacted quickly, and a number of changes ensued.

From a reformist perspective the most significant changes advocated in *Lessard* included (a) the guarantee of full adversarial rights, (b) the establishment of the 'least restrictive alternative' principle, and (c) the acknowledgement of serious deficiencies in the knowledge base and scientific expertise of mental health professionals. In our view the courts have done an admirable job in reforming the legal abuses (e.g. limiting hearsay evidence and requiring adversarial representation—but see Poythress, 1978, for an example of the failure due to reluctance on the part of attorneys to act against their client's *parens patriae* interests). Even in this area it should be noted that the lack of training of key persons involved in the process (i.e. attorneys, judges) may limit the effective application of legal reforms. For example, Stier and Stoebe (1979) lay part of the blame for the failure of civil commitment legislation in Iowa on their finding that lawyers were not properly trained for their roles in the civil commitment process. The courts have done less well, somewhat naturally, on psychological/psychiatric issues. We wish to argue that this is so because the courts have been provided with incomplete, misrepresented data, and that the social science reformers who have provided this information let their ideological objections to the *parens patriae* principle cloud their scientific judgement. This is most easily demonstrable with respect to the issue of dangerousness and its prediction.

Almost every analysis of civil commitment procedures contains the seemingly obligatory review of 'dangerousness prediction' and concludes by paraphrasing Cocozza and Steadman's 'there is *no* empirical evidence to support the position that psychiatrists have any special expertise in accurately predicting dangerousness' (1976, p. 1099). The continued repetition of this litany has had, we believe, a substantial impact on a whole generation of scholars, lawyers, judges, and mental health professionals. With a few notable exceptions (e.g. Monahan, 1981) no authors have stressed the fundamental irrelevance of most of this research to the problems faced by a commitment court or forensic mental health professional.

This claim may seem outlandish, but it is easily defended. First, to the extent that data exist, it seems clear that very few commitments are sought only on the basis of dangerousness to others. Monahan *et al.* (1982) report that only 4 per cent of a cohort of 589 consecutive evaluations for emergency commitment were referred for evaluation solely on the basis of dangerousness to others. (When conjoint referrals were tabulated, dangerousness to others was mentioned in a total of 35.8 per cent of all referrals.) Warren (1977) has presented similar data.

Second, the studies upon which the 'inability to predict' conclusions are based, whatever other serious methodological problems they may have (see Monahan, 1981, for a partial review), are irrelevant because they are based on data from a radically different type of population than is of concern in civil commitment cases. That is, the populations heretofore studied are almost invariably either persons convicted of serious felonies *and* having significant mental disturbance now facing release back to the community; or they are defendents acquitted of serious crimes by virtue of a successful NGRI (not guilty by reason of insanity) plea or found unfit to stand trial with serious charges outstanding and who are facing dispositional questions within the corrections/mental health system. For example, the well-known Cocozza and Steadman (1976) study analysed data on 257 indicted felony defendants found unfit and facing mandatory treatment in a correctional facility (if found dangerous) or in a mental hospital (if found non-dangerous). The famous *Baxstrom* and *Dixon* studies took advantage of class action suits that mandated the re-evaluation of a group of convicted felons who had been transferred to psychiatric facilities while serving prison terms, and where prison terms had expired. In fact, none of the classically cited 'failure to predict' studies concern themselves with either an appropriate target population or an appropriate prediction context.

We seem to have constructed an entire generation of court rulings and social policy debate in response to an unknown reality. The lack of relevant data can be illustrated by the following scenarios:

1. The police receive a complaint that a woman's new next-door neighbour has been disturbing and frightening her in the following ways: (a) he has been making lewd gestures to her; (b) she is concerned because 3 days ago her daughter, aged 5, came home with mud on her inner legs and genital area—the girl claims she and the man were playing together making mud houses and he suggested they cover their legs with mud as a game (but he did not touch her); (c) 2 days ago all of their garbage cans were spilled over her clothes line in the back yard; and (d) last night someone painted a vagina, in what appeared to be blood, on her front door. She suspects the man to be involved but has no proof. The duty officer, sufficiently alarmed, asks the nearest patrol officer to talk to the man. Upon doing so, the officer reports that (e) the man strenuously denies any wrong-doing, calling the woman a 'filthy slut who smells of all the come from men—one's even a priest', (f) the man loudly challenges the officer to arrest him if he has any proof, otherwise to 'get the hell out of my home—this is my castle, my church'; (g) other than his somewhat crude manner and piercing looks, the officer noted nothing unusual; and (h) the man reports that he was playing with the child (whom

he likes), but denies any wrong-doing with her as well, 'I don't like her to get into filth and such'. Based on the facts, the duty officer would not be reasonably able to take any action, but he is worried, so he calls the forensic consultant, wanting to know if he should be worried.

2. A young street person, well known to the police with a history of nuisance crimes (falsely obtaining meals, begging, drunkenness), was recently committed for observation because he was walking naked in the street, daring women to look at him. He was briefly hospitalized (36 hours), and released with an injection of Prolixin and a recommendation to attend a day-hospital (which he did not do). During his hospitalization he manifested a clear sensorium, spoke in a moderately disorganized manner, made frequent allusions to his religious mission, but denied all major psychotic symptoms. He was non-violent, but did seem quite restless and behaved as if hallucinated. Twenty days later he is observed by the police shouting obscenities at women on the street and mumbling to himself. The duty officer, worried because of the continuing problem and its apparent escalation, calls the forensic consultant asking if he should (a) warn the person, (b) proceed with arrest (for another nuisance charge); or (c) try another emergency commitment (or perhaps an extended one).

3. A 28-year-old man is brought to the attention of a forensic psychologist who is on call to the police department. The man has been arrested for creating a public disturbance, namely shouting wildly at two repairmen from the local cable television service. On examination at the city jail, the man is dishevelled in appearance, disoriented, and rather uncooperative. He is very vague about himself, glances frequently about the rooms, particularly at the light and power sockets, but will not explain why. He does admit that he has a history of physical difficulties, particularly with his stomach, which he is constantly holding. Only once during the interview does he reveal anything of overt significance. When questioned about his stomach he blurts out 'It's terrible ... the pain ... I can't sleep at night ... I can hear them with their microwave guns ... they're irradiating me.' When questioned further about this, he refuses all further comment. The interviewer, while convinced that there is a probable connection between the public disturbance and the suspected delusional system, is unable to proceed further. The man, according to existing policies, is held overnight and fined $50.00 at court the next day. The duty officer, wise in the ways of the street, but untrained in forensic psychology or psychiatry, asks the consultant for experiential or research data on the chances this person will commit a more serious assault.

These scenerios (which are, by the way, factual composites) illustrate an important, but infrequently recognized, point: the clinical and research literature on dangerousness and its prediction is almost totally useless in real civil commitment situations. The courts have reformed civil commitment procedures in partial response to data about the unpredictability of dangerousness that is not relevant to the civil commitment situation. We are not trying to argue that any of these cases are obvious in the manner in which they should be resolved. Rather, we present them because they illustrate the real lack of data we have about the prediction of dangerousness. Let us consider each of these scenarios as a way of illustrating the state of current knowledge and the type of data that is lacking.

Most of us would (or should) get chills reading scenario 1. The first problem that we face is that much of the 'evidence' for a clinical formulation is either circumstantial or hearsay. Therefore, in a contested civil commitment hearing under 'hardball rules' most of it would either be excluded outright or the fact that the professional had relied upon it in reaching a conclusion would be noted, and the conclusion weighed in light of that reliance. Quite rightly, and in response to numerous procedural abuses, the courts have come to view commitment hearings as requiring full due process protection because of the potential deprivation of liberty. The author of an evaluation report must be in the courtroom so that he or she can be cross-examined. The potential committee needs advance notice of the hearing, competent representation by adversarial counsel (not just a guardian *ad litem*), and so forth (see *Lessard* v. *Schmidt* for an excellent analysis of many of the due process issues).

It may be the case that, in balancing the interests of society (to protection) and those of the potential committee (to liberty) the standards of evidence need not be *identical* to those at a criminal trial. The individual's liberty interest involves a 72-hour commitment, disruption of his life for 3 days, the stigma of hospitalization (if confidentiality, tortuously we might add, is breached), the possibility that he may be innocent of (c) and (d), and other negative consequences. The woman's interests are less certain (nothing may happen to her or her daughter), but far more serious if they do occur (violent assault or death). This is a difficult situation, and its resolution is not clear, but we believe that the clinician is likely to assume a connection between the factual evidence, the circumstantial evidence, and the hearsay. This assumed connection should be admitted, for the limited purpose of a presumption of dangerousness warranting time-limited commitment for evaluation, *if* the clinician can provide actuarial data that rise to some level of credibility ('In my experience', will not do) that ties these three types of evidence together.

Even assuming that the man in scenario 1 has done all these things, of what are they indicative? Most clinicians would believe (perhaps correctly) that individuals with (a) behavioural indications of paranoid ideation and moderate thought disorder who (b) appear to be preoccupied with sexuality, religion, and cleanliness, and who (c) may have committed nuisance crimes of a highly symbolic–aggressive nature (the lewd gestures), would be 'high assaultive risks'. This would particularly be the case if the behavioural and circumstantial evidence indicated a time-course marked by increasing symbolic dyscontrol. Belief systems aside, however, what evidence for such an assertion exists? Rofman *et al.* (1980) conducted a study of the prediction of dangerousness with a clinical population. This study found that 41 per cent of a committed group, compared to 8 per cent of an unmatched control group, carried out an assault while in the hospital. This study has been criticized (Morse, 1982), and even if it were flawless it is likely that it is one of only a small number of empirical studies that try to examine the prediction of dangerousness with clinical populations. As far as we are able to determine, little pertinent empirical literature exists.

Scenario 2 raises still other policy- and data-oriented issues. The evidence issues are clearer than in scenario 1, and there certainly are legal grounds for proceeding against the individual. This scenario illustrates a different sort of problem, namely our lack of real data on the tracking of mentally disordered individuals and the quality of care they receive over time. What available data we do have would suggest that the police are unlikely to continue to charge him criminally and he is unlikely to be committed again, or, if committed, is unlikely to be held more than the minimal period. If untreated (it is unlikely that he will voluntarily attend a day-hospital or consent to medication), how likely is he to deteriorate to the point where he places himself in situations where he is physically at risk (e.g. wandering in the cold of winter without clothes)? How likely is he to put himself (legally) or others (physically) at risk by physically or sexually assaulting women? Do the unknown probabilities of these events legitimate an intervention *now*? What is known of the temporal cause and outcome of this sort of individual? What future behaviours are likely, given a change from a passive (appearing naked) to an active (shouting obscenities) mode of confrontation? Regrettably, the answer to all of these questions is an uninformed shrug of the shoulders. After several incidents like this the police will simply come to ignore this person unless something untoward does happen to him or someone else.

Scenario 3 is similar to both 1 and 2 but more difficult, because there is almost no evidence. The hint is of a person in the early stages of a paranoid schizophrenic process. What is most disturbing is that, if the hint is correct, the person has gone to the point of connecting his perceived bodily damage (somatic delusion?; real physical ailment?) to a source (microwave guns) and has begun to seek out the 'owners' of the guns (the cable repairmen). Given the current law there is no mechanism for monitoring this person, nor any data to turn to in order to answer the duty officer's question. Even if this person began to carry a knife (or, where legal, a handgun), no action could be taken. Obviously, this is the kind of situation where we need much better data on the 'natural history' of various forms of mental disorder and personality disturbance. The published literature on violence prediction and the association between mental disorder and violence has failed to answer any of the real questions that the courts and mental health professionals who work in civil commitment contexts must face on a daily basis.

THE EFFECT OF COMMITMENT LAW CHANGES ON MENTAL HOSPITAL ADMISSIONS

The changes in commitment laws were intended to deal with the perceived problem that many mental patients had been unnecessarily detained in mental hospitals. The new laws were expected to reform the admission procedures so that this would be less likely to occur. As a consequence of the tightening of the commitment procedures, one would expect a reduction in the involuntary admission rates and perhaps in admission rates in general. In this section we will examine some studies that have looked at the effects of this legal reform.

Kiesler (1982) recently provided a review of US data on hospitalization rates in psychiatric facilities. Drawing on information from several national data bases, Kiesler confirmed that the rate of hospitalization was indeed stable over the past 15 years, as a number of researchers had argued (e.g. Klerman, 1979; see also Goldman *et al.*, 1983a, for a recent discussion), but that the length of stay had decreased. Kiesler goes on to suggest, however, that this presents a misleading picture of psychiatric hospitalization rates because general hospitals with psychiatric units were typically excluded from these studies. When they are included, Kiesler reports that the rate of mental hospitalization has increased. Kiesler adds that private and state mental hospitals now account for only 25 per cent of the total number of psychiatric facility admissions.

In terms of research methodology, the most appropriate design to examine changes in hospitalization practices is an interrupted time series (Cook and Campbell, 1979), a quasi-experimental design. This allows one to look at commitment practices for an extended period of time, both prior to and after reform. Studies that use only a pre-post design, in which commitment rates are examined for the year prior to the change and compared to the year after, are not adequate. This is because one needs to examine the stability of commitment rates over a considerable period of time. It is possible, for example, that commitment rates in a particular state had been dropping for many years prior to the actual change in the law. The pre–post design would show that the rate in the year after the change was less than the year before. Policy-makers might well be mistaken, however, if they concluded that the decrease was due to the statutory change, since it may have been due to the downward trend that had been occurring for some years. An interrupted time-series design would address this possibility and allow the researcher to reach more definite conclusions about the effects of the legal reform.

Fortunately, there are a few studies that have used the time-series design. One study was conducted by Luckey and Berman (1979). Their data consisted of 30 observations (of 21-day intervals) prior to the change in the Nebraska commitment law and 20 observations after the change. Each observation period included all involuntary admissions to the three Nebraska state hospitals. The major finding was that the involuntary admission rate did drop, but this effect was only temporary, since the admission rates increased over time to the former level. They also found that the readmission rate after the law change reversed a downward trend and began to increase. One other finding is worth noting. Luckey and Berman found a highly significant decrease in the length of commitment, but the length of stay had been declining for some time prior to the law. Thus, it is unclear whether these same results would have been obtained in the absence of the law.

The Luckey and Berman study raises a number of questions about the effect of the legal reform, at least in one state. Why did the data demonstrate stability in involuntary admission rates, contrary to expectations, since commitment was supposed to become more difficult? One hypothesis is that the courts ignored the legal changes and continued to commit individuals it believed were in need of treatment. A rival hypothesis, of course, is that patients had always (at least in recent times) been committed using the tighter criteria, with the statutory change simply conforming to the existing practice. Another rival hypothesis is that commitment rates would have *increased* at a higher rate had the laws not changed. Support for this hypothesis comes from a study by Durham and Pierce (1982). In 1973 the state of Washington changed its commitment law to incorporate the dangerousness criterion, but in 1979 revised it by expanding the definition of gravely disabled to allow commitment of anyone who could not function independently in the community. The serious-harm concept was also expanded to include destruction of property. Durham and Pierce found a 56 per cent rise in involuntary admissions in the 6-month period after the 1979 change, and a smaller decrease in voluntary admissions. The total admission rate rose 12 per cent.

Two other results from the Luckey and Berman study worthy of comment are the increased readmission rate and the decreased length of stay. One concern about the changes in civil commitment laws is that mentally ill individuals would not be able to gain admission to mental hospitals or, if they did, would not be held long enough to be treated successfully. Furthermore, there was concern that the community treatment alternatives would not be able to deal with the increased treatment load. The Luckey and Berman data suggest that this concern may be valid, as demonstrated by the readmission and length-of-stay data. However, they conclude (and we concur) that the problem is not in the legal reform but in the lack of alternative treatment methods. As they suggest, 'the challenge now is to develop more efficacious and rapid treatment methods in both inpatient and outpatient settings. The new law also highlights the need for effective transition to and care in the community' (p. 159).

The main findings in the Luckey and Berman study are duplicated in the study of California data before and after the Lanterman–Petris–Short Act (LPS) took effect. Lamb *et al.* (1981) found that involuntary admissions remained fairly stable over time, but that the length of commitment has decreased. The decrease in length of stay has resulted in a significantly reduced mental hospital census, even though the admission rates have not changed. In a study of the Worcester State Hospital in Massachusetts, Morrissey *et al.* (1979) found a 54 per cent reduction in the census, as well as a 32 per cent reduction in the admission rate. In this study they also found a dramatic increase (47 per cent) in the 'seen but not admitted' category. This finding, of course, raises questions about whether this group was able to find treatment elsewhere, assuming of course that this group needed treatment. It may well be that they did not and, consequently, unnecessary intervention was avoided. Furthermore, it may also be the case that, even if they were admitted, these individuals would not have received adequate or effective treatment in the institution, given the treatment success rates of most mental hospitals.

TRANSFER TO THE CRIMINAL JUSTICE SYSTEM

One potential outcome of changes in civil commitment laws is that other procedures will be used to deal with persons viewed as mentally ill. There are a certain number of individuals in the community for whom some intervention is necessary and, if traditional pathways are blocked, then, it is argued, other methods will be employed. One such possibility is through the use of the criminal justice system to arrest and detain persons who under different commitment laws might have been committed to a mental hospital.

Gunn (1977), in his study of the rates of mental disorders in prisons, made an important point for those interested in examining the relationship between crime and mental disorder. Gunn suggested that, as other alternatives are blocked off, it would be expected that more people would end up in prisons, including greater numbers of persons who had previously been detained in mental institutions. But does this suggest that there is a relationship between crime and mental disorder? Gunn argues that one should be cautious in making such an interpretation. We would agree. It is our position that, if indeed more mentally ill persons are ending up in prisons, it is because of institutional and public policy practices that have nothing to do with individual deviance *per se*. In fact, the individual behaviour may not have changed at all. What has changed, however, is the manner in which the institutions of our society react to that individual behaviour.

Dickey (1980) made the case that 'in the absence of an organized system for dealing with the deinstitutionalized, the response to their mildly self-destructive and disruptive behaviour is frequently an improvised one' (p. 35). Police are,

Dickey suggested, relatively untrained to deal with such persons and, if traditional (e.g. mental hospital) avenues are not possible, they will resort to arrest. There is little question that the police receive minimal training about how to respond to possibly mentally ill individuals. Snibbe (1973), for example, reported that police in Los Angeles receive about 8 hours (of a total of 840 training hours) on how to deal with the mentally ill. More extensive training, however, may in fact be of limited value. If mental health resources are unavailable or not usable (because the individual does not appear to be dangerous), then the police may have little recourse but to arrest.

Once these individuals are arrested they frequently present a problem to the jails and the courts. They may act out in the jail or the courtroom and be viewed as in need of mental health intervention. If traditional alternatives are not possible the courts may resort to other means to get treatment for these persons. It is quite possible that judges and other criminal justice system personnel are not simply trying to rid themselves of a problem, but may well be acting out of a genuine concern for the individual. A case illustration from an article by Dickey (1980) demonstrates this:

> The parents of Glenn, age 32, reported that his mental illness began three years before commitment. He began smoking marijuana and taking pills and, according to his parents, became troublesome in their home. He refused to abide by any household rules and was belligerent and remote at home. He repeatedly accused his parents of not being his real parents and of treating him like a child. When Glenn refused to take his parents' advice to see a psychiatrist, they attempted to have him involuntarily committed. This failed because dangerousness was not established, and the parents ordered Glenn to leave the home. When he refused to do so, the parents called the police and had him arrested for criminal trespass. He was subsequently committed as incompetent to stand trial. The social service admission history at the institution to which Glenn was committed contained the following comment: 'A judge in Milwaukee told the parents that the only way for them to get help for Glenn was to have him charged with a crime. Therefore, they had him charged with criminal trespass, and the judge sent him to the Winnebago Mental Health Institute. The parents are hoping that he will receive treatment' (pp. 36–37).

A recent review by Teplin (1983) of empirical studies on the issue of increased involvement of mentally ill persons in the criminal justice system provides some confirmation that this has occurred, although Teplin found that so many of the studies were methodologically flawed that they only provided tentative support.

In the remainder of this section we will examine the issue of how many persons are now entering the criminal justice system who, in the past, might have been committed to a mental hospital.

Arrest versus Commitment

A study by Jacobson *et al.* (1973) demonstrates the latitude police have in responding to the mentally ill, provided that alternatives exist. Their study was of 48 cases brought by police to a psychiatric unit within a university medical centre. The officers were interviewed to determine how they reached the decision to refer the individuals to the mental health system. The behaviours which prompted police attention included potentially criminal ones such as assault, nude exposure, and drug-induced behaviour, as well as non-criminal ones such as confused behaviour and attempted suicide. While almost one-half of the cases could have resulted in a criminal charge, charges against only one individual were being considered. In response to a question about why they chose a civil rather than a criminal disposition, the officers indicated that they believed that the person was not responsible for his acts or that hospitalization was more helpful than jail. The responding officers also indicated that they frequently looked for alternatives to hospitalization as well, such as contacting a responsible person, counselling the family, or not taking any action at all. This study points to the fact that the police are a primary contact point for many mentally ill individuals and, further, that the police exercise considerable discretion in their decision-making. It is likely that the majority of cases are handled through means other than arrest, with arrest being used only as a last resort. Jacobson *et al.* (1973) found that 21 per cent of their police officer sample indicated that they would never arrest a mentally ill person even if a crime had been committed, while 51 per cent said they would sometimes arrest such individuals.

A recent study by Monahan *et al.* (1979) also addresses this issue. They conducted interviews with 100 police officers in a California community, one-half after they had petitioned a person for involuntary civil commitment and the remainder after they had made an arrest. The study focused on police decision-making as well as police perceptions of the two populations. One of the findings was that, while arrests could have been made in 30 per cent of the commitment cases, they were seriously considered in less than one-half of these. The officers reported that civil commitment was a possible option but one not pursued, because they believed that these individuals were not severely mentally ill or dangerous. Monahan *et al.* point out that over two-thirds of all the cases entering one system were seen as inappropriate for the other system and conclude that

> this study has produced little evidence that seriously mentally disturbed persons are being 'criminalized' by placement in jail as an alternative to civil commitment or that serious law breakers are being 'psychiatrized' by being shunted into hospitals instead of jails (p. 517).

One method for examining the question of whether the criminal justice system is being used to detain persons who cannot be civilly committed is to determine whether there have been increases in the prevalence of mental illness in jail or prison populations.

Whitmer's (1980) article on a California jurisdiction's practices presented some sketchy data on an undefined sample of 500 defendants in need of treatment in a local jail. Whitmer tries to make the case that people are being shifted from the mental health system to the criminal justice system, but in fact he provides very little data. His data are mostly in the form of a few case histories, although he does note that nearly all the 500 cases had prior psychiatric hospitalizations. He did not provide any specific data about prior arrests. Swank and Winer (1976) also provide some county jail data, indicating that a large number of psychotic persons were seen, but providing no data on whether the population had increased over time. Furthermore, most of their data were based on a select group of inmates who were referred for or requested a psychiatric evaluation. Their data on a smaller but more representative number of inmates suggested that the overall incidence of psychosis was not that high, probably no more than about 5 per cent. The methodological problems with studies such as these are easy to list, but the general difficulty is that there are many assumptions about what has happened to the deinstitutionalized but very little hard data.

Monahan and Steadman (1983) recently reviewed a number of studies addressing the issue of prevalence and concluded that the rates of mental illness in jails or prisons were no higher than those in the general population, controlling, of course, for social class. Unfortunately, all the studies are based on data collected at a single point in time in one facility. Thus, while the data provide information on prevalence, they are not helpful in determining whether the rates have increased following changes in commitment laws. We could not locate any studies that provided such data.

It is also possible to determine the arrest rates of former mental patients in an attempt to understand whether more mental patients are entering the criminal justice system. Studies and reviews on arrest rates have suggested that they have increased over time and that mental patients are arrested more often than the general population (Rabkin, 1979; Sosowsky, 1978; Zitrin et al., 1976), although perhaps very few of these arrests are for violent crimes (Cocozza et al., 1978). The interpretation of this rather consistent finding is problematic. While it might be attributable to the problems created by deinstitutionalization (e.g. Sosowsky, 1980), it has also been argued that the primary reason for the increase is the fact that the number of mental patients with prior arrest histories has increased (Lamb and Grant, 1983; Steadman et al., 1978). Thus, the increase may simply be due to the change in the population of released mental patients. The difficulty in interpreting the data on arrest rates points to the need for a long-term research project that would track subjects as they move in and out of both the mental health and criminal justice systems. We will elaborate on this point at the end of this chapter.

Another method for examining this issue is to look at the rates of prior mental hospitalization among offenders. Monahan and Steadman (1983) were able to identify only three studies, the most important of which was their own recent national one. They reported prior mental hospitalization rates for inmates entering state prisons in six states in two time periods, 1968 and 1978. The 1978 percentages varied across states, from 3.9 per cent in Arizona to 16.7 per cent in Iowa. In three of the states the percentages were higher in 1978 compared to 1968, while in the remaining three states there were no significant differences. In no state was the difference greater than 10 per cent.

One conclusion that can be drawn from these studies is that it is not possible to understand fully how the mentally ill are treated in a complex system by looking only at jail rates or prison statistics. One must also look at how police exercise their discretion. Evidence that it is the institutional response rather than the behaviour of mentally ill individuals that has changed can be found in a study by Levine (1970). Using a random sample of 100 mental hospital patients, he asked a prosecutor to read the summary of events leading to the hospitalization and to determine if any crimes had been committed. No crime had been committed in only 29 cases, with the majority of the remaining cases being potentially guilty of misdemeanours and a small percentage guilty of felonies. This study was based on pre-1970 data, when commitment was less difficult. Obviously, there were grounds for arrest if the police did not have hospitalization as an alternative. What is unclear, however, is how many would have actually been arrested and how many would have simply been left alone or had non-institutional dispositions if commitment were not possible.

Lamb (1982) completed one of the more recent studies of mentally ill persons in a jail. He randomly selected 102 inmates who had been referred to a forensic unit within a county jail. A number of his findings are worth noting, although the conclusions are limited because the data are drawn from a single point in time. The sample was composed of persons who had extensive histories of both prior psychiatric hospitalization and prior criminal activity. Ninety per cent had a history of prior hospitalization and 92 per cent had prior arrests. The majority had at least one felony arrest (75 per cent), while 17 per cent had a misdemeanour arrest only. Thus, only 8 per cent had no prior arrests. The breakdown for the current charge was interesting. Slightly over one-half were charged with felonies, with one-half of these being crimes of violence. There was a significant relationship between the seriousness of the charge and the living situation prior to the arrest. Over one-half of those charged with misdemeanours had been living on the streets, in missions, or in cheap hotels. Only 14 per cent had received any form of outpatient treatment. Lamb suggested that 'it may be that many of this group of uncared-for mentally ill persons are being arrested for minor criminal acts that are really manifestations of their illness, their lack of treatment, and the absence of structure in their lives' (p. 114).

Lamb also attempted to determine why the police chose to arrest rather than hospitalize these individuals. For the felony cases the answer was simple, as persons who have allegedly committed more serious crimes are almost uniformly arrested, regardless of mental condition. Mental health treatment may well be appropriate, but the primary concern of the police is to ensure that the person is securely detained. Lamb suggests that the police are reluctant to take these persons, as well as persons charged with misdemeanours, to local emergency rooms because they have learned through experience that the hospitals frequently release them because of bed shortages or because they do not satisfy commitment criteria. Lamb concluded that 'the police may well book the person into jail—which is less time-consuming and ensures the person's removal from the community pending further evaluation—rather than take him to the hospital' (p. 117).

In his concluding comments Lamb argues for changes in the commitment laws so that these people can get appropriate treatment, which would 'begin to interrupt the continual pattern of jail and hospital and help these persons achieve some measure of order and security in their lives' (p. 120). Lamb fails to note, however, that his own data indicate that nearly all of his sample had been hospitalized in psychiatric facilities at some time in the past, apparently with little positive effect. Lamb does acknowledge that a number of changes in the community will also be needed, such as more community residential facilities.

Use of Competency Procedures

One method for getting individuals charged with crimes into the mental health system is to use the statutes allowing for the evaluation of defendants whose ability to stand trial is questionable. The concept of competency to stand trial is an important one in the legal system because it provides for the postponement of a trial of defendants who are unable to understand the proceedings against them and adequately participate in the defence (see Roesch and Golding, 1980, for a review). When used properly it provides a safeguard of the rights of a defendant to a fair trial. In practice, however, the competency procedures may provide a convenient method for the courts to obtain mental health intervention for certain defendants.

Abramson (1972) was one of the earliest writers to suggest that one side-effect of the civil commitment law changes (California's LPS act) was the increased use of the criminal justice system. He cited a 36 per cent increase in competency evaluations in 1970 (in San Mateo, California) compared to 1968, and a 100 per cent increase in commitment as incompetent to stand trial. While Abramson's conclusion may well be correct, the data he cites are ambiguous and do not provide empirical support for it. His article is illustrative of a design problem that abounds in mental health law research and commentary. While Abramson cites a 36 per cent increase in competency evaluations, this statistic is meaningless without knowing if there was an increase in the arrest rate during that period. It is necessary to know whether the 36 per cent increase was greater than the increase in the arrest rate. If it was not, then the increase in evaluations can be explained by the increased arrest rate, and thus does not provide any support for the hypothesis that changes in civil commitment laws lead to increased use of competency evaluations. Similarly, the increased use of incompetency commitments could be explained as a consequence of the increase in evaluations, or changes in the decision-making personnel (e.g. a psychiatrist who finds defendants unfit more often). Furthermore, the 100 per cent increase is based on a total sample of only 33, and the increase may simply have been due to yearly fluctuations in the rates. Abramson's data, like most in the area, are cross-sectional and confined to one branch of the 'megasystem'. To answer questions such as he posed, one must have multiple time-series and some measure of the 'cross-correlation' between the series (i.e. how many individuals flow from one system to another).

Two more recent studies on this issue present similar problems. Dickey (1980) examined the Wisconsin practices following changes in civil commitment laws in that state. The percentage of commitments after a determination of incompetency rose 42 per cent in the year following changes compared to the year before. Furthermore, he reported an increase in the percentage of incompetency commitments charged with misdemeanours. In 1976, 28 per cent of the commitments were for misdemeanours, compared to 42 per cent in 1978. A significant portion of these were charged with disorderly conduct. The increased percentage of persons charged with minor crimes would presumably support the hypothesis that the police are arresting more mentally ill persons and charging them with misdemeanours because they do not have alternative means for detaining these individuals in the mental health system. The courts, Dickey adds, then use competency procedures to get them into treatment. Dickey argues that this is further supported by his finding that all persons committed as incompetent ($n = 24$) during a 2-month period in 1977 had their charges dismissed when they were finally returned to court as competent.

Another study examining the impact of restrictive civil commitment practices was conducted by Bonovitz and Guy (1979). Their study, of a Philadelphia prison with a 60-bed forensic unit, tested two hypotheses: '(1) there would be a marked increase in the number of referrals to a prison psychiatric service, and (2) there would be discernible changes in the psychiatric and criminal profiles of people in a prison psychiatric unit' (p. 1046). They used a 1-year pre- and post-test design to compare the number of requests for psychiatric consultation as well as the admission rates. Their results supported both hypotheses. Significant increases in the referral and admission rates were found, as well as differences in the types of crime. Defendants admitted to the forensic unit after implementation of the new law tended to be charged with less serious crimes and had committed fewer crimes in the past.

Again, however, there are methodological problems that make this kind of pre/post analysis difficult to interpret. The design of both of these studies is subject to a number of threats to internal validity (see Cook and Campbell, 1979), and one would also need data from the criminal justice system showing what general changes occurred during the same time period (e.g. Did the percentage of misdemeanours increase?; What was the increase, if any, in arrest rates?). What is needed is a multiple time-series design (Cook and Campbell, 1979), which would demonstrate the pattern of commitments over a longer period of time. For example, in the Dickey study it may have been the case that in 1976 there was an unusually small number of incompetency commitments. Thus, the apparent increase in 1978 may simply have been a return to the more stable base-line pattern.

COMMUNITY TREATMENT

The movement to deinstitutionalize the mentally ill also carried with it the promise that treatment alternatives would be provided in the community. Has this promise been met?

There is little question that, when community alternatives are available, they can be as effective—and sometimes more effective—in treating mental patients. There have been a number of studies that randomly assigned persons to inpatient treatment or treatment as an outpatient in the community (e.g. Braun et al., 1981; Dellario and Anthony, 1981; Kiesler, 1980; Stein and Test, 1980). Such studies have generally concluded that community alternatives can be effective. One good example of research on alternatives is the study by Delaney et al. (1978). They used an interrupted time-series design to examine the effectiveness of a crisis intervention programme designed to provide community alternatives to psychiatric hospitalization. Compared to a matched non-equivalent control community, they found that such a programme was effective in reducing the mental hospital admission rates as well as in arranging for appropriate community resources.

There appears to be little question, then, that effective alternatives to hospitalization are available. The dilemma is that, while programmes like the one described by Delaney et al. (1978) are effective, they also may be expensive. While such programmes may make efficient use of existing resources, as Delaney et al. did, the problem created by deinstitutionalization is that the needed community treatment programmes are often unavailable, inadequately funded, and simply not reaching the population in need. As a consequence, many individuals who might benefit from intervention are not able to gain access to treatment resources. The problem is especially acute in rural areas (Bachrach, 1972) and it differentially affects the poor and minorities, who will be more at risk, because of the lack of services for them (Williams et al., 1980).

Bassuk and Gerson (1978) as well as Brown (1980) argue that deinstitutiona-lization has not been effective, because the community mental health movement has failed to meet its promise of prevention and treatment of mental illness. A primary reason is the lack of adequate funding for community treatment facilities. State legislators who closed down state hospitals did not shift the funds to the community treatment centres. On the other hand, some entrepreneurs were able to take advantage of increased state funds to provide boarding home facilities for persons discharged from mental hospitals. In fact, it was a common practice simply to transfer patients from the hospitals to the boarding homes. This situation created a new group of 'profiteers' (Lerman, 1982) who saw boarding homes as an opportunity to make a good deal of money with little investment. Brown (1980) noted that nursing and boarding homes accounted for, in 1974, nearly 30 per cent of direct mental health costs in the United States. Whether these transfers resulted in improvements in the quality of life for these individuals is questionable, as indeed is whether the new placement is really much different from the old institution (Felton and Shinn, 1981). Reich and Siegel (1973), for example, suggested that boarding homes were often no different and sometimes worse than mental hospitals:

Under the facade of community service they refurbished unsuccessful old hotels and motels and arranged with the state hospitals to accept any patients the hospitals wished to discharge. The result is that many of these proprietary homes have become unsupervised state hospitals. Many of the patients were on high doses of tranquillizers, causing them to be apathetic, disinterested, and unable to function on any level. Young mental hospital dischargees became isolated in the homes because they were unable to relate to the average age of the other residents (over 65). Patients gathered in the lobby, gazing blankly into space, rocking back and forth, staring at a television set which has been turned off. If the clients deteriorated in the proprietary homes, they were often turned out on the street when the state hospitals did not readmit them (p. 46).

Bachrach (1980) questioned whether these boarding homes are indeed 'less restrictive alternatives' to mental hospitals. She suggested that the principle of the least restrictive alternative is difficult to define operationally and asked the question: 'Is living in a halfway house in the community on long-term psychoactive medication injected intramuscularly a less restrictive alternative to institutionalization?' (p. 97). Many would argue that it is more restrictive and less effective. Patients may be on high dosages of medication because there are no staff or treatment. Brown (1980) refers to this as the 'New Custodialism', in which reliance on high doses of psychiatric medication has replaced any form of therapy. Scull (1981) concluded that, 'for the majority of the chronically mentally ill, what appears to have changed is the packaging rather than the reality of their misery' (p. 17).

Another influence that had an effect on deinstitutionalization was an economic one. Price and Smith (1983) suggest that the structure of the medicare system forced patients out of the hospital because payments stopped after 60 days of hospitalization. However, patients who were subsequently readmitted were covered for an additional period, thus contributing to the 'revolving door' policy.

The implication of all of the above commentaries is that the deinstitutionalization movement may have resulted simply in a good deal of reinstitutionalization for many and no treatment for most. Bassuk and Gerson (1978) come to the conclusion that deinstitutionalization may represent an abdication of responsibility rather than the enlightened revolution many hoped it would be. Not all agree with this conclusion, however. DeLeon (1982) argues that the deinstitutionalization movement should be regarded as a constructive response to the many abuses of the past. He also chides psychology for not providing alternatives to current approaches to treatment, including alternatives to boarding homes as well as medication.

Christenfeld (1982), in responding to Brown's (1980) article, argued that a primary difficulty faced in treating the deinstitutionalized is created by the failure to treat in the past. He suggested that the problem of reintegration is made more difficult because of the mental patients' 'own loss, over years of confinement, of basic coping skills and the disappearance of their natural support system of relatives, neighbors, and friends' (p. 176). Given this situation, DeLeon (1982) is quite correct—psychology has had all too little to contribute to the effective treatment and reintegration of the chronic mental patient. From a prevention standpoint it is obviously too late to provide anything but tertiary care for current chronic patients. Even in this area, however, psychology can become more centrally involved in ensuring that community treatment facilities are more available and offer humane treatment, perhaps through the use of paraprofessionals and other citizen involvement in the homes. We can also, of course, mount more primary and secondary prevention programmes designed to minimize the number of individuals who end up in chronic situations.

Test (1981) reviewed the type of community treatments needed to treat effectively the chronically mentally ill in the community. She pointed out that we cannot rely on residential facilities by themselves to provide effective treatment. Placement in such facilities may keep patients out of mental hospitals, but they rarely have any positive effect on the behaviour of the residents (e.g. Anthony et al., 1972). What is needed, Test argued, are special supports to help these individuals improve their quality of life. These include mental health services that focus less on traditional therapy and more on problem-solving interventions that help individuals deal more effectively with their environment, less reliance on drugs as the sole type of treatment, and greater use of natural support systems.

An example of the latter comes from the work of Fairweather and his colleagues (1969) who set up a community lodge in which chronic mental patients were given an opportunity to take greater control of their own lives as well as support the other residents in the lodge. The lodge model is an excellent example of a programme that departed from the typical boarding home approach to chronic patients. Whereas boarding homes often assume that the residents could not function independently, Fairweather *et al.* gave the lodge residents considerable autonomy in making decisions for themselves as well as in the operation of the lodge. It is perhaps with these more challenging programmes that psychologists can make a contribution to the effective treatment of chronic patients.

Unfortunately, there are too few examples of successful treatment, a result that accounts for the view that the deinstitutionalization movement has been a failure. We have provided inadequate services and, all too often, no services at all, to individuals in need of support. While there has been a great deal of talk about the need to keep mental patients in the community, it has been the sad case that many members of the community do not want them integrated (Estroff, 1981).

We suggest that, if the deinstitutionalization movement is to be regarded as a failure, it is because we as a society have failed to recognize the complexity of the problem and the need for various groups to coordinate their important contributions. It was not enough for legal reformers to change the laws regarding commitment to mental hospitals. This has simply created a situation where we pay considerable attention to the *rights* of individuals but ignore their *needs* (Rappaport, 1981). Monahan (1982) has discussed this issue by making a distinction between *negative rights* (in which an individual is free from control imposed by others) and *positive rights* (in which the individual has access to resources). Monahan suggests that the achievement of one right may actually hinder the other. In order to avoid problems created by this issue, legislators also needed to, but did not, appropriate adequate funds for community services, mental health professionals needed to provide more creative treatments instead of relying heavily on medication, and researchers needed to evaluate various treatment alternatives, and so on. To some extent all of these things happened, but not to the degree necessary to have a substantial impact. This failure to provide appropriate funding to community treatment programmes supports Scull's (1977) theory that the state was motivated by financial interests, rather than treatment or civil liberty issues, in supporting the deinstitutionalization movement. Put simply, the state viewed community treatment as a less expensive method for dealing with mental patients. To the extent that this is true, the effectiveness of treatment or the quality of life of affected individuals may not have been the primary concerns of the state.

One reason that the chronic mental patient did not fare well in the community following release from a mental hospital is that the hospital invested little effort to prepare patients for release, be it to boarding homes or other community placements. Patients were often simply transferred to a home, and typically were appraised of the transfer on the day of the placement. The high recidivism rates are not at all surprising given this lack of preparation. There are, however, two notable exceptions that provide evidence that effective intervention is possible. One is from the work of Fairweather and his colleagues (1969), whose research was mentioned earlier in this chapter. Prior to their release to the lodge, patients in this study participated in a series of workshops and group problem-solving sessions to prepare them for the task of living in and operating the lodge in an autonomous fashion (without the need for hospital staff intervention). These sessions were seen as critical to the ultimate success of the lodge model.

The other example comes from the work of Gordon Paul (Paul and Lentz, 1977). This research examined the effectiveness of two interventions (a social learning programme and a milieu therapy group) in comparison with the traditional hospital treatment programme for chronic mental patients (who had been hospitalized for 17 years on the average). The two programmes developed by Paul had considerably more success in preparing patients for release to the community, although most went to boarding homes. The social learning programme was particularly effective, with 39 of 40 patients being released (36 to boarding homes). The milieu programme had 22 of 31 released (20 to boarding homes), compared to only 13 of 29 patients in the traditional hospital programme. Furthermore, the recidivism rate for the two experimental programmes was only 3 per cent after 18 months, compared to 41 per cent after 12 months for state hospital patients. One other finding from Paul's research is worth noting. In a 'triple-blind' drug withdrawal study he found that most patients did not require the maintenance psychotropic drugs that the hospital routinely administered. As a consequence, approximately 85 per cent of the patients in the two treatment programmes were not receiving drugs at the end of the programme.

The Fairweather and Paul studies demonstrate that it is possible to initiate interventions in the lives of chronic mental patients that have a high likelihood of enhancing their success upon release to community settings. The fact that these programmes have not routinely been adopted is discouraging. In fact, Fairweather attempted to have his lodge model adopted throughout the United States, but his efforts did not result in any significant use of the model (Fairweather et al., 1974). It is clear that, without such treatment, the deinstitutionalization movement will never achieve any measure of success.

CONCLUSION

Our brief overview of some effects of the deinstitutionalization movement has provided few answers about its effectiveness. While there have been some quite good studies, the amount of information available on the system-wide effects is negligible. The available studies provide some hints that the reform has not quite achieved its projected success. Unfortunately, the research does not provide us with any definitive answers, because any single study typically addresses itself to only one part of the system. A study of boarding homes in one community, for example, does not tell us anything about the ex-mental patients who did not get transferred to boarding homes and were arrested or are simply living on the streets. What is needed, of course, is information on an entire cohort of persons potentially affected by changes resulting from the deinstitutionalization movement. In the remainder of this chapter we will outline a method for gathering such data.

While we pride ourselves, as social scientists, on belief systems and social policy proposals that are 'rational' and 'data-based', most policy change in the mental health–law arena seems to have been formulated on the basis of personal belief and rhetoric. We believe that this state of affairs can no longer be tolerated. Each year tens of thousands of our more unfortunate citizens are affected by the decisions of ever-changing policy-makers who operate in a system where the personal, social, and financial consequences of their decisions remain fundamentally unknown.

We do not mean to suggest that valuable individual research projects that have policy implications have not been attempted or accomplished; obviously, this is so. However, in reviewing the literature and in talking with other colleagues we have been struck by the enormous waste of person-power entailed in most of these efforts. Most mental health and criminal justice agencies, in response to cost-cutting pressures, have limited evaluation resources, and even when individual projects have been attempted the chances of the project being incorporated into the daily life of the institution are close to zero. The failure of such projects (which we will, below, label as evaluation and client-tracking) is not because the idea has not been competently voiced before; nor is it because of insurmountable technical problems (although, to be sure, confidentiality and the public's fear of data banks must be reckoned with). Rather, we have come to the conclusion that a major reason for the failure has been that empirical efforts at policy reform have remained fragmented and individualistic. As empirically oriented social scientists whose promotion, tenure, and reputation depend upon our own individual products, we are loath to participate in collective efforts, but this has been our Achilles' heel. We can only attack this problem through collective effort.

THE NEED FOR INTEGRATED CLIENT TRACKING AND EVALUATION

While most of us frequently speak, lecture, and write about such concepts as the 'megasystem', the 'revolving door', the 'criminal justice–mental health interface' or the 'amoeba-like system', it is worthwhile to note that we have no ability to track clients through one system (e.g. mental health) or between systems (police discretion–community care–criminal justice–mental health–welfare–etc.). In addition, not one of these systems (or sub-systems) has an ongoing evaluation programme whose product is used to formulate policy, allocate resources, or to evaluate current or past policy. (We do not deny that individuals have set up such systems in a particular place—it is just that they have never lasted.)

As our overview of literature on the radiating impact of reforms in such areas as deinstitutionalization and civil commitment has made clear, it is almost impossible to answer our initial impact evaluation question with existing data. Such data as exist suggest that criminal justice systems are receiving more mental patients as the traditional mental health system changes under the impact of various reforms. The data in this area will never be of much use until some basic methodological difficulties are addressed. Most systems are not able to follow patients/clients/prisoners/defendants over time within their own 'territory', much less across various institutional boundaries. Moreover, any data routinely collected tend to be extremely crude and in general do not contain any information beyond simple case-identifying demographics. When data have been collected they have tended to reflect the extraordinary efforts of a given research group in a particular local context. This means that the results have little generalizability and hence have little to say about the operation of the system as a whole.

Moreover, since the data are collected in a particular locale, the results tend to be inordinately influenced by a few decision-makers and other selective factors. Thus, a local mental health centre may have the capacity to know how many individuals have been referred from it for civil commitment on the grounds of dangerousness to others (although usually such a count, if made, would be done at the request of an external agent, by hand, by a research assistant, relying upon faulty records). Such a typical centre would not ordinarily receive feedback from the rest of the megasystem regarding the outcomes of its various decisional strategies. They are therefore important decision-makers in a highly complex and interactive system without any information control (either feedback or feed-forward) over their decisions. A clinician working in this environment would not know the consequences for the individual and/or society if he or she decided to arrange for some group of support services as an alternative to brief hospitalization. Similarly, if the hospitalization option were chosen, long-term follow-up is again unlikely. Small wonder, then, that neither the on-line clinician nor the external researcher is able to generate much data that are helpful in analysing the impact of various policies.

To cite a small example, Schuerman and Kobrin's (1981) recent work in California showed that a substantial portion of referrals to the mental health system appeared on the 'books' of the criminal justice system either currently or subsequently. However, they were (apparently) unable to determine why these individuals were referred in the first place (as a condition of probation?), nor did they have the capacity to trace the fate of these individuals in either system. All that was possible was a simple cross-tabulation in one time frame with sub-analyses by standard demographic information (race, sex, crime charged). Similarly, Monahan *et al.*'s (1982) recent analysis of the Stone–Roth model of civil commitment contains excellent data on agreement between initial decision-makers and their grounds for the decision, but they were unable to gather data on the prior histories or subsequent fates in the community of civilly committed individuals. (They did have limited data on the percentage who were held for longer periods of time.) Note that, if they had had the resources, they would have been able on an 'extraordinary measures' case-wise basis, to collect these data, but such data would not be available routinely.

This brief discussion of the evaluation and tracking problem leads to the following conclusion: *Researchers and decision-makers in the criminal justice–mental health supersystem must now cooperate in the construction and utilization of a confidential, longitudinally based, tracking and evaluation system. At a minimum such a data base must be able to track not only the individual's social adjustment and level of psychological functioning, but also his or her quality of life and the resources contributed by and to such a person.*

If such a system, even in its rudimentary form, were available, many of the questions posed, but unanswered, in this chapter would be resolved. For example, it surely should be possible to discover how cohorts of deinstitutional-ized patients have fared over a given time period, and how many have made what kind of social/personal adjustment at what cost and for how long. We also should be able to determine what has happened over a 3-year period to the cohort that was denied emergency admission under current civil commitment criteria. These are elementary questions and can be easily answered if such an evaluation and client-tracking system were available. Obviously, to answer sophisticated questions it would be necessary to obtain exhaustive personal, social, and vocational resource information collected at multiple points in time, but, in reality, far simpler information would be quite valuable. As the systems now stand, legions of social workers, community care workers, probation officers, nurses, psychologists, psychiatrists, physicians, unemployment counsellors, judges, occupational therapists, and police officers have monthly contact with these populations. If data at each source were rationally and routinely collected, summarized, and collated, we would be a long way towards answering the questions posed in this chapter.

We make this proposal with full appreciation for the arguments that will be raised against it. We believe, however, that such a system, in some form or another, is critical, and wish to initiate a public dialogue and debate. In this chapter we have laid what we believe to be a rational basis for concluding that such a system is necessary. As a matter of conscious decision we have chosen *not* to present the details of the system we would personally propose because that would undermine our overall goal—to stimulate debate within the community—by allowing critics to focus on the undesirability of a particular aspect of the proposal without considering the idea *per se*. Obviously, at some future date, it will be incumbent upon us to summarize the debate and to offer our own proposal, but for now we believe the idea is clear enough to have its intended effect.

ACKNOWLEDGEMENTS

Preparation of this chapter was in part supported by a grant from the Ministry of the Solicitor General of Canada to the first author. The authors wish to thank Edward Seidman for his insightful comments on an earlier draft, and Denise Foisy for her extensive library research and comments on previous drafts.

REFERENCES

Abramson, M. F. (1972) The criminalization of mentally disordered behaviour: possible side effect of a new mental health law. *Hospital and Community Psychiatry*, 23, 101–105.

Anthony, W. A., Buell, G. J., Sharratt, S. and Althoff, M. E. (1972) Efficacy of psychiatric rehabilitation. *Psychological Bulletin*, 78, 447–456.

Bachrach, L. L. (1972) Deinstitutionalization of mental health services in rural areas. *Hospital and Community Psychiatry*, 28, 669–672.

Bachrach, L. L. (1980) Is the least restrictive environment always the best? Sociological and semantic implications. *Hospital and Community Psychiatry*, 31, 97–103.

Bachrach, L. L. and Lamb, H. R. (1982) Conceptual issues in the evaluation of the deinstitutionalization movement. In G. J. Stahler and W. R. Tash (Eds) *Innovative Approaches to Mental Health Evaluation*. New York: Academic Press.

Barnes, G. E. and Toews, J. (1983) Deinstitutionalization of chronic mental patients in the Canadian context. *Canadian Psychology*, 24, 22–36.

Bassuk, E. L. and Gerson, S. (1978) Deinstitutionalization and mental health services. *Scientific American*, 238, 46–53.

Baxstrom v. *Herold*. 383 US 107 (1966).

Bennett, D. and Morris, I. (1983) Deinstitutionalization in the United Kingdom. *International Journal of Mental Health*, 11, 5–23.

Bonovitz, J. C. and Guy, E. B. (1979) Impact of restrictive civil commitment procedures on a prison psychiatric service. *American Journal of Psychiatry*, 136, 1045–1048.

Braun, P., Kochansky, G., Shapiro, R., Greenberg, S., Gudeman, J. E., Johnson, S. and Shore, M. F. (1981) Deinstitutionalization of psychiatric patients: a critical review of outcome studies. *American Journal of Psychiatry*, 138, 736–749.

Brown, P. (1980) Social implications of deinstitutionalization. *Journal of Community Psychology*, 8, 314–322.

Christenfeld, R. (1982) Deinstitutionalization and its critics: a commentary on Brown. *Journal of Community Psychology*, 10, 176–180.

Cocozza, J. J., Melick, M. E. and Steadman, H. J. (1978) Trends in violent crime among ex-mental patients. *Criminology*, 16, 317–334.

Cocozza, J. J. and Steadman, H. J. (1976) The failure of psychiatric predictions of dangerousness: clear and convincing evidence. *Rutgers Law Review*, **29**, 1084–1101.

Cook, T. D. and Campbell, D. T. (1979) *Quasi-experimentation: Design and Analysis Issues for Field Settings*. Chicago: Rand McNally.

Delaney, J. A., Seidman, E. and Willis, G. (1978) Crisis intervention and the prevention of institutionalization: an interrupted time series analysis. *American Journal of Community Psychology*, **1**, 33–45.

DeLeon, P. H. (1982) Commentary on Brown, 'Social implications of deinstitutionalization'. *Journal of Community Psychology*, **10**, 84–87.

Dellario, D. J. and Anthony, W. A. (1982) On the relative effectiveness of institutional and alternative placement for the psychiatrically disabled. *Journal of Social Issues*, **37**, 21–33.

Dickey, W. (1980) Incompetency and the non-dangerous mentally ill client. *Criminal Law Bulletin*, **8**, 22–40.

Durham, M. L. and Pierce, G. L. (1982) Beyond deinstitutionalization: a commitment law in evolution. *Hospital and Community Psychiatry*, **33**, 216–219.

Estroff, S. E. (1981) Psychiatric deinstitutionalization: a sociocultural analysis. *Journal of Social Issues*, **37**, 116–132.

Fairweather, G. W., Sanders, D. H., Cressler, D. L. and Maynard, H. (1969) *Community Life for the Mentally Ill*. Chicago: Aldine.

Fairweather, G. W., Sanders, D. H. and Tornatzky, L. G. (1974) *Creating Change in Mental Health Organizations*. New York: Pergamon.

Felton, B. J. and Shinn, M. (1981) Ideology and practice of deinstitutionalization. *Journal of Social Issues*, **37**, 158–172.

Goldman, H. H., Adams, N. A. and Taube, C. A. (1983a) Deinstitutionalization: the data demythologized. *Hospital and Community Psychiatry*, **34**, 129–134.

Goldman, H. H., Morrissey, J. P. and Bachrach, L. L. (1983b) Deinstitutionalization in international perspective: variations on a theme. *International Journal of Mental Health*, **11**, 153–165.

Gunn, J. (1977) Criminal behaviour and mental disorder. *British Journal of Psychiatry*, **130**, 317–329.

Guy, W. A. (1869) On insanity and crime; and on the plea of insanity in criminal cases. *Journal of the Royal Statistical Society*, **32**, 159–191.

Hiday, V. (1977) Reformed commitment procedures: an empirical study in the courtroom. *Law and Society Review*, **11**, 651–666.

Humphrey v. Cady. 405 US 504 (1972).

In re Winship. 397 US 358 (1970).

Jacobson, D., Craven, W. and Kushner, S. (1973) A study of police referral of allegedly mentally-ill persons to a psychiatric unit. In J. R. Snibbe and H. M. Snibbe (Eds) *The Urban Policeman in Transition: A Psychological and Sociological Review*. Springfield, Illinois: C. C. Thomas.

Kiesler, C. A. (1980) Mental hospitals and alternative care: noninstitutionalization as potential public policy for mental patients. *American Psychologist*, **35**, 349–360.

Kiesler, C. A. (1982) Public and professional myths about mental hospitalization: an empirical reassessment of policy related beliefs. *American Psychologist*, **37**, 1323–1329.

Klerman, C. A. (1982) New trends in hospitalization. *Hospital and Community Psychiatry*, **30**, 110–113.

Lamb, H. R. (1982) *Treating the Long-Term Mentally Ill*. San Francisco: Jossey-Bass.

Lamb, H. R. and Grant, R. W. (1983) Mentally ill women in a county jail. *Archives of General Psychiatry*, **40**, 363–368.

Lamb, H. R., Sorkin, A. P. and Zusman, J. (1981) Legislating social control of the mentally ill in California. *American Journal of Psychiatry*, **138**, 334–339.

Leon, C. A. (1983) Perspectives on mental health care for Latin America. *International Journal of Mental Health*, **11**, 84–97.

Lerman, P. (1982) *Deinstitutionalization: A Cross-Problem Analysis*. Washington, DC: US Department of Health and Human Services.

Lessard v. Schmidt. 349 F. Supp. 1078 (E. D. Wise, 1972).

Levine, D. (1970) Criminal behavior and mental institutionalization. *Journal of Clinical Psychology*, **26**, 279–284.

Lipsitt, P. (1980) Emergency admission of civil involuntary patients to mental hospitals following statutory modification. In P. Lipsitt and B. D., Sales (Eds) *New Directions in Psycholegal Research*, pp. 246–264. New York: Van Nostrand Reinhold.

Luckey, J. W. and Berman, J. J. (1979) Effects of a new commitment law on involuntary admissions and service utilization patterns. *Law and Human Behavior*, **3**, 149–161.

Monahan, J. (1981) *Predicting Violent Behavior: An Assessment of Clinical Techniques*. Beverly Hills: Sage.

Monahan, J. (1982). Three lingering issues in patient rights. In B. Bloom and S. Asher (Eds) *Psychiatric Patient Rights and Patient Advocacy*. New York: Human Sciences.

Monahan, J. and Steadman, H. J. (1983) Crime and mental disorder: an epidemiological approach. In M. Tonry and N. Morris (Eds) *Crime and Justice: An Annual Review of Research*, vol. 4. Chicago: University of Chicago Press.

Monahan, J., Caldeira, C. and Friedlander, H. (1979) Police and the mentally ill: a comparison of committed and arrested persons. *International Journal of Law and Psychiatry*, **2**, 509–518.

Monahan, J., Ruggiero, M. and Friedlander, H. D. (1982) The Stone–Roth model of civil commitment and the California dangerousness standard: an operational comparison. *Archives of General Psychiatry*, **39**, 1267–1271.

Morrissey, J. P., Tessler, R. C. and Farrin, L. L. (1979) Being 'seen but not admitted': a note on some neglected aspects of state hospital deinstitutionalization. *American Journal of Orthopsychiatry*, **49**, 153–156.

Morse, S. J. (1982) A preference for liberty: the case against involuntary commitment of the mentally disordered. *California Law Review*, **70**, 54–106.

Mosher, L. R. (1983) Radical deinstitutionalization: the Italian experience. *International Journal of Mental Health*, **11**, 129–136.

Note (1974). Civil commitment of the mentally ill. *Harvard Law Review*, **87**, 1190–1406.

Odejide, A. O., Olukayode Jegede, R. and Sijuwola, A. O. (1983) Deinstitutionalization: a perspective from Nigeria. *International Journal of Mental Health*, **11**, 98–107.

Paul, G. L. and Lentz, R. J. (1977) *Psychosocial Treatment of Chronic Mental Patients*. Cambridge: Harvard University Press.

Poythress, N. (1978) Psychiatric expertise in civil commitment: training attorneys to cope with expert testimony. *Law and Human Behavior*, **2**, 1–23.

Price, R. H. and Smith, S. S. (1983) Two decades of reform in the mental health system (1963–1983). In E. Seidman (Ed.) *Handbook of Social Intervention*. Beverly Hills: Sage.

Rabkin, J. G. (1979) Criminal behavior of discharged mental patients: a critical appraisal of the research. *Psychological Bulletin*, **86**, 1–28.

Rappaport, J. (1981) In praise of paradox: a social policy of empowerment over prevention. *American Journal of Community Psychology*, **9**, 1–25.

Reich, R. and Siegel, L. (1973) The chronically mentally ill shuffle to oblivion. *Psychiatric Annals*, **3**, 35–55.

Richman, A. and Harris, P. (1983) Mental hospital deinstitutionalization in Canada: a national perspective with some regional examples. *International Journal of Mental Health*, **11**, 64–83.

Roesch, R. and Golding, S. L. (1980) *Competency to Stand Trial*. Urbana, Illinois: University of Illinois Press.

Rofman, E. S., Askinazi, C. and Fant, E. (1980) The prediction of dangerous behavior in emergency civil commitment. *American Journal of Psychiatry*, **137**, 1061–1064.

Schuerman, L. A. and Kobrin, S. (1981) 'Criminal population and mental patient activity risks: client/criminal or patient/prisoner?' Paper presented at the annual meeting of the American Society of Criminology, Washington, DC.

Scull, A. (1977) *Decarceration: Community Treatment and the Deviant: A Radical View*. Englewood Cliffs, NJ: Prentice-Hall.

Scull, A. (1981) Deinstitutionalization and the rights of the deviant. *Journal of Social Issues*, **37**, 6–20.

Seidman, E. (1978) Justice, values and social science: unexamined premises. In R. J. Simon (Ed.) *Research in Law and Sociology*. Greenwich, Conn.: JAI Press.

Seidman, E. (1983) Unexamined premises of social problem solving. In E. Seidman (Ed.) *Handbook of Social Interventions*. Beverly Hills: Sage.

Siegenthaler, L. A. (1983) Deinstitutionalization in Switzerland: the incrementalist model. *International Journal of Mental Health*, **11**, 137–152.

Smith, R. (1981) *Trial by Medicine: Insanity and Responsibility in Victorian Trials*. Edinburgh: University of Edinburgh Press.

Snibbe, J. R. (1973) The police and the mentally ill: practices, problems, and some solutions. In J. R. Snibbe and H. M. Snibbe (Eds) *The Urban Policeman in Transition: A Psychological and Sociological Review*. Springfield, Ill: C. C. Thomas.

Sosowsky, L, (1978) Crime and violence among mental patients reconsidered in view of the new legal relationship between the state and the mentally ill. *American Journal of Psychiatry*, **135**, 33–42.

Sosowsky, L. (1980) Explaining the increased arrest rate among mental patients: a continuing debate. *American Journal of Psychiatry*, **137**, 1602–1605.

State v. *Strasburg*, 110 P.1020 (1910).

Steadman, H. J., Cocozza, J. J. and Melick, M. E. (1978) Explaining the increased arrest rate among mental patients: the changing clientele of state hospitals. *American Journal of Psychiatry*, **135**, 816–820.

Stein, L. I. and Test, M. A. (1980) Alternative to mental hospital treatment. I: conceptual model, treatment program, and clinical evaluation. *Archives of General Psychiatry*, **37**, 392–397.

Stier, S. D. and Stoebe, K. J. (1979) Involuntary hospitalization of the mentally ill in Iowa: the failure of the 1975 legislation. *Iowa Law Review*, **64**, 1284–1458.

Stone, A. A. (1982) Psychiatric abuse and legal reform: two ways to make a bad situation worse. *International Journal of Law and Psychiatry*, **5**, 9–28.

Swank, G. E. and Winer, D. (1976) Occurrence of psychiatric disorder in a county jail population. *American Journal of Psychiatry*, **133**, 1331–1333.

Teplin, L. A. (1983) The criminalization of the mentally ill: speculation in search of data. *Psychological Bulletin*, **94**, 54–67.

Test, M. A. (1981) Effective community treatment of the chronically mentally ill: what is necessary? *Journal of Social Issues*, **37**, 71–86.

Volovik, V. M. and Zachepitskii, R. A. (1983) Deinstitutionalization in Soviet psychiatry. *International Journal of Mental Health*, **11**, 108–128.

Warren, C. A. B. (1977) Involuntary commitment for mental disorder: the application of California's Lanterman–Petris–Short Act. *Law and Society Review*, **11**, 629–649.

Watzlawick, P., Weakland, J. H. and Fisch, R. (1974) *Change: Principles of Problem Formation and Problem Resolution*. New York: Norton Press.

Wexler, D. B. (1983) The structure of civil commitment: patterns, pressures, and interactions in mental health legislation. *Law and Human Behavior*, **7**, 1–18.

Whitmer, G. E. (1980) From hospital to jails: the fate of California's deinstitutionalized mentally ill. *American Journal of Orthopsychiatry*, **30**, 65–75.

Williams, D. H., Bellis, E. C. and Wellington, S. W. (1980) Deinstitutionalization and social policy: historical perspectives and present dilemmas. *American Journal of Orthopsychiatry*, **50**, 54–64.

Zitrin, A., Hardesty, A. S., Burdock, E. I. and Drosaman, A. K. (1976) Crime and violence among mental patients. *American Journal of Psychiatry*, **133**, 142–149.

Aggression and Dangerousness
Edited by D. P. Farrington and J. Gunn
© 1985 John Wiley & Sons Ltd.

CHAPTER 10

The Management of Dangerous Patients in Zimbabwe

TERRY BUCHAN and PETER SPARLING

Dangerousness has been defined in the Butler report (1975) as the propensity to cause physical injury or lasting psychological harm, but in practice the term 'dangerous' is usually restricted to cases of personal injury or sexual assault. This particular study is concerned with the former. It is apparent that there is considerable controversy concerning the role played by mental illness in the genesis of dangerous behaviour in this restricted sense. On the one hand it has been argued that the mentally ill contribute proportionately little to the problem (Gillis *et al.*, 1968); on the other hand it has been urged that the popular perception of the mentally ill as dangerous has some justification (Lagos *et al.*, 1977). Some of the issues which obfuscate this issue would seem to be conceptual.

In some Third World countries physical violence is often an important criterion for the diagnosis of mental disorder (Westermeyer and Wintrob, 1979). A sample survey in our own practice (Buchan *et al.*, 1981) showed that 46.8 per cent of cases admitted were brought to hospital because of violent behaviour and there was a tendency to regard anybody manifesting such behaviour as suitable for admission, which was not always the case. The hospital was expected to control the behaviour, but not to deal with the root cause of the disorder, which is believed to stem from a supernatural force, such as angry ancestral spirits or witchcraft. In fact 76.5 per cent of cases who were violent prior to admission became quiet and cooperative within 24 hours.

In a more subtly disguised form, the same conceptual confusion persists in the British 1959 Mental Health Act, which defines psychopathic disorder as 'a persistent disorder or disability of mind (whether or not including subnormality of intelligence) which results in abnormally aggressive or socially irresponsible conduct on the part of the patient and requires or is susceptible to medical treatment'. This definition has had many critics. For example McCrae (1973), quoting Lady Wootton, has pointed out that the definition is circular: mental disorder is diagnosed on the basis of antisocial behaviour and then antisocial behaviour is excused on the grounds of mental disorder.

Gunn (1975a) has also had some serious reservations. Firstly, the term 'psychopath' implies hopelessness and unpleasantness, which are associated with considerable temptation to reject such people, many of whom have been rejected all their lives; secondly, there may be a tendency to provide a 'hospital' to which unwilling psychopaths could be sent for compulsory detention, in some countries, without trial.

This procedure would have the unfortunate effect of removing the patient from the protection of the sentencing system, which at least ensures that his detention is no longer than the offence warrants (Editorial, *Psychological Medicine*, 1974). In Zimbabwe, prior to the amendment of the Mental Health Act in 1976, a patient found mentally disordered prior to arraignment was detained until such time as he had recovered from the disorder for which he was committed. As the criteria for recovery from psychopathic disorder are even more uncertain than those for diagnosis, it was possible for a patient to spend long periods in hospital without being brought to trial. Fortunately the amending legislation now permits a patient to go on trial as soon as he 'becomes able to understand the nature of the criminal proceedings during which such order was issued and properly to conduct his defence therein' (section 30(1)). It is no longer necessary for him to have recovered from his disorder.

Stern warnings have been issued against the medicalization of social deviance. For example, the editorial of a responsible journal (*British Medical Journal*, 1968) asserted:

Antisocial behaviour must not be equated with mental illness and psychiatrists must beware of having forced upon them the role of controlling misfits or regarding it as their function to normalise the abnormal or non-conforming. The doctor's duty is to diagnose and to treat his patient, not to enforce the society's rules.

Some nine years later the substance of this view, prompted by Dr Denis Leigh, found expression in the Declaration of Hawaii (1977) which states (Article 7) 'the psychiatrist must not participate in compulsory treatment in the absence of any psychiatric illness'.

Nevertheless, the psychiatrist is often called upon to examine those found guilty of offences and to offer an opinion as to whether medical or penal treatment would be more appropriate (Wootton, 1963). This is often an all but impossible exercise. As Scott has remarked (1970),

Since no one is very clear where mental illness finishes and disturbed or deviant behaviour begins, it is inevitable that there will be doubts whether certain sorts of persons should be in prisons or hospitals. The choice is often arbitrary and many years ago Penrose showed that the utilisation of prisons and asylums varies inversely.

Because of this difficulty in defining illness, the definition of treatment becomes comparably problematical. Scott continues:

Treatment is best regarded not as a passive process applied only by a doctor but as any approved measure used by anyone or any group (staff member, inmate, or relative) to change a person in the desired direction. It is hoped that it will be the person himself who desires the change, otherwise the change must extend only to abandonment of unlawful or manifestly self-damaging behaviour. This definition of treatment clearly includes that variety of punishment (perhaps better called conditioning) which is rationally applied according to the rules of learning, and must sometimes include solitary confinement.

In Britain the Royal College of Psychiatrists seemed to accept this view in its report (1975), which suggested that forensic psychiatrists are equipped by interest, reading, and experience to act as consultants in the management of behaviour disorders in settings where management is difficult and specialized methods of treatment may be required.

Nevertheless, despite Scott's caveat, not all would accept this broadening of the concept of treatment. In the United States, although a Missouri Court did sanction custody and observation as a form of mental health treatment in the case of Davee, the New York Court of Appeals reached the opposite conclusion in the case of Robert Torsney (Roth, 1979). In 1977, Torsney, a white police officer, was found not guilty by reason of insanity after he shot and killed a black Brooklyn youth. The medical evidence described him as showing a tendency to hysterical dissociation under stress. Subsequently an appeal was made for his release on the grounds that he was not psychotic and no longer a danger to himself or others. The appellate division of the court noted that he was not receiving treatment—he had been 'warehoused'—but declined to release him on the grounds that 'we may not shirk our responsibility to the community by prematurely releasing Mr. Torsney whilst he continues to suffer from a dangerous personality disorder'.

The Court of Appeals

rejected as constitutionally suspect the interpretation of the law given by the appellate division which would permit a detainee's continuing institutionalisation on a vague concept of dangerousness unrelated to mental illness or defect and for which no immediate in-patient treatment is required.

Continuing mental illness was defined as a necessary, if not sufficient, condition for a patient to be detained. As a corollary the role of psychiatry was defined as being to treat mental illness and not merely to provide custody for those whom society may continue to fear.

With such contradictions evident, one cannot but sympathise with Sir Roger Ormrod's gloomy view (1975): 'In other words, the observer might say that the courts have come, rather suddenly, to take psychiatrists at their word, only to find, when called upon, the resources of psychiatry prove to be inadequate'. In Zimbabwe the phrase 'and requires that the patient should be detained in an institution for treatment' was omitted from the Act in the 1976 amendment of the definition of psychopathic disorder.

Various attempts have been made to clarify the situation by proposing operational definitions of mental illness. For example, it has been suggested that illness should have as its necessary and sufficient condition the experience of therapeutic concern of a person for himself and/or the arousal of therapeutic concern in his social environment. This would seem to apply that, *ipso facto*, any person brought to hospital is ill, which has not proved to be the case in our own practice. As an alternative, Kendell (1975) offered the concept of biological disadvantage, which was defined as a reduction in fertility and/or life expectancy. Evidence was adduced that schizophrenia, manic depressive disorders, some sexual disorders, and various kinds of drug dependency can be justifiably classified as illnesses; the evidence was not strong enough to include neurotic illness or personality disorder. Great care must also be taken to avoid attaching the label 'schizophrenia' to a patient inappropriately, as the labelling process itself may lead to the appearance of symptoms which seem to confirm the diagnosis (Wing, 1979).

Even when it can be established that the patient suffers from a recognizable mental illness the relationship between the illness and the dangerous behaviour remains complex. Tennent (1975) has suggested that there are three possibilities:

1. Dangerous behaviour may occur as the result of mental illness (e.g. from persecutory delusions). Successful treatment of patients in this category will be expected to alter behaviour so as to make repetition of the dangerous acts unlikely.
2. Dangerous behaviour may occur in those with mental illness but in whom the illness is only one of a number of factors in the life pattern.
3. Dangerous behaviour may occur in those without any evidence of mental disorder.

In the latter two categories, dangerousness may be seen not as a lasting disposition but as a potential reaction which may be triggered by particular situations leading to frustration (Home Office, DHSS, 1975). This means that treatment will be largely ineffective and that prediction of recurrence with any degree of certainly will be impossible. Notwithstanding these difficulties, there are several studies of arrest rates which show that discharged psychiatric patients commit certain violent acts, including homicide, more often than the general population (Rappeport and Lassen, 1965; Giovannoni and Gurel, 1967; Zitrin *et al.*, 1976; Gruneberg *et al.*, 1977; Rollin, 1969).

In this context some cynics have blamed the treatment itself for the emergence of violence. Indeed benzodiazepines have been shown to cause rage reactions occasionally (Tobin and Lewis, 1960; Ingram and Timbury, 1960;

Guldenpfenning, 1973) and to increase hostility in groups of normal volunteers (Salzman *et al.*, 1974; Kochansky *et al.*, 1975, 1977). Solid evidence to the contrary was found in Laos, a country without either psychiatrists or psychiatric services, where violence was common amongst the mentally disordered (Westermeyer and Kroll, 1978).

Most Western countries have experienced a marked increase in violence against the person during the past two or three decades. Between 1950 and 1975 homicides and attempted homicides in England and Wales almost doubled from 531 to 1014 per annum. The corresponding increase in Scotland was almost four-fold, from 45 to 175 (McClintock, 1978). The mentally ill made their contribution to this upsurge, for in England and Wales, during the 11-year period 1967–1977, 84 out of the 3616 (2.3 per cent) confirmed homicides were found unfit to plead whilst a further 871 (24.1 per cent) were found to have diminished responsibility by virtue of mental disorder, and were convicted of Section 2 manslaughter (Bluglass, 1979).

McClintock (1978) was of the opinion that similar trends are now affecting the Third World, and evidence has been adduced that the incidence of murder amongst the Xhosa of the Transkei may be as high as 8124 per 100,000 per annum or 69 times the rate for the UK (Thomson, 1980). Whilst it has not been possible to establish whether or not this is true for Zimbabwe, there are two surveys which give some idea of the contribution made by the mentally disordered. During the 5-year period 1970–1974 a total of 316 persons of all races were arraigned by the High Court in Bulawayo on charges of murder or culpable homicide; 22 (7.0 per cent) were found to be mentally disordered (Buchan, 1978). A more recent survey of persons convicted for the same two offences in the High Court, Harare, during the 4-year period 1979–82 showed that 67 of 549 (12.2 per cent) were found to be mentally disordered (Ratcliffe, 1983).

Conventional mental hospitals are unable to provide security for potentially dangerous patients (Rollin, 1974), and the trend in Britain has been to establish regional secure units as alternatives to either special hospitals or the prisons (Bluglass, 1978). However, in view of the disconcerting conceptual uncertainties surrounding definitions of mental illness and treatment and the lack of firm guidance from elsewhere in the world, it was decided to deal with our problems in Zimbabwe from first principles. Accordingly, a survey was undertaken of 256 criminal mental patients admitted consecutively to Ingutsheni Hospital during the 5-year period 1970–74 (Buchan, 1976). Patients found to be mentally disordered either prior to arraignment or whilst undergoing trial (i.e. unfit to plead) numbered 189 (73.8 per cent).

It was found that 95 (37.1 per cent) of the patients were admitted pursuant to charges of violent crime (i.e. murder, attempted murder, assault with intent to do grevious bodily harm, or culpable homicide). Most patients were male and were managed in the 58-bed male admission ward, which was a locked ward.

Despite the lack of any serious incidents this state of affairs was considered unsatisfactory and a recommendation was made that a new secure unit should be constructed. This recommendation, along with others, was accepted and plans were put in train for a 70-bed secure unit at Ingutsheni Hospital for the management of these patients. It was originally envisaged that this unit would also cater for psychopaths (a term which appeared in the legislation in 1967) but patients diagnosed as 'pathological personality' totalled only 21 out of 256 (8.2 per cent). Amongst these 21, only six were charged with crimes of violence against the person, so that the numbers were too small to warrant special consideration.

Because of the enormous investment required, in terms of both capital expenditure and manpower, in a developing country with meagre resources, a further study was undertaken in an attempt to determine the optimum size and precise functions of this projected unit. The results of this study of 41 patients convicted of homicide (Buchan, 1978) suggested that there was a pattern to their crimes and that preventive measures could be predicated upon this pattern. By the time the study was concluded it had also become clear that considerable difficulties were being experienced in the development of regional secure units in Britain (Bluglass, 1978). There was a general lack of agreement about the type of patient who would be admitted, and little thought had been given to the relationship between the secure units and the other elements of the service (the special hospitals, the NHS hospitals, and forensic services within the community).

With these considerations in mind it was concluded that the recommendation for a secure unit had been premature (Buchan, 1978). However, it was recognized that the study was small and confined to Ingutsheni Hospital in Matabeleland. A larger survey, covering patients from the whole country, was therefore undertaken and is reported here.

MATERIALS AND METHODS

During the 3-year period 1 May 1978 to 30 April 1981, 267 patients were treated by the authors at Mlondolozi Prison. This is a secure unit for about 200 criminal mental patients situated at Khami Prison near Bulawayo, which roughly fulfils the function of a special hospital. At the beginning of this period there were 187 patients in the unit. During the study period, 81 cases were admitted, 68 were discharged, and 12 died, leaving a total of 188 at the conclusion. Only one of the patients discharged during the survey was readmitted. He was a Black male, first admitted on 5 May 1977 having been convicted of a robbery. A diagnosis of acute brain syndrome due to alcohol was made; he rapidly became normal and was released on the 23 January 1980. On 29 January 1980 he committed a murder, again in a state of pathological intoxication, and was readmitted following his trial on 19 June 1980. There were therefore 268 cases.

Patients found to be mentally disordered prior to arraignment or during trial were usually committed to a mental hospital for examination and assessment, but two patients in this category charged with murder were admitted to Mlondolozi for security reasons. All other patients were admitted in terms of a President's Warrant (Section 28(5) of the Mental Health Act 1976) pursuant to a Special Verdict, i.e. having been found 'guilty of the act or omission charged against him but was mentally disordered at the time he did the act or made the omission' (Section 28(3)). The crimes relating to the 268 cases are set out in Table 1.

Since Mlondolozi is the only institution of its kind in the country virtually all the subjects of Special Verdicts are eventually admitted there. It was distressing to find that in 57 cases (21.3 per cent) there was no danger of personal injury, although in 33 of these (12.3 per cent) there was some damage to property. The Special Verdict would seem to be totally inappropriate for trivial offences; the point has already been made that this removes the

Table 1   Crimes relating to 268 cases

Crime	No. of cases		Percentages
Murder	126		
Culpable homicide	10		
Attempted murder	11		
Assault with intent to do grievous bodily harm	39		
Assault	12		
Rape and attempted rape	10		
Robbery	3		
		(211)	78.7
Arson	17		
Malicious injury to property	16		
Theft	9		
Stock theft	1		
Criminal injury	2		
Indecent assault	3		
Forging and uttering	1		
Contravening the Road Traffic Act	1		
Housebreaking	2		
Attempting to administer poison	1		
Recruiting terrorists	1		
Violating a grave	1		
Unknown	2		
		(57)	21.3
	268		

patient from the protection of the sentencing system. As an alternative, the Mental Health Act in Zimbabwe specifically empowers a magistrate to issue a Reception Order, committing the patient to a mental hospital as a civil patient even if he 'has committed or attempted to commit any crime or offence or has acted in a manner offensive to public decency' (Section 8(1)(d)).

Because the number of patients made the amount of information available unwieldy, it was decided to focus on the most dangerous: those convicted of homicide. Excluding the two patients who had not completed their murder trials, there were, amongst the 267 patients, 124 convicted of murder and 10 of culpable homicide in the High Court. Cases of culpable homicide are usually heard in the Regional Magistrate's Court and it is probable that those heard in the High Court were initially charged with murder but the charge was subsequently reduced; this was known to have been the case for six patients.

Patients who had already been to trial were selected for study because it was considered that statements about the previous history made under oath would be reliable. For example a patient was not recorded as having been previously treated by a traditional healer unless this was specifically stated in evidence or in the statement of agreed facts.

RESULTS

Amongst the 134 patients were nine females, all Black, and 125 males, of whom 121 were Black, two White and two Coloured.

Victims

In 124 cases the patient killed one victim, in eight cases two victims, in one case three victims and in one case four victims, making a total of 147 victims. Details are set out in Table 2. Amongst the nine female patients one killed her husband, one her sister-in-law, one her aunt, and one her neighbour; the remaining five women all killed small children, their own in two cases. In five cases (two at Harare, two at Esigodini, and one at Plumtree) the victim was a hospital inpatient killed by another patient. Three victims were traditional healers; in two cases the healer was killed by patients whom he was attempting to treat for mental disorder and in the third case by a young man who was being trained by the healer to follow the art.

Weapons and Site of Injury

Details of the weapons used in killing the 147 victims are set out in Table 3. Firearms were used by six patients, causing seven deaths. The five patients who used a rifle were all members of the Armed Forces; the victims were an old lady who was a complete stranger and five fellow-servicemen (two policemen, two

Table 2   Details of 147 victims

Description	No. of victims
Children under 10 years	24
Children (age unspecified)	6
Neighbour	14
Stranger	14
Mother	11
Wife	11
Father	11
Brother	7
Grandmother	6
Sister-in-law	5
Fellow-soldier	5
Fellow-patient	5
Employer	4
Husband	3
Traditional healer	3
Fellow-worker	3
Railway passenger	2
Aunt	2
Sister	2
Mother-in-law	1
Brother-in-law	1
Grandfather	1
Uncle	1
Kraal head	1
Girl friend	1
Unknown	3
	147

soldiers, and a District Assistant). In the remaining case a White male killed his girl friend with a shotgun. In the one instance of a motor car being used as a weapon, a drunken driver collided with another vehicle, killing one of the occupants; he was charged with culpable homicide.

Details of the site of injury for the 147 victims are set out in Table 4. The commonest method of killing was to hit the victim over the head with an axe or pole, often a stamping pole or a fence pole (usually about 1.5 m long and 75 mm or more in diameter). Where a knife was used the victim was usually stabbed in the chest or abdomen. Occasionally the throat was cut; for example one woman cut the throat of her 2-year-old daughter whilst another decapitated four of her own children aged 15 months to 7 years whilst they were sleeping.

Location of Homicide

Only 24 patients (17.9 per cent) killed their victims in urban areas

Table 3   Weapons used in 147 killings

Weapon	No. of victims	Weapon	No. of victims
Axe	32	Cattle yoke	1
Knife	19	Panga	1
Pole	12	Plank	1
Stick	10	Crutch	1
Knobkerrie	8	Walking stick	1
Hoe	6	Metal pipe	1
Metal bar	6	Fist	1
Foot	6	Brick	1
Rifle	6	Pick handle	1
Rock	5	Bottle	1
Axehandle	5	Swinging child by legs	1
Spear	2	Shovel	1
Hammer	2	Anvil	1
Log of wood	2	Fatally burned	1
Strangling	2	Shotgun	1
Unknown	7	Motor car	1
		Hoe handle	1
		Total	147

Table 4   Site of injury in 147 victims

Site	No. of victims
Head	87
Neck	18
Abdomen	7
Chest	6
Back	4
Body (including burn)	3
Unknown	22
	147

(excluding hospitals); they numbered eight in Harare, six in Bulawayo, four in Mutare, three in Kwekwe, one in Masvingo, one in Shabani and one in Kadomah. Apart from the five deaths in hospitals, the homicides by the remaining 110 patients were scattered over rural areas throughout the country. Since about 80 per cent of the population in Zimbabwe live in rural areas, this is more or less what would be expected in terms of population distribution. There was no evidence that urbanization increased the incidence of homicide. On the other hand, amongst the 267 patients studied there were also 11 convicted of attempted murder (13 victims) and 39 of assault with intent to do grevious bodily harm (48 victims). No fewer than 20 of these 50 patients (40.0 per cent) attacked their victims in urban areas; seven in Harare, six in Bulawayo, four in Mutare, two in Kwekwe, and one in Masvingo. The difference is statistically significant ($\chi = 8.23, p < 0.01$, 1 d.f.).

Diagnostic Categories

Diagnostic categories for the 134 patients are set out in Table 5, and are, in every case, outcome diagnoses (i.e. based on a period of observation and treatment). Focal epilepsy can be extremely difficult to distinguish from other disorders. For this reason 28 of the 37 epileptics had EEGs taken; the findings are summarised in Table 6. A further 22 patients also had EEGs which were within normal limits. The eventual outcome diagnoses for these are set out in Table 7. Despite the difficulties in differentiating schizophrenia from other disorders which have been encountered in Zimbabwe (Buchan and Chikara, 1980) it was considered that the diagnoses were fairly firmly based.

It was also possible to establish that the onset of the illness preceded the crime in 92 (68.7 per cent) patients. Thirty had previously been admitted to a mental hospital and 12 more had been treated by a traditional healer for mental illness. Sixty-four had exhibited warning symptoms, usually in the form

Table 5   Diagnostic categories for 134 patients

Diagnosis	No. of Patients	Percentages
Schizophrenia	46	34.3
Paranoid schizophrenia	16	11.9
Epilepsy	37	27.6
Pathological personality	12	9.0
Acute brain syndromes	8	6.0
Alcohol 4		
Cannabis 3		
Infection 1		
Chronic brain syndromes	2	1.5
Depression	2	1.5
Dissociated state	2	1.5
Somnambulism	1	0.75
Hypomania	1	0.75
Subnormality	3	2.2
Unknown	2	1.5
Not mentally disordered	2	1.5
	134	100.0

Table 6   EEG findings in 28 of the 37 epileptics

Findings	No. of patients
Right temporal focus	6
Left temporal focus	6
Right frontal focus	1
Left frontal focus	1
Focus (unspecified)	1
Borderline abnormal	4
Diffusely slow	2
Paroxysmal	3
Within normal limits	4

Table 7   Outcome diagnoses for 22 patients with normal EEGs

Diagnoses	No. of patients
Schizophrenia	14
Pathological personality	4
Dissociated state	1
Depression	1
Acute brain syndrome	1
Not mentally disordered	1
	22

of disturbed behaviour, for a period of hours or days before the crime; 28 of them had received previous treatment, either by a hospital or traditional healer. Only 42 (31.3 per cent) gave no warning either in terms of premonitory symptoms or previous episodes of illness.

DISCUSSION

The Law in Zimbabwe

An important difference from the law in Britain is that Zimbabwe has no concept of 'diminished responsibility'; the accused cannot plead that he is 'not guilty of murder but guilty of manslaughter on the grounds of diminished responsibility'. The accused may contend that he was 'mentally disordered or defective so as not to be responsible according to law for his actions at the time when the act was done or the omission made'. If this defence proves successful then a Special Verdict will be returned by the Court.

The criteria for establishing insanity are based on the McNaughton Rules but have been considerably widened in an important series of judgements. For example, in the case of the *State* vs. *Senekal* it was ruled in the Appeal Court (AD 281 of 1969) that the cause of the mental disorder, whether organic or functional, is irrelevant in law and that the disorder need not be of a permanent or recurrent nature. In Senekal's case it was ruled that, having established that Senekal acted in a state of automatism as a result of concussion, a Special Verdict should be returned. On the basis of this ruling it has been successfully argued that a patient with depression (CRB 11873/6a) and another with somnambulism (CR 777-77) were mentally disordered and entitled to a Special Verdict. Murder trials are usually held before a judge and two assessors, who are usually persons with extensive knowledge of local customs and mores, and the psychiatrist's opinion is usually given considerable weight, although it was ruled in 1968 by Mr Justice Young (R. V. Dube) that medical evidence is not necessary for proof of insanity.

The Victims

There were some remarkable similarities between our own findings and those elsewhere, confirming that homicide is very much a family affair the world over. Immediate family members (i.e. husband, wife, mother, father) accounted for 36 (24.5 per cent) of our victims, as compared with 28.0 per cent in a study at Matteawan State Hospital, NY (Lanzkron, 1963). Children accounted for 30 (20.4 per cent) of our victims, but were not always killed by their own parents. Neighbours accounted for a further 14 victims (9.5 per cent) in our study, compared with 7.6 per cent in the USA. Similar findings were reported in Nigeria where 21 out of 53 victims (39.6 per cent) were related to the killer by blood or marriage (Asuni, 1969), and also in Britain where one study showed that half the victims were family members, 25 per cent friends or acquaintances and 25 per cent strangers (Bluglass, 1979).

Method of Killing

The principal pattern of killing in our study was for the victims to be hit over the head with some handy domestic implement such as an axe, pole, stick, hoe, axe handle, hammer, or traditional knobkerrie (ostensibly used for herding cattle). Some 77 victims (52.4 per cent) were despatched by means of these implements. Firearms accounted for only seven victims (4.7 per cent) as compared with 29.9 per cent in the US study and 8 per cent in the British. Sharp instruments, such as a knife, were used in about a third of the homicides studied in Britain and 35 per cent of those in the US, but in Nigeria 36 victims (67.9 per cent) were killed by such instruments, mostly machetes. It would seem that the choice of weapon is determined by whatever is readily available in the particular culture.

Psychiatric Diagnosis

Schizophrenia was our largest diagnostic category, accounting for 62 (46.3 per cent) patients. This compared with 42.6 per cent in the US study and 70 per cent of the 30 mentally abnormal killers in Nigeria, and would seem to contrast with Britain where the commonest diagnosis was depression which often led to subsequent suicide.

Only two of our patients, both Black males, were depressed. One killed his 2½-year-old daughter by dashing her onto a log and fracturing her spine. This occurred in July 1977 and there was corroborative evidence that he had been depressed at least since April; in May he had consulted a traditional healer. Previously he had been a stable personality and happily married. The second killed his 8-month-old son by stabbing him in the abdomen. Subsequent investigation revealed that he had become depressed because of doubts over the paternity of the child; because of these doubts he had assaulted his wife about a week previously. There were hysterical traits in his personality; he exhibited episodes of aggressive behaviour towards the nursing staff, during which he claimed to hear voices, which he attributed to ancestral spirits. He frequently attempted to manipulate his discharge in order to consult a traditional healer. This latter case illustrated the point that mental illness can be compatible with motivated crime (Rollin, 1974) and whether or not the court takes the illness into account depends upon whether a voluntarist or determinist discourse is selected as the method of approach (Smith, 1980).

An unusual feature of our series was the large number of epileptics (37, or 27.6 per cent) which would seem to be very different from Britain. In one Scottish survey, for example, only two epileptics were found amongst 80 abnormal killers (65 male and 15 female) (Gillies, 1976). Soundly based and cogent arguments have been advanced to show that the association between epilepsy and crime is largely mythical (Gunn, 1979). Two local factors may account for this discrepancy. Firstly, epilepsy is common amongst our Black patients because of aetiological factors such as birth injury, cysticercosis, and syphilis (Rachman, 1970) which would be rare in Britain. Secondly, when faced with an apparently motiveless and incomprehensible crime, the courts will often accept psychiatric evidence that an association between the crime and epilepsy is possible as sufficient grounds to return a Special Verdict. Rigorous proof that crime occurred during a focal attack or post-ictal confusional state is not essential, as it would be in Britain (Pond, 1980).

CONCLUSIONS

There are three important conclusions to be drawn:

1. The study corroborated the findings of the earlier one that most homicides by the insane in Zimbabwe are committed in rural areas as opposed to urban, that the weapons used are handy domestic implements, and that the victims are usually relatives or friends of the killer, often children.
2. The majority of patients (73.8 per cent) suffer from potentially treatable illnesses such as schizophrenia or epilepsy.
3. The majority of patients (68.7 per cent) give some warning of mental disorders prior to the crime.

Taking into account the disproportionate amount of non-fatal violence in the cities and the readiness with which violent patients are brought to the hospital, it would seem reasonable to infer that ready access to psychiatric treatment permits urban dwellers to take advantage of the warning signs and seek treatment before the violence reaches lethal intensity. Alternative interpretations of the data are of course possible.

If one accepts this inference as valid it follows that making psychiatric treatment facilities available at the primary health care level should prevent a significant number of homicides. Other advantages would also accrue. Firstly, it has been shown that removal of a patient from his home environment to a remote mental hospital tends to alienate him from his family and friends, making it much more difficult to reintegrate him into the community after he has recovered (Buchan and Baker, 1974). Secondly, maintenance medication for discharged patients should be much easier to supervise, thus reducing the relapse rate.

These two factors should help to keep the patient in his home environment where the resources of the extended family—which is still the norm for rural areas of Zimbabwe—can be utilized in his rehabilitation. Certainly there is evidence that there is a reduced tendency for the schizophrenic patient to deteriorate into a withdrawn blunted state when living in an extended as opposed to a nuclear family (Fahkr el-Islam, 1979).

For these reasons it is mandatory that the development of psychiatric primary health care is the first priority and tentative beginnings have been made in this area which have been summarized elsewhere; considerable care has been taken to avoid some of the pitfalls encountered in Britain (Buchan, 1983). Plans for the construction of a regional secure unit have been indefinitely postponed. Nevertheless the provision of secondary and tertiary facilities is vital to the efficient functioning of the system as a whole. At the secondary care level the quality of expertise in some district hospitals would seem to have been inadequate; some three deaths occurred in these settings. In none of these cases was adequate medication given, and in one case there had been reliance on physical restraint.

To remedy this deficiency a start has been made on developing the undergraduate teaching of psychiatry, which became a barrier exam for the first time in July 1983. A new postgraduate Diploma in Psychiatric Health has been introduced and the first two candidates graduated in July 1983 and July 1984. This is a 12-month course aimed at providing general duties medical officers who are interested in the subject with sufficient psychiatric know-ledge and expertise to develop regional psychiatric sub-centres at selected district hospitals. Such sub-centres are intended not only to provide a few beds (1 per 10,000–15,000 adult population has been suggested) and appropri-ate nursing staff for the treatment of common acute conditions, but also to develop the infrastructure by training staff at all levels throughout the district.

With this in mind, a series of educational objectives have been prepared for village health workers, medical assistants, and nurses (Chawla, 1979). Medical officers are expected to be familiar with these objectives and to be able to teach towards them. The role of the village health worker in educating the public in such matters as the availability of services, the consequences of alcohol and cannabis abuse, and the care of the mentally disordered or subnormal in the community, is particularly emphasized.

Several studies have emphasized the significance of neurotic illnesses presenting at primary health care facilities (Giel and van Luijk, 1969; Ndetei and Muhangi, 1979; Harding et al., 1980; Dhadphale et al., 1982) and experience in Zimbabwe has been no different (Buchan and Chikara, 1980). Unravelling the underlying psychopathology of such disorders is both difficult and time-consuming, but does not necessarily require medical expertise. Accordingly, in cooperation with the Department of Psychology and the School of Social Work, my Department of Psychiatry is engaged in teaching postgraduate courses in Clinical Psychology (leading to an M.Sc.) and Clinical Social Work (leading to B.Sc.Hons.). It is hoped that some of these graduates will be posted to regional psychiatric sub-centres. At the tertiary care level, it should be mentioned that there were two deaths at Harare Hospital. One was caused by overcrowding and understaffing in one of the wards, and the other by attempting to manage a patient with personality disorder (social deviance dimension) in an open ward. Both of these issues have been dealt with previously (Buchan, 1976) and the situation has been remedied.

Work is proceeding on the upgrading of the 60-bed psychiatric unit at Harare Hospital. Adequate day space will be provided and four small rooms which can be locked and made secure are to be retained. The rationale for this plan is based on two considerations: firstly the finding that only a very small proportion of hospital inpatients require secure facilities because of violent behaviour (Fottrell, 1980), even when selected because of a potential for violence (Bowden, 1977). Other factors conducive to violence include overly authoritarian attitudes on the part of the nursing staff, and lack of involvement of medical staff in ward activities. Group work with staff is being undertaken with a view to minimizing these factors. Secondly, there is the finding that the establishment of a separate facility leads inevitably to 'banishment pressure' (Gunn, 1977).

An important link in the chain of care is the provision of easy access to psychiatric consultation so that workers in primary health care can feel supported and confident that if a problem passes beyond their range of expertise they can readily pass on the responsibility. Such a situation requires an adequate number of psychiatrists, and plans are in hand to introduce postgraduate training at this level. In the long term it is hoped that by the time a significant number of psychiatrists become available there will also have been considerable development of psychiatric services at the primary health care level. At that stage it should be possible to graft onto the infrastructure the kind of community forensic service which has been envisaged for Britain (Gunn, 1975b).

REFERENCES

Asuni, T. (1969) Homicide in Western Nigeria. *British Journal of Psychiatry*, **115**, 1105–1113.

Bluglass, R. (1978) Regional secure units and interim security for psychiatric patients. *British Medical Journal*, **1**, 489–493.

Bluglass, R. (1979) The psychiatric assessment of homicide. *British Journal of Hospital Medicine*, **22**, 366–377.

Bowden, P. (1977) The current management of the mentally disordered offender. *Proceedings of the Royal Society of Medicine*, **70**, 881–884.

Buchan, T. (1976) Some problems in the hospital management of criminal mental patients. *South African Medical Journal*, **50**, 1252–1256.

Buchan, T. (1978) Some clinical and cultural correlates of violent death. *South African Medical Journal*, **54**, 536–540.

Buchan, T. (1983) Development of community care in psychiatry. *Central African Medical Journal*, **29**, 17–21.

Buchan, T. and Baker, A. P. (1974) Psychiatric services in Matabeleland. *South African Medical Journal*, **48**, 925–930.

Buchan, T. and Chikara, F. B. (1980) Psychiatric outpatient services in Matabeleland, Zimbabwe. *South African Medical Journal*, **57**, 1095–1098.

Buchan, T., Nyamuswa, R. L. and Futter, G. E. (1981) Community psychiatric services in Mashonaland, Zimbabwe. *Central African Journal of Medicine*, **6**, 111–116.

Chawla, S. (1979) Integration of mental health services in primary health care. *Report to the Ministry of Health, Government of Zambia*.

Declaration of Hawaii (1977) *British Medical Journal*, **2**, 1204–1205.

Dhadphale, M., Ellison, R. H. and Griffin, L. (1982) Mental disorders among outpatients at a rural district hospital in Kenya. *Central African Journal of Medicine*, **4**, 85–89.

Editorial (1968) Compulsive gambler. *British Medical Journal*, **2**, 69.

Editorial (1974) Criminology, deviant behaviour and mental disorder. *Psychological Medicine*, **4**, 1–3.

Fahkr el-Islam, M. (1979) A better outlook for schizophrenics living in extended families. *British Journal of Psychiatry*, **135**, 343–347.

Fottrell, E. (1980) A study of violent behaviour among patients in psychiatric hospitals. *British Journal of Psychiatry*, **136**, 216–221.

Giel, R. and van Luijk, V. N. (1969) Psychiatric morbidity in a small Ethiopian town. *British Journal of Psychiatry*, **115**, 149–162.

Gillies, H. (1976) Homicide in the West of Scotland. *British Journal of Psychiatry*, **128**, 105–127.

Gillis, L. S., Lewis, J. B. and Slabbert, M. (1968) Psychiatric disorder amongst the coloured people of the Cape. *British Journal of Psychiatry*, **114**, 1575–1587.

Giovannoni, J. F. and Gurel, L. (1967) Socially disruptive behaviour of ex-mental patients. *Archives of General Psychiatry*, **17**, 146–153.

Gruneberg, F., Klinger, B. I. and Grumet, B. (1977) Homicide and de-institutionalisation of the mentally ill. *American Journal of Psychiatry*, **134**, 685–687.

Guldenpfenning, W. M. (1973) Clinical Experience with a new Benzodiazepine in the treatment of epilepsy (Clonazepam). *South African Medical Journal*, **47**, 998–1000.

Gunn, J. (1975a) Management of patients who have committed offences. *Medicine SA*, **30**, 1595–1597.

Gunn, J. (1975b) Forensic psychiatry and psychopathic patients. In T. Silverstone and B. Barraclough (Eds) *Contemporary Psychiatry*, pp. 302–307. Ashford, Kent: Headley Bros.

Gunn, J. (1977) Management of the mentally abnormal offender: integrated or parallel. *Proceedings of the Royal Society of Medicine*, **70**, 877–880.

Gunn, J. (1979) Forensic psychiatry. In K. Granville-Grossman (Ed.) *Recent Advances in Clinical Psychiatry*: No. 3. London: Churchill Livingstone.

Harding, T. W., de Asango, M. V., Baltazar, J., Climent, C. E., Ibrahim, H. H. A., Ladrido-Ignacio, L., Srinivasa Murthy, R. and Wig, N. N. (1980) Mental disorders in primary health care: a study of their frequency and diagnosis in four developing countries. *Psychological Medicine*, **10**, 231–241.

Home Office, Department of Health and Social Security (1975) *Report of the Committee on Mentally Abnormal Offenders*. London: HMSO, Cmnd. 6244.

Ingram, T. M. and Timbury, G. D. (1960) Correspondence. *Lancet*, **2**, 766.

Kendell, R. E. (1975) The concept of disease and its implications for psychiatry. *British Journal of Psychiatry*, **127**, 305–315.

Kochansky, G. E., Salzman, C., Shader, R. I., Harmatz, J. S. and Ogletree, A. M. (1975) The differential effects of chlordiazepoxide and oxazepam on hostility in a small group setting. *American Journal of Psychiatry*, **132**, 861–863.

Kochansky, G. E., Salzman, C., Shader, R. I., Harmatz, J. S. and Ogletree, A. M. (1977) Effects of chlordiazepoxide and oxazepam administration on verbal hostility. *Archives of General Psychiatry*, **34**, 1457–1459.

Lagos, J. M., Perlmutter, K. and Saexinger, H. (1977) Fear of the mentally ill: empirical support for the common man's response. *American Journal of Psychiatry*, **134**, 1134–1137.

Lanzkron, J. (1963) Murder and insanity: a survey. *American Journal of Psychiatry*, **119**, 754–758.

McClintock, F. H. (1978) Criminological aspects of family violence. In J. P. Martin (Ed.) *Violence and the Family*. Chichester: Wiley.

McCrae, A. K. (1973) Forensic psychiatry. In A. Forrest (Ed.) *Companion to Psychiatric Studies*, vol. II, pp. 488–510. London: Churchill Livingstone.

Ndetei, D. M. and Muhangi, J. (1979) The prevalence and clinical presentation of psychiatric illness in a rural setting in Kenya. *British Journal of Psychiatry*, **135**, 269–272.

Ormrod, Sir Roger (1975) The debate between psychiatry and the law. *British Journal of Psychiatry*, **127**, 193–203.

Pond, D. A. (1980) Responsibility. *Bulletin of the Royal College of Psychiatrists*, Jan., pp. 10–15.

Rachman, I. (1970) Epilepsy in African hospital practice. *Central African Journal of Medicine*, **8**, 201–204.

Rappeport, J. R. and Lassen, G. (1965) Dangerousness—arrest rate comparisons of discharged patients and the general population. *American Journal of Psychiatry*, **121**, 776–783.

Ratcliffe, C. A. (1983) Personal communication from the office of the Secretary for Justice, Zimbabwe.

Rollin, H. R. (1969) *The Mentally Abnormal Offender and the Law*. London: Pergamon Press.

Rollin, H. R. (1974) The Mental Health Act, 1959, with special reference to the mentally abnormal offender. *British Journal of Hospital Medicine*, **12**, 272–277.

Roth, L. H. (1979) Judicial action report. *Psychiatric News*, **14** (21), 3.

Royal College of Psychiatrists (1975) Norms for medical staffing of a forensic psychiatry service within the National Health Service in England and Wales. *Supplement to British Journal of Psychiatry*, June, pp. 5–10.

Salzman, G., Kochansky, G. E., Shader, R. I., Porrino, L. J., Harmatz, J. S. and Swett, C. P. Jnr. (1974) Chlordiazepoxide-induced hostility in a small group setting. *Archives of General Psychiatry*, **31**, 401–405.

Scott, P. D. (1970) Punishment or treatment: prison or hospital? *British Medical Journal*, **2**, 167–169.

Smith, R. (1980) Scientific thought and the boundary of insanity and criminal responsibility. *Psychological Medicine*, **10**, 15–23.

Tennet, T. G. (1975) The dangerous offender. In T. Silverstone and B. Barraclough (Eds) *Contemporary Psychiatry*, pp. 308–315. Ashford, Kent: Headley Bros.

Thomson, I. G. (1980) Homicide and suicide in Africa and England. *Medicine, Science and the Law*, **2**, 99–103.

Tobin, J. M. and Lewis, N. D. C. (1960) New psychotherapeutic agent, chlordiazepoxide. *Journal of the American Medical Association*, **174**, 1242–1249.

Westermeyer, J. and Kroll, J. (1978) Violence and mental illness in a peasant society: characteristics of violent behaviours and 'folk' use of restraints. *British Journal of Psychiatry*, **133**, 529–541.

Westermeyer, J. and Wintrob, R. (1979) 'Folk' criteria for the diagnosis of mental illness in rural Laos: on being insane in sane places. *American Journal of Psychiatry*, **136**, 755–761.

Wing, J. K. (1979) The concept of disease in psychiatry. *Journal of the Royal Society of Medicine*, **72**, 316–321.

Wootton, the Baroness of Abinger (1963) The law, the doctor, and the deviant. *British Medical Journal*, **3**, 197–202.

Zitrin, A., Hardesty, A. S., Burdock, E. and Drossman, A. K. (1976) Crime and violence amongst mental patients. *American Journal of Psychiatry*, **133**, 142–149.

Author Index

Aarvold. Sir C., 173
Abraham, K., 140
Abramson, M. F., 225
American Psychiatric Association, 30, 116
Andy, O. J., 37
Ankles, T. M., 123
Anthony, W. A., 227, 229
Asuni, T., 253

Bachrach, L. L., 210, 227, 228
Bach-Y-Rita, G., 20, 36, 37
Bagshaw, M. H., 33
Baker, A. P., 255
Bancroft, J. H. J., 14
Barnes, G. E., 209
Bassuk, E. L., 228, 229
Beleslin, D. B., 27
Bennett, D., 209
Berger, P. A., 26, 35
Berlin, F. S., 14
Berman, J. J., 219, 220
Bernstein, I. S., 9
Bertilson, H. S., 67
Bion, W. R., 144, 145
Blackburn, R., 29–31, 35
Blake, W., 124
Bluglass, R., 185, 207, 245, 246, 253
Blumer, D., 16
Bohm, E., 107
Bond, A., 88
Bonovitz, J. C., 226
Boranga, G., 110
Bowden, P., 256
Bowlby, J., 133
Brain, P. F., 20
Braun, P., 229
Brodie, H. K. H., 26, 35

Bronson, F. H., 20, 21
Broome, A. K., 205
Brotherstone, J., 84
Brown, G. L., 28
Brown, P., 228, 229
Brown, W. A., 11, 18, 19, 29
Buchan, T., 3, 241, 245, 246, 251, 255, 256
Burgess, P. K., 28
Butler, Lord, 2, 185, 241, 244

Campbell, B. A., 39
Campbell, D. T., 218, 227
Candland, D. K., 20
Carlton, P. L., 39
Carney, M. W. P., 2, 187, 188, 191, 193, 198, 199, 206
Chawla, S., 256
Chesno, F., 59, 67
Chessick, R. D., 129, 132
Chikara, F. B., 251, 256
Christenfeld, R., 229
Christiansen, K. O., 31
Cleckley, H., 1, 30, 57, 60, 70, 84, 96, 98
Cobb, J., 114
Cochran, C. A., 9
Cocozza, J. J., 161, 213, 214, 223
Cohen, J. A., 70
Conner, R. L., 9, 20, 25
Cook, T. D., 218, 227
Cooper, A. J., 15, 18
Copas, J., 84
Coppock, H. W., 33
Cox, D. N., 32, 25, 69
Coyle, G. S., 14
Craddick, R., 68

Dahlstrom, W. G., 68

261

Daizman, R. J., 35
Dalton, K., 17
Davis, G. H., 11, 18, 29
Davis, W. M., 88
De Abovitz, F. S., 60
Delaney, J. A., 227
DeLeon, P. H., 229
Dell, S., 185, 205
Dellario, D. J., 227
Dengerink, H. A., 77
Descartes, R., 103
Desjardins, C., 20, 21
Deutsch, H., 131
Dhadphale, M., 256
Dickey, W., 220, 221, 226, 227
Dickinson, R., 7
Dixson, A. F., 9, 19
Doering, C. H., 10, 18
Dombrose, L. A., 85
Dominik, M., 107
Douglas, R. J., 33, 38
Durham, M. L., 219

Edelberg, R., 32
Edmunds, G., 87
Ehlers, C. L., 17, 18
Ehrenkranz, J., 11, 12, 16
Eichelman, B. S., 27
Ekkers, 24
Eleftheriou, B. E., 20
Ellison, G. D., 27, 39
Emmons, T. D., 35
Ervin, F. R., 8, 37
Estroff, S. E., 230
Ey, H., 113
Eysenck, H. J., 28, 31, 59, 65, 85, 86, 91
Eysenck, S. B. G., 59, 65, 85, 86, 91

Fahkr el-Islam, M., 255
Fairbairn, W. R. D., 130, 133, 144
Fairweather, G. W., 229, 230, 231
Farrington, D. P., 86
Feldman, M. P., 31
Felton, B. J., 228
Fenz, W., 31
Flor-Henry, P., 34
Floud, J., 2
Forsham, P. H., 33, 34
Fottrell, E., 186, 201, 206, 256
Foulds, G. A., 96, 98
Freud, S., 8, 112, 131–133, 151

Friel, C. M., 60
Funkenstein, D., 24

Gabrielli, W. F., 34
Gagne, P., 14, 15
Gallwey, P. L. G., 148
Garner, J., 2
Gayford, J. J., 120
Geller, I., 28
Gerson, S., 228, 229
Gibbens, T. C. N., 186, 205
Giel, R., 256
Gillies, H., 254
Gillis, L. S., 241
Giovannoni, J. F., 244
Glusman, M., 37
Goddard, G. V., 33
Golding, S. L., 2, 3, 210, 225
Goldstein, M., 29, 38
Golla, F. L., 12
Goldman, H. H., 218
Gordon, M., 27
Gough, H. G., 58, 69, 85
Grant, R. W., 223
Gray, J. A., 29
Green, R., 9
Greene, R., 17
Griffiths, A. W., 135
Grinker, R. A., 130
Grossman, S. P., 37
Gruneberg, F., 244
Gudjonsson, G. H., 1, 84, 86, 88, 91, 94, 96
Guldenpfennig, W. M. 245
Gunderson, J. G., 129
Gunn, J., 220, 242, 254, 257
Gurel, L., 244
Guy, E. B., 226
Guy, W. A., 212
Gynther, M. D., 67

Hafner, R. J., 118
Halleck, S. L., 14
Hamburg, D. A., 17
Harding, C. F., 20
Harding, T. W., 256
Hare, R. D., 1, 31, 32, 35, 36, 59, 67–70, 98
Harris, P., 209
Hartmann, R. J., 28
Harvey, J. A., 20

Hawk, S. S., 68
Heath, R. G., 38
Heilbrun, A. B., 67
Henderson, D. K., 82
Hepworth, D. R., 2, 155, 156, 158, 166
Herbert, J., 9
Hiday, V., 213
Higgins, J., 201, 203
Hinton, J. W., 2
Hodge, R. S., 12
Hodges, W. F., 94
Hogarth, J., 174
Holmberg, M., 86
Holland, T. R., 98
Hollingshead, A. B., 61, 74
Houts, M., 30
Hundleby, J. D., 67, 77
Hutchings, B., 31

Ingram, T. M., 244
Isaacson, R. L., 38, 39

Jacobson, D., 221, 222
Jaremko, M. E., 107, 108
Jarrard, L. E., 38, 39
Jaspers, K., 112, 113
Jeffery, C. R., 31
Johnson, V. E., 7
Jones, E., 107
Joslyn, W. D., 9

Kaelber, W. W., 37
Karli, P., 25
Karpman, B., 31, 98
Kendell, R. E., 244
Kendenberg, D., 11
Kendler, K. S., 113
Kendrick, D. C., 87
Kernberg, O., 130, 132
Keverne, E. B., 9
Kiesler, C. A., 218, 227
Kilmann, P., 59, 67
Kimble, D. P., 38, 39
Kinsey, A. C., 7
Klein, M., 2, 105, 130, 144, 151
Klerman, C. A., 218
Klerman, C. L., 129, 130
Kling, A., 9, 16, 18, 19
Knesper, D. J., 187, 206
Knight, R., 8, 132, 140, 185
Kobrin, S., 233

Kochansky, G. E., 246
Konner, M., 19
Korn, J. H., 39
Kostowski, W., 26
Krafft-Ebing, R. von, 107, 109
Kretschmer, E., 114
Kreuz, L. E., 11, 12, 15, 16, 18, 19
Kroll, J., 245
Kunce, J. T., 25, 29

Lader, M., 88
Lagache, D., 110, 112, 120
Lagos, J. M., 241
Lamb, H. R., 210, 220, 223–225
Langfeldt, G., 110
Lanzkron, J., 253
Lassen, G., 244
Latane, B., 31
Leaton, R. N., 39
Le Boit, J., 130
Lemert, E., 174
Lentz, R. J., 231
Leon, C. A., 209
Lerman, P., 228
Lerner, L. J., 13
Leshner, A. I., 9, 17, 20–22
Levander, S. E., 32
Levine, D., 224
Lewin, R., 29, 35
Lewis, N. D. C., 244
Lion, J. R., 36, 37
Lindsey, R., 107, 108
Lipsitt, P., 213
Loeb, J., 32
Logan, F. A., 9
London, H., 60
Lorentz, K., 8
Lorimer, F. M., 30
Lorr, M., 30
Luckey, J. W., 219, 220
Lykken, D. T., 32, 59

Maack, L. H., 2, 120
Mabry, P. D., 39
Maclean, P. D., 8
Manning, N., 83
Mark, V. H., 8, 37
Marks, I. M., 96, 98
Martin, C. E., 7
Marx, J. L., 34
Mason, J. W., 21, 23

Masters, W. H., 7
Mattson, A., 10, 11
Mawson, A. R., 31
Mawson, C. D., 31
Mayer, A., 17
Mazur, A., 9
McClintock, F. H., 245
McCrae, A. K., 241
McEwen, B. S., 22, 23, 34
McPhail, N. I., 186, 201
Mednick, S. A., 1, 31–34, 38
Meehl, P. E., 161
Megargee, E. I., 29, 30, 40, 69, 161
Meinecke, C. F., 14
Mello, N. K., 12
Melmon, K. L., 23
Mendelson, J. H., 12
Menninger, K. A., 37
Meyer-Bahlburg, H. F. L., 10, 19
Mirsky, A. F., 9
Molinoff, P. B., 23
Molof, M. J., 30
Monahan, J., 213, 214, 222, 223, 230, 234
Monden, Y., 16, 18
Monello, J., 60
Money, J., 13
Monroe, R. R., 30, 37
Mooney, H., 114
Moos, R. H., 17
Morrissey, J. P., 220
Morse, S. J., 217
Morton, J. H., 17, 18
Morris, I., 209
Mosher, D. L., 108
Mosher, L. R., 209
Moss, R. L., 40
Mowat, R. R., 109, 120
Moyer, K. E., 8, 17, 18, 25, 27, 41
Muhangi, J., 256
Mullen, P. E., 2, 117, 120
Muller, M., 32
Murphy, D. L., 35
Murray, M. A. F., 12, 14

Ndetei, D. M., 256
Nelson, G. M., 25, 39
Nemiah, J. C., 146
Neri, R. O., 13
Neu, J., 119
Neumann, F., 12, 13
Newman, J. P., 1, 59

Nolan, P. A., 187, 188, 191, 198, 199, 206
Norris, M., 84, 98

O'Brien, M., 83, 98
Odegaard, J., 109
Odejide, A. O., 209
Olweus, D., 10, 11, 19
Ormrod, Sir, R., 243
Osgood, C. E., 97

Panksepp, J., 37
Parlee, M. B., 17
Passingham, R. E., 28
Paul, G. L., 231
Perachio, A. A., 9
Percy, Baron E. S. C., 176, 177
Perry, R. C., 129, 130
Persky, H., 10
Peterson, R. A., 68
Petrie, A., 29
Phillips, N., 188
Pierce, G. L., 219
Pinta, E. R., 111
Ploog, D. W., 8
Pomeroy, W. B., 7
Pond, D. A., 254
Post, R. D., 123
Potegal, M., 26
Poythress, N., 213
Prentky, R., 1
Preu, P. W., 30
Pribram, K. H., 33
Price, J. H., 185
Price, R. H., 228
Psarska, A. D., 120
Pucilowski, O., 26

Quay, H. C., 31, 32
Quinn, M. J., 67

Rabkin, J. G., 223
Rachman, I., 254
Rachman, S., 28
Rada, R. T., 10, 13, 18, 19
Rapoport, R., 83
Rappaport, J., 230
Rappeport, J. R., 244
Redmond, D. E., 35
Reich, R., 228
Reik, T., 107
Reitan, R. H., 88

Rettersol, N., 109, 113
Richman, A., 209
Roberts, J. C., 1, 84, 86, 88, 96
Robertson, G., 186, 205
Robichaud, R. C., 28
Robins, L. N., 63, 64, 66, 70, 71–75, 83
Rocky, S., 13
Roeder, F., 37
Roesch, R., 2, 3, 210, 225
Rofman, E. S., 217
Rollin, H. R., 244, 245, 254
Rose, R. M., 9–12, 15, 16, 18, 19, 22
Rosen, A., 161
Rosenfeld, H., 131
Ross, B., 67, 77
Roth, L. H., 243
Royal College of Psychiatrists, 186, 201, 204, 207, 243
Rubin, R. T., 23
Ruin, R., 120
Rundle, A. T., 135
Rushton, J. P., 28

Salzman, G., 245
Sano, K., 37–39
Sassenrath, E. N., 17
Scaramella, T. J., 11, 19
Schachter, S., 31
Schalling, D., 31, 86, 98
Schmauk, F. J., 32, 59
Schmideberg, M., 123
Schooler, C., 35
Schuerman, L. A., 233
Scott, J. P., 8
Scott, P. D., 164, 242
Scull, A., 228, 230
Sedvall, G. C., 23
Seeman, M. V., 108, 123
Seidenberg, R., 124
Seidman, E., 211
Selmanoff, M. K., 9
Shah, S. A., 1
Shapland, J., 28
Sheard, M. H., 25, 27
Sheffield, B. F., 193
Shepherd, M., 110, 118
Shinn, M., 228
Siddle, D. A. T., 31, 32
Siegel, L., 228
Siegenthaler, L. A., 209
Siegman, A. W., 60

Sifneos, P. E., 146
Sigg, E. B., 20
Silver, A. W., 68
Simon, N. G., 18
Singer, H. T., 129
Sjoerdsma, A., 27
Sledge, K. L., 28
Slobin, M. S., 85
Slusher, M. A., 22
Smith, M., 9
Smith, R., 212, 254
Smith, S. S., 228
Smythies, J. R., 33, 39
Snibbe, J. R., 221
Solomons, R. C., 106
Sorenson, C. A., 27
Sosowsky, L., 223
Sparling, P., 3
Spellacy, F., 88
Spielman, M. D., 105
Spinoza, B., 103
Spitz, R. A., 133
Spitzer, R. L., 68, 69
Spodak, M. K., 14
Staub, E., 30
Steadman, H. J., 161, 213, 214, 223
Stein, L., 38
Stein, L. I., 227
Stern, A., 131
Stevens, D. A., 28
Stier, S. D., 213
Stoebe, K. J., 213
Stone, A. A., 210
Stone, M. H., 130
Sturup, G. K., 163, 164
Sullivan, H. S., 105
Swank, G. E., 223
Syndulko, K., 33
Szara, S. I., 26

Tagliamonte, A., 26, 29, 35
Teismann, M. W., 108
Tennent, T. G., 185, 244
Teplin, L. A., 221
Test, M. A., 227, 229
Thiessen, D. D., 8, 9, 17
Thoa, N. B., 27
Thomson, I. G., 245
Thorne, G. L., 35
Timbury, G. D., 244
Tipton, R. M., 107

Tobin, J. M., 244
Todd, J., 109
Toews, J., 209
Tov-Ruach, L., 108
Turbott, J., 118

Ulrich, J., 9
US Bureau of the Census, 66

Valzelli, L., 25–28, 40, 41
Van Luijk, V. N., 256
Vauhkonen, K., 107, 110, 113, 118, 119
Venables, P. H., 32, 33, 38, 39
Vergnes, M., 26
Vernikos-Danellis, J., 26, 35
Virkkunen, M., 33
Vogt, M., 43
Volavka, J., 1
Volovik, V. M., 209

Warburton, D. M., 35
Warren, C. A. B., 214
Watzlawick, P., 211
Weaver, S. N., 202
Webb, W. W., 35
Weil-Malherbe, H., 26
Weinberger, D. A., 94
Weinstein, J., 94
Weiss, J. M., 24, 25

Welch, A. S., 20, 24, 25, 35
Welch, B. L., 20, 24, 25, 35
West, D. J., 135
Westermeyer, J., 241, 245
Wexler, D. B., 212
Wheatley, M. D., 37
Wheeler, M., 17
White, W. C., 30
Whiteley, S., 81, 84
Whitmer, G., 223
Widom, C. S., 1, 57–59, 63–66, 69, 78
Williams, A. H., 142
Williams, D., 30
Williams, D. H., 227
Wilson, J. G., 187
Wilson, J. Q., 66
Winer, D., 223
Wing, J. K., 244
Winnicott, D., 130, 132, 140
Wintrob, R., 241
Woodside, N., 187, 190
Wootton, Baroness B., 242
Wurtman, R. J., 43

Young, W., 2

Zachepitskii, R. A., 209
Zitrin, A., 26, 223, 244
Zuckerman, M., 29, 32, 35, 60

Subject Index

Aarvold Advisory Board, 173–174
Admissions to mental hospitals, *see* Mental hospitals, detention in
Adrenaline/noradrenaline, *see* Catecholamine
Age, 11, 19
  of puberty, 9, 19
Aggression, 7–55
  and biology, 7–55
  and endocrine factors, 9–11
  and overcontrolled personality type, 29–30, 39–40
  and sex, 1, 7–55
  and sexual excitement, 17, 26–27, 29–35
  and undercontrolled personality type, 29–30
Aggressive behaviour and personality, 85–88
Androgen depletion, 13–15
  pre- and post-natal, 9, 18–19
  see also Aggression and endocrine factors
Antisocial behaviour, self-report inventories, 67–69
Antisocial personality disorder, *see* Psychopathy
Anxiety, 1, 10, 16–18, 24, 31, 36, 37, 40, 65, 75, 84, 94, 96, 98, 133–135, 138
Arrow-Dot test of personality disorder, 85–89
Automatism, 253

Banishment pressure, 257
Biological disadvantage, 244
Borderline personality, 127–151
  and offending, 135, 136, 140, 142–144, 146, 147, 149
  and schizophrenia, 128–129, 131, 137, 141, 143, 146, 148

diagnostic categories, 129–130
episodic disturbance, 128, 144, 146
role of fantasy, 134–135, 137
treatment, 127, 136–142, 144, 148–150
see also Dual personality
Buss–Durkee Hostility Inventory, 10, 11, 13, 19
Butler Report, *see* Committee on Mentally Abnormal Offenders

California Psychological Inventory (CPI)
  Socialization (So) Scale, 58, 69, 70–72, 75–77, 85–87, 89
Catecholamine, 23–25, 27–29, 35, 39
Commitment
  and charge, 224–226
  evidence for clinical decision-making, 216–218
  hearings and due process, 216, 225, 230
  procedures, hypothetical scenarios, 214–217
Commitment law
  and the criminal justice system, 220–227
  reform, 209–239
  shortcomings, 210–212
Commitment to mental institutions, studies of, 209–239
  methodological shortcomings, 3, 213–219, 221, 223–227, 231–234
  recommendations, 232–235
Committee on Mentally Abnormal Offenders, 2, 185, 241, 244
Competency to stand trial, 210, 225–227, 242
Criminal history, 10–12, 82, 84, 121, 161, 223, 224
Criminality and mental disturbance, 220–227

267

Criminal justice system personnel and
    mental disorder, 213, 221
Cross-cultural comparisons of patient
    management, *see* Patient management

Dangerousness
    and commitments to hospital, 213–214
    and criminal history, 160–161
    and mental illness, 241–259
    and nature of offence, 160–161
    and prediction of future criminality,
        161
    and severity of offence, 160–161
Dangerousness, assessment of
    and care and control objectives, 2,
        163–168, 176
    and resource availability, 163–171
    and using objective criteria, 162–163,
        173, 174, 177
Dangerousness, potential, 244, 256
    prediction, 3, 213–218, 251–252, 255
Decision-making
    as a human process, 174–178
    function of doubt, 171–172, 174, 177,
        181–183
    models, 158–172, 174–178
Declaration of Hawaii (1977), 242
Defensive personality, 133–136
Deinstitutionalization of mental patients,
    see Mental patients, deinstitutionaliza-
    tion
Department of Health and Social Secur-
    ity, 157, 167, 185, 204
Depersonalization, 131, 132, 142, 146
Destructive impulses, schizoid encapsula-
    tion, 133, 140–144
*Diagnostic and Statistical Manual of the
    American Psychiatric Association*
    (DSM III, 1980), 113, 116–117, 129
Diminished responsibility, 252–253
Discharged psychiatric patients, violence
    in, 244–245
Dopamine, *see* Catecholamine
Dual personality, models, 132–150
    'false self' organization, 133–140, 148–
        150
    'split ego' organization, 133, 140–146,
        147–150
Due process and commitment hearings,
    216, 225, 230

Electrodermal measurement, concord-
    ance with self-report study results,
    90, 91–96, 98
Electrodermal skin response, 32–33, 36,
    88, 90–91, 92–93
Emotions, 105–106, 133–134
Envy, 103, 104–105
    see also Jealousy
Epilepsey, temporal lobe, 23, 37
Eysenck Personality Inventory (EPI),
    85–87, 89, 96
Eysenck Personality Questionnaire
    (EPQ), 58–59, 86

False personality organization, 133–140,
    148–150

'Gault' case, 212
Glancy Report (1974), 185
Gough Socialization Scale, *see* California
    Personality Inventory
Group therapy, 81–83, 98
Guilt, 1, 84, 112
    and transgressive behaviour, 85, 96–98

Henderson hospital, 81–98
    evaluation studies, 83–88
    patients' characteristics, 82, 84
Home Office, 2
Home Secretary, 157, 158, 170, 172–174
Homicide rates and mental illness, 245
Hormone levels and psychological influ-
    ences, 21–22
    see also Oestrogen, Progesterone, Tes-
    tosterone
Humphrey v. Cady (1972), 212

Infantile deprivation, 133–140
Integrated client tracking, 232–235
International Classification of Diseases,
    116, 117

Jealous delusions, 109–113
Jealousy
    and aggression, 2, 103–105, 107, 109–
        111, 120–123
    and alcohol, 109–111
    and anxiety, 107
    and behaviour, 106–107, 109–112
    and domestic violence, 103, 120, 124
    and homosexuality, 112–113

and marital infidelity, 106–114, 117, 118, 121–124
and psychoanalysis, 105, 106
and relationships, 117–124
and sexual dysfunction, 119
cultural norms, 110
displacement of, 124
morbid, 2, 108–112, 115–118
pathological, 2, 103–126, 133

Lanterman–Petris–Short Act (LPS), 212, 220, 225
Law and mental illness in Britain and Zimbabwe, 252–253
'Least restrictive alternative' principle, 213, 228
Legal Dangerousness Scale, 161
Lessard v. Schmidt (1972), 212, 213, 216
'Lodge' model of community treatment of mentally ill, 229–230

Management of dangerous patients, and education personnel, 255–256
Marital infidelity, see Jealousy
Masturbation, 8, 12, 14, 15
Maternal deprivation, see Infantile deprivation
McNaughten Rules, 253
Medicalization of social deviance, 242
Mental abnormality
  and assessment of dangerousness, 155–183
  and criminal offending, 157
  and management of violence, 185–188, 191, 198–199, 201–202, 207
  compulsory treatment of, 156–157
  danger of physical harm, 159
  see also Mental illness
Mental Health Act (1959), 155–157, 167, 176, 192, 193, 199, 241
Mental Health Act (1983), 2, 178
Mental Health Act (1976) (Zimbabwe), 242, 247, 248
Mental Health (Amendment) Act (1982), 176, 177
Mental Health Review Tribunal, 2, 155–183
  acquisition of information, 167–169
  and the Home Secretary, 172–174
  decision-making criteria, 158–172
  effectiveness, 176

power of adjournment, 166–167, 169, 170, 173, 176, 177
  Rules (1960), 166, 169
Mental hospitals
  detention in, 218–220
  hospitalization of offenders, 223–224
  management of violence, 185–188, 191, 198–199, 201–202, 206–207
Mental illness
  and alcohol, 246–247
  and definitions of dangerousness, 241–259
  and homicide rates, 245
  and physical violence, 241–259
  in the Third World, 241–259
  in Zimbabwe (national study), 246–257
  operational definitions, 244
  treatment of, 242–244
Mental patients, deinstitutionalization, 2, 209–239
  and community alternatives, 219–220, 225, 227–231
  and public policy, 218, 220–221, 227–233
  and re-institutionalization, 3, 228–229
  management of, 241–259
  see also Violence in hospitals
Mentally ill, arrest of the, 209, 215, 221–222
  and arrest rates, 223, 226, 244
  and commitment, 221–225
Mentally ill in prison, 214, 220–221, 223–224
Mentally ill offenders in Zimbabwe, 246–259
  diagnostic categories 251–252, 254
  previous mental history, 248, 251, 252
  relationship with victim, 248, 249, 253, 255
  warning symptoms, 251–252, 255
  weapons used by, 248–250, 254, 255
Minnesota Multiphasic Personality Inventory (MMPI)
  Psychopathic Deviate (Pd) Scale, 58, 68–69, 70–72, 75, 77
Mosher Morality-Conscience Guilt Scale, 96

Negative therapeutic reaction, 131
Neurotic extraversion and offending, 28–29

Neurotic jealousy, 114, 118
Neuroticism, 84, 86
    extrapunitive, 84
New custodialism, 228

Oedipus complex, 105, 112
Oestrogen, 13, 17
    see also Hormone levels
Olweus Aggression Inventory, 10–11

Parens patriae, 163, 212–213
Passive-avoidance learning, 59–60, 74–75
Patient management, cross-cultural com-
    parisons of, 3, 241–259
Penile erection, 8, 12, 14, 38
Percy Commission, see Royal Commis-
    sion on the Law relating to Mental
    Illness and Mental Deficiency
Personality disordered patients, self-
    concept, 88, 91–96, 98
Personality inventories, 58–59
Personality models, see Dual personality
Physical violence and mental illness,
    241–259
Pituitary–adrenal cortical hormones, 20–
    23, 32–35
Police discretion and commitment to
    mental institutions, 221–222, 224
    Premenstrual tension, 17–18
    as defence in law, 18
Preventive medicine, 3, 246, 255–257
Primary psychiatric care, see Preventive
    medicine
Progesterone, 17–18
    see also Hormone levels
Psychoanalysis, 2, 24, 129–133
Psychodynamic modelling of borderline
    personality, 127–151
    bimodal, 145–147
    linear, 144
    see also Dual personality
Psychopaths
    incarcerated, 57, 66, 68, 77–78
    institutionalization of, 242–244
    psychological and physiological charac-
    teristics, 1, 57–60, 73–78, 85–88,
    96–98, 246
    reaction to deception, 88, 90–96, 98
Psychopaths, non-institutionalized, 57–80
    antisocial characteristics, 61–62, 66
    demographic characteristics, 62–4, 66
    psychometric characteristics, 64–66

Psychopathy, 1, 16, 18, 24, 30–36, 127
    and antisocial behaviour, 32–33, 241
    and antisocial personality disorder, 57,
    70–73, 75, 77–78, 127–130
    arrest as an indicator of, 57, 63, 66, 68,
    72–74
    biological roots of, 31–36
    definitional problems, 241, 245
    diagnostic criteria, 1, 67, 69–78, 127–
    129
    inheritance of, 32
    primary and secondary, 1, 30, 35, 84,
    98
    psychological and physical characteris-
    tics, 81–101
Psychotherapy, 2, 81–82, 98, 127, 130,
    136–142, 144, 148–150

R. v. Dube (1968), 253
Reconviction, 84
Regional Secure Unit (RSU), 2, 3, 82,
    185–208, 245–246, 256
    characteristics of follow-up cohort,
    193–198
    characteristics of hospital, 188–191
    characteristics of patients, 192–193
    characteristics of temporarily transfer-
    red patients, 199–200
    contacts with community, 203
    need for, 183–186
Reitan Trail Making Test, 88
Research Diagnostic Criteria (RDC) of
    Psychopathy, 69–78
Rivalry, 103–104, 113
Robins diagnostic criteria for sociopathy,
    63, 64, 66, 70–78
Royal College of Psychiatrists report
    (1975), 243
Royal College of Psychiatrists report
    (1980), 186, 201, 204–205, 207
Royal Commission on the Laws relating
    to Mental Illness and Mental De-
    ficiency (1957), 176, 177

Secure unit, local/crisis, 201–202, 204,
    207
    see also Regional secure unit
Self-report studies, 11, 12, 19, 88
Self-report study results, concordance
    with electrodermal measurement,
    90–96, 98

Sensory deprivation, 24–25
Serotonin, 25–27, 34–36, 39
Sex differences in the experience of
    jealousy, 107–108, 118
Sexual aggression, *see* Aggression
Sexual offences/offenders, 8, 12–15, 37
Skin resistance tonic level (SRL), *see*
    Electroderman skin response
Social learning and aggression, 8, 20, 28,
    29, 31, 36, 41
    and response hierarchies, 28, 31, 33
Somnambulism, 253
Special (Secure) Hospitals, 2, 157, 158,
    164–167, 185–186, 205
Special verdict (Zimbabwe), 247–248,
    252–254
'Split ego' organization, 140–151
    forensic/'ego dystonic', 140, 142–150
    non-forensic, 140–142
State v. Senekal (1969), 253
State v. Strasburg (1910), 212
Stress, 15–16, 18, 21–25, 31, 35, 98, 137,
    148, 243
Suicide and attempted suicide, 28, 110,
    117–118

Testosterone
    and aggression, 9–19, 22
    and alcohol, 12
    and dominance in social hierarchies, 9
    and tranquillizers, 12, 14
    response to stress, 15–17
    see also Hormone levels
Therapeutic communities, 1, 81–101
Time estimation, 60–61, 75

Violence in hospitals
    management of, 185–188, 191, 198–
        199, 201, 202, 206–207
    potential, 198–203
    seclusion as a criterion of, 198–199
    sex differences, 186, 198–199, 206
    see also Mental patients
Violent offenders, 8, 11–12, 15, 17–19,
    37, 158

'Winship' case, 212

Zimbabwe, management of dangerous
    patients, 241–259